W9-ABZ-921

SPURR'S BOATBOOK

UPGRADING THE CRUISING SAILBOAT

Carl—

one of us—should know
what the hell is going on... in these
boats— and I think it best if it was
you!!! Please memorize entire book,
for next year's cruise—

Thanks—

Nولمار (wetboek)'85

SPURR'S BOATBOOK

Daniel Spurr

Upgrading The Cruising Sailboat

Illustrations by Bruce Bingham

SEVEN SEAS

SEVEN SEAS PRESS, INC.   *Newport, R.I.*

SEVEN SEAS PRESS, INC.

Newport, Rhode Island
Edited by James R. Gilbert

Copyright © 1983 by Daniel O. Spurr
Illustrations, except where noted, by Bruce Bingham Copyright © 1983
Portions of this book appeared previously in *Cruising World* magazine

First printing, 1983
Second printing, 1984

All rights reserved. No part of this book may be reproduced in any
form or by any electronic or mechanical means including information
storage and retrieval systems without permission in writing from the publisher.

   3   5   7   9   HL/HL   0   8   6   4   2

Library of Congress Cataloging in Publication Data

Spurr, Daniel, 1947-
   Spurr's Boatbook.

   Includes index.
   1. Sailboats.   I. Title.   II. Title: Boatbook.
VM351.S63   1983   623.8′223   83-18404
ISBN 0-915160-57-9

Book trade distribution by Simon and Schuster,
a division of Simon & Schuster, Inc.,
1230 Avenue of the Americas, New York, NY 10020

Designed by Irving Perkins Associates
Printed in the United States of America by Haliday Lithograph

Dedication

This book is dedicated to my great-grandfather, Alfred Spurr, who ran away from his Nova Scotia home at the plucky age of 14 to become a Gloucester fisherman. Eventually he became part-owner and captain of the *John F. Wonson,* but she was lost at sea with all hands, save my great-grandfather, who for some odd reason had temporarily taken up farming. Later he purchased the *Silver Dart,* smaller than the *John F.* but a solid vessel nonetheless and capable of bringing in a sizable catch. Later the *Silver Dart* was wrecked in a fog, though this time the captain and crew were all saved.

I never knew the man, he having passed away years before I came into the world. But if you believe in bloodlines, roots and all that, and even if you acknowledge the geno-primal longing in all of us to embrace the source of life, I still suppose my great-grandfather is as much responsible for my fascination with the sea as the sea itself.

But no great purpose is served by dwelling too long on the past—there is the now and the future of our lives as well. And so this book also is dedicated to my children Peter and Adriana, and to Lynda—partly because they share with me the things I love, but mostly because they give me reason to "keep on keepin' on."

Acknowledgements

The acknowledgement page of a book seems much to me like the acceptance speeches of Academy Award winners—name too few persons who've helped and you T-off the others; name too many and you put the audience to sleep. In any case, there are friends and acquaintances who've done me invaluable service by sharing their knowledge, and I would feel remiss in neglecting to mention their names.

Gerard Pesty introduced me to the many ways of generating alternative power; Aaron Jasper explained some of the mysteries of sailmaking; Henry Keene made available Edson's excellent drawings of steering systems; Bob Wilkinson elucidated the chemistry of paints; Tom Colvin challenged the convention of my thinking on a host of topics; Kim Houghton showed me how to fasten wire terminal fittings; Louie and all the folks at JT's Ship Chandlery scrounged through their inventories and let me take apart equipment; Roger Marshall allowed me the use of his tankage formulas; Frank Mulville shared the wisdom of his many years singlehanding across the oceans; Danny Greene instilled in me an appreciation for utility and safety; Bob Dobbins helped me put the crowbar to many a board when I was timid; Ron Barr gave me free use of his incomparable bookstore; Joanne Oakes cheerfully typed the manuscript—several times over; Murray and Barbara Davis gave me the break I really wanted by hiring me at *Cruising World;* Dale Nouse, with the patience of Job and skill of a great teacher, improved my writing; Gene and Anne Correll got me going on my first boat and taught me the first rules of seamanship; and Bruce Bingham . . . well, without him this book just would not have been the same. Not only was every drawing three times better than what was asked for, his technical editing helped refine a piece of coal into a stone of at least some small value. Jim Gilbert and Andrew Rock of Seven Seas Press deserve commendation for picking me off the floor when I was tired and overwhelmed, pouring a shot of Tequila down me and sending me back to the typewriter. And to Herb McCormick, also writing a book, who shared the office on countless nights when we'd rather have been anyplace else—misery loves company!

Looking back, it was a tremendous experience —to have met so many people and learned so much about boats in so little time. The result is the book I wish had been available to me 15 years ago. And if it helps one person get to sea a few months sooner or brings one more boat safely through a storm, it will have accomplished its purpose.

Contents

Introduction

Cruising in a sailboat involves a strange amalgam of skills and materials that, independent of the joys and sorrows, is probably one of the major reasons that adventures under sail are pursued by so many tinkerers, adventurers, mystics and ordinary people.

Beyond the live-aboard skills necessary for comfortable cruising, becoming a good seaman requires years of varied experiences on different boats in different conditions. Coastal and celestial navigation are sufficiently deep and murky subjects to obsess numbers fanatics for the rest of their lifetimes.

This book concerns what philosophers would term, "the thing in itself," the boat. It is a study of a material object composed of both organic and inorganic substances—wood, steel and plastic. That we tend to anthropormorphize boats is a natural manipulation, and even if absurd, it honestly represents the trust and affection we feel for the thing that we live in, that carries us from one port to the next, that is our partner in other romantic experiences with members of our own species—men, women and children who sit with us in the cockpit as the sun goes down, anticipating the green flash, a sky streaked with pastel colors, a warm breeze, a rising moon.

While there is no such thing as an "ideal cruiser," there are hundreds of boats capable of going to sea and making good, safe passages. Few of these boats, however, are equipped for offshore work at the time of construction. Eric Hiscock, Hal Roth, Don Street, Lin and Larry Pardey and others have written excellent books describing what, to their minds, ought to be done to make a boat a suitable cruiser. It would be difficult and presumptuous to suggest here that their recommendations are somehow deficient or incorrect. Indeed, the accumulated wisdom of these voyagers is worth its weight in gold to the beginning coastal or offshore cruiser.

On the other hand, many of the boats described in these books are custom-built especially for offshore work, and are enormously expensive to design, build, commission and fit out. There are a growing number of used boats on the market that may be modified and customized for cruising, even though they were originally built and sold as family weekend coastal cruisers. Which boat to select—new or used—and how to upgrade it for offshore sailing are the principal subjects of this book. To this end, the book is divided into two sections. The first deals with the basic structure of the boat—hull, interior, deck, engine and rig. The second part discusses the ancillary systems and gear necessary for cruising in a variety of conditions—generators, electronic instruments, galley gear, heating and cooling devices, and paint.

Many of the ideas and projects discussed here were the results of a major renovation effort I undertook over a period of years with a 1967 Pearson Triton. And through my work as an editor with *Cruising World* magazine I have had the opportunity to sail on and inspect dozens of ocean cruisers and racers—entrants in the Observer Singlehanded Race (OSTAR), the Two-Star, Bermuda Singlehanded and One-Two races, BOC Challenge and many others, not to mention the many inauspicious small cruisers which, following major ocean passages, quietly drop their hooks in Newport Harbor, and a few days later, just as unostentatiously depart.

Some of us sit in our offices and dream, some go out there and do it—we learn best from those who have.

Dan Spurr
Newport, Rhode Island

PART ONE

The Basic Boat

CHAPTER 1

The Anatomy of a Cruising Sailboat

And all I ask is a tall ship
And a star to steer her by.

JOHN MASEFIELD

Murray Davis, publisher of *Cruising World*, has a saying that there's no such thing as a bad boat, just ones used for the wrong purpose.

My first boat was a Snipe, a 15-foot daysailer. She was a great boat to knock about Michigan's small inland lakes, and on several occasions she was packed with a tent, sleeping bags and camping gear and was cruised across the frigid waters of northern Lake Michigan to Beaver Island and the Manitous. The Snipe was not designed for open-water sailing—but then neither was the sailboard designed for the Frenchman who sailed it around Cape Horn. Fortunately there always will be spirited fools and adventurers seeking to increase their fun—what a dull world it would be without them.

Because successful ocean passages are made in such a variety of crafts, it follows that there is no such thing as the "ideal cruiser". But, just as ancient Greek philosophers sought the perfect form of beauty, we too believe that somewhere there exists a perfect boat, one that sails well, gives us all the room we require, and pleases our senses as we look over our shoulders rowing towards her in the dinghy. Each of our boats must fit that ideal.

The truth is, one man's meat is another man's poison. Catamarans and trimarans successfully cruise around the world, even Cape Horn itself, the Everest of the blue-water sailor. You can find motor-sailers tied stern-to in Papeete that have made seamanlike passages from Southern California. Fin-keel, spade-rudder racers have passed beneath the five great capes making circumnavigations at breakneck speeds. And floating gypsy voyagers have lumbered among the islands in heavy displacement boats, finding pleasure and security in their turtle pace, even though their vessels may be hard pressed to claw away from a lee shore.

Some of us set off in a "radical" or otherwise unsuitable boat with a naïveté that later we find alarming.

But we survived, emerging, we hope, as Coleridge's "older, wiser man," a mariner not too ancient. Others engage in a diligent apprenticeship, owning progressively larger boats, methodically building upon a rudimentary knowledge until one day we realize that we do, indeed, know something about boats and seamanship.

During the learning process, I suppose most of us have taken inordinate risks. I sailed *Culculine*, the Snipe I named for a vixen in Guillaume Appollonaire's fiction, across Lake Michigan when I was 22. Back then it was the only boat available to me, and I would rather have risked the drowning than denied myself the adventure. Today, I am older, more conservative, and I hope wiser. My *Adriana*, a 28′6″ Pearson Triton sloop, is a tough little cruiser, meticulously fitted out and maintained as best I can to take what the sea delivers. Sometimes I yearn for the thrill of putting to sea in a minimal boat, which would enable me to confront nature on a more elemental level.

But when I pause to reflect, I do not wish to die. I do not wish to subject my beautiful children, who often cruise with me, to any unnecessary dangers. Comfort—my favorite music on the stereo, a library of good books, a dry bunk, a nip of brandy with my mate after a passage—has become more important. This is not to say I *need* these things to cruise, just that I prefer them that way.

This developmental process has repeated itself in the souls and minds of sailors for centuries, and there is an accumulated wisdom there, a body of knowledge if you will, that is available to the men and women who wish today to learn what they can before they themselves set out. While most of this book concerns hands-on projects to upgrade a boat to satisfy this "body of knowledge," it also is sensible to begin with a firm foundation, that is, a boat with a reasonably good chance of doing the things we ask of it. Whether we choose to gunkhole down the Intracoastal Waterway, nose around the Caribbean Islands, or make long blue-water passages to the South Pacific, there are certain design parameters, which if embodied in our boat, will make our cruising more successful. And by successful I mean safer and more comfortable.

THE CRUISING IMPERATIVES

At the risk of didacticism and with all due respect to the supra-scholarly texts on designing cruising sailboats, let's put forward a few cruising imperatives, recognizing, of course, that the designer has wide latitude in deciding how best to satisfy them.

Ability to Take the Ground Without Fear

Everybody runs aground. It's a simple fact of cruising. The more time spent cruising unfamiliar coastal waters, the more frequently you'll run aground. To avoid grounding would mean to avoid going anyplace new. If you live in constant fear of holing the boat or being unable to kedge off, you begin to place restrictions on the places you go and your pleasure is correspondingly diminished. This is not to say that every boat must be able to withstand pounding on a coral reef. But it should be able to hit sand and even small rocks without causing disabling damage.

Full-length keels give better protection to rudders than fin keels. But the latter allows the boat to pivot easier if it's necessary to turn the boat around before kedging off. Keels with vertical leading edges won't allow lines or floating debris, such as logs, to pass underneath easily. In either case, heavy ground tackle and a windlass are essential.

Ability to Survive a Knock-down

No one relishes the prospect of putting the mast in the water. And while circumnavigations have been made without knock-downs, it is a possibility (if not a probability) for which one should be prepared.

Gear commonly damaged by knock-downs are rigs and sails (Chapter 10), ports (Chapter 9) and just about anything inside the boat (Chapter 3) that is struck by flying pots, batteries and persons. Gear stored on deck, such as dinghies and ground tackle, must be securely lashed to keep it from being swept overboard or doing damage to pulpits, rigging and crew.

Ability to Balance Boat for Self-Steering

Short-handed crews on cruising boats will have more fun under way and enter port far more rested if the boat can self-steer at least part of the time. With just a couple aboard, self-steering is almost essential. Mechanical wind vanes and electronic autopilots (Chapter 7) can be fitted to just about any type of boat, but they will perform better if the design of the boat enables a fairly balanced helm. Ketches are admired for their ability to balance well, as are some yawls and schooners. The degree to which single-masted rigs balance is a function of the design of the hull and rig. A boat that doesn't balance well fights the self-steerer every inch of the way and promotes the likelihood of running off course and breaking gear.

Ability to Beat Off a Lee Shore

Even the best navigators and weather prognosticators sooner or later find themselves caught near a lee shore with a gale brewing. In this situation a boat that sails sideways is in peril of striking bottom. While a good cruising boat need not be able to point as high as a one-design racer, it should be able to make distance to windward in all but the worst conditions.

Again, the ability to beat to windward is largely a function of design. This entails the shape of the hull, the ends of the boat, the shape and size of the keel, and the kind of rig. A boat that sails well on all points isn't arrived at by chance on the architect's drafting board, but rather is the product of much skill and wisdom in bringing together many diverse factors, such as wetted surface area, prismatic coefficient, longitudinal plane, center of buoyancy, center of gravity and so forth.

Ability to Carry Sufficient Stores

Regardless of boat size and crew, a good cruising boat should be able to carry enough water, fuel, food, medical supplies, line, spare parts and other necessary gear to meet all the crews' needs for the duration of a passage, plus a safety margin.

Planning for extended cruises outside one's home country should take into account premium prices for supplies and services and the likelihood that many other goods won't be available at all. If you must have several beers a day, and if beer in the Caribbean costs $1 a can, then you'd be foolish not to fill the bilge with as many cases as possible. What, the space beneath the cabin sole is smaller than the cutlery drawer? How about under the bunks? Oh, you planned to store tools there. Maybe the lazarette. Full of life jackets, lines and fenders? Well, perhaps you'd better learn to like lemonade at happy hour!

Ability to Ride Comfortably at Anchor

Most cruising boats spend more time at anchor than under way. A well-known cruising family once told me that during their years of cruising, the highest ratio of sailing to anchoring was about 50–50, and usually much less. Even if you're just cruising for several weeks, you'll rest easier in a boat that has the ability to stay put.

A boat with high freeboard at the bow will tend to blow off and "sail" more at anchor than a boat with more moderate freeboard. Underwater, the distribution of lateral plane determines the resistance to this tendency; a boat with a deep forefoot and long keel will ride more comfortably at anchor.

Protected Propeller

Sadly, the oceans are no longer as clean as they used to be. Blue-water voyagers today report seeing half-submerged oil drums, logs, nets and just about every type of conceivable floating garbage. Coastal waters are worse. Discounting junk, there are legitimate hazards such as fish traps, lobster pots and research buoys that often are poorly marked.

Fouling the propeller with a line or bending the blades by striking a solid object has all the makings of a nightmare, pure and simple. With luck, the weather will be fair, the seas calm and the water warm. You can secure the boat, lower yourself over the side with a face mask and attempt to cut away the line with a sharp knife. But these conditions cannot always be guaranteed.

The best precaution is preventive planning. A boat without a prop aperture poses a significantly greater risk. On boats with separated keels and rudders, a strut of bronze pipe or length of wire extending between the keel and rudder skeg helps lines and other objects pass safely astern.

The snagging of lines by spade rudders or wind vane rudders is a cause for concern. At the start of the third leg of the 1982/83 BOC Challenge singlehanded round the world race, Richard Broadhead caught an inflatable buoy around his windvane rudder. His 52-foot cutter stopped dead in the water. Broadhead was forced to luff his sails to disentangle himself, but only after several minutes of panic and help from spectators. The same thing happened to me while sailing off Newport, Rhode Island, when the wind vane rudder snared a fish float. Try as I might to push the float and line under the rudder with my feet, it eventually required a cold swim to extricate ourselves.

Comfortable Accommodations

When I first met Tom Colvin during a cruising seminar at which we were both speaking, he emphasized the importance of bringing the comforts of home aboard the cruising boat. "I like a big, sumptuous aft cabin," he said. "When you reduce cruising to tenement living, I don't want any part of it."

Well, not everyone likes aft cabins, or may own a boat large enough to have one. But the point is well taken. My 28-foot Triton is very comfortable for two persons for extended periods. But substantial interior modifications were necessary. Cushions were recovered, book shelves

built, a stereo installed, large lounge pillows purchased, comfortably angled backrests added, and a five-inch-thick foam mattress cut for the double berth in the forward cabin. I can sleep as well there as in any bed. And in the main cabin I can read a book, watch television or listen to music as comfortably as in any cushy wingback chair. Who needs back pain?

DESIGN AND CONSTRUCTION CONSIDERATIONS

Designing a successful cruising boat is such a complex process, with so many variables to marry, that it is virtually impossible to make dogmatic statements about displacement, underwater shape, type of rig or hull material without knowing something about the other variables.

Some persons aren't happy unless they're making 12 knots on a ULDB (ultra-light displacement boat); others don't feel secure unless they're sitting deep inside a heavy-displacement, full-keel Colin Archer-type monohull. Despite the impassioned claims of "experts", who's to say one is better than the other?

A good percentage of us, however, are less apt to go wrong if we observe the old maxim, "all things in moderation." Defining a "moderate" cruising boat is certainly easier than attempting to define the "ideal" cruising boat.

Underbody Profiles

If we can imagine the various types of sailboat underbodies as a continuum (Figure 1-1) ranging from a small fin keel with a spade rudder at one end to a full keel extending from bow to stern at the other end, and if we understand that just about any configuration *may* be effective if the designer has done his job well, then we begin to get a picture of what constitutes moderate underbody profile.

Advocates of full keels cite, sometimes erroneously, characteristics such as greater tracking ability, greater stability, and better ability to absorb a grounding. In fact, a full keel guarantees nothing if the boat is poorly designed. This is not to discredit full keels at all. I own a boat with

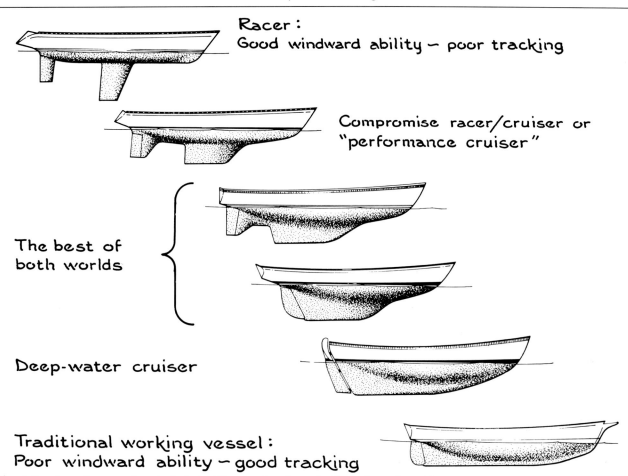

Racer:
Good windward ability – poor tracking

Compromise racer/cruiser or "performance cruiser"

The best of both worlds

Deep-water cruiser

Traditional working vessel:
Poor windward ability – good tracking

Fig. 1-1 *A continuum of underbody profiles ranging from the fin keel, spade rudder lightweight racer to the full keel attached rudder, heavy displacement cruiser*

a large keel, but it has a cutaway forefoot to make turning easier and reduce wetted surface area. It terminates at the rudder stock, about four feet from the stern. She tracks well and turns easily.

A fin keel is not a fin keel is not a fin keel, as Figure 1-1 illustrates. In many instances, a fin keel has less wetted surface, but this depends upon the length and depths of the two keels one is comparing. The fin keel may point higher, but is dependent to some extent on the shape of the leading edge and the amount of lift obtained from the keel's shape.

In recent years, Seattle naval architect Bob Perry has popularized the "performance cruiser", characterized in part by large fin keels with flat bottoms, and skeg-mounted rudders mounted well aft. They have sufficient lateral plane for good tracking ability, and the skeg strengthens and protects the rudder.

Many other factors contribute to the handling

characteristics and stability of a given boat, including center of gravity, firm or slack bilges, rolling period and location of garboards. If one is in doubt as to the seaworthiness of his boat, he would do well to consult a naval architect or at least read books such as *Skene's Elements of Yacht Design*.

Rudder Types

Considering that the rudder steers the boat, and without it the boat is left to the vagaries of weather and the skipper's ingenuity to carry on, utmost attention should be given to its type and method of construction (see Chapter 2).

Full keels facilitate attaching the rudder at the trailing edge, either inboard (stock emerging through hull) or outboard (rudder and stock hinged on trailing edge of keel and/or transom). Loads on the full-keel rudder are well distributed and the keel, especially if it is an inch or so deeper than the rudder, will take the brunt of a grounding. The few times I've been aground in my boat, even when careened over almost to the point where the turn of the bilge touched bottom, the rudder was still free to move a short distance. It has never been damaged.

When the keel and rudder are separated, it is best to have the rudder fixed to a full skeg, though a partial skeg is better than none.

Spade rudders, while often the most responsive, are often also the weakest. Not only can a bent stock disable steering, but striking an underwater object can push the stock up into the hull, breaking the interior supports. Many cruising boats with spade rudders have made successful voyages, but some extra caution is required. One should not hesitate to beef up the stock supports inside the hull if they are not sufficiently strong.

The Displacement/Length Ratio

The comparative heaviness of a yacht is determined by its displacement/length ratio. The formula is

$$\text{D/L ratio} = \frac{\text{Displacement in long tons}}{(.01 \text{ DWL})^3};$$

or, displacement-to-length ratio equals displacement in long tons divided by one hundredth the designed waterline length to the third power. (A long ton equals 2,240 pounds.)

Here are a few popular boats and their D/L ratios:

Olson 40	91
Santa Cruz 40	102
Freedom 40	208
Pearson 530	211
C&C 39	228
Nor'Sea 27	257
Valiant 40	264
Pearson 323	275
Mason 63	285
CT 37	343
Pearson 35	371
Southern Cross 31	388
Allied Seawind II	396
Westsail 32	435

For the purposes of general discussion, we can consider any D/L ratio under 200 as light, between 200 and 300 as moderate, between 300 and 400 as moderately heavy, and any number above 400 as heavy.

Bruce Bingham, the illustrator of this book and a naval architect who has designed, among other boats, the 20-foot Flicka and 35-foot Fantasia, believes that too much emphasis is placed on the D/L ratio. There are those who argue that heavy displacement boats have more seakindly motion and can carry greater amounts of stores; others point out the greater speed of moderate displacement boats, lighter and therefore less expensive rigs, and the ability to ride over waves rather than crash through them.

Bruce believes, and rightly so, that there are many other factors that deserve consideration in conjunction with the D/L ratio. While it is true that a high D/L ratio is generally more compatible with a blue-water cruiser than a coastal cruiser, naval architects are also concerned with the prismatic coefficient (a measure of relative fullness of the ends of the boat compared to the middle), the angle of entry of the waterline, angle of the buttocks lines, hull shape, length/beam ratio, and so on. In fact, in recent years acceptable minimum D/L ratios have lowered dramatically. Robert Perry says when he designed the Valiant 40 in 1973, its D/L ratio of 260 was considered by many as too light for ocean cruising. Yet several have made safe, comfortable circumnavigations. The upshot is that in evaluating a boat one must look at a variety of factors; it's foolish to grab one number, such as the D/L ratio, and conclude that boats measuring above this number are good, and boats below it are bad.

Weight is one thing, the shape of the hull quite another. Bruce's graph of D/L ratios for different type boats (Figure 1-2) suggests moderation and is consistent with the thinking of many other naval architects who believe that a D/L ratio of about 300 is close to ideal for a live-aboard, ocean cruising boat.

Bow and Stern

In the past decade or so there has been a trend toward widening and flattening the stern of the boat to give, among other things, more cockpit space and seat locker stowage. This practice has followed on the heels of wider beams to give greater living space below. These are all pluses

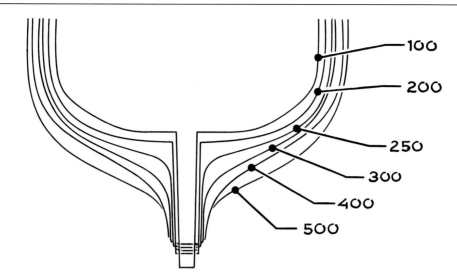

100: Strictly racing, thrill sailing and overnighting
200: Racing, weekending and light cruising
250: All-around good sailing, motoring, long and short cruising with moderate liveability
300: Fair sailing for long cruises but excellent motoring with good liveability
400: Poor sailing but excellent motoring, seakindliness and liveability
500: Terrible sailing but superb liveability. Motoring is good with high power.

Fig. 1-2 *The displacement/length ratio is calculated by dividing the boat's displacement in long tons (2,240 lbs.) by .01 times the design water line to the third power. An appropriate D/L ratio depends in part upon the intended use of the boat.*

certainly and, because a boat derives a good deal of her stability from her beam, it would seem that wide beam and a wide stern would make a very good cruising boat. However, to give the boat a bite on the water and an ability to point high, the bows on these boats are often quite hollow and narrow. The result is a bow and stern out of proportion to one another, and especially when coupled with a relatively flat, shallow bottom, there is often a tendency for such a boat to display excessive weather helm when heeled over.

On a reach, a wide stern can give the boat greater power by moving the stern wave further aft. On a run with following seas, however, a wide stern can cause the boat to slew off. Looking still closer, full ends do provide reserve buoyancy enabling the boat to rise with the waves and not plunge. Tony Lush's *Lady Pepperell,* a 54-foot entrant in the BOC Challenge, was severely rolled in the Southern Ocean and ultimately lost. One theory suggested that the bow was too fine, with insufficient buoyancy to keep it from nosediving into a trough as she slid down a steep wave. Again, a safe conclusion is that moderate beam and ends contribute to a good cruising boat.

Double-enders have enjoyed something of a renaissance among production builders since the introduction of the Westsail 32 (Figure 1-3) in the early 1970's. Of course, there is really nothing new about this design, adapted as it was from North Sea pilot boats of the previous century. The pointed stern is favored by some for its reputed ability to part following seas, thus avoiding the yawing motion of boats with wide, flat transoms. While this may be true to an extent, some speed is sacrificed. And, if the stern is too narrow, reserve buoyancy also may be dangerously diminished.

Fig. 1-3 *The Westsail 32, designed by William Crealock, was based on several generations of Colin Archer-type cutters used in the North Sea. The Tahiti Ketch was another famous offshoot of these boats. The Westsail 32 in many ways started the current popular interest in cruising. She was offered with both ketch and cutter rigs.*

Draft

In considering beam, we should not forget draft. Maxi ocean racers frequently have deep fin keels drawing 10 feet and more. This contributes to their tremendous windward ability and stability. But double-figure drafts are impractical for the cruiser who wants to sail around reefs and islands. In the Bahamas and Florida Keys, any draft greater than four feet will severely limit where a boat can sail without hitting bottom. What shoal keels give away in windward performance is regained by their ability to cruise many beautiful places off limits to deeper draft boats. In the 1950's, Carleton Mitchell's *Finnisterre* dispelled the myth that centerboard boats were not practical for ocean sailing, though they are seldom seen nowadays on any major ocean racing circuit. The possibility of jamming the board up or down is just one more potential headache that many cruising sailors can do without.

Twin Keels

It might be pertinent to mention here that twin keels have much to recommend themselves for shoal-water cruising. Long popular in England, even on such well-known production boats as the Westerly line, twin keels have the advantage of keeping the boat upright on the flats when the tide goes out. While they often have more wetted surface area than single keels, and won't point as high, they do give a damping motion off the wind that is quite pleasing. And, because the keels are generally angled outward from the bilges, the twin-keeled boat draws more heeled than when perfectly upright—a twin-keeled boat drawing say three feet, might actually draw 3½ feet when heeled 25 degrees.

During a cruise in New Zealand's Bay of Islands, I met Shelly and Jane DeRidder, who live aboard *Magic Dragon* (Figure 1-4), a 40-foot

twin-keeled cutter. Shelly is a very innovative, if seat-of-the-pants designer of cruising boats and gear, including a self-steering wind vane. His *Magic Dragon* is the largest twin-keel cruising boat I have seen, and while Shelly is not unaware of the sacrifices he made to have this particular keel configuration, he and Jane are more than pleased with the boat.

Inverse Stability

Several tragedies in the yachting world in the past few years have raised serious questions about exceptionally beamy boats with shallow bottoms and shoal or insufficiently ballasted keels. The late English naval architect, Angus Primrose, ironically appears to possibly have been the victim of design problems with one of his own boats.

Fig. 1-4 *Shelly and Jane DeRidder built their 40-foot* Magic Dragon *with bilge keels and have sailed her thousands of miles across the Pacific. Following a flood where she was moored in New Zealand's Kerikeri River, they brought her to Opua in the Bay of Islands to inspect the damage.*

Following the 1980 U.S. Sailboat Show in Annapolis, Maryland, Angus and one crew member were caught in a gale a few hundred miles offshore. According to the crew member, who survived by hanging onto a life raft for several days, the boat was knocked down and then rolled over. The crew member stated that the boat did not right itself for about five minutes, during which time water entered the cabin through hatches. When a wave finally rolled the boat upright, it was too full of water to save and it was abandoned.

The boat had the following specifications: LOA 33′; LWL 28′5″; beam 11′5″; draft 4′5″; ballast 3,815 pounds; displacement 10,525 lbs.

Beam resists the righting moment of the keel, which is also competing with the weight and resistance of the rig under water. Expanding on this in the 1975 *Cruising World* annual, naval architect John Letcher wrote:

"It is worth noting on this question of self-righting ability, that typically beamy modern

hulls have a limited range of stability, and a stable equilibrium position upside down. (Figure 1–5.) Even if it is unlikely that the hull would remain in this relatively narrow stable range for more than the time of one sea passing, this property undoubtedly gives a tendency to hesitate in the 180° position, allowing more time for water to come in through available openings.

"Once a substantial amount of water is inside, the resulting free surface greatly reduces the stability in the inverted position (especially with a flush deck), so righting follows quickly. At the design stage, a small reduction in beam from modern standards can greatly improve righting ability from angles near 180°."

Primrose's boat did right itself with water inside, but was dangerously low in the water and could not be handled to negotiate the waves. Primrose and his crew member believed that the boat was sinking and that the best course of action was to take to the life raft.

The 1979 Fastnet Race disaster, which claimed the lives of 15 sailors, prompted a thorough investigation of yacht design, equipment and crew experience. In summing up the RYA-RORC report, Dale Nouse, *Cruising World*'s editor, wrote, "The report observed that in cases of severe knockdowns (past horizontal and even 360°

Fig. 1-5 *It is possible for a boat, especially a beamy one with shallow draft, to achieve stability upside down.*

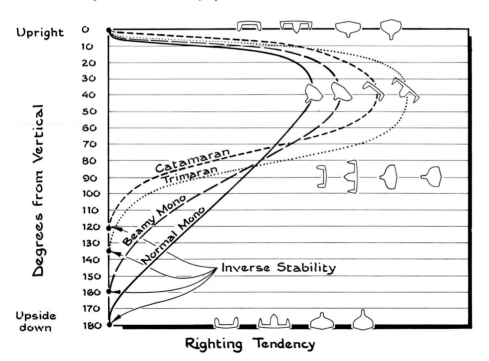

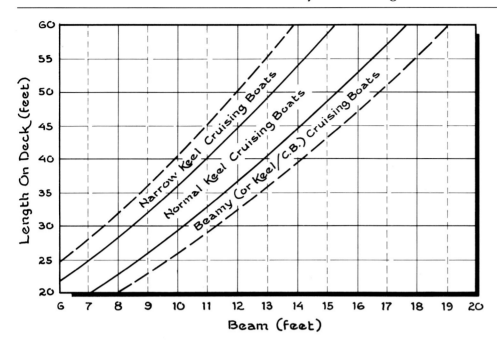

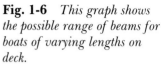

Fig. 1-6 *This graph shows the possible range of beams for boats of varying lengths on deck.*

rolls) the design characteristics which appeared to increase the likelihood of a knockdown include lack of initial stability, wide beam and wide, shallow hull form. There was little indication of any tie between knockdowns and either ballast ratios or length/displacement ratios."

Because wide beam can mean more space below, and because space is so important to the live-aboard couple, it is difficult to dissuade anyone from purchasing a wide-beamed boat. By coupling deep garboards, firm bilges and deeper draft, however, the chances of achieving inverse stability are lessened.

If one were to follow Letcher's advice and reduce beam from "modern standards", it might appear that interior volume would be correspondingly less. But, if freeboard is high and the garboards deep, the narrow boat can have as much interior volume as the beamier, more shallow boat. Figures 1-6 and 1-7 offer some suggested beam and draft relationships according to waterline length and length on deck.

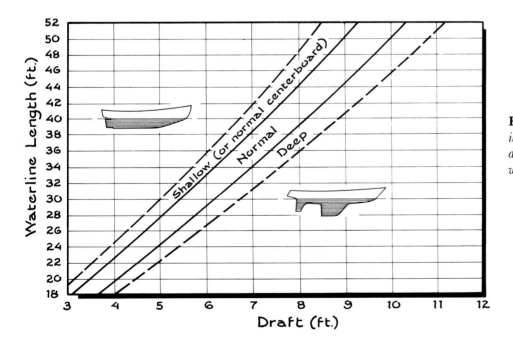

Fig. 1-7 *This graph illustrates the possible range of drafts for boats of varying waterline lengths.*

Internal or External Ballast?

In wood boat construction, common practice is to pour molten iron or lead into a female mold until it cools. The keel is then fitted onto the hull or stub keel and fastened by large bolts sunk into the ballast at the time it was made. The bolts protrude through heavy floor timbers and are held in place by washers and nuts. This practice is less frequently used in fiberglass boats, except with some fin keels. More and more builders are molding the entire keel with the hull and dropping the ballast into the hollow mold. There are advantages and disadvantages to each method (Figure 1-8).

The main argument for external ballast is that, with lead at least, the keel is sufficiently soft to absorb the blow caused by the boat striking a rock or other obstacle. Lead keels may be severely dented in such instances, but the hull remains intact and no water enters. . . . unless the keel bolts are wrenched and water finds its way through a fissure between the ballast and keel, then into the bilge. This can and does happen, though much depends on the methods used to fasten the ballast and the way in which the keel bolt loads are distributed inside the boat. It is possible to glass over the lead keel and fair the laminations into the hull for extra strength and protection.

With internally ballasted boats, keel bolts cease to become causes of concern because there aren't any. The fiberglass hull totally supports the weight of the ballast. When an underwater object is struck, the fiberglass around the ballast may be fractured, and water could enter the area between the ballast and the fiberglass keel. The problems are minimized, though, if the builder has been careful to eliminate air pockets inside the keel. But this is not always an easy thing to do. In fact, I know of quite a few boats that have required major keel reworking because of these voids. Discounting the possibilities of running

Fig. 1-8 *In externally ballasted boats, large keel bolts are sunk into the metal to fasten the ballast to the hull. Internally ballasted boats built in fiberglass have hollow molded integral keels into which the ballast is dropped. Resin is poured in around the keel to fill voids and then the area is glassed over to seal it off.*

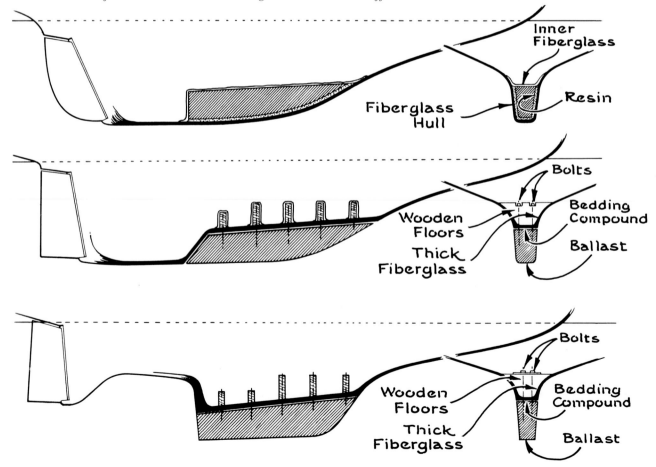

aground, internally ballasted keels give less cause for concern and are basically maintenance free, whereas externally ballasted keels must be watched to make sure the keel bolts are tight and that no water is leaking in.

All in all, either method of fixing ballast to the hull is entirely satisfactory for any type of sailing. It is much more a question of how well the builder has done his job than the method he has chosen.

HULL MATERIAL

For centuries, wood was just about the only material used for small boats. The Dutch began using steel in the 19th century for boats as small as nine feet. Only in the past few decades has fiberglass become dominant, and while its virtues are many, it is not the only viable boatbuilding material. Figure 1-9 compares the basic engineering properties of the most commonly used materials.

Fiberglass

One of the first production fiberglass sailboats in the U.S. was the Pearson Triton (Figure 1-10). It was introduced at the 1959 New York Boat Show by cousins Clint and Everett Pearson, and was an immediate success. Other good boats, like the Invicta (1960), Bounty II (1961), Vanguard

(1962), and Countess 44 (1965), soon followed to round out the Pearson line.

It is common to hear the owners of these boats say that the early Pearsons were built "before they knew fiberglass," meaning that hull thicknesses were based on engineering knowledge for appropriate thicknesses for wood. "My hull is this thick!" a Triton or Vanguard owner will say, spacing his thumb and finger an inch apart. These guesstimates are about as accurate as fish stories, but there is a little bit of truth to the notion.

The hull thickness of my Triton (#603) is about one-half inch at the sheer, increasing slightly at the turn of the bilge to about ⅞-inch thick at places in the keel. This certainly is a heavier lay-up than many new boats. But Pearson officials are quick to say that their new boats are just as heavily laid up. Would you expect them to say anything else?

In comparison, the Tatoosh 42, a good cruising boat designed by Bob Perry and built by Ta Yang, a good yard in Taiwan, is about .36 inches thick at the sheer, .47 inches at the turn of the bilge, and .59 inches at the keel.

When buying a boat, it's always a good idea to research the lamination schedule, because the type and weight of cloth, mat and woven roving, use of cores, internal reinforcements and ratio of glass fiber to resin are also important. Some builders refuse to give this information, saying the lay-up is "thick enough". Thick enough for what? To withstand a bump from a floating log? To withstand a collision with another boat? Here's the lamination schedule for the Corbin 39, built in Canada by Corbin Les Bateaux Inc. Note that more than one layer of each material may be used in every step, depending on the part of the boat being laminated.

Gel coat (22mm)
1-oz. mat
1½-oz. mat
24-oz. woven roving
1½-oz. mat
24-oz. woven roving
1-oz. mat
1-oz. mat
¾"-Airex core
1½-oz. mat
24-oz. woven roving
1½-oz. mat
24-oz. woven roving

Fig. 1-9 *Properties of common boatbuilding materials*

Material	Weight lb/cu. ft.	Tensile Strength (psi)	Compressive Strength (psi)	Modulus of Elasticity (psi)
GRP Mat	94	10,000	15,000	900,000
GRP W/R	106	35,000	25,000	2,000,000
Douglas Fir (12% moisture)	34	2,150	2,000	1,600,000
Aluminum	166	42,000	32,000	10,000,000
Steel	490	60,000	60,000	28,900,000
Ferrocement	168	1,600	10,000	1,300,000

Fig. 1-10 *The 28'6" Pearson Triton was the first production sailboat built in fiberglass in the United States. More than 700 were completed before production ceased in 1967. Though not as beamy as more modern 28-footers, the Triton was heavily glassed and performed well.*

Twenty-five layers were used in the center of the Corbin 39, and 35 layers were used at the keel—exceptionally strong! Figures 1-11 and 1-12 give suggested hull thicknesses for solid skin hulls and those with cores according to displacement.

Today, core materials like Airex® and Contourkore® end-grain balsa (Figure 1-13) are frequently used to stiffen hulls and reduce weight. The actual thickness of fiberglass mat, cloth and resin will not be as great as in a solid fiberglass hull, but the stiffening, weight-reducing and in-

Fig. 1-11 *This graph suggests a lamination schedule and hull thickness for solid skin fiberglass boats by displacement.*

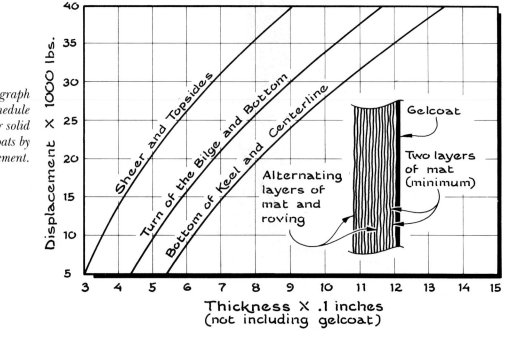

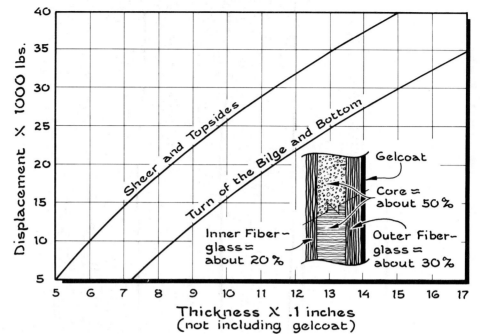

Fig. 1-12 *This graph suggests a lamination schedule and hull thickness for cored fiberglass hulls by displacement.*

sulating properties make it worthwhile. Also, core materials are less expensive than resin. While few 10- to 20-year-old boats used core materials in the hull, many boats built in the 1980's not only employ cores but also incorporate molded floor grids that have been engineered to further stiffen the hull in critical areas. Studying Figure 1-14 gives some clues as to how one might consider strengthening a hull that is too thin and/or has insufficient athwartship and lon-

Fig. 1-13 *Baltek Corporation manufactures an end-grain balsa product called Contourkore that is commonly used nowadays as a hull core material. The boat being laid up here is a J/24.*

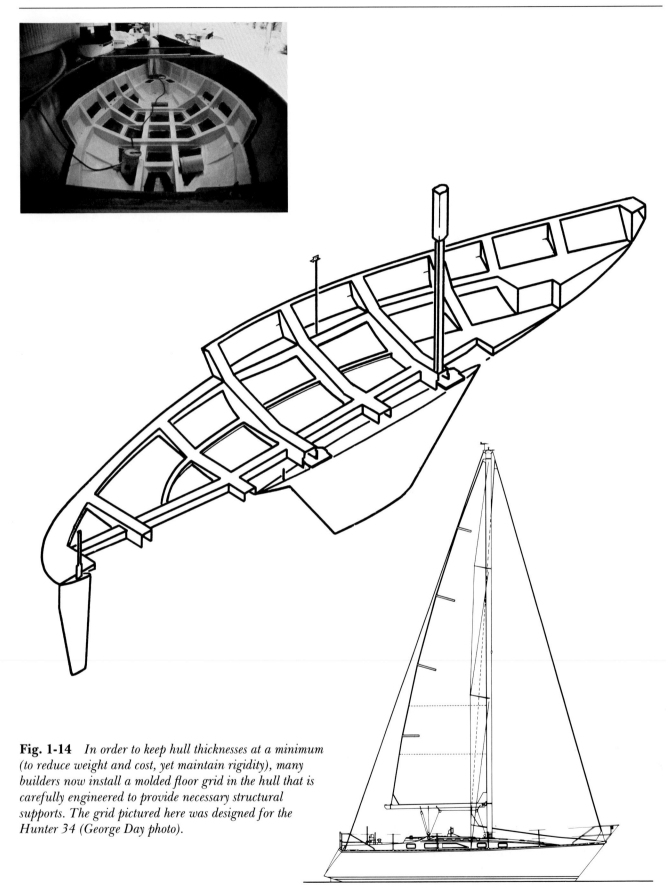

Fig. 1-14 *In order to keep hull thicknesses at a minimum
(to reduce weight and cost, yet maintain rigidity), many
builders now install a molded floor grid in the hull that is
carefully engineered to provide necessary structural
supports. The grid pictured here was designed for the
Hunter 34 (George Day photo).*

gitudinal stiffeners. If this describes your hull, you might already be aware of the problem by having observed the following:

- Doors won't close
- Bulkheads cracking or delaminating where they are glassed to the hull
- Standing rigging that is perpetually loose
- Hull panel deflecting when struck with force (push on it with the palm of your hand)

Wood

Fiberglass has been the dominant boatbuilding material during the last 20 years and is an obvious choice for many sailors. Fewer and fewer major production yards built in wood during the late 1960's and 1970's, though a few, like Dickerson and Hinckley, continued for a time before making the switch to fiberglass. If considering a wood boat, retain the services of a competent marine surveyor to check the boat before purchase. Wood is a wonderful building material, just make certain you aren't buying a hull riddled with rot or weakened by broken ribs. And be realistic in assessing the hours required for repair and annual maintenance.

Cold-molded boats saturated with epoxy resin, such as those built by the Gougeon Brothers W.E.S.T. System (Figure 1-15), are lightweight, rigid and more resistant to abrasion than bare planking. This method is especially ideal for multihulls. Typical construction might call for multiple-veneer laminates of ⅛-inch western red

Fig. 1-15 *A typical W.E.S.T. System cold-molded hull. Note how the thin veneers are stapled at cross angles to increase strength. Epoxy resin saturates each lamination and prevents moisture from entering the wood (Gougeon Brothers, Inc.).*

cedar with a final skin thickness of ⅝-inch, depending on the type of mold used.

Steel

Steel pleasure boats are a relatively new phenomenon in America. But in Holland, a country without abundant timber, steel has been the preferred material for more than 100 years. Many of those boats are still sailing (Figure 1-16). Today a growing number of yards in North America are building quality steel boats. But steel construction is just as labor intensive as fiberglass and one can't expect to save much by looking for a used steel production sailboat. A few custom steel boats are around, but most were built overseas. If they pass survey, they

Fig. 1-16 *Because of the sparsity of trees in Holland, the Dutch have been building boats in steel for over 100 years—everything from small dinghies to large leeboard sailing barges, such as this one powering along a canal near Vollenhove.*

Fig. 1-17 *The Meta Company of Tarare, France, has patented a process called "Strongall," in which aluminum boats are built with plates about three times the usual 4 to 5mm thicknesses. This design, by Michel Joubert, is the JNF 38.*

could be good buys, indeed. Without a doubt, steel provides the greatest resistance to holing by reefs or floating debris.

Aluminum and Other Metals

Aluminum is an excellent material for boatbuilding, and contrary to some persons' thinking, can be suitable for homebuilding. The principal objection to amateurs working in aluminum is that different skills are required than for steel to cope with oxidation and linear expansion. On the other hand, the average-size plate is much lighter than a comparatively sized steel plate, and so is easier to move around. And, a good marine-grade aluminum doesn't rust the way steel does, so there is less concern for exposing the metal to the elements, and no need to sandblast prior to painting. In fact, the French, who have a predilection for aluminum "escape machines", often don't paint their hulls at all above the waterline.

The Meta Company of Tarare, France, has experienced favorable results building aluminum cruising boats triple the usual 4mm to 5mm thicknesses of most other conventionally plated aluminum boats. The patented "Strongall" process is viewed by the developers as an answer to the problems of weldment fracture, plate distortion and electrolysis. Designer Michel Joubert could not have tripled the thicknesses of similar size steel hulls because of excessive weight. But because of the low specific gravity of aluminum, he could design a 39-footer (Figure 1-17) displacing 25,000 pounds.

A few cruising boats have been built of Monel, a metal long used for fuel tanks and sometimes for propeller shafts. It is more corrosion-resistant than steel and is quite strong. Copper-nickel alloy (90/10) has been used in the construction of several commercial vessels in Third World countries. While it is about eight to 10 times more expensive than mild steel, it is supposedly antifouling, and costs are recouped by never having to haul the boat or spend money on bottom paint. *Cruising World*'s Danny Greene is considering building a 34-foot double-headsail yawl or ketch using this metal to avoid haulouts and for protection against the three greatest threats to the offshore cruiser—large breaking waves, large floating objects, and the occasional grounding.

Ferro-Cement

Although a few yards dabbled in ferro-cement during the 1970's, most boats built of this difficult material were home-built, many according to plans offered by Samson Marine Designs in Canada. A professionally plastered hull can be sufficiently strong for ocean sailing, although abrasion resistance is not as great as steel or fiberglass. But it's not an easy job, mainly because the wire mesh, which is laid over frames to form the shape of the hull, has so many tiny corners it is hard to get all the bubbles out of the plaster when it is applied. Expansion and contraction due to temperature changes eventually cause cracks to appear in the hull.

If considering buying a ferro-cement hull, determine whether professional plasterers were used. Again, retain a marine surveyor to check it for you.

RIGS

Cruising sailors argue the various merits of different rigs to no end. I suppose this is only to be expected, because just as there is no ideal cruiser, there is no ideal rig, either. A few observations:

Proponents of two-stick rigs make a good point when they say that if one spar is lost, there's always one left to jury rig. For this reason, the triatic stay, which connects the two mastheads, should be avoided if at all possible, even if it means using running backstays and split or double backstays on the main and jumper struts on the mizzen.

On the other hand, two-stick rigs (yawl, ketch and schooner) are usually not as weatherly as sloops and cutters. And they cost more because of the number of spars, extra fittings, rope and wire. Their best point of sail is reaching, when they can put up more canvas. The fore and aft distribution of sails often makes them balance very well.

The Freedom line of boats (Figure 1-18) has popularized the cat ketch rig in recent years, and for several good reasons. First, eliminating stays means you no longer have to worry about losing the rig if even just one of several dozen terminals

or tangs breaks (corrosion is often the culprit, and difficult to detect, even if the terminal fitting is at the deck). Free-standing spars are being built of aluminum, steel and carbon fiber. Of these, the latter is the preferred material due to its combination of strength and light weight. They are expensive, but price is mitigated to an extent by the fact that standing rigging is eliminated. Carbon fiber spars also are quite strong, as evidenced by the fact that when Tony Lush's *Lady Pepperell* rolled over in the Southern Ocean, the spars survived intact.

Sloops and cutters generally demonstrate superior windward performance, but for them to

Fig. 1-18 *The Freedom line of cat ketches has gained notoriety by virtue of their freestanding spars and self-tending rigs. The Freedom 44 pictured here won the 1981 Bermuda One-Two Race.*

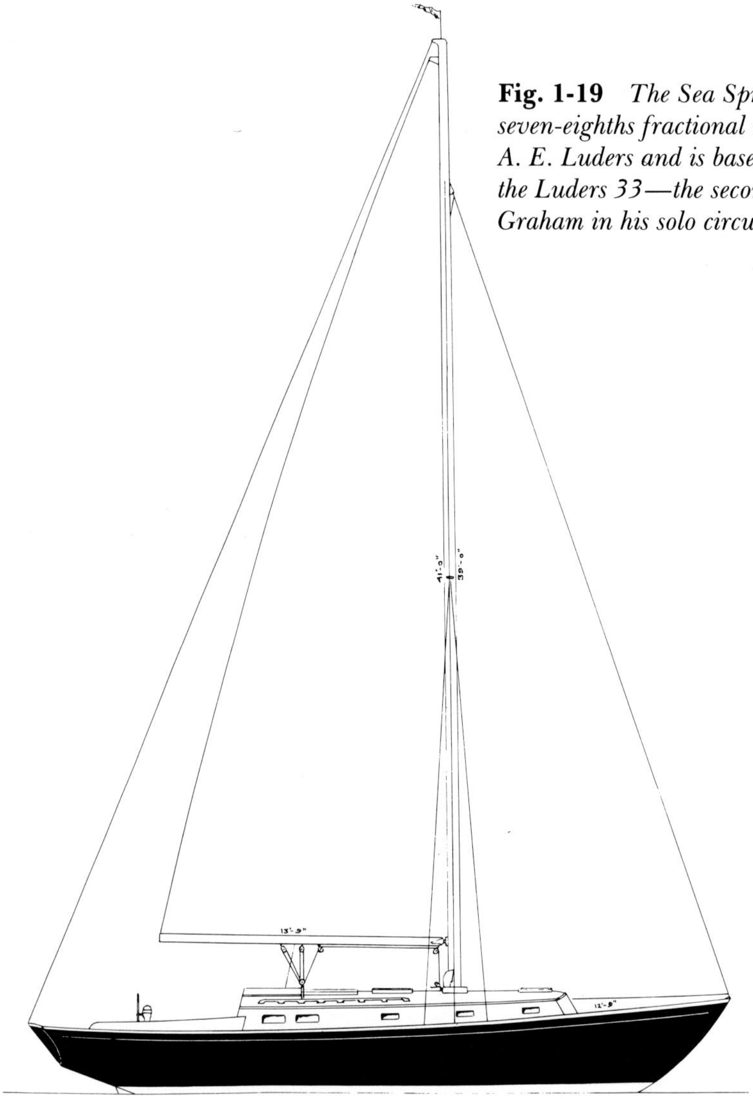

Fig. 1-19 *The Sea Sprite 34, which sports a tall seven-eighths fractional rig, was designed by A. E. Luders and is based on another of his designs, the Luders 33—the second boat sailed by Robin Lee Graham in his solo circumnavigation.*

handle winds ranging from light to gale force, their sail inventories should include everything from drifters to trysails and storm jibs. The cutter is preferred because the foretriangle is divided among two sails instead of just one; this decreases the size of sails that must be handled —instead of changing sails in heavy weather, you just start reefing or taking them down. Clubfooted staysails, however, must be viewed with suspicion, as they are capable of rapping someone on the skull or knocking him overboard if the sail backwinds unexpectedly. A safer arrangement is to eliminate the club and lead the sheet from a block at the clew to a block on the traveler (Chapter 10).

Fractional rigs (Figure 1-19) have become popular once again, primarily on racing boats because the spar can be bent backwards to op-

timize sail shape. Yet veteran sailors such as Tristan Jones, who claims more singlehanded miles at sea than any other man, have said that the simple masthead rig is hard to beat for cruising. They tend to be slightly shorter than fractionl rigs for the same size boat, and consequently offer less weight and wind resistance high up. The top of the mast also is more rigidly stayed, thereby being less subject to whipping when slamming into head seas. Jumper struts are not required, either.

SUMMARY

There is no such thing as the "ideal" cruiser, but moderate design and dimensions can be regarded as intelligently conservative when choosing a boat. Regardless of specific design features, the good cruising boat should be expected to:

- Take at least minor groundings without disabling the steering or threatening the integrity of the hull.
- Survive a knockdown without losing the rig or suffering broken ports or other major structural damage.
- Balance sufficiently well to permit self-steering, either by mechanical wind vane, electronic autopilot or trimming of sails (such as by utilizing sheet-to-tiller steering).
- Beat off a lee shore in all but the worst conditions.
- Carry sufficient fuel, water and food for the duration of the passage plus a safety margin.
- Ride comfortably at anchor so the boat doesn't hobbyhorse or sail from side to side, posing the potential danger of striking another boat or possibly fouling the rode.
- Sail over floating debris and markers without damaging or wrapping the propeller or impairing steering.
- Provide comfortable accommodations to minimize crew fatigue, enhance their enjoyment of the cruise and protect them during bad weather.
- Return quickly to an upright position if rolled 180°.
- Have a rig and sail plan that is manageable by the available crew.

FURTHER READING

The Ocean Sailing Yacht, Vols. I and II, by Donald M. Street, Jr.; W. W. Norton & Company, 500 Fifth Avenue, New York, New York 10110.

Choice Yacht Designs, by Richard Henderson; International Marine Publishing Company, Camden, Maine 04843.

Best Boats, by Ferenc Maté; Albatross Publishing House, 5934 Marine Drive, West Vancouver, B.C., Canada V7W 2S2.

Understanding Boat Design, by Edward S. Brewer and Jim Betts; International Marine Publishing Company, Camden, Maine 04843.

Sailing Yacht Design, by Douglas Phillips-Birt; Adlard Coles Ltd., Frogmore, St. Albans, Hertfordshire, England AL2 2NF.

The Sailing Yacht, by Juan Baader; W. W. Norton & Company, 500 Fifth Avenue, New York, New York 10110.

Fiberglass Boat Survey Manual, by Arthur Edmunds; John de Graff, Inc., Clinton Corners, New York 12514.

Skene's Elements of Yacht Design, revised and updated by Francis S. Kinney; Dodd, Mead & Company, 79 Madison Avenue, New York, New York 10016.

CHAPTER 2

Strengthening Major Structural Components

There is a pleasure in being in a ship beaten about by a storm, when we are sure that it will not founder.

PASCAL

Ondine, a well-known maxi ocean racer, was built in aluminum of plating that wasn't thick enough to withstand the pounding of the seas. Before long, the plating buckled inward between the frames. Filler compound was used several times to fair the hull, but ultimately it was necessary to replate major portions of the hull. The yard bill, of course, was astronomical, suggesting that even good designers are not necessarily infallible. In the quest for speed or a good rating, shortcuts are calculated risks willingly undertaken. But the cruising sailor, whose only interest is safety, wants only the strongest boat his means allow.

IDENTIFYING WEAK AREAS

The most certain way to determine whether a hull/deck is weak is simple observation. Eric Goetz, a boatbuilder in Bristol, Rhode Island, is a protégé of the Gougeon Brothers specializing in cold-molded wood boats. He tests the decks of his boats by having his heaviest employee jump on the deck. If it deflects (oil-cans), he adds deck beams until it stops.

Naval architect Roger Marshall says that a boat built in this manner will be overbuilt, because a deck that deflects may indeed be strong enough. But framing to eliminate all deflection means the boat will be strong enough to withstand the immense forces to which a hull is subjected. And it also will give the crew that subtle confidence of knowing that the surface beneath their feet is as firm and rigid as the Earth on which they walk.

Observing the deflection of hull panels is trickier. Pounding on the side of the hull with your fist is a bit like kicking the tires of a used car. A panel that deflects with the push of a hand *may* in fact be quite strong. But for my boat, I like to know that everything will stay in place as much as possible. A boat that works excessively at some point will begin to show the effects of fatigue: cracking of the gel coat, bulkheads separating from the hull, loose fittings, and cabinet doors that won't close.

Of course, a daysail in light winds won't show the problems as readily as a hard beat into heavy seas. But if you've sailed your boat in rough conditions and haven't experienced problems, then perhaps it is strong enough. Compare your boat's scantlings with those recommended by established authorities such as Lloyds of London. Figures 1-11 and 1-12 in the previous chapter give an idea of what minimum hull thicknesses to expect for a given size fiberglass boat. Herreshoff's and Nevins' rules should be consulted for wood boat scantlings. *Skene's Elements of Yacht Design* (see "Further Reading" at end of Chapter 1) includes these, plus Wyland's aluminum scantlings. A marine surveyor could help you be more certain of your hull's integrity.

A Cost/Benefit Decision

The strength of a hull/deck structure is derived from several factors: the strength (tensile, impact, compressive, etc.) of the skin, building material, hull shape, size and the reinforcing network of ribs, longitudinals stringers, bulkheads and attached furniture. With fiberglass boats, it is generally easier to add a bulkhead, knee, hull stiffener or deck beam than to add fiberglass laminations to a hull that is too thin or improperly laid-up. I am tempted to say that if a hull is inadequately built, one might be better off buying a different boat than attempting any major strengthening. But often circumstances won't allow purchasing a different boat, or the boat meets all the owner's requirements save this one problem.

GLASS FIBERS

Before launching into identifying structural weaknesses and their remedies, you should have a basic familiarity with the different types of fiberglass fabrics and resins used in boatbuilding. You should have some experience performing minor fiberglass repairs—such as patching a hole in the dinghy—before attempting the larger jobs suggested in this chapter. Also take a look at the books listed at the end of this chapter, especially Jack Wiley's *The Fiberglass Repair and Construction Handbook*, and Ken Hankinson's *Fiberglass Boatbuilding for Amateurs*. They are excellent primers on working with fiberglass.

There are three types of glass fibers commonly used by boatbuilders (Figure 2-1). Each has unique properties that make it better for some jobs, worse for others.

Cloth

Fiberglass cloth is a closely woven fabric available in weights ranging from about two to 30-plus ounces a yard. Ten-ounce cloth is one of the most frequently used weights in boatbuilding, and is the one most often recommended for the various projects described in this book.

Compared to the other fabrics—woven roving and mat—cloth possesses the greatest strength, yet is the thinnest. It requires less resin to wet out, and so is not as stiff as the others, nor as watertight. The ratio of glass fiber to resin is

Fig. 2-1 *The most commonly used types of fiberglass fabric for repair and strengthening are: a) chopped strand mat, b) cloth and c) woven roving.*

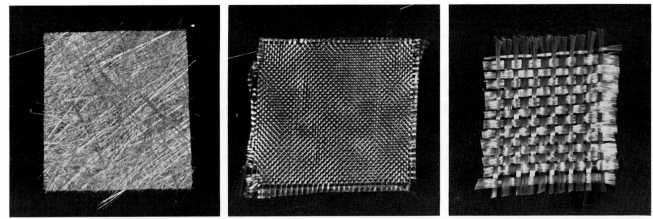

about 50/50. Cloth is frequently used as a sheathing or finishing layer in a laminate because it gives a fairly smooth surface when the resin has cured. However, it is seldom used in hull laminates or in major structural members. It is available in widths from about 38 to 60 inches, or in rolls of "tape" in widths from about one to 12 inches. The tape comes with selvedged edges to prevent unraveling, which is a good thing because cloth is the most expensive of the three kinds of fabric.

Woven Roving

Woven roving is a thick, loosely woven fabric available in weights ranging from about 14 to 36 ounces a yard, though 24-ounce woven roving is the weight most commonly used in the industry. Because of its higher fiber content, it has more tensile strength than mat, but less than cloth. Because of its loose weave, it does not leave a very smooth finished surface. It is usually sandwiched between layers of mat in building up a laminate. The ratio of glass fiber to resin is about 45/55.

Mat

Mat consists of chopped strands of glass fiber about ¾″ to 1½″ long. These are laid down in a random pattern that gives omnidirectional strength. Typical weights range from ¾ to three ounces a square foot. One and a half and two-ounce weights are commonly used in the industry. Mat is the least expensive of the three fabrics and takes the most resin to wet out, thereby also making it the most waterproof. The ratio of glass fiber to resin is about 30/70. This means that mat is a weaker laminate than cloth or woven roving —though it does have good bonding characteristics. In a laminate, mat builds up thickness quickly, thereby reducing the number of layers of other fabric required—and labor costs.

Thicknesses of Glass Fiber Laminates

Figure 2-2 will help determine how many layers of a certain fabric it will take to achieve a certain thickness. Variations of up to 10 percent

can be expected as a laminate is built up due to changes in the ratio of glass to resin and due to differences in individual laminating techniques.

RESINS

There are many different types of plastic thermosetting resins formulated for a wide variety of uses in industries today. While boatbuilders use only a few of these, it is important to know how they differ, and to use the right resin for the right job.

Polyester

Almost all sailboat hulls are laid up with polyester resin. An accelerator is usually already added during manufacturing, so all that you need to do is add a catalyst to start the chemical reaction that causes the individual molecules to start linking together in chains. This process is called polymerization and, incidentally, is the same principle behind the new generation of copolymer topside and anti-fouling bottom paints.

A difference exists between "laminating" polyester resin and "finishing" resin. The former is air-inhibited, meaning it does not completely cure when in contact with air. These resins tend to remain tacky, thus forming better bonds with additional layers in the glass fiber laminate. Finishing resin is non-air-inhibited, meaning it does cure in air. This is achieved by adding a wax to the resin, which rises to the surface and seals the resin from the air. The wax must be removed before attempting any additional bonding or painting. Boatbuilders use laminating resin for all but the last layer, which is laid on with finishing resin. There are, however, resins that have been specially formulated to perform both functions.

Most polyester resins are formulated to cure between 70° and 80°F with the specified amount of catalyst (methyl ethyl ketone peroxide— MEKP) added. It is possible to work at temperatures as low as 60° and as high as 100° by using more or less catalyst. Never work in direct sunlight as this causes the resin to cure too rapidly. Practice is necessary to correctly gauge the right amount of catalyst to be added to the resin.

Laminate	Plies	Type of Construction Material	Thickness (ins.)	% Glass Content	Tens. (psi)	Flex. Str. (psi)	Mod. x 10⁶ (psi)	Wgt. Lam./sq. ft.
1	2	2 oz. mat.	.11	28.2	14,050	23,400	0.92	14.2 oz.
2	1	10 oz. Cloth	0.100	28.4	10,500	18,550	0.89	10.9 oz.
	1	2 oz. Mat						
3	1	10 oz. Cloth	0.110	32.0	13,850	22,100	1.10	12.8 oz.
	2	1.5 oz. Mat						
4	1	10 oz. Cloth	0.130	30.1	14,950	21,400	0.95	16.9 oz.
	2	2 oz. Mat						
5	1	10 oz. Cloth	0.180	32.0	13,200	18,750	0.92	22.2 oz.
	3	2 oz. Mat						
6	1	10 oz. Cloth	0.120	24.9	9,090	37,600	1.47	14.9 oz.
	1	1.5 oz. Mat						
	1	10 oz. Cloth						
7	1	10 oz. Cloth	0.180	22.6	10,500	28,400	1.20	23.0 oz.
	2	1.5 oz. Mat						
	1	10 oz. Cloth						
8	1	1½ oz. Mat	0.254	39.2	30,300	42,800	1.59	36.0 oz.
	3	2415 Fabmat						
9	1	10 oz. Cloth	0.092	42.5	18,500	28,500	0.78	11.7 oz.
	1	24 oz. W.R.						
	1	10 oz. Cloth						
10	1	10 oz. Cloth	0.125	38.3	17,050	22,850	1.25	14.0 oz.
	1	1.5 oz. Mat						
	1	24 oz. W.R.						
11	2	24 oz. W.R.	0.080	52.7	38,950	44,900	1.85	9.5 oz.
12	1	24 oz. W.R.	0.100	53.2	29,000	45,900	2.20	13.2 oz.
	1	1.5 oz. Mat						
	1	24 oz. W.R.						
13	1	2 oz. Mat	0.125	36.0	11,500	23,000	0.73	16.4 oz.
	1	24 oz. W.R.						
	1	10 oz. Cloth						
14	1	1.5 oz. Mat	0.1294	47.0	22,200	41,800	1.90	16.6 oz.
	2	24 oz. W.R.						
15	1	1.5 oz. Mat	0.100	47.9	24,900	31,400	1.11	14.3 oz.
	1	24 oz. W.R.						
	1	1.5 oz. Mat						
	1	10 oz. Cloth						

Fig. 2-2 *Table of laminate thicknesses*

Acetone is the chemical solvent generally used for cleaning brushes and tools, but it can't dissolve resin that's hardened. If thinning of the resin is required, use styrene, not acetone, as the latter inhibits curing. Acetone is highly flammable, so don't smoke or introduce open flames in its vicinity.

Epoxy

Like polyester resin, epoxy requires an outside agent to produce the exothermic reaction necessary to produce a cure. Instead of a catalyst, however, a hardener is used, although the mixing ratios are different than with polyester and catalyst. The Gougeon Brothers W.E.S.T.™ System epoxy resin is one of the best known of this type, and is used for both laminating and finishing.

Epoxy resin is considerably more expensive than polyester. It is used most often for repair jobs or when bonding glass fibers to wood and metal because of its better bonding properties. It is compatible with polyester resin and can be laminated on top of existing polyester surfaces. Catalyzed epoxy resin eventually will go off in a wide range of temperatures; 70°F is close to ideal. It is best to purchase the solvent marketed by the company formulating the resin.

Core Materials

Many boatbuilders today are using core materials in their hulls to reduce weight, cut down on the high cost of solid fiberglass and to improve rigidity. Airex® and Klegecell® polyvinyl chloride (PVC) foams and Contourkore® end-grain balsa are the most commonly used materials (Figure 2-3). In addition to the above-mentioned properties, they also provide thermal and acoustical insulation. Plywood is still seen in deck sandwiches. It has better compressive strength, an important characteristic when adding thru-bolting cleats, fairleads and other fittings. Core materials are sometimes used in subassemblies, such as the sea hood described in Chapter 9.

Mold Release Agents

Anytime a mold is used to fabricate a hull or subassembly, it is necessary to coat the mold with a material that prevents the resin from sticking to the mold. Wax, petroleum jelly and specially formulated parting agents all do the job. But purchasing a product specifically intended for this use probably gives the best results. Most suppliers of fiberglass fabrics and resins also can sell you a parting agent.

Distributing Stress

As you read through the projects in this book, you will notice that the individual layers of cloth and mat must be varied in width and length. There are several reasons for this. By varying the widths, each layer is placed in direct contact with the bonding surface, ensuring a better bond. This technique also prevents creating stress at the edge of the laminate (Figure 2-4).

Similarly, when bonding a structural member or piece of furniture to a fiberglass surface, loads on that member should be distributed over as much surface area as possible. Tapering the ends of hull stiffeners and rounding the corners of backing blocks will distribute stress loadings better than squared ends that create "hard spots" (Figure 2-5).

Health

The chemicals used in resins, hardeners and catalysts can be dangerous. They never should be swallowed or allowed to touch the eyes. Some persons develop skin irritations from contact with epoxy resins, so rubber surgical gloves are advisable.

During the chemical resin-curing reaction, fumes are given off that are dangerous to breathe. Working outdoors is generally safe. But if you're working in the basement or inside the boat, use exhaust fans to remove as much of the fumes as possible, and don't hesitate to leave the work area if you feel threatened. Styrene fumes given off by polyester resin can cause brain damage and can even kill.

If proper safety precautions are observed, however, there is no reason why the amateur builder or handyman cannot work successfully with fiberglass. It is messy, but it does possess some truly remarkable properties that make it quite suitable for modern boatbuilding and repair.

Fig. 2-3 *Typical core materials are from top to bottom, Airex, Contourkore end-grain balsa, and Klege-Cell.*

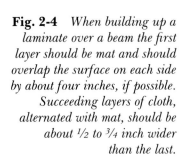

Fig. 2-4 *When building up a laminate over a beam the first layer should be mat and should overlap the surface on each side by about four inches, if possible. Succeeding layers of cloth, alternated with mat, should be about ½ to ¾ inch wider than the last.*

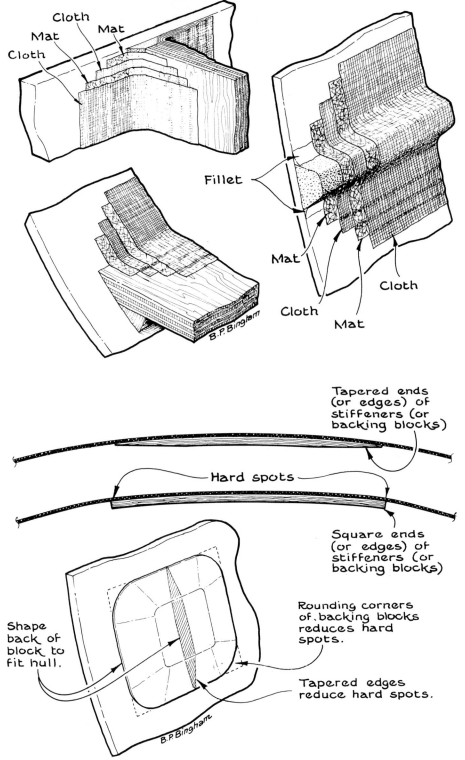

Cloth
Mat
Cloth
Mat
Fillet
Mat
Cloth
Cloth
Mat
B.P.Bingham

Tapered ends (or edges) of stiffeners (or backing blocks)

Hard spots

Square ends (or edges) of stiffeners (or backing blocks)

Fig. 2-5 *Hard spots in the hull or other panel, which can cause stress cracking, can be avoided by tapering the ends of hull stiffening beams, and rounding the corner of backing blocks.*

Rounding corners of backing blocks reduces hard spots.

Shape back of block to fit hull.

Tapered edges reduce hard spots.

B.P.Bingham

DECK REINFORCEMENTS

I once owned a 19-foot English twin-keel sloop that I sailed all over the Great Lakes. She was over-rigged, (large diameter twin backstays, upper and double lower shrouds), had a bridge deck (unusual on a small boat), and had a beautiful and massive outboard rudder fashioned out of solid mahogany. The hull was perhaps a ¼-inch thick, and the round shape made it rigid enough. But there was no deck or cockpit sole core to provide stiffening. The result was a disconcerting "sproing!" whenever someone stood on them. Instead of using a core, the builders had laminated layers of fiberglass mat over ½-inch wood moldings under the deck. This turned out to be insufficient, as one step on the foredeck quickly demonstrated.

Oilcanning Decks

Nothing is quite so disconcerting as bounding forward under sail to handle a jib and feeling the deck bounce like a trampoline. Perhaps such a deck is strong enough. But if it doesn't *feel* strong, then corrective measures are in order. Crowned decks are stronger than flat decks because there is better distribution of loads. This is an important principle to remember in building any large, load-bearing surface (Figure 2-6).

Fiberglass Decks

There are several ways to stiffen an oilcanning fiberglass deck. In many instances the most effective method is glassing in one or more athwartship deck beams (Figure 2-7). Beams may be wood sawn to shape and length and then covered with fiberglass mat. Or, thin wood veneers can be laminated over a form and then glassed over. Another method uses fiberglass mat, woven roving or cloth laid up over another material, such as foam, that functions purely as a mold. A final method is to glass in a core material to the underside of the deck.

Making a Deck Beam

To begin, find the location of greatest flex; it probably will be in the center of the largest unsupported area. The foredeck is a likely place, because often it is built without coring or reinforcing bulkheads.

Fashion a pair of hardwood knees (if you'd like to leave part of the beam exposed) or plywood knees (if you intend to cover them entirely) about ¾ to one-inch thick. Cut the shape with a band saw or, if it is thin enough, with a heavy-duty saber saw. Sand to an attractive finish. Locate them opposite one another at the

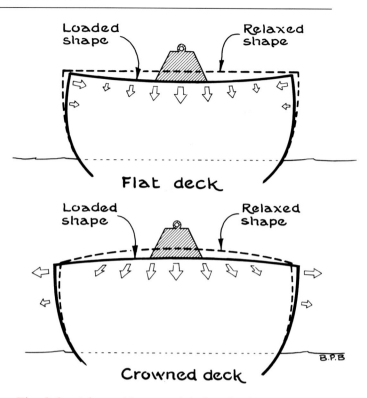

Fig. 2-6 *A boat with crowned deck and cabin generally is stronger, all other factors being equal, than one with flat decks, because it distributes loads over a greater area.*

hull/deck joint, and sand the hull surface where it will be bonded. All paint and dirt must be removed. A final wipe with acetone will get the surface really clean.

Mix some epoxy putty or, better yet, epoxy resin mixed with ¼-inch chopped strand—you can cut up small pieces of mat to make your own. The latter is popularly called "mush", and should be spread with a putty knife between the knee and hull and deck to form a primary bond and to seal the wood from moisture.

With the knee held in place, apply more mush where the hull and wood meet. Cut a piece of furring strip or a sail batten and round one end. Pull the stick across the mush to form a nicely radiused fillet (Figure 2-8). A pop bottle bottom also can be used. Use your wet finger to smooth small ridges you can't get flat with the stick. Epoxy is hard to sand, so the smoother you get it now, the easier it will be to finish later.

The Gougeon Brothers suggest making fillets by mixing W.E.S.T. System 105 resin with 406 Colodial Silica for a high-density, high-strength bond. But when the strength of the fillet vastly

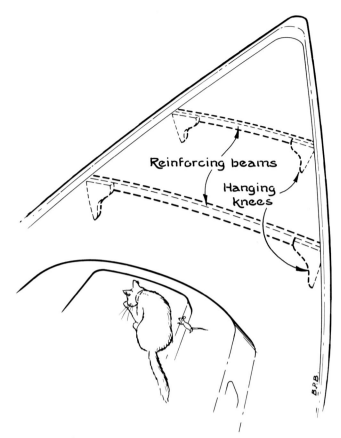

Fig. 2-7 *An internal deck beam can be glassed in under the foredeck area, fastened at each end to knees that are also glassed to the hull. Furniture, such as these V-berths, can be integral structural members, especially if they are glassed to the hull.*

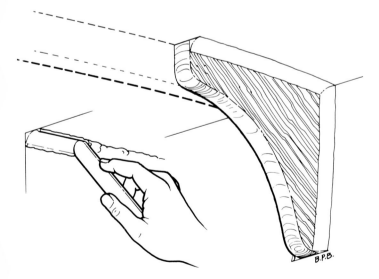

Fig. 2-8 *A fillet functions as a bond between two surfaces. When radiused, it permits fiberglass mat and cloth to conform easier to the bend. A bottle or batten rounded at one end forms a nice curve.*

exceeds the strength of the wood fiber, a combination of 406 Colodial Silica and 409 Microspheres is suggested for a lower-density fillet. In either case, the fibers thicken the resin and prevent sagging.

A fillet not only provides a basic bond between the knee and hull, but also forms a gentle curve to which the fiberglass mat and woven roving can conform more easily. This reduces stress cracking. Without a fillet, mat tends to pop out of right angle corners, thereby reducing strength and producing air pockets.

Once the epoxy fillet has cured, cut short "tabs" of mat, about 3″ x 5″. Be sure that both surfaces have been sanded and wiped with a cleaner compatible with your resin. Coat the hull with resin where the tabs go, then lay the tabs in place and dab on more resin until you're satisfied it is thoroughly wetted out. Wetting out means dabbing the mat with catalyzed resin until all whiteness has disappeared from the fibers. The resin will run, so be careful not to put on more than the mat can hold.

Once the resin has cured or "kicked", and the knee is securely in place, you're ready to apply a layer of mat over the entire joint.

Cut alternate strips of 1½-ounce mat and 24-ounce woven roving (or 10-ounce cloth) to the length of the joint and in varied widths. Where possible, overlap the knee and hull about four inches. The first layer should be the narrowest, with each subsequent layer about ½-inch to ¾-inch wider (Figure 2-4). Don't stack layers of the same width on top of each other.

If the curve of the hull makes the strip bunch up, cut slits or darts (triangle shapes) halfway into the mat (Figure 2-9) as close together as is necessary to allow the mat to lie flat on both surfaces.

Wet out the strips of mat on a piece of Formica or other non-absorbent material (Figure 2-10). Brush a coating of resin on the hull, too, before laying on the mat. This will help ensure a good bond and minimize the amount of resin needed to wet out the mat. Once the mat is wetted out in place, stop. Excessive brushing will only bunch up the fibers and create uneven thicknesses.

Add a wider second layer of woven roving while the first layer of mat is still wet. Continue alternating mat and woven roving or cloth until

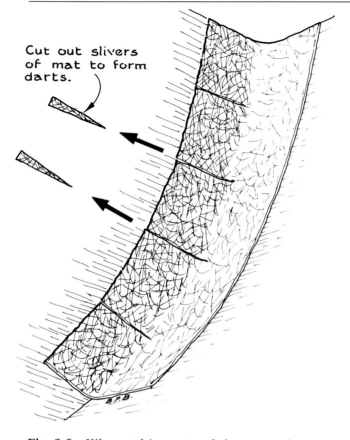

Cut out slivers of mat to form darts.

Fig. 2-9 *When applying mat or cloth to a curved surface, it usually is necessary to cut small slits or darts every few inches so the material won't buckle.*

a thickness is achieved equal to about half the thickness of the hull. The table on laminate thicknesses earlier in this chapter will help you determine how many layers are necessary.

When the resin cures, the knee will be a strong structural member. The fiberglass laminate may not look like much. But resin and fiber together are incredibly strong—after all, it's the same stuff as your hull.

Next, cut a piece of wood to form a beam between the two knees (Figure 2-7). An attractive hardwood finished without a fiberglass covering could be used. But it won't be as strong as a beam glassed to the deck. And, if it's covered with glass, the beam might as well be made of cheaper softwood. There are several ways to make the beam (Figure 2-11):

A. Cutting from a single piece of wood.
B. Laminating and bending thin veneers of wood over a form.

C. Gluing sawn planks together.
D. Cutting strips of urethane foam.

A laminated beam is stronger than a solid one, but *if* the beam is to be glassed over, the fiberglass cloth and resin will do most of the work. Refer to Figure 2-12 for final beam thicknesses according to the size of boat.

SAWN BEAMS

To draw the cutline for a single sawn piece, hold the beam up as high as you can, flat against the knees on either side. Using a compass with a pencil in one end, put the metal end against the deck. Put the pencil against the beam. Pull the compass across the deck keeping the compass angle uniform so that the pencil scribes a line on the wood as you go. See Figure 9-33 in Chapter 9 for a clearer understanding of this technique.

GLUED BEAMS

If laminating the beam by gluing several standard 1-inch planks together, use the first plank as a pattern to cut several more.

Fig. 2-10 *Wetting out means brushing the fiberglass with catalyzed resin until all the fibers are saturated and no longer white. Brush out bubbles, but avoid excessive brushing, which causes the fiberglass to come apart.*

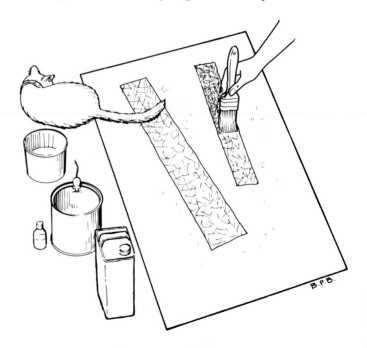

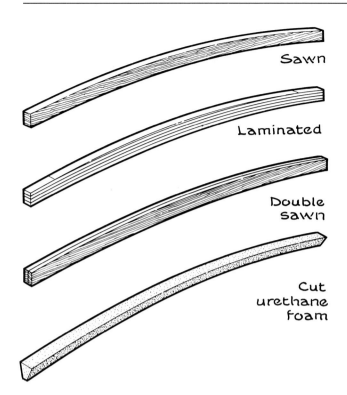

Fig. 2-11 *The deck beam can be (from top to bottom), cut from solid hardwood, laminated from thin veneers of wood, made from sawn planks glued together, fashioned out of shaped blocks of foam.*

Glue all the pieces together with epoxy glue or resin or a good waterproof glue such as resorcinol. Clamp with C-clamps, inserting small pieces of wood in between the clamp and beam to help distribute the pressure of the clamp over a greater surface area. When the glue has cured, sand off the glue that has ooozed from between the planks. Coating the entire beam with a finishing resin will prevent moisture from rotting or expanding the wood. Also, knock off the sharp edges and corners of the beam with a rasp or router so the fiberglass mat will conform better.

LAMINATED BEAMS

To laminate a beam from thin (⅛-inch) veneers, a mold can be made from several pieces of cheap fir cut to the shape of the deck (use a compass as described earlier) and Masonite or Formica nailed over the tops for a fair curve (Figure 2-13). Or, if the topside deck directly above where you want to install the beam has a fair curve and is unobstructed by deck gear, you can use it as a laminating form. Cover the deck with a thin sheet of plastic or Mylar so resin doesn't stick to it.

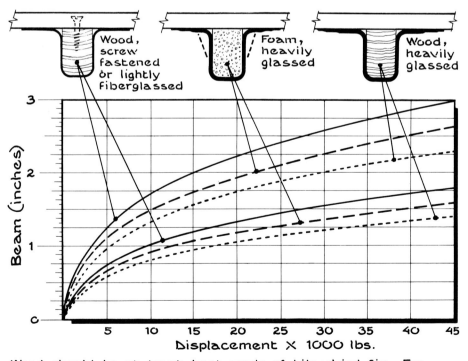

Fig. 2-12 *Beam thicknesses increase with the size of boat, as this graph illustrates. Use it as a guide.*

Wood should be at least best grade of kiln-dried fir. For heavy glassing, fiberglass should equal at least ⅛ of short dimension of beam using polyester resin.

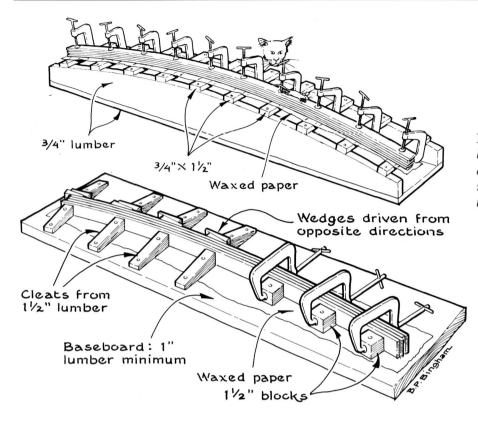

3/4" lumber

3/4" × 1½"

Waxed paper

Wedges driven from opposite directions

Cleats from 1½" lumber

Baseboard: 1" lumber minimum

Waxed paper

1½" blocks

B.P.Bingham

Fig. 2-13 *C-clamps are used to bend thin stock over a form or jig and a strong glue or fiberglass resin is used to laminate the pieces together.*

Any wood laminated over a form will experience some springback when released. The amount of springback is difficult to calculate accurately, but the greater the bend, the greater the springback. With experience, a builder can compensate by slightly overbending the laminate, hoping the springback will return the member to the desired shape. Alternatively, the member can be planed to shape after the resin is well cured and all springback finished. For this reason and because of the difficulty in accurately lofting the lines, it is easier to laminate in place than over a form.

FASTENING BEAM TO KNEES

Now, glue the beam to the knees with epoxy; a few nails will hold it in place until the glue cures. Bronze or stainless steel bolts also can be used, but won't really add much strength if the beam is to be glassed over.

GLASSING IN THE BEAM

Form fillets between the beam and deck with mush as described previously. When they've cured, glass over the entire beam. Alternate lay-ers of the same weight mat and woven roving used for the knees, and to the same thickness. To prevent them from sagging, it may be necessary to add only one layer at a time. A layer of cloth will give a nicer finished appearance than mat or woven roving. When it has cured for a few days, sand and paint.

When you consider the surface area of the fiberglass bond, you'll understand why it is stronger than a beam merely bolted to knees and screwed to the deck.

FOAM BEAMS

Long strips of urethane foam or Airex can be cut in long wedge shapes to form very adequate forms over which are laid alternate layers of mat and woven roving. The wedge shape gives a better bonding angle for the mat and woven roving to conform to. The foam almost can be considered sacrificial as the covering laminate performs most of the stiffening function. Airex conforms easily to most any shape, though stiffer foam may have to be cut with kerfs to make it lie flush against the deck. The foam can be held in place with a quick-setting glue, but test the compatability of the glue on a small piece of foam first—some glues will dissolve the foam. The same lamination schedule used for wood beams can be used for foam, too.

Wood Decks

Wood decks generally are made of planks, plywood covered with canvas or plywood covered with a single or double layer of fiberglass cloth.

If a wood deck flexes when walked on, it is less likely to be a problem with the original construction than it is with rotting deck beams or loose fastenings. In either case, it is necessary to examine the existing deck beams closely and determine whether they should be left in place and new beams added, or if they should be removed altogether and new beams installed in their place. Needless to say, if a beam shows any sign of rot, it should be removed. And if one beam is rotten, suspect all others.

In most types of construction, the beams will be supported on either side by shelves. It may be necessary to remove several deck planks to gain access to where the deck beam and shelf join (Figure 2-14). Already you can see you've got a big job on your hands. If deck planking must be

removed, the glass or canvas covering the deck must first be torn away to expose the fastenings. Hopefully, only one or two planks at the sides of the deck must be removed.

The old deck beam is most easily removed by sawing it in half. To avoid cutting into the deck, try springing the beam loose from the deck with a wedge. Then insert a thin material such as Formica against which the saw can cut without damaging the deck. If the beam has been screwed to the deck along its entire length, first remove the deck covering and take out those fastenings.

The new deck beam can be cut from well-seasoned oak or laminated from smaller thicknesses as described for fiberglass decks.

Unless the deck problem is an isolated one, which can be repaired in this manner, you may find it wise to remove all deck planking and install new beams everywhere. At the same time, you may decide to strengthen the hull/deck joint with hand-sawn knees or welded metal hanging knees (Figures 2-23, 24, 25).

Ripping out wood is often like opening Pandora's Box—it exposes new problems such as rot more extensive than previously thought. You begin rationalizing additional repairs that are fa-

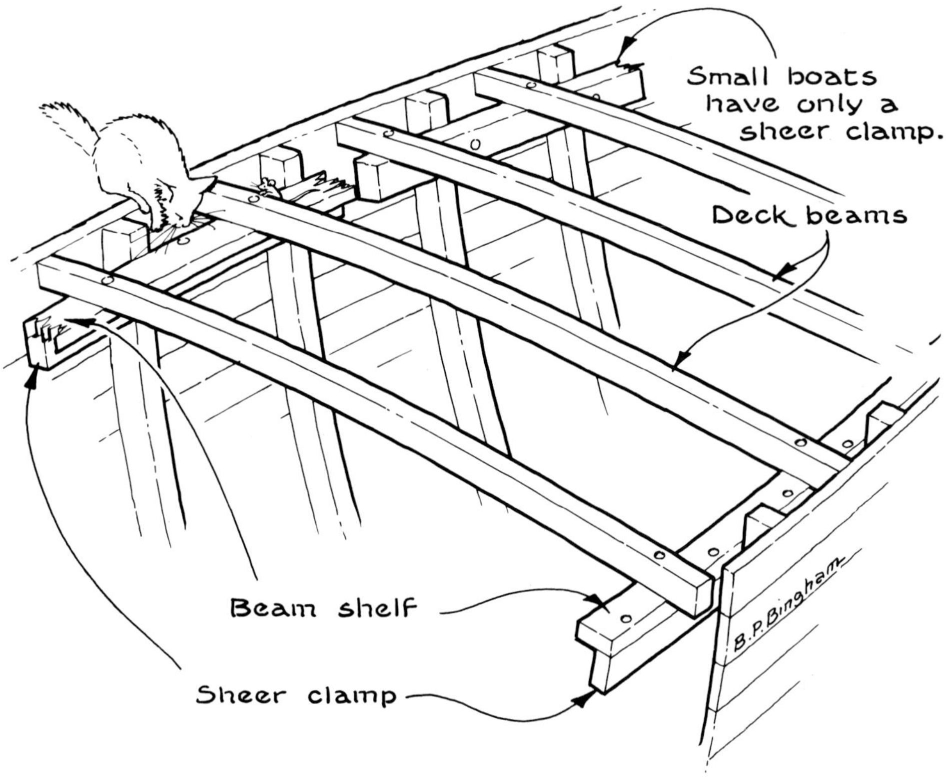

Fig. 2-14 *Deck beams are attached at the ends to shelves running beneath the decks. Depending on the configuration, it may be necessary to remove the outer deck plank to remove a rotted beam.*

cilitated by preparations for the first job. What you end up with is a major restoration project, a season or more out of the water, and many hours of labor. The alternative is a boat of dubious strength.

Steel and Aluminum Decks

An insufficiently stiffened metal deck is more easily repaired than wood or fiberglass. Unless corrosion is the culprit, the problem is either deck plating that is too thin, or beams spaced too far apart. Assuming you are a handy welder (which you ought to be if you own a metal boat), cutting new beams and welding them in place is largely a matter of copying the method of installation used during original construction. Leave the old beams unless they are corroded.

HULL FLEX

Flexing the hull, which is probably most common in the forward area, can be corrected much in the same manner as oilcanning decks, but without using knees or shelves. In fiberglass boats, this problem can be eliminated without wood altogether, if one chooses.

Fiberglass Hulls

Four ways to strengthen fiberglass hulls are adding extra laminations (with or without coring), glassing in longitudinal stringers or ribs, adding partial bulkheads, and glassing in bilge floors. The correct remedy depends on the location and severity of hull flex.

EXTRA LAMINATIONS

If you can clear a fairly large area of the hull of furniture and other impediments, it is possible to add extra laminations of fiberglass mat, cloth and woven roving to the hull. This is an extreme measure to bolster a poorly built hull or one that simply wasn't intended to be sailed hard.

The techniques of sandwich construction can be applied here. Add a layer of a core material between any new laminations (Figure 2-15). Airex, Klegecell and Contourkore end-grain balsa core are all materials regularly used by boatbuilders in the lay-up of hulls. They decrease weight and increase stiffness. And, be-

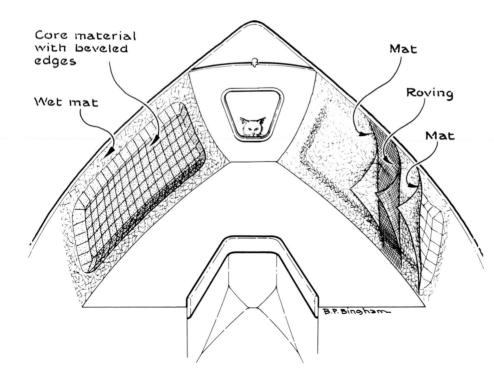

Fig. 2-15 *A core material such as Airex can be laminated to inside hull surfaces to increase stiffness. It should be bonded to both sides of the hull to prevent uneven loading.*

cause they are less expensive than fiberglass cloths and polyester resins, they help keep costs down.

To reinforce a hull or deck in this manner, it is important that whatever you do to one side of the hull, you replicate on the opposite side. This is to prevent the unequal distribution of loads on the hull.

Inner liners will make it virtually impossible to add layers of matted cloth, or employ core materials as stiffeners. Liners inhibit access to the hull, except in small areas such as through the locker lids underneath berths.

Carpeting, vinyl, paint or any other hull lining material will have to be removed. Once you're down to bare fiberglass, sand the hull with a coarse grit paper, about #50 to #60, and then wash with acetone. Depending on how vertical the hull is, you may decide to apply only one or two laminations at a time, as they tend to sag. With or without a core, the reinforcement should extend over as much of the panel as possible to avoid creating a hinge point (due to unequal skin thicknesses) that could cause cracking under load. Extending the laminate from the deck to the bilge is safer than reinforcing just part of the area.

When core materials are to be included, lightly coat one side of the sheet (say ½-inch Contourkore) with resin before sticking it against one or two still-wet layers of 1½-ounce mat already laid on the hull. (The mat will ensure a strong bond between the core and hull, and make the core more watertight.) You may find it necessary to contrive some means to hold the foam or balsa in place until the resin kicks. When it has, finish the job with the last alternate layers of mat and 18-ounce woven roving—perhaps one at a time to prevent sag. See Chapter 9, under making a sea hood, for further details on working with core materials.

LONGITUDINAL STIFFENERS AND RIBS

Vertical, ribbed stiffeners running vertically tend to duplicate the job of bulkheads and floors. And, because more of the loads on a sailboat tend to be longitudinal or diagonal anyway, longitudinal stiffeners generally give better results. Also, longitudinally placed stiffeners are

less obtrusive, and might be worked into some sort of cleat (brace) for shelving.

There are several ways to form this type of stiffener (Figure 2-16):

A. Garden hose
B. Plastic or metal pipe
C. Cardboard tube cut in half
D. Half-round softwood stock
E. Top hat sections made from wood or foam.

Top hat stiffeners can be pre-formed outside the boat or made in place using urethane foam or wood. They need not be continuous though; especially with wood, a tapered end eliminates the possibility of a hard spot that can cause stress cracking. Also, pad the wood with a thin strip of foam for this same reason. The American Bu-

Fig. 2-16 *Longitudinal hull stiffeners can be fashioned from: a) garden hose, b) plastic or metal pipe, c) cardboard tube cut in half, d) half-round softwood stock and e) top hat sections made with wood or foam. These function as forms, over which fiberglass mat and woven roving or cloth are laid.*

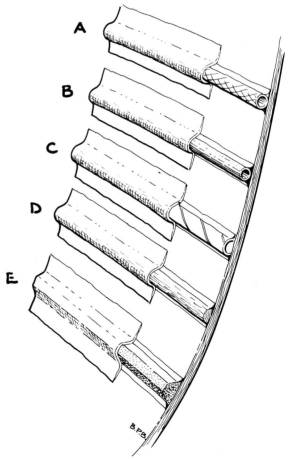

reau of Shipping recommends that the height of the stiffener be 30 times its skin thickness (a 7½-inch tall stiffener should have a ¼-inch skin thickness). Wedge shapes widen the base proportionate to the top, and form better bonding angles. Fillets still may be necessary. Remove paint or any other covering; clean and abrade the surface with sandpaper, and wipe with acetone.

The wood or foam can be held in place by a compatible quick-setting epoxy glue until the layers of mat and woven roving are laid on. Covering the stringer with four alternating layers of 1½-ounce mat and 18-ounce woven roving should do the trick, though achieving a thickness equal to half the thickness of the hull remains a good rule of thumb.

Where possible, longitudinal stiffeners should be carried forward to the stem and joined together. Often, however, bulkheads get in the way. Avoid abrupt ends in favor of tapering the stiffener at each end to prevent hard spots.

CIRCLE AND HALF-CIRCLE SECTIONS

Hose, tubing or pipe and cardboard tubes cut in half are held in place with glue or duct tape. The bond is not critical, as once it has been glassed over the laminate will do the stiffening, not the form material. Again, the surface should be sanded clean before work commences.

Coat the hull with resin on either side of the form, and coat the form itself. Then lay on precut strips of 1½-ounce mat and 18-ounce woven roving, overlapping the hull a minimum of four inches. Increase the width of each successive layer by ½ to ¾ inch. Consider using 10-ounce cloth for the final layer for a neater, smoother appearance. Sand lightly and paint to finish.

PARTIAL BULKHEADS

If adding a bulkhead seems to be the answer (it couldn't hurt on a boat with an open interior), you get the added benefit of a new place to mount lighting, instruments or bookshelves. Adding a bulkhead rather than a hull or deck stiffening beam also has the advantage of tying together the hull, deck and cabin floors.

A tick stick is the tool used to make a bulkhead pattern. Figure 2-17 shows how to use one to transfer hull lines to the piece of wood. (This accomplishes the same thing as the compass shown in Chapter 9, Figure 33 and also described earlier in this chapter. However, because of hull/cabin shapes and the size of full or even half bulkheads, it would be difficult to use a compass to transfer lines.)

Fig. 2-17 *A tick stick is one way of transferring hull curves to a piece of wood to be cut into a bulkhead. The point of the stick is moved a few inches down the hull and the end of the stick traced onto a piece of wood (not necessarily the bulkhead). When the wood and stick are removed to the workshop, lay the bulkhead wood next to the wood with the tracings on it. Place the stick over the tracings and mark where the tip ends on the bulkhead. Connect all the dots and you've recreated the hull line.*

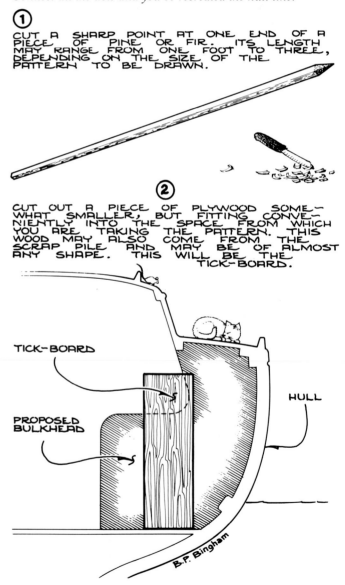

① CUT A SHARP POINT AT ONE END OF A PIECE OF PINE OR FIR. ITS LENGTH MAY RANGE FROM ONE FOOT TO THREE, DEPENDING ON THE SIZE OF THE PATTERN TO BE DRAWN.

② CUT OUT A PIECE OF PLYWOOD SOMEWHAT SMALLER, BUT FITTING CONVENIENTLY INTO THE SPACE FROM WHICH YOU ARE TAKING THE PATTERN. THIS WOOD MAY ALSO COME FROM THE SCRAP PILE AND MAY BE OF ALMOST ANY SHAPE. THIS WILL BE THE TICK-BOARD.

TICK-BOARD

PROPOSED BULKHEAD

HULL

B.P. Bingham

③ TEMPORARILY ERECT THE TICK-BOARD IN THE SAME POSITION TO BE OCCUPIED BY THE PROPOSED BULKHEAD.

⑦ MOVE THE POINT OF THE STICK TO THE NEXT CRITICAL CUTTING POINT. DRAW A NEW LINE ON THE TICK-BOARD AND NUMBER THE STICK AND BOARD AGAIN.

⑧ CONTINUE MOVING THE STICK TO NEW POSITIONS, LINING AND TICKING AS YOU GO, UNTIL YOU HAVE TICKED OFF THE ENTIRE PERIMETER OF THE SHAPE TO BE TRANSFERRED.

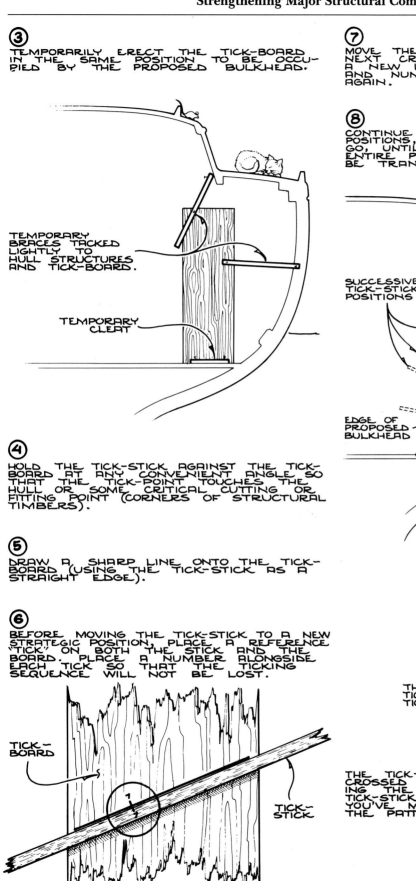

TEMPORARY BRACES TACKED LIGHTLY TO HULL STRUCTURES AND TICK-BOARD.

TEMPORARY CLEAT

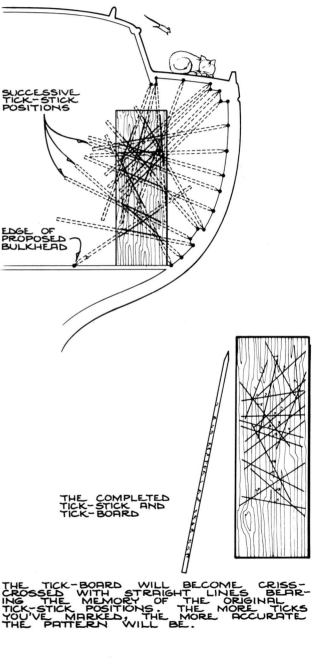

SUCCESSIVE TICK-STICK POSITIONS

EDGE OF PROPOSED BULKHEAD

④ HOLD THE TICK-STICK AGAINST THE TICK-BOARD AT ANY CONVENIENT ANGLE SO THAT THE TICK-POINT TOUCHES THE HULL OR SOME CRITICAL CUTTING OR FITTING POINT (CORNERS OF STRUCTURAL TIMBERS).

⑤ DRAW A SHARP LINE ONTO THE TICK-BOARD (USING THE TICK-STICK AS A STRAIGHT EDGE).

⑥ BEFORE MOVING THE TICK-STICK TO A NEW STRATEGIC POSITION, PLACE A REFERENCE "TICK" ON BOTH THE STICK AND THE BOARD. PLACE A NUMBER ALONGSIDE EACH TICK SO THAT THE TICKING SEQUENCE WILL NOT BE LOST.

THE COMPLETED TICK-STICK AND TICK-BOARD

TICK-BOARD

TICK-STICK

THE TICK-BOARD WILL BECOME CRISS-CROSSED WITH STRAIGHT LINES BEARING THE MEMORY OF THE ORIGINAL TICK-STICK POSITIONS. THE MORE TICKS YOU'VE MARKED, THE MORE ACCURATE THE PATTERN WILL BE.

(continued on next page)

DRAWING THE PATTERN

⑨
IT'S BEST TO LAY OFF THE PATTERN ON MEAT WRAPPING PAPER SO THAT YOU CAN ADJUST ITS POSITION ATOP THE LUMBER LATER TO MINIMIZE WASTE.

LAY THE TICK-BOARD, FACE UP, ON TOP OF THE PAPER.

⑩
PLACE THE TICK-STICK ONTO THE TICK-BOARD SO THAT THE STICK ALIGNS WITH ITS ORIGINAL #1 POSITION (AS DICTATED BY THE LINE AND TICK DRAWN ON THE BOARD).

⑪
PLACE A DOT ONTO THE PAPER DIRECTLY BELOW THE POINT OF THE TICK-STICK.

⑫
MOVE THE TICK-STICK TO SUCCESSIVE POSITIONS ON THE BOARD, MAKING DOTS ON THE PAPER AT THE POINT OF THE STICK AS YOU GO, UNTIL ALL OF THE TICK REFERENCES HAVE BEEN USED.

⑬
REMOVE THE BOARD FROM THE PAPER. NOW CONNECT THE DOTS USING A FLEXIBLE WOODEN OR PLASTIC BATTEN (OR STRAIGHT EDGE AS CIRCUMSTANCES DICTATE).

⑭
REFERRING TO YOUR CONSTRUCTION DRAWING OR SKETCHES, DRAW ALL REMAINING DETAILS REQUIRED FOR CUTTING THE FINISHED PIECE ACCURATELY.

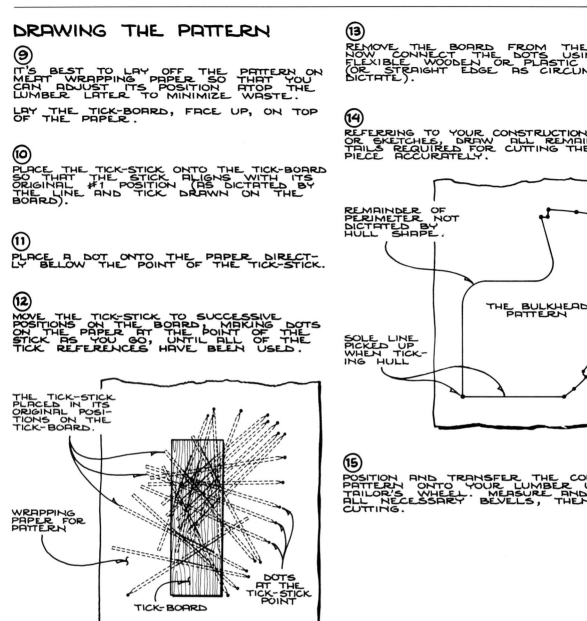

THE TICK-STICK PLACED IN ITS ORIGINAL POSITIONS ON THE TICK-BOARD.

WRAPPING PAPER FOR PATTERN

TICK-BOARD

DOTS AT THE TICK-STICK POINT

REMAINDER OF PERIMETER NOT DICTATED BY HULL SHAPE.

THE BULKHEAD PATTERN

SOLE LINE PICKED UP WHEN TICKING HULL

⑮
POSITION AND TRANSFER THE COMPLETED PATTERN ONTO YOUR LUMBER USING A TAILOR'S WHEEL. MEASURE AND NOTE ALL NECESSARY BEVELS, THEN START CUTTING.

A third method is to cut a piece of stiff cardboard by trial and error until the correct lines are obtained. Lay the cardboard on the piece of wood that is to become the bulkhead. Trace the line with a pencil and cut with a saber saw.

Because bulkheads form major structural supports for the hull and deck, considerable loads can be exerted upon them, particularly where the hull meets the bulkhead. This is another possible location for a hard spot. In this instance, water exerting force on the outside of the hull causes the unsupported areas to flex, however minutely. The thin edge of the bulkhead supports the hull in a very small area only. The hull here will not flex like the panel sections to either side. Consequently, some hull cracking or delamination can occur at this spot—unless the bulkhead is installed without creating a hard spot. This is best accomplished by cutting a thin strip of urethane foam the width of the bulkhead (¾-inch bulkheads are standard in the industry for 30 to 40-foot boats). Resting the bulkhead on the foam will provide a cushion between the wood bulkhead and fiberglass hull (Figure 2-18). Cutting the foam at a 45-degree angle might obviate the need for fillets.

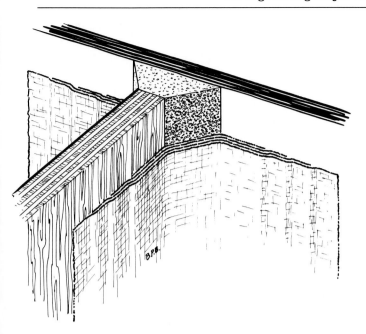

Fig. 2-18 *A strip of urethane foam can be cut the width of the bulkhead and used as a cushion between the bulkhead and the hull so as not to make a hard spot. Increasingly wider layers of mat are used to bond the hull. Cut the foam at a 45-degree angle to save the step of making a fillet.*

After securely clamping the bulkhead in place at right angles to the centerline of the boat in both axes, bond the bulkhead to the hull and deck, overlapping the hull a minimum of four inches, increasing the width of each succeeding layer of 1½-ounce mat and 18-ounce woven roving.

STRENGTHENING THE BILGE AREA

If there is hull flexing in the bilge areas, the cabin sole can be removed and a series of fiberglassed plywood floors added (figure 2-19). The greater distance they extend up the hull, and the more surface area bonded, the stronger the reinforcement.

Refer back to the Hunter 34 grid in Chapter 1, Figure 1-14. This shows a network of athwartship and longitudinally molded beams used to provide stiffness. In adapting these principles to your job at hand, longitudinal beams can be glassed in and interconnected to the floors. This would greatly stiffen the hull, though again, if these steps were necessary to create a strong hull, I think I'd buy another boat that didn't require such a massive effort.

Fig. 2-19 *Plywood floors glassed to the hull help stiffen the critical bilge area. Longitudinal stringers can be glassed to the hull and floors at right angles to form a structural grid.*

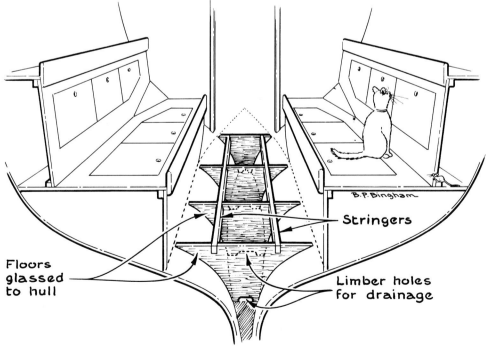

Floors glassed to hull

Stringers

Limber holes for drainage

CHECK BOND OF FURNITURE TO HULL

In the forecabin, V-berths glassed to the hull give rigidity to the forward hull area. The same is true of cabinets and furniture in other cabins. If the fiberglass bond between the wood and hull has been broken, you should reglass the joint using four to six alternating layers of 1½-ounce mat and 10-ounce cloth (for a thinner laminate than woven roving).

Wood Hulls

Hull flex normally occurs in wood hulls when one or more of the ribs or frames is cracked. This is not uncommmon in old wood boats, especially those with steam-bent frames. Sawn and grown frames are stronger, but rarely seen these days.

The easiest method of strengthening a hull plagued by broken frames is to laminate sister frames in situ beside the old ones. Bob Vaughn, proprietor of the Seal Cove Boatyard in Brooksville, Maine, used this method to repair *Desperate Lark*, a 49-foot Herreshoff designed and built yawl. She was constructed in 1903 with long-leaf pine planking on oak frames. Because she once belonged to a friend's grandfather, I dropped in at the yard during a visit to Maine.

As Bob and I watched two carpenters installing the new frames, he said to me, "If Herreshoff had had epoxy, he'd have used it."

Two-inch by ⅜-inch strips of white oak (red oak doesn't bond as well because of a higher acid content) were cut and worked into place under the bilge and sheer clamps, and beside the frame each was replacing. Strips of cardboard were placed between the old frame and new to prevent resin from forming a bond between the two. Resin was not used to bond the new frame to the hull as this would not allow the planks to expand evenly when swelling. Holes were drilled through the entire laminate and temporary 2½-inch #8 screws run into the hull skin to hold the new frames in place until the Cold Cure Epoxy™ used between the layers had cured. Shims were wedged in between the bilge and sheer clamps to help hold the new frames flush to the hull while the holes for the temporary fasteners were being drilled. Bob said that a good deal of "cussedness" helped, too.

When the resin cured, the screws were removed, the holes extended through the hull, larger holes drilled and 2¼-inch #12 silicon bronze wood screws used from the outside to fasten the planking permanently to the new frames. They were ¼-inch shorter than the temporary screws because they were countersunk and plugged. The holes on the inside were then filled with the epoxy. The eventual thickness of the new frames was slightly less than the old ones, 1¾ inch by two inches (Figure 2-20), as compared to 1½–2½ inches by 1⅞ inches.

In the bilge area, new floor timbers were sawn

Fig. 2-20 *New frames were laminated in situ on* Desperate Lark, *a 49-foot Herreshoff designed and built yawl. Seal Cove Boatyard of Brooksville, Maine, did the work.*

from four-inch thick pieces of oak and bronze bolts were used to fasten each to the wood keel. This was necessary because the keel bolts had corroded and needed replacement, requiring removal of the old floors. Beneath the mast step, four-inch laminated oak floors were lofted on the shop floor and made up. In the boat, they extended up three planks on either side.

Desperate Lark has one bronze floor timber aft to keep the cabin sole low for head room. For this same reason, Lin and Larry Pardey cast their own bronze floor timbers for their new 30-foot *Taleisin*.

As an aside, Bob Vaughn also cautioned on refastening hulls by simply removing the old fasteners and screwing in larger diameter fasteners. He said there is always some damage to the wood caused by electrolytic action between the wood and the old fastener, and that a stronger repair results by drilling new holes into new wood, and just plugging the old holes.

Desperate Lark was well built, and had bronze diagonals throughout the hull running between the hull and frames. This is an excellent method of further strengthening the hull structure.

Steel Hulls

Frames on steel boats are made of either angle bar (T-bar) or flat bar, the latter being specified on all Bruce Roberts designs. Frames are placed on centers ranging from about 15 to 24 inches. Adding frames will do little to strengthen the hull, though they will help prevent the plates from pushing inward.

Adding frames isn't an easy task, primarily because of the difficulty in bending the flat bar to the hull curvature. (Panels between frames ultimately do tend to cave in. This is a common phenomenon, and doesn't weaken the skin. If a fair hull is desired, fillers can be used. It's not necessary to add dozens of frames halving the distance between centers.) A professional welder will do a better job, and unless you're willing to develop your skills through a welding course offered at a local community college or vocational school, don't attempt critical repairs yourself.

Rather than trying to bend the stock, it often is easier to buy or have cut two-inch strips of

steel from a large plate. Weld one piece on edge, perpendicular to the hull in the desired location, then weld the second strip on top of the first at right angles. It may be necessary to cut notches in the second strip to make it conform to the proper shape. Weld up the cuts on completion (Figure 2-21a). Never weld a long continuous bead all at once as this may distort the plates. Instead, make several randomly placed short beads, let them cool, and then complete the weld in between.

Another method is to use "wiggle rod," formed from round bar stock (Figure 2-21b). Tack weld the points of the rod to the hull, and then a strip over the points on top.

Fig. 2-21 *Easier than trying to bend angle bar or T-bar is to cut strips of plate, weld one piece to the hull, then weld the second at right angles. The use of "wiggle" rod is yet another method.*

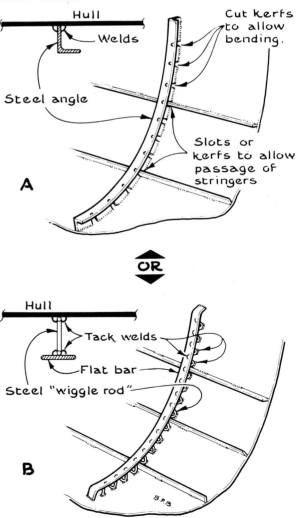

HULL/DECK JOINTS

Fiberglass Boats

Hulls and decks are typically joined in several ways. Figure 2-22 shows some of them. Rivets and screws are definitely inferior to stainless steel thru-bolts. It's probably worth the effort to replace them if there is any cracking or excessive leaking at the joint.

Polysulfide compound is frequently used by builders to seal the joint before the fastenings are drilled. Before applying a compound, be certain the area is bone dry. Use fans and lamps, if necessary. Wiping alcohol over the crack will assist in evaporating any remaining moisture. If the joint hasn't been glassed over, and the seam leaks, fill in the cracks with polysulfide or glass over with a strong laminate.

By removing the toe rail or rub rail (depending on the type of hull/deck joint) you can gain access to the outside of the hull/deck joint. You might consider sealing the joint with polysulfide, or glassing it over from the outside. A functional and attractive rub rail can be thru-bolted over some types of joints. This would protect the joint to a degree, and at the same time keep the topsides from getting scuffed up at the dock.

Wood Boats

As mentioned earlier, the hull/deck joint on wood boats is an area particularly subject to distortion by waves. Traditionally, grown oak knees were cut and fitted horizontally between deck beams and shelves, and vertically between the beams and frames. If the hull/deck area seems to be working, the simplest solution is to replace the knees (Figure 2-23).

Because grown knees are difficult to come by (they are sawn out of the trunks of trees where they lead into the root system), it is far easier to laminate new ones. Carefully measure the angles between the beams and shelves and between beams and frames; make a jig, and lay up new knees that equal the dimensions of the old ones (Figure 2-24).

Another solution is to weld up braces from steel and then bolt them to the beams, frames and shelves (Figure 2-25). An advantage of welded knees is that there is less likelihood of creating dead air spaces where rot can grow.

COMPRESSION OF THE DECK AT THE MAST STEP

Most forces of the rigging on deck-stepped masts are directed straight down the spar and are transferred to the deck. Not only must the deck be as strong as possible here, the load must be distributed over as wide an area as possible. Boats with beams wider than about nine feet can have the cabin walkway offset to one side of the hull so that a compression post may be inserted between the deck and keel. Of course, masts

Fig. 2-22 *There are several conventional methods of attaching the hull to the deck. Regardless of the type of joint on your boat, a layer of glass over the inside of the joint strengthens the area and helps prevent leaks.*

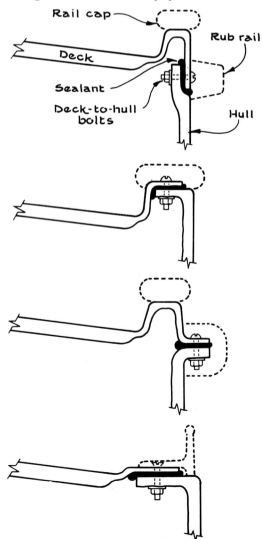

Rail cap

Rub rail

Deck

Sealant

Deck-to-hull bolts

Hull

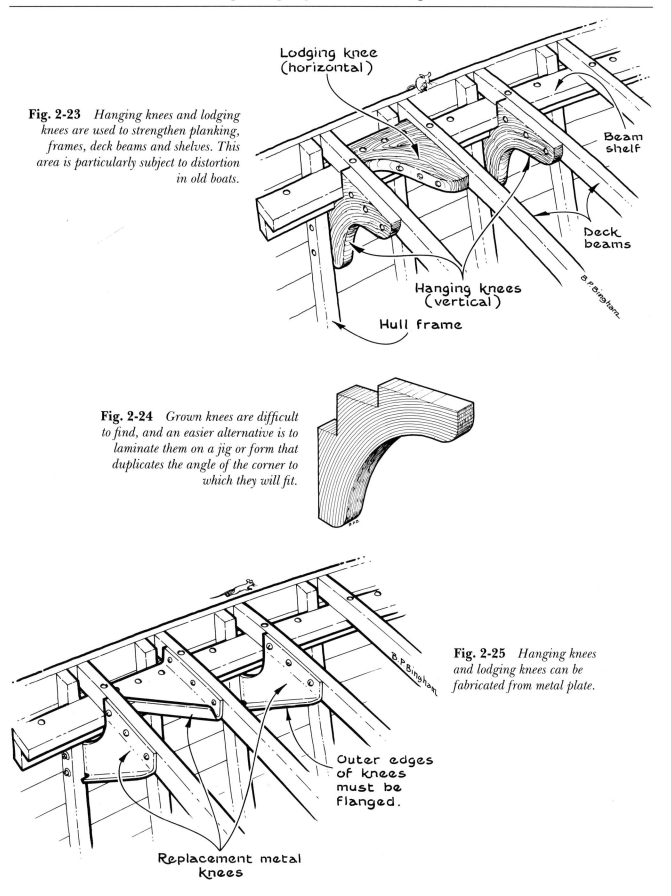

Fig. 2-23 *Hanging knees and lodging knees are used to strengthen planking, frames, deck beams and shelves. This area is particularly subject to distortion in old boats.*

Lodging knee (horizontal)

Beam shelf

Deck beams

Hanging knees (vertical)

Hull frame

Fig. 2-24 *Grown knees are difficult to find, and an easier alternative is to laminate them on a jig or form that duplicates the angle of the corner to which they will fit.*

Fig. 2-25 *Hanging knees and lodging knees can be fabricated from metal plate.*

Outer edges of knees must be flanged.

Replacement metal knees

stepped on the keel won't cause problems with the deck, other than occasional stress around the collar if the fit is tight and the rigging loose. Figure 2-26 shows several ways in which the loads from the mast can be transferred to something more substantial than the deck—including beams—which is how these loads are handled on my Pearson Triton.

The deck of my 19-foot twin-keeler deflected from the mast compression loads so that several cabinet doors wouldn't open unless I jammed in a compression post between the cabin sole and deck. But then I couldn't get into the forward bunk, so a deck beam seemed to be the right solution. The same techniques can be used for adding this beam as were described for the foredeck reinforcing beam project (Figure 2-27). If there are bulkheads to either side in the appropriate place, these could be used to thru-bolt the beam in lieu of knees. In the Triton, the beam is supported by four posts, fastened flush to the bulkheads, and run all the way down to the hull. This gives better support to the beam than just knees or bulkheads.

Another possible solution is to install a pad beneath the base of the mast (Figure 2-27). This can be metal—stainless steel or, even better, aluminum plate thru-bolted to the deck—or plywood glassed to the deck. The greater the

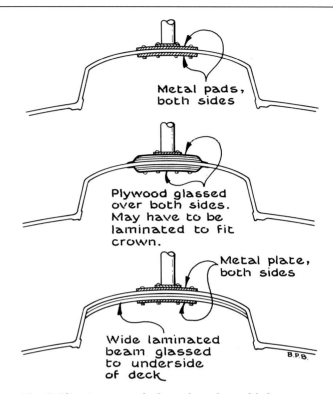

Fig. 2-27 *A mast pad of metal or plywood helps distribute the load of the mast over a larger area.*

thickness the stronger it will be. And the larger it is, the better it will distribute loads over the deck. Of course, whatever thickness is added beneath the mast will add to the height of the mast,

Fig. 2-26 *Compression posts transfer the load from the mast to the keel. Sometimes the post runs through the cabin sole directly to the keel; other times a reinforced cabin sole is used to support the post. Narrow-beam boats may rely on the bulkheads and an internal deck beam to carry the load.*

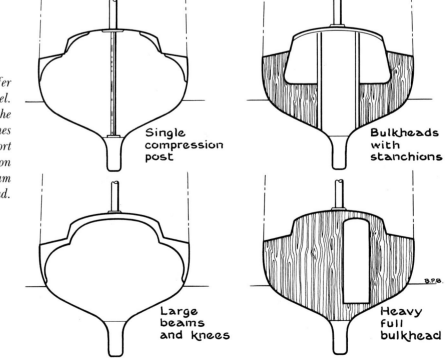

and toggles will have to be added to the chainplates, or longer tangs installed on the mast if the turnbuckles can't absorb the difference.

CHAINPLATES

When chainplates, which link the rigging turnbuckles to the bulkheads or knees, are leaking or working, you may decide to do some work on them. The loads on chain plates and structural members is significant—a ¼ inch 1 x 19 shroud has an 8,200-pound breaking strength. Even if there is a four-to-one safety factor, loads approaching or exceeding a ton can be exerted on the chainplates and structural members. The more inboard the shrouds, the more this load is increased (see Chapter 10). On racing boats, moving the shrouds inboard enables the skipper to sheet headsails in closer, thereby pointing higher. However, on a cruising boat, strength of the rig is more important than narrow sheeting angles. That is why some boats, such as the Westsail 32 and Morgan Out Island series, have their chainplates attached to the hull sides with thru-bolts. This is the widest staying base possible, unless channels are fitted to the hull to move the tops of the chainplates outboard of the hull. Wood backing plates glassed to the inside of the hull will reinforce this critical area (Figure 2-28).

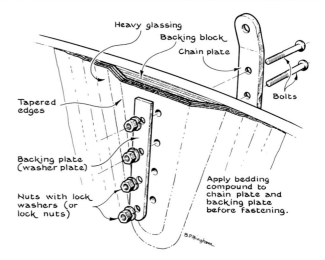

Fig. 2-28 *If chainplates appear to be working loose, reinforce them with a backup plate of plywood glassed to the bulkhead or hull. In this drawing, the chainplates are thru-bolted to the outside of the hull.*

If a chainplate is working, one remedy is to increase its size (see Chapter 10) and that of the structural member to which it's fastened—knee or bulkhead. If the structural member is a knee, consider increasing its size. If the structural member is a bulkhead, probably ¾-inch plywood, either replace with a thicker bulkhead (messy) or reinforce by adding shiplap planking or another piece of plywood to one side, or by using wood or metal backing plates where the chainplates are fastened. Figure 2-29 illustrates these possible solutions.

Fig. 2-29 *These illustrations show several ways to beef up the chainplate installations. They include enlarging the knee, doubling the thickness of the bulkhead and adding a backing plate.*

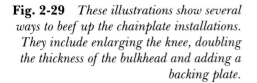

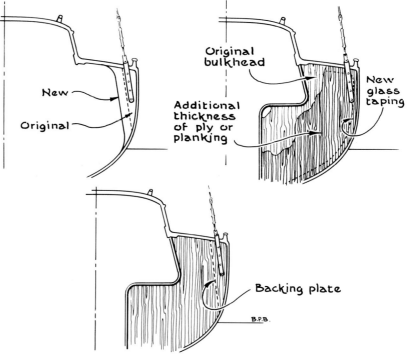

EXTERNAL REINFORCEMENTS

The internal reinforcements we have discussed so far are probably the most effective means of making the hull and deck more rigid. However, there are several options for attacking the problems of flexing from the outside.

Handholds

One simple trick is to thru-bolt a longitudinal stiffener to the deck or cabin roof that doubles as a handhold or toe rail. These can be solid hardwood, such as teak or mahogany, or can be laminated from thinner pieces. With a table saw, you can rip a larger plank into strips from about 1/8" to 1/4" thick and between one and two inches wide. They can be laminated in place by drilling the bolt holes and bolting the stiffeners to the deck at the same time you glue the individual pieces together (Figure 2-30). However, it will be more difficult to finish the stiffener after it's installed. The utility of an external deck stiffener is enhanced if you can place them where they also function as footholds for working around the mast or at the bow. Be certain to properly bed all thru-bolts.

Teak Decks

A dubious and far more expensive and time-consuming solution is to cover the decks with teak planks (Figure 2-31). They must be bedded in polysulfide and screwed to the deck if it has a core (which it probably doesn't if you're installing teak decks to correct oil-canning), or bonded to the deck with epoxy resin mixed with talc or microfibers to thicken it, and then fastened. Use a grooved cement trowel to achieve a uniform coating and reduce waste. In his book, *From A Bare Hull*, Ferenc Maté has an excellent chapter on installing teak decks. It would be worthwhile reading for anyone considering the job. He recommends using polysulfide to fill the grooves on top. But some builders of cold-molded boats, like the Gougeon Brothers, are using epoxy resin mixed with graphite (to make it black and protect the resin from ultra violet attack). But after you've read about what Maté calls "200 hours of screamingly frustrated labor," and after considering the difficulty of doing a good job, it's probably wisest to save teak decks for your next boat.

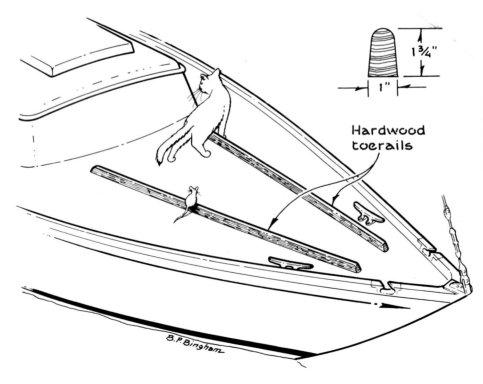

Hardwood toerails

Fig. 2-30 *An external deck beam laminated from thin pieces of hardwood and both thru-bolted and screwed to the deck helps stiffen areas that oilcan.*

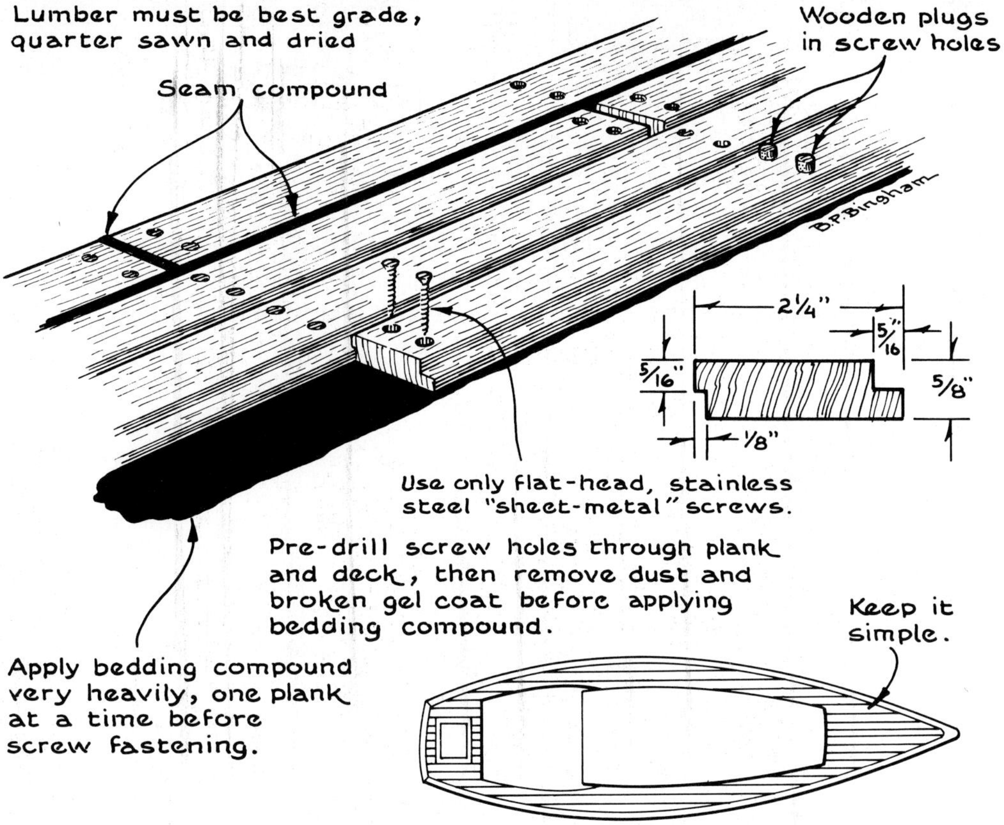

Lumber must be best grade, quarter sawn and dried

Seam compound

Wooden plugs in screw holes

B.P.Bingham

2¼"

5/16"

5/16"

5/8"

1/8"

Fig. 2-31 *Teak planks help stiffen uncored decks. They may be epoxied and/or screwed to the existing deck. An epoxy/graphite mix to fill the seams has the look of Thiokol or polysulphide without the mess.*

Use only flat-head, stainless steel "sheet-metal" screws.

Pre-drill screw holes through plank and deck, then remove dust and broken gel coat before applying bedding compound.

Keep it simple.

Apply bedding compound very heavily, one plank at a time before screw fastening.

WHY I HATE INNER LINERS

If strengthening the hull is just the beginning of your upgrading efforts, it certainly would make sense to do these jobs before remodeling furniture or anything else, because you may have to rip out bunks and cabinets to get at the places of the hull or deck requiring reinforcement.

There are two types of inner liners and both make working on the boat much more difficult; unfortunately, they are all too commonplace. The deck liner is a molding of fiberglass that fits the underside of the deck and cabin top. It's purpose is to replace the rough inside of the bare fiberglass hull with a glossy white gel coated surface.

As this idea took hold, some builders got really crafty and molded a pan with all the bunks, galley and cabinets figured in. This pan was dropped into the hull before the deck was put on and then it was glassed to the hull in several places. All the workmen had to do then was trim the pan with pieces of teak and, presto, the interior was done.

It may sound like a good idea, but these pans seriously interfere with access to the hull. A friend of mine in Newport, who owns a Pearson

32, ran the externally ballasted keel into a rock during a cruise to Woods Hole. The keel and keel bolts twisted, necessitating replacing and reinforcing the structural floors that support the keel via the keel bolts. The boat has a fiberglass pan and the workers had to cut large sections of it away just to get at the hull so they could do the work. Then, once they'd fixed the keel, they had to fix the holes they had cut in the liner—without the benefit of a mold.

What all this boils down to is that a plywood interior is easier to remove or modify. Except for major bulkheads, berths and shelving, most other pieces of interior wood can simply be screwed together so that when you really have to get at something, you aren't sawing up your boat. And, if you care at all about how your boat looks inside, remember that it was these pans that led to the unflattering epithets about fiberglass boats looking like Clorox bottles and the insides of refrigerators.

REINFORCING RUDDERS

Tremendous forces are constantly at work against your rudder, under way and even at anchor or at the dock. Sooner or later in the life of many boats, the rudder will need reinforcing or replacing. Unfortunately, you often can't go out and buy a new rudder the way you buy a new starter or water pump for your car. If the company that built your boat is still in business, they may be persuaded to make a new one for you. But, unless you are convinced that they have properly engineered the rudder, you may decide to beef up the old rudder yourself.

Reinforcing Wood Rudders

Your plan will depend on what type of rudder you have—wood or fiberglass, attached, spade or outboard (see Chapter 1, Figure 1-1). *Adriana's* attached rudder is made of ¾-inch mahogany planks held together by pins or drifts inside, much the way an orthopedic surgeon pins a broken leg. The gudgeon straps also help hold the planks together. Hauling the boat in the winter and exposing this wood to the dry cold air causes some shrinking and cracking. But unless the planks are working loose it won't hurt to let the small cracks go as they'll disappear back in the water when the planks swell. Glassing over or screwing in metal straps should strengthen a failing wood rudder satisfactorily (Figure 2-32). If glassing over metal straps, use epoxy resin, as it bonds much better to metal than polyester resin. Use 1½-ounce mat and 10 or 14-ounce cloth.

Fiberglass Rudders

Making a new fiberglass rudder is another matter. Steel rods commonly are welded to the stock and a foam core is often laid in and around the rods before covering the whole network with fiberglass.

The reason for using foam is that rudders should be as near to neutrally buoyant as possible. A solid fiberglass rudder would be too heavy and could cause a lee helm. Likewise, an overly buoyant rudder could cause weather helm. While a new all-wood rudder may be positively buoyant, the additional weight of fittings, and the water it absorbs over the years eventually makes it nearly neutrally buoyant.

Other fiberglass rudders incorporate metal plates welded to the stock. Both types are strong. But if these welds break inside, the fiberglass bond to the rudder stock will break in short order and leave you without any control. An offshore cruising skipper must be able to rely on his rudder . . . *always*.

A fiberglass rudder can be made from male or female molds, though the former is easier for the amateur. To make a male mold, fashion two pieces of plywood to the size and shape desired, and smaller than the final product by the thickness of the laminate that will cover it. Use 1½ or two-ounce mat and 24-ounce woven roving or 10-ounce cloth (cloth is to be preferred on the

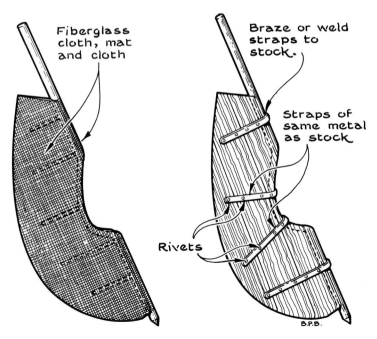

Fiberglass cloth, mat and cloth

Braze or weld straps to stock.

Straps of same metal as stock

Rivets

B.P.B.

Fig. 2-32 *A wood rudder, made up from several boards, may use drift pins run through the rudder's width to hold it together. If the boards begin to work, glassing the entire rudder and adding metal straps will strengthen the rudder.*

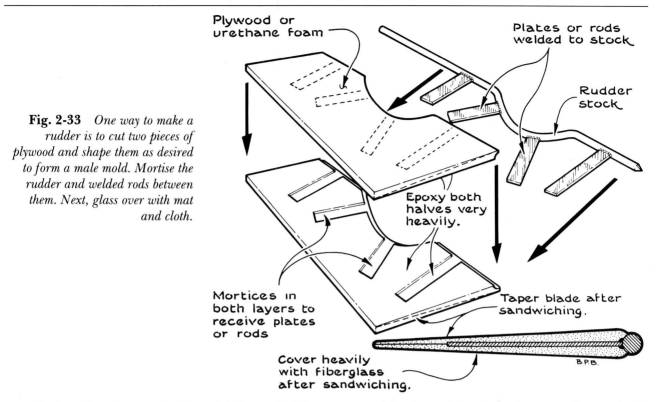

Fig. 2-33 *One way to make a rudder is to cut two pieces of plywood and shape them as desired to form a male mold. Mortise the rudder and welded rods between them. Next, glass over with mat and cloth.*

Plywood or urethane foam

Plates or rods welded to stock

Rudder stock

Epoxy both halves very heavily.

Mortices in both layers to receive plates or rods

Taper blade after sandwiching.

Cover heavily with fiberglass after sandwiching.

outside layer) to cover the board (Figure 2-33). Of course, the rudder stock and stiffening rods must be incorporated into the design. Notch the wood so that the two pieces can enclose the hardware and lie flush. One possible method is shown.

Rudder Supports

Vertical rudder stocks should enter the hull either through a glass or stainless steel tube bolted through a substantial block of wood (Figure 2-34). A stuffing box is fitted to the hull or tube to center the stock and make the opening watertight. It wouldn't hurt to strengthen the hull here, either by glassing in a heavier piece of plywood against the hull, adding extra layers of mat and woven roving in the area, or glassing in a few beams, between which the backing block can be glassed. (You'll need to remove any existing block to do these repairs.)

Additionally, the stock should be supported higher up, where it passes into the cockpit or wherever else it emerges above deck. There should be a strong collar to support the stock and a bearing plate firmly supported by structural members glassed to the hull.

This reinforcment will protect the hull against

normal loads and, in the sad event of a grounding, will even help prevent the rudder from being shoved up through the hull. Losing the rudder is one thing, losing the whole boat a catastrophe!

Whether gudgeons and pintles are used to hang the rudder, or gudgeon straps, they should

Fig. 2-34 *Wherever the rudder enters the hull should be reinforced by glassing in a block of wood with a hole cut for the shaft. Additional strengthening of this critical area can be achieved by glassing in short beams around the block.*

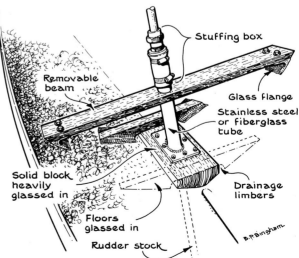

Stuffing box

Removable beam

Glass flange

Stainless steel or fiberglass tube

Solid block heavily glassed in

Floors glassed in

Rudder stock

Drainage limbers

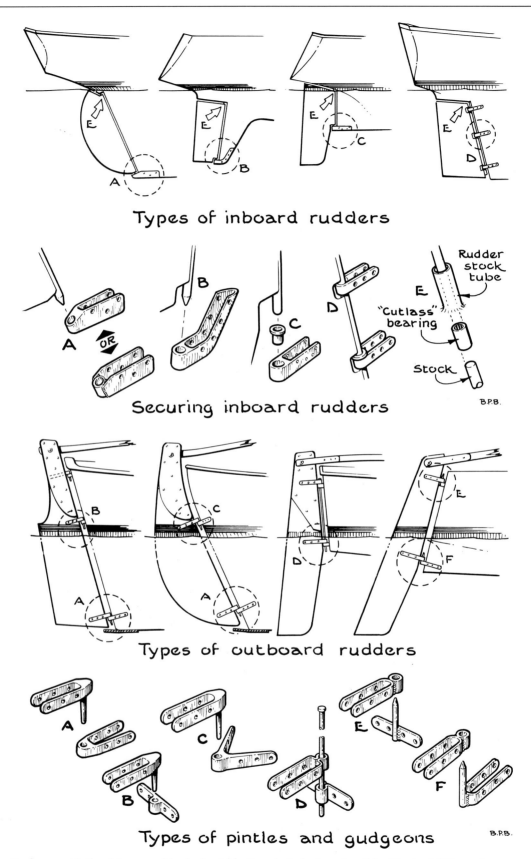

Types of inboard rudders

Securing inboard rudders

Types of outboard rudders

Types of pintles and gudgeons

Fig. 2-35 *Gudgeons, pintles, hinges and heels should be thru-bolted where possible. The heel fittings shown are thru-bolted to the skeg and help distribute the load of the rudder over a wide area.*

be thru-bolted to the rudder and hull or keel. Backing blocks should be glassed in as well, if the skin is thin. Skeg-mounted rudders and rudders attached to full keels should have a heel bearing (usually bronze) that supports the weight of the rudder and also acts as a rudder-to-keel attachment (Figure 2-35). The heel bearing should extend along the base of the keel or skeg, to which it is thru-bolted to help distribute the loads imposed by the rudder on it.

SUMMARY

These, then, are some of the ways in which a boat can be fortified and prepared to withstand the awesome power of the sea. Over-engineering hull structures and rudders gives better than a fighting chance in severe storm conditions. If something seems weak, fix it now, not after it has broken—the lives of you and your crew are at stake.

You may have some qualms about changing the structural design of the boat, as well you should. Don't move bulkheads without assuring yourself that the hull can stand rigid without it, or with it in a new location. It never hurts to contact and question your boat's designer. Failing that, talk the project over with another designer, an experienced builder, or a qualified marine surveyor. Asking the right person the right question may give you some useful tips to consider before jumping in.

FURTHER READING

Fiberglass Boatbuilding for Amateurs by Ken Hankinson; Glen-L Marine Designs, 9152 Rosecrans, Bellflower, California 90706.

Fiberglass Boats by Hugo du Plessis; John de Graff, Inc. Clinton Corners, New York 12514.

From A Bare Hull by Ferenc Maté; Albatross Publishing House, 5934 Marine Drive, West Vancouver, B.C., Canada V7W 2S2.

Wooden Boat Repair Manual, by John Scarlett; International Marine Publishing Company, Camden, Maine 04843.

Own A Steel Boat by Mike Pratt; International Marine Publishing Company, Camden, Maine 04843.

Gougeon Brothers On Boat Construction; 706 Martin Street, Bay City, Michigan 48706.

The Fiberglass Repair And Construction Handbook by Jack Wiley; Tab Books, Inc., Blue Ridge Summit, Pennsylvania 17214.

CHAPTER 3

A Seagoing Interior Layout

Possibly this love for a small cabin was atavistic, derived from our remote ancestors for whom a cave was the only safe, indeed the only possible, dwelling.

Samuel Eliot Morrison

In considering the seaworthiness of a cruising boat, emphasis is often placed on the integrity of the hull and strength of the rig. A close third is the nature of the interior accommodations. After all, in bad weather one or all of the crew may be inside. In survival conditions, the helm is lashed and all hands are ordered below where they should be strapped to their bunks to await fairer weather.

Though no statistics are available, it is entirely possible that more injuries occur belowdecks than above. Being thrown against a cabinet corner, having a heavy pot land on your head, or getting scalded by a tipped pan of hot water are just a few of the ways that someone can be injured. The interior plan of your boat should be designed with a vision of the worst that can happen.

TYPICAL PRODUCTION BOAT LAYOUTS

The "dinette" and "standard" layouts of most production boats have evolved in part from what works, and in part from what the public has demanded, however, ill-informed it may be.

For example, shag carpeting looks cozy, but provides poor footing and once damp is difficult to dry. Dinette tables mounted on flimsy pedestals are nice for coffee hour on the mooring, but are in the way at sea and frequently broken when crashed into by a stumbling body. V-berths forward seem practical enough, but in any kind of sea are sickenly uncomfortable. These kinds of features may work on weekends, but not for extended cruising.

MY IDEAL LAYOUT

There is certainly room for considerable freedom and personal preference in designing one's

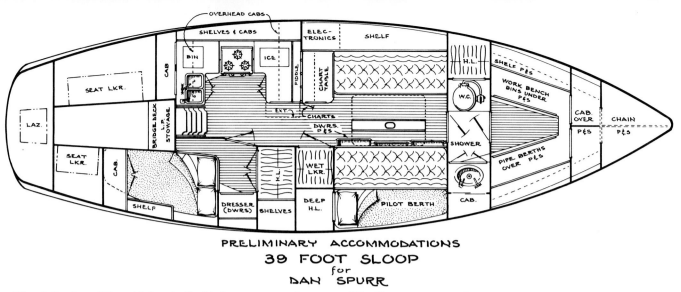

PRELIMINARY ACCOMMODATIONS
39 FOOT SLOOP
for
DAN SPURR

Fig. 3-1 *In a 35 to 40-foot hull, this layout comes close to my "ideal" arrangement plan.*

ideal interior layout, especially on larger boats. And, of course, there are innumerable restrictions: the shape of the hull, length of the hull, positioning of bulkheads, location of chainplates, type of deck (flush or coachroof), headroom, etc. But as long as we're dreaming, giving thought to an ideal layout is at least instructive, and at most a goal to attempt achieving in your own boat.

Figure 3-1 illustrates many of the points I consider important and possible in a boat of about 35 to 40 feet LOA. Beginning at the bow, there is a large forepeak for stowage of seldom-used items that aren't too heavy—sea anchors, cockpit awning, anchor buoys, etc. The forward cabin, usually used for V-berths, has a fold-up pipe berth to port with an oak-topped workbench underneath. To starboard are storage bins for tools, paint, sails, sewing machine and other odds and ends.

In the main cabin there is a settee to port and navigation station. If the settee isn't long enough to sleep on, because of a foot well for the navigation station, a drop-leaf board with cushion could be fashioned to extend the foot of the berth beneath the chart table. To starboard there is a narrow settee and pilot berth up underneath the deck that makes an excellent sea berth on port tack.

Moving aft there is a U-shaped galley to port with deep double sinks, a gimballed stove/oven mounted athwartships, and large counter surfaces for food preparation. Opposite the galley is a private quarter cabin with double berth and bureau for neat storage of clothes.

A bridge deck in the smallish cockpit gives ad-

ditional seating space and has the added benefit of opening up more space in the quarter cabin. And it allows the galley to extend a few extra feet underneath the cockpit. There might also be room here for a wet locker to hang dripping foul weather gear. Sharp corners are rounded, handholds are everywhere, the cabin sole is not so wide that one can't always find a surface to brace a hip against, and all sea berths are fitted with lee boards or heavy canvas lee cloths.

Obviously, I haven't thought of everything, and almost infinite acceptable variations are possible. But this layout does meet these major requirements:

- Safety for sleeping and sitting crew
- Adequate storage space
- A safe galley area
- Usable navigation station
- A strong and unobtrusive dining table

Let's now take a look at the major considerations in redesigning an interior, and then study the changes I made to my 28-foot Pearson Triton as a case history.

BERTHS

Most production boats are designed for weekend cruising by crews in multiples of two. One couple sleeps in the forward cabin V-berths, the other on a folded down dinette. Extra kids can be stuffed in pilot or quarter berths and, in desperation, still others could put their sleeping bags in the cockpit. It works, but for the cruising single or couple, too much space is wasted by all these berths. It makes good sense to plan your new interior around the number of people who'll actually be living aboard, then make some provision for visits by two more persons. If the setup for guests isn't ideal, remember that they'll probably be sailing with you for only a week or two at a time and that your comfort comes first.

If you have a dinette model and decide to keep the arrangement, then the problem of where to put your brother and his girlfriend is solved. However, it can be a nuisance to have to clear the table every time the berth is made—some things you just learn to live with.

Most dinette tables are notoriously flimsy. A number of very strong stainless steel or aluminum table pedestals are on the market (Figure 3-2), and one of these would be a worthwhile investment if your existing pedestal has excessive wobble. The base should be thru-bolted to the cabin sole with large stainless steel bolts and, if the sole looks too thin, a backing plate of plywood, aluminum or stainless steel should be fitted. Stainless steel is tough to drill with

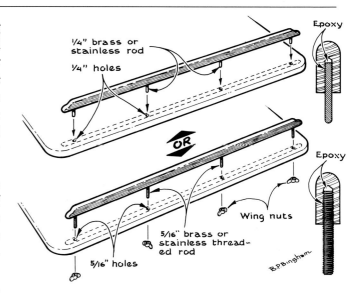

Fig. 3-3 *Removable fiddles on a dinette make berth cushions fit better when the table is lowered for sleeping, to say nothing about the comfort of your back.*

Fig. 3-2 *Dinette table pedestals should be thru-bolted to the floor and must provide plenty of support. This one, made by the Dutch firm of Zwaardvis, is hydraulically operated. Pushing the table down compresses the "gasspring," which effortlessly returns the table to the up position when ready (D. W. Follansbee, Inc.).*

household tools. Since you'll encounter other metal-working jobs you probably won't be able to handle alone, search out a local metal worker/ welder and establish a friendly relationship. With his tools, it'll take just seconds to do what would frustrate you for hours.

Two-inch fiddles help keep plates and glasses from sliding off the dinette table at dinner or cocktail hour, but they're tough to sleep on. Removable fiddles (Figure 3-3) can be fashioned by fitting ¼-inch wood pegs or brass rods into the bottom of the fiddles and then drilling appropriately spaced holes into the table. Experiment with sizes to get a snug fit. At bedtime, pull off the fiddles and stow them on a shelf. If the inboard fiddle also functions as a handhold, a stronger method is to sink threaded rod stock in place of the pegs. Use wing nuts under the table to keep the fiddles tight.

The forward V-berths offer many possibilities for customizing. If you plan to sleep nightly in the main cabin, consider converting the forward cabin to a sail stowage and rope locker by removing the tops of the bunks. Alternatively, one bunk could be converted to a workbench with drawers and bins for tools underneath. Eric Hiscock, when I visited him in Opua, New Zealand, was proud to show me how he could convert the forward cabin to a darkroom to develop black and white photographs.

Boatbuilders frequently offer V-berth inserts to convert the entire forward cabin into an enormous double berth. This arrangement has its obvious merits, but unless the couple has the shoulders of linebackers, much space on both sides is wasted. On a small cruiser, you just can't afford not to put that space to good use. In my 28-foot Triton, with a beam of just 8′4″, there was sufficient room to build an offset double berth with the foot aft and head forward. There is still room to walk into the cabin, sit on the edge of the bunk and rest your dogs on the floor while undressing. To starboard there is about six square feet of bunk space on which to build clothes bins.

Pilot berths tucked like stair steps under the side decks outboard of the settees are nifty for kids because they give a sense of security much like hiding in a tree fort. They are up and out of the way under deck, so adults still awake or moving about aren't stumbling over the errant little legs and arms. And when not in use, pilot berths can be stuffed with bedding, pillows and other gear. A lee board or heavy lee cloth (Figure 3-12) can be fitted across the face of the berth to keep these items from tumbling out. A possible disadvantage of pilot berths on boats without great beam is that they force the settees inboard, thereby reducing the width of the cabin sole, and perhaps the width of the settees themselves.

Quarter berths are excellent sea berths, and one would be wise to pause and consider their value before converting this space to some other use. Dropping yourself into one is sometimes like crawling feet first into a coffin, but they are snug. If only the head of the berth protrudes into the cabin, lee cloths or bunk boards may not be necessary. Quarter berths occupy little space and can accomodate all sorts of bedding and gear during the day, or at night, depending on the watch hours of its occupant.

My friend Dave Markell bought a Pearson Vanguard with the dinette arrangement amidships. The production version had two quarter berths aft, but the previous owner had removed the port-side bunk, added a bulkhead between the under-cockpit area and cabin, and installed a large navigation station (Figure 3-4). Under the bridge, atop the engine box, he fitted a Tiny Tot solid fuel stove. Coal storage was con-

structed under the port cockpit seat with a special hatch (Chapter 14, Figures 14-7, 14-8, 14-9). Inside, beneath the chart table, a small door allows Dave to dump out just enough coal to fill the stove and keep his cabin warm on cool and clammy Newport nights.

Beneath his starboard quarter berth he has dozens of small drawers for spare parts and tools, all organized for instant identification. Drawers are sometimes more practical than top-loading hatches and bins. It isn't necessary to pull up the cushion to get at things (all the more an irritation if someone is on the bunk) and with large finger or hand holes drilled in the drawers, the growth of mildew is minimized.

Fig. 3-4 *The port quarter berth of this Pearson Vanguard has been converted to a navigation station. Also, a wood/coal stove has been fitted under the bridge deck.*

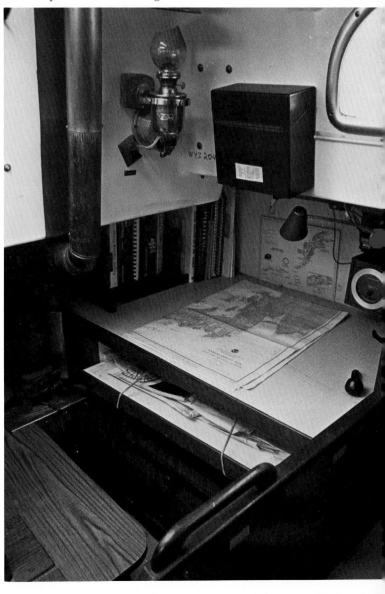

STOWAGE

You can't have too much storage space on a small boat. Building drawers and bins out of wood is very labor intensive and only the higher-priced production boats even approach having adequate built-in stowage space. However, this is one area in which you can use your creative genius to great effect, and at little risk of botching up the boat. Areas under the deck and outboard of bunks are almost always the best places to build bookshelves, instrument boxes, can storage, etc. Drawers can be fitted under bunks; hanging lockers and forepeaks can be improved by adding shelves with tall fiddles or facings; nets can be strung underneath the decks; and unused bunks can be turned into navigation stations, bureaus or extra galley space.

Drawers and cabinets are better stowage areas than the bins under bunks, which are usually unpartitioned and poorly ventilated. These spaces can be converted to drawer storage by cutting openings in the facing of the bunk sides and constructing runners and drawers (Figure 3-5).

Only when you've moved aboard for a period of time do you begin to realize the amount of stowage space necessary for comfortable, organized living. It's a nusiance to continually have to dig through layers of clothes or gear to find the item you want, or to have things sitting out on bunks for lack of places to stow them. Consider your needs carefully, study the space available, and make sketches of alternatives. Think through each step carefully before cutting up old furniture or buying materials and tools. Try to picture each piece, how you will measure it, how it will be supported. For example, will there be enough room to use a screwdriver between it and an adjacent surface? If possible, consult with a friend; he may give you time-saving ideas that never would have occurred to you. If you can plan several projects before buying materials, you can save time and money by doing all your shopping at once. And don't hesitate to purchase new tools when necessary; any job is easier with the right tool, the finished product more attractive, and you'll have it for future use.

The galley should have room for pots and pans, tableware, and bins or cabinets for food that are dry and ventilated. Don't forget drawers

Fig. 3-5 *Drawers fitted beneath berths are much more useful and handy than the hatches that require lifting the cushions to gain access.*

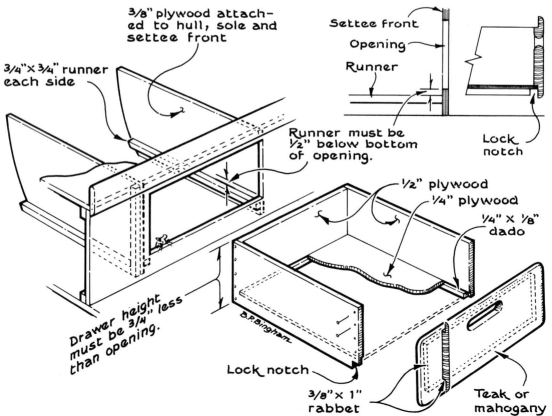

for the dozens of necessary small cooking utensils.

Counter surfaces of sufficient size for laying out cans and cabbages, cutting vegetables and mixing soups are essential. The dinette table can be used for this purpose. But this means occupying the space your crew may be using for writing letters, reading or, in the case of kids, drawing and pasting.

Heavy pots must remain secure when the boat is bucking around. Thin veneer facings and shock cord will not stop a 10-pound iron skillet from launching itself to the other side of the cabin. Nor will an icebox lid without a lock keep the contents inside during a rollover. Visit as many ocean cruising boats as possible and study how best to solve these problems on your own boat. Also, read the practical sections of sailing magazines and technical boating books, for there are dozens of useful tips to be found there.

On small boats, it may be impossible to always have every item safely stowed. Danny Greene, a *Cruising World* editor who lives aboard a Mystic 10-3 26-foot cutter, keeps his cutlery in a wood holder near the galley. His pots and pans are kept in a bin under the twin Sea-Swing stoves. When it gets really nasty, he throws everything into a box and stows it under the cockpit where,

at least, the knives won't stab the skipper and the pots won't brain the mate.

HEAD

On a cruising boat, the simpler the toilet the better. Even the simplest systems that pump through the hull can become jammed with human waste, toilet paper, sanitary napkins and cigarette butts. And no task on board is more onerous than cleaning out discharge lines. Add macerators, chemical rinses and the other devices used for legalizing heads, and the potential for problems mounts astronomically. That's why some wise old sailors keep espousing the virtues of the ordinary bucket (Figure 3-6). If you need the feel of a real toilet seat under your bottom, mount one on a board with the bucket underneath—it's no different than using the portable johns at concerts and carnivals (Yeah, I know, they stink!). If you don't plan to empty it after every use, dump in some of the deodorizing chemicals used for portable toilets.

Offshore, a holding tank is neither practical nor required by law. For use in harbor, a small

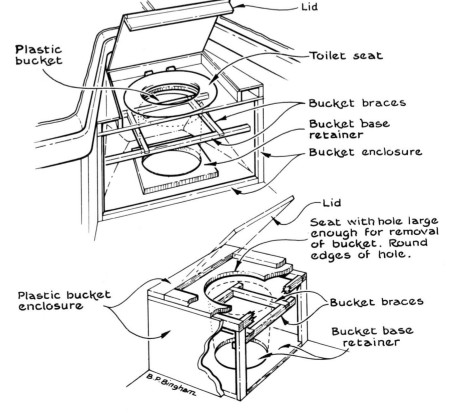

Fig. 3-6 *The traditional cedar bucket, though illegal in coastal waters, is a head of the utmost simplicity. Actually, a plastic bucket is much more sensible.*

Plastic bucket

Lid

Toilet seat

Bucket braces

Bucket base retainer

Bucket enclosure

Lid

Seat with hole large enough for removal of bucket. Round edges of hole.

Bucket braces

Bucket base retainer

Plastic bucket enclosure

B.P.Bingham

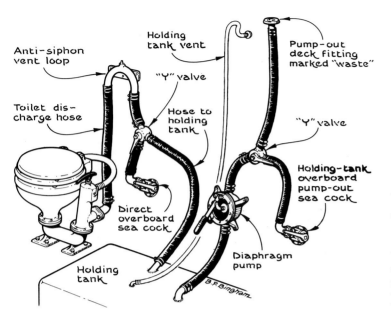

Fig. 3-7 *One of the simplest legal heads uses a small flexible holding tank. A Y-valve allows pumping wastes into the tank or over the side.*

holding tank can be installed beneath a berth or wherever else space is available and connected to the head with a Y-valve that permits either direct overboard dumping or depositing into the holding tank. Pump-out stations are not found everywhere in the world, let alone in the United States. So the system should be designed so the tank can be emptied with a manual pump or carried ashore for discharge. You can install a small flexible holding tank, thus meeting the letter of the law and providing a place to hold wastes when anchored in a crowded harbor (Figure 3-7).

THE METAMORPHOSIS OF *ADRIANA:* A CASE HISTORY

I lived with my Pearson Triton sloop *Adriana* for five years before making major changes to her interior. Most of that time I daysailed her on weekends and spent one and two-week vacations around the Great Lakes or along the East Coast. I did a few things to her, such as installing a pipe berth for a fifth person (Figure 3-8). But all the other alterations I had planned were never af-

fected until the spring I decided to move aboard. Prior to this, everytime I picked up a crowbar and hammer I chickened out. But when push came to shove, I was ready.

The preceding winter I had lent the boat to a friend, Kathy Lash, who after two years of cruising the Caribbean, said she couldn't live ashore any longer. Faced with the prospect of wintering in Newport, and without any boat of her own, she asked if she could live on *Adriana* at the Newport Yachting Center. In the middle of October we moved the boat off its mooring and into the dock. She purchased a 110-volt space heater (that automatically shut off if it fell over), an Aladdin kerosene lamp and an electric blanket. About once or twice a week I trudged down through the snow in the yard, knocked on the hatch, and went below for a visit. The biggest surprise was that Kathy was indeed keeping warm. "Everyone thinks I must be freezing," she told me more than once. "I may be many things, but cold is not one of them!"

Thanking Kathy for serving as my guinea pig, I decided that next spring to move aboard . . . permanently. In April, I hauled the boat at a yard in Bristol, Rhode Island, owned and operated by Clint and Carolyn Pearson. Clint and his cousin Everett had founded the Pearson Yacht

Fig. 3-8 *A pipe berth set up over a settee in the main cabin provides a comfortable berth for an extra guest, and is quickly stowed out of the way in the morning.*

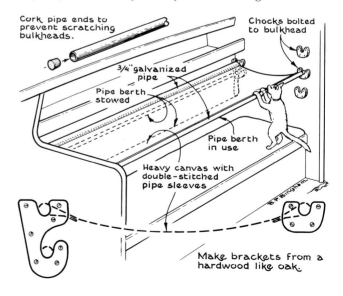

Company in the late 1950's, and were the ones who built *Adriana* along with more than 700 other Tritons. It was the first production fiberglass sailboat built, and following its introduction at the 1959 New York Boat Show, it enjoyed unparalleled success. Later, Everett and Clint split up. Everett ran Pearson for a while before selling out to Grumman and then linking up with Mr. Tillotson to build a variety of boats—Freedom 40's, J 24's, Fales Navigators—as well as aluminum truck bodies and telephone poles. Clint started Bristol Yacht Company and runs it to this day.

I allotted six weeks to complete the modifications I had planned. My tentative list looked like this:

- Convert V-berths to one double berth
- Install sink and mirror in place of hanging locker
- Install thru-hull head in place of Porta-Potti
- Rip out old side-loading icebox and install new top-loading icebox
- Install a table that won't block access throughout the cabin

- Replace companionway stairs to create more galley space
- Build in bookshelves and storage space for food and miscellaneous gear
- Recover all cushions
- Replace curtains and rods
- Locate stoves for easier cooking at anchor and under way

At the end of the six weeks, all these jobs had been completed, including new bottom paint and topside paint, a windvane and a few smaller jobs on the rig. I worked on weekends and after work on weekdays. It seemed like half the time was spent buying screws from Paul Letendre, who runs the chandlery at the yard, or talking over a project with Bob Dobbins, another Triton owner who'd been this route before.

Weston Farmer wrote that the boatbuilder's most valuable tool is a thinking chair. If this is so, the second best must be a friend with whom to discuss the pros and cons of doing something a particular way. Anyhow, Figure 3-9 shows the before and after arrangements of *Adriana's* interior.

Fig. 3-9 *These two drawings show* Adriana's *interior before and after the changes were made, including relocation of the icebox, an offset double berth forward, removal of the companionway stairs and conversion of the hanging locker to a sink and vanity. The removable table over the starboard berth is not shown.*

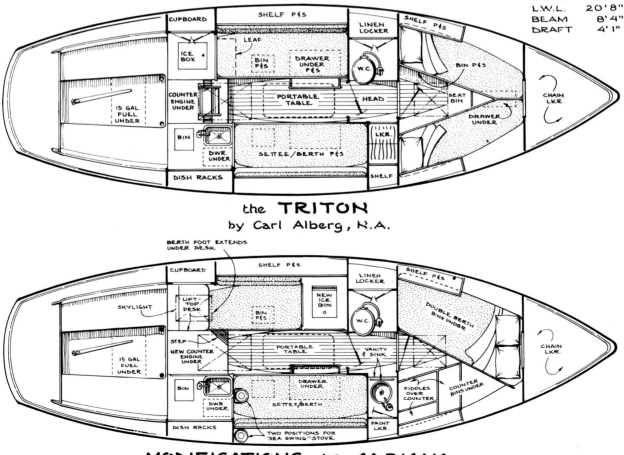

the TRITON
by Carl Alberg, N.A.

MODIFICATIONS to ADRIANA

Converting V-Berths to a Double Berth

The simplest way to make a double berth forward is to make an insert to fill the spaces between the V-berth singles. This is the method most often used by manufacturers. Lower the fiddles that hold the cushions in place, cut a piece of plywood to fit the opening, screw a fiddle to the aft end of the insert board to hold the cushion in place, cut a piece of four or five-inch foam to fit over the board, cover and you've got a king-size playpen (Figure 3-10).

The only problem with this double berth is that you have to dive in head first and often there's no floor space to walk or turn around, nor any place to sit down while undressing. Also, the berth is so wide at the after end that much of the space goes unused—except on those nights when the crew is miffed at one another, and go to bed hugging their respective sides of the hull.

A better solution—to my mind—is an offset berth, either to port or starboard. Remove both V-berth cushions, cut a piece of plywood to angle across the opening, then cut a new piece of foam to fit. Again, a fiddle will hold it in place. Planned correctly, there will still be room to walk into the forward cabin, sit on the edge of the bunk or the after end of the unused berth, and contemplate the hedonistic joy of sleeping in a large, comfy berth (Figure 3-11).

I wanted to be able to reconvert the berth back to two singles when my children visit in the summer, so I decided to keep things simple. I merely remove the foam double and plywood underneath and replace them with the original two V-berth cushions. To keep the kids from rolling out or invading each other's space, lee cloths fitted to the inboard edge of each bunk does the trick (Figure 3-12). These same type of cloths or lee boards should also be fitted to those berths in the main cabin that will be used for sea berths. Lee boards can be padded on one side and used as backrests during the day. Install one set of mounts (such as U-shaped blocks of wood screwed into bulkheads or furniture) at the inboard head and foot of the berth, and another set at the outboard edge. For sleeping, remove the board from its backrest mount, flip it over so the padded side faces the berth, and insert it in the lee board mounting position.

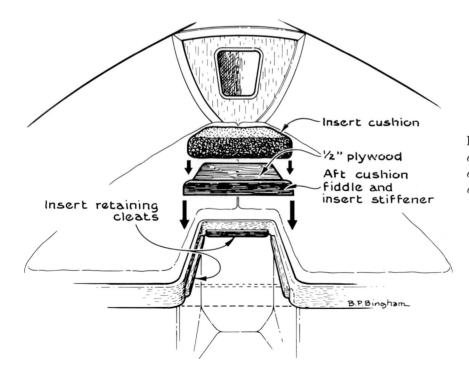

Insert cushion

½" plywood

Aft cushion fiddle and insert stiffener

Insert retaining cleats

B.P.Bingham

Fig. 3-10 *The easiest way to convert forward V-berths to a double is by cutting an insert board and cushion to fit between the two.*

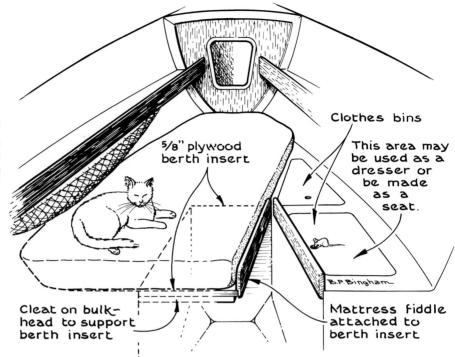

Fig. 3-11 *On* Adriana, *I chose to install an offset double berth on the port side. This left the starboard side for a seat and clothes bins.*

5/8" plywood berth insert

Clothes bins

This area may be used as a dresser or be made as a seat.

B.P.Bingham

Cleat on bulk-head to support berth insert

Mattress fiddle attached to berth insert

Installing a Sink & Mirror in Hanging Locker

On a small cruiser, it is almost axiomatic that all clothes will be wrinkled—even if there is a hanging locker to hang dress shirts and jackets. The hanging locker on *Adriana* was opposite the head, but it was narrow and difficult to use. It took me about three seconds to decide that the space would better be used as a sink for washing up, shaving, combing hair and brushing teeth.

Adding a sink, however, is not a simple or inexpensive job. Materials required include the sink, sea cock, hose to connect them, a pump, hose and T-fitting to connect the pump to the water tank, and a board to mount them on (Fig-

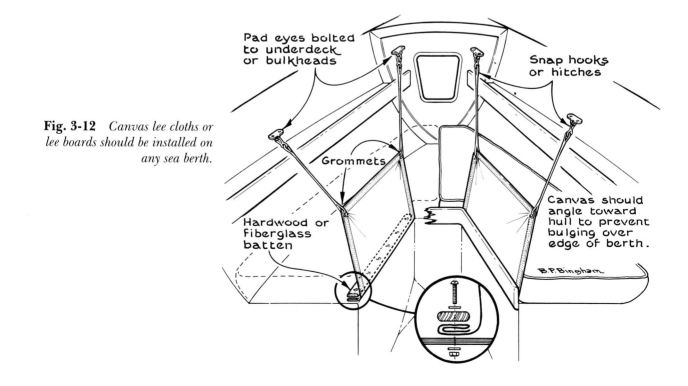

Fig. 3-12 *Canvas lee cloths or lee boards should be installed on any sea berth.*

Pad eyes bolted to underdeck or bulkheads

Snap hooks or hitches

Grommets

Canvas should angle toward hull to prevent bulging over edge of berth.

Hardwood or fiberglass batten

B.P.Bingham

ure 3-13). The cost of these items easily could approach $100. If possible, route the sink drain to an existing sea cock in the head or galley. This will save expenses and eliminate an additional thru-hull.

Begin by screwing in cleats (¾″ x 2″ lenghs of wood) to the sides of the hanging locker. When positioning them, make sure the sink is at a comfortable height, and allow for the thickness of the plywood top and Formica. Cut the plywood vanity top to size. Paint, varnish or otherwise seal the edges to prevent moisture from creeping in and causing delamination. Use a fine-toothed (e.g., 32-point) saber saw to cut a piece of Formica to the approximate size, but larger. A hack saw with a "blindcut" handle also works well; it's slow but accurate. Cut with the Formica upside down to minimize chipping, and keep your blade close to the edge of the workbench or other supporting surface.

With a brush, spread contact cement on both the wood and the underside of the plastic. Two coatings are necessary as there is some absorption. Let it dry for a few minutes. If the pieces are small, you can probably eyeball the placement of the plastic onto the wood; this is impor-

tant because once the two touch it's nearly impossible to separate them. If the pieces are larger than about two square feet, lay two dowels on top of the wood and lay the Formica on top of them. Look straight down onto the Formica and when it is positioned correctly, just slide out the dowels. Seal the two firmly by placing a block of wood on top and hitting it with a hammer. Let it dry before filing the edges smooth and flush with the wood. Exposed edges that can't be covered with wood trim look best with a bevel (Figure 3-14).

Now draw a cutline for the sink and pump holes. Drill a hole inside the circle large enough to accept your saber saw blade. Using a coarse-cut blade or pushing the saw too rapidly causes the thin surface of the plastic to chip off, so be patient. Soon you learn to appreciate any cut edge that is covered by a fixture. In this instance, both the sink and pump overlapped the cut edges and obscured the tiny chips in the Formica.

The mirror was hinged behind the sink to permit access to the paint locker and a space was cut in the vanity front below the sink to give access to the seacock (Figure 3-15). It's also a well-ven-

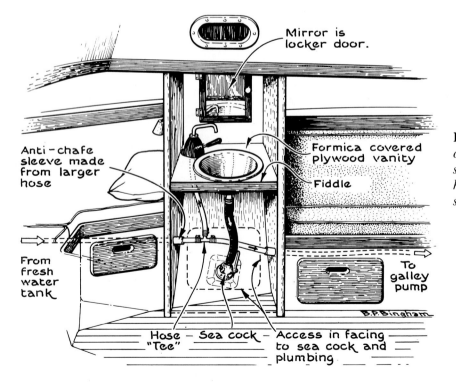

Fig. 3-13 *Acknowledging that clothes are always wrinkled on small boats anyway, Adriana's hanging locker was converted to a sink and vanity.*

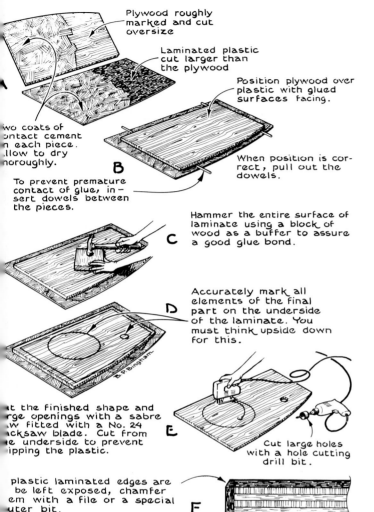

Plywood roughly marked and cut oversize

Laminated plastic cut larger than the plywood

Position plywood over plastic with glued surfaces facing.

Two coats of contact cement on each piece. Allow to dry thoroughly.

B

To prevent premature contact of glue, insert dowels between the pieces.

When position is correct, pull out the dowels.

C

Hammer the entire surface of laminate using a block of wood as a buffer to assure a good glue bond.

D

Accurately mark all elements of the final part on the underside of the laminate. You must think upside down for this.

E. P. Bingham

Cut the finished shape and large openings with a sabre saw fitted with a No. 24 hacksaw blade. Cut from the underside to prevent chipping the plastic.

E

Cut large holes with a hole cutting drill bit.

If plastic laminated edges are to be left exposed, chamfer them with a file or a special router bit.

F

Fig. 3-14 *Wilson Art laminated plastic (similar to Formica brand) was glued to a piece of plywood. Dowels were used to keep them separated until aligned perfectly. A saber saw was used to cut the holes for the sink and pump.*

tilated storage bin for carrying bags, ice nets and foul weather gear. The hanging locker has never been missed.

Installing a Thru-Hull Toilet

For years, my solution to the head problem was a Thetford Porta-Potti, which is a self-contained unit containing a five-gallon water compartment and separate waste receptacle. It was inexpensive, easy to operate, and satisfied the letter of the law, at least in the United States.

During our trip from Lake Michigan to Newport several years ago, we traversed the Trent-

Severn Waterway through Ontario, and learned that Canada had outlawed portable heads in the Great Lakes. Apparently they doubted that sailors would empty them ashore. They were right; it was a nuisance to lug the apparatus through the cabin, into the dinghy, and then search out a public facility that wouldn't object to our flushing the waste in their toilets.

I traded my Porta-Potti to a friend for a leaky thru-hull toilet. The biggest chore involved in making the conversion was installing the two seacocks—one for overboard discharge, the other for sea water flush. How to do this is described in detail in Chapter 4. If possible, mount the toilet on a platform above the waterline; moving it outboard may also help elevate it. Screw the toilet to the floor with large square-head lag bolts, or, if you can reach underneath it, use bolts, nuts and washers. Cut the reinforced hose

Fig. 3-15 *Although the area below the sink is crammed with foul weather gear, it enables quick access to the sea cock if trouble should develop.*

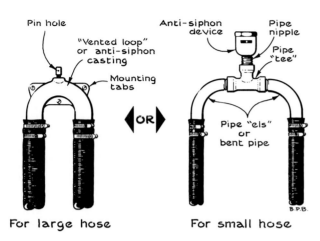

Fig. 3-16 *This drawing shows a vented loop, which should be installed above water level in the head compartment.*

to the proper length and smear an appropriate sealant over the fitting opening and on the inside of the hose to prevent leaking and make later removal easier.

Fasten each hose with stainless steel hose clamps. The schematic of my system is shown earlier in this chapter in Figure 3-7.

If the toilet sits below water level, install a vented loop in the discharge hose to prevent water from siphoning in (Figure 3-16). This requires elevating the lines above water level and placing the anti-siphon device at the apex of the line. It should be screwed to a sturdy surface. Use sealant and hose clamps in all hose connections. I also have one of these on the sea water cooling hose for my diesel engine (see Chapter 8).

Install Top-Loading Icebox

The Pearson Triton was built with a seemingly ingenious side-loading icebox under the bridge deck on the port side. Ice was loaded through a deck hatch in the cockpit. This compartment was above the food storage area. The food storage area was accessible from the cabin and the two were connected by a small opening in the upper compartment, the idea being that the cold air would fall into the food area below. It was a nice idea, but it didn't work very well for several rea-

sons. First, the ice melted quickly in the hot cockpit (the lid to the ice compartment was only one-inch foam encapsulated with fiberglass). One-inch foam was also used around the entire icebox below, only one quarter of the minimum thickness required for decent insulation. Further, the side-loading door, while handsome and remindful of grandfather's icebox 60 years ago, was grossly inefficient. Because cold air sinks to the lowest possible level, every time the door was opened all the cold air fell out.

Partly because I was short on counter space, and partly because putting the new top-loading icebox under the bridge wouldn't have allowed enough room to take off the lid, I resolved to relocate the icebox forward on the port side, next to the bulkhead separating the main cabin from the head.

The first thing I had to do was rip out the old icebox, a task that I approached with not a little trepidation. Fortunately, my friend Bob Dobbins had extricated his unit the year before and knew its vulnerable joints and screws. Peeling off the fake teak veneer on the front revealed wood screws that kept the whole thing together. Prying deeper into the mysteries of the icebox required a crowbar to separate the wood frame from the fiberglass liner. The foam was so paltry and half-disintegrated that it was no wonder ice lasted so short a time. The icebox was tacked to the hull in a few places with one layer of glass cloth, and this was easily broken with a hammer and cold chisel. The entire unit was too bulky to remove from the cabin through the main hatch, so it was necessary to smash it into pieces. As it turned out, the box was already in pieces by the time it emerged from its berth beneath the bridge.

What to do with the deck-loading hatch? Either glass it permanently to the cockpit, glass in a six-pack-size box underneath, or . . . make a sky light! A piece of half-inch Plexiglas® was easily screwed to the cockpit seat and furnished excellent lighting above the schoolboy desk top that I screwed to an improvised bulkhead where the old icebox once resided (Figure 3-17).

A new icebox was purchased from Bristol Yachts for a modest price, and herein is a very useful tip. If you can't find the item you need from your local chandlery or discount mail

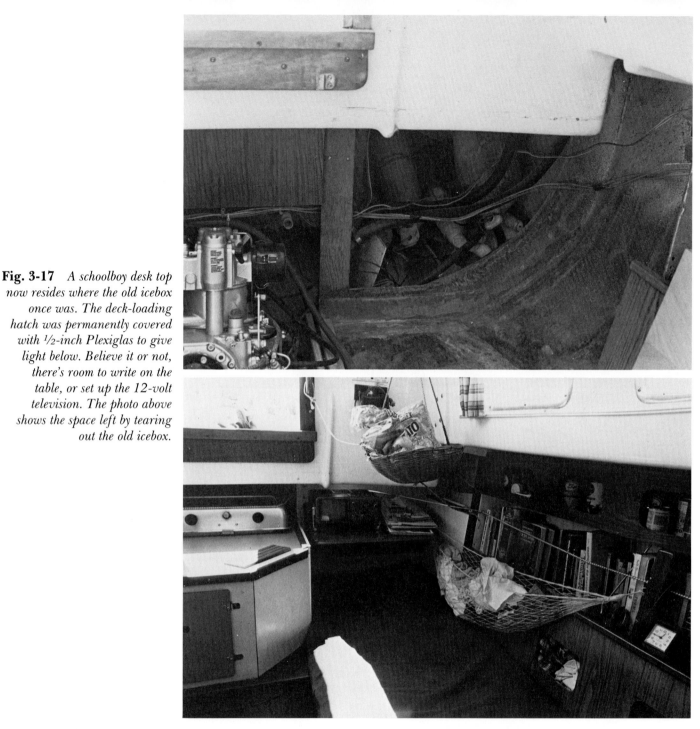

Fig. 3-17 *A schoolboy desk top now resides where the old icebox once was. The deck-loading hatch was permanently covered with ½-inch Plexiglas to give light below. Believe it or not, there's room to write on the table, or set up the 12-volt television. The photo above shows the space left by tearing out the old icebox.*

order catalog, call or write or visit the nearest boatbuilder. In my experience, these people are invariably happy to sell you almost any item they keep in stock, from teak trim to sinks and sail track, providing they are well stocked. Some of these items, such as icebox molds, they manufacture themselves. Given the economics of new boat sales these days, they are quite willing to part with them—at a slight profit. Fair is fair. Clint Pearson's right hand man, Sandy Towne, sold me the icebox mold and mahogany lid.

But you could make your own lid in a few hours (Figure 3-18). Cut the lid from a piece of mahogany or teak-faced plywood (or any other wood you like). Glass at least two inches of foam to the underside using one layer of six or 10-ounce cloth. Leave space around the edges for the lid to rest on the top of the icebox, or if you want it flush, screw in strips of wood to the underside of the plywood icebox top, or make two tops, the first ½-inch narrower all around than the second, which is just a hair larger than the lid.

In order to locate the new icebox forward on

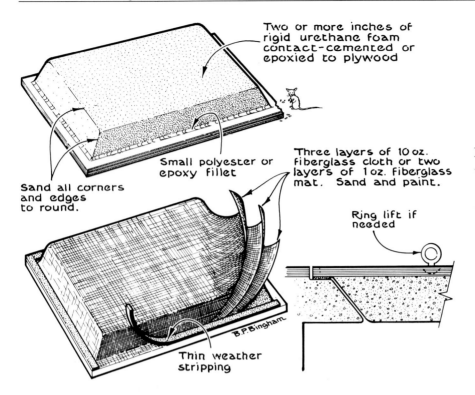

Two or more inches of rigid urethane foam contact-cemented or epoxied to plywood

Small polyester or epoxy fillet

Sand all corners and edges to round.

Three layers of 10 oz. fiberglass cloth or two layers of 1 oz. fiberglass mat. Sand and paint.

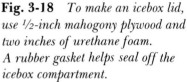

Ring lift if needed

B.P.Bingham

Thin weather stripping

Fig. 3-18 *To make an icebox lid, use ½-inch mahogony plywood and two inches of urethane foam. A rubber gasket helps seal off the icebox compartment.*

Adriana, the port berth had to be moved aft into the space vacated by the old icebox. This cost me about two feet of seating space, but the additonal counter space was well worth the trade-off. Besides, two people still can sit comfortably on that bunk, so overall very little was lost.

To install the new icebox, I cut a hole in the bunk to receive the deep end of the box (Figures 3-19 and 3-20). Being careful to allow four inches of room on either side for insulation, I

screwed in one-inch by two-inch strips of fir cleats to the bunk board and backrest. Half-inch plywood formed the aft side and front of the icebox, as well as the top on which the flanges of the icebox mold were thru-bolted. A second layer of plywood covered the flange. But since many of you may not have access to a premolded liner, we'll take a closer look at making one from scratch. The principles of installing the foam are the same.

Fig. 3-19 *The icebox I purchased from Bristol Yachts has two compartments, one lower than the other. I cut a hole in the bunk board to recess the deep end.*

Fig. 3-20 *This is how the icebox looked just before covering the surfaces with Wilson Art laminated plastic.*

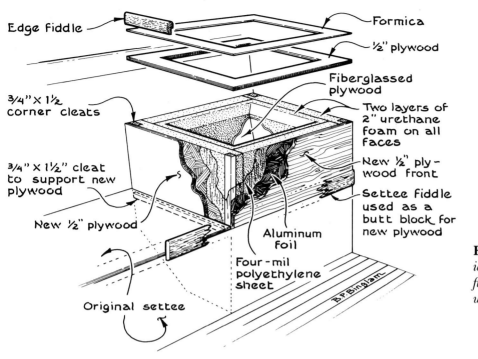

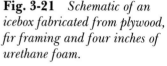

Fig. 3-21 *Schematic of an icebox fabricated from plywood, fir framing and four inches of urethane foam.*

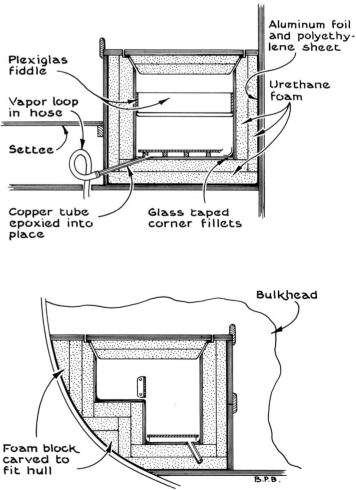

Figure 3-21 illustrates the main points of constructing a new icebox without benefit of a premolded liner. Two-inch foam is used all around, doubled for a total thickness of four inches. The more the better. (If it hadn't meant shortening my port bunk by another four inches, I would have placed six inches on each side.) Avoid butt joints, using glued staggered joints instead to help retain water vapors (Figure 3-22). Both a vapor-proof and heat-reflective barrier should be incorporated. Mylar and tinfoil can be stuck to the insides of the plywood housing box with polyester resin. (Bruce Bingham says that polyethylene sheeting is more workable than Mylar). A "space blanket" functions as both.

The seams can be glued, caulked with contact cement and polysulfide, and the seams taped with a metal-type tape. Cut plywood to form all surfaces of the box, fit in place, fillet and glass over with 1½-ounce mat. Paint the cured surfaces with pigmented gel coat or epoxy.

The drain deserves some consideration. Mine empties into the bilge, though some folks complain that this makes the bilge smell. To date, this fresh water run-off is the least offensive smell in my bilge! But a better long-term arrangement would pump the water overboard or into a container. A small pump can be fitted out-

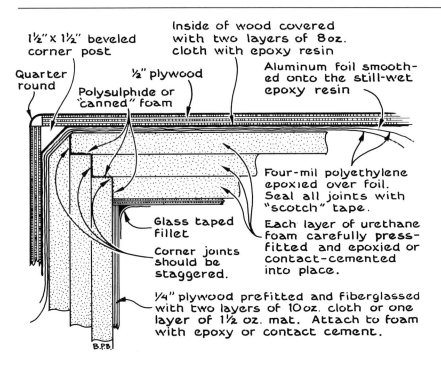

1½" x 1½" beveled corner post

Quarter round

½" plywood

Polysulphide or "canned" foam

Inside of wood covered with two layers of 8 oz. cloth with epoxy resin

Aluminum foil smoothed onto the still-wet epoxy resin

Four-mil polyethylene epoxied over foil. Seal all joints with "scotch" tape.

Each layer of urethane foam carefully press-fitted and epoxied or contact-cemented into place.

Glass taped fillet

Corner joints should be staggered.

¼" plywood prefitted and fiberglassed with two layers of 10 oz. cloth or one layer of 1½ oz. mat. Attach to foam with epoxy or contact cement.

B.P.B.

Fig. 3-22 *Joints in the foam should be staggered and glued to prevent the escape of water vapors. Avoid butt joints.*

side the icebox to drain water. But this does require your attention at periodic intervals. If you go ashore for a day, the ice melts and then sits in its own water until pumped and few things, besides poor insulation, make ice melt faster than sitting in water. Bruce says his studies show that ice melts about 15 percent faster if standing in water. On the other hand, it does avoid the possibility of leaks and algae forming in the drain hose's water trap (a U-shaped loop in the hose that traps water and keeps cold from flowing out).

Some persons tap the icebox drain for fresh water drinking, though it seems to me that the water used for making ice is not of the purest quality. One solution is to build a sump into the drain that can be pumped dry when it becomes full (Figure 3-23).

Formica (or another brand of laminated plastic) was used to cover the plywood shell of the icebox. I chose an ice blue color that worked nicely with the red seat cushion covers. Bristol Yachts sold me mahogany fiddle material to fit along the edges of the icebox, so low flat objects can be left on top of the icebox while under way. Also, this minimizes the number of Formica edges that must be cut without error. The one vertical corner of the box was beveled with a fine-toothed file and looks quite nice. Fiddle ma-

terial can usually be found at a well-stocked chandlery, or made from regular stock with a router.

The upshot of all this is that 15 pounds of ice now lasts for four days and longer, depending on how many times the lid is opened, and how many cans of warm beer my friends stash directly on the ice. This is a melt-rate of just under four pounds a day. Acceptable performance is about six pounds a day, four to five pounds good, and under four superior. Later, I pur-

Fig. 3-23 *John Campbell, who lives aboard a 35-foot junk-rigged schooner in the West Indies, installed a drain tube attached to a hand pump in his icebox to avoid leaks around the drain.*

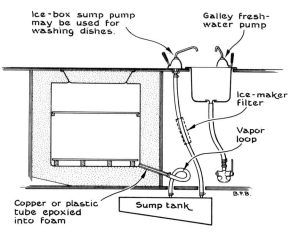

Ice-box sump pump may be used for washing dishes.

Galley fresh-water pump

Ice-maker Filter

Vapor loop

Copper or plastic tube epoxied into foam

Sump tank

B.P.B.

chased a Cold Blanket ® from Mainstay Designs to cover the ice and food; this functions as extra insulation (the lid is still the weak link, being only two inches thick) and reduces the size of the compartment being cooled. The new icebox also makes an excellent backrest for me and my big pillow when I turn on the 12-volt television, which I keep on the schoolboy desk top. With the tube in front of me, and cold brews within an arm's reach behind, I truly have all the comforts of home!

Install a Removable Table

The Triton is a narrow (8′4″) boat. The usual table arrangement is a removable affair that in position hooks onto either side of the door to the head and is supported by a leg to the cabin sole. The only way to get forward is to remove the table, crawl under or go forward on deck and descend through the forward hatch—a real pain at dinner time. And kids, of course, always pick this time to go wee wee. Some Triton owners have cut their bunks in half and built dinette tables in the conventional manner. The problem on a narrow boat, especially one like the Triton with firm bilges, is there is little room for one's feet while seated at the table. Being under six feet tall, I don't mind sitting crosslegged facing fore or aft on the berth with a table in front of me. Living on a small boat teaches you how to scrunch yourself up into compact packages!

Murray-Clevco, the New Zealand company, makes a hinge that has a spring-loaded pin enabling the two halves to separate (Figure 3-24). These ingenious devices can be used in a multitude of places on a boat—seat lockers, engine compartment boards, companionway ladders and removable dinette tables—on anything you want to hinge and remove. These hinges were just what I needed to mount my dinette table to the backrest of my starboard berth (Figure 3-25). The removable support leg was cut short so it rested on the inboard edge of the berth, just inside the board that holds the cushion in place. The thru-bolted hinges support all the weight one could possibly place on it.

When the bunk is needed for sleeping, the table can be taken off by simply popping the

Fig. 3-24 *The Murray Snap-Apart Hinge works like a clevis pin, and is an ideal fitting for anything you want to be securely mounted, yet removable (South Pacific Associates).*

hinge pins; the table is then stowed under the bunk along with the removable support leg.

Had any of the bulkheads been large enough, or better situated, I might have permanently fastened a fold-down table with piano hinges to function as extra surface area for food preparation, navigation or just odds and ends. Chain fastened to either corner of the table and to the bulkhead would be one way to hold it up. A less obstructed method would be a pivoting brace—the kind used for extra leafs on dining room tables—that folds up flush to the bulkhead when not in use.

Fig. 3-25 *The Snap-Apart hinges were fitted to* Adriana's *dinette table so it could be removed when the settee was used for sleeping or lounging.*

Replace Companionway Stairs With Galley Space

As can be seen from the drawing of *Adriana*'s standard interior layout, there isn't much galley counter space. This space was doubled by removing the companionway stairs and extending the galley counter from the sink under the bridge and companionway hatch.

One by two-inch stock was screwed to the side of the galley and aft bulkhead (Figure 3-26). Half-inch plywood was used to construct the sides and ¾-inch "lumber stock" plywood veneer with solid ½-inch by ½-inch boards inside on top. (Regular plywood would work as well.) The lower step, under which the batteries are stored, was retained as a support for the new engine box/counter top. A corner of the step was left open to serve as a second step when coming down from the counter. Space also was available for a trash bin with an access door. Fiddles and a foot pad finished off the trim (Figure 3-27).

Because water inevitably is spilled on the counter, it's a good idea to paint the edges of all wood before assembly. This will prevent water getting into the end grain and eventually delaminating the wood. This practice should be followed on every interior construction job, whether the project seems to be near a source of water or not—sooner or later, everything inside a boat gets wet.

Add Bookshelves and Extra Storage Space

Nothing makes a boat look more homey than a good selection of books. Navigation books and nautical almanacs are, of course, a necessity, and books for pleasure are just as vital to the mental and spiritual well-being of the crew. On most boats, even new ones, little book space is provided. A rack for 10 volumes above the navigation station is insufficient.

Like many production boats, the Triton has shelves running the length of the main cabin beneath the side decks. These had short fiddles to retain things, but when heeled over, everything tumbled out. The spaces behind the bunk backrests were also wide open, and while they were handy for storing frying pans and aluminum foil, it was always a chore to pull out everything on top to get at something you wanted at the bottom.

My solution was to put a teak veneer facing on the shelves with four-inch by six-inch cutouts for access (Figure 3-28). Cleats were nailed to the inboard edge of the original shelf, and glued to the underside of the deck with epoxy, and the facing screwed into the cleats. Below these I built another set of shelves at the same height as the backrests. This closed off the space behind the bunks, but again, access was obtained by cutting out rectangular holes. Drill a pilot hole and then insert a saber saw to make the cut. If you decide

Fig. 3-26 *The companionway ladder was removed to give more space to the galley. This construction also encloses the new BMW diesel and provides secure footing as well as a small trash bin.*

Fig. 3-27 *The new galley counter was an attractive and functional change to Adriana's interior.*

Fig. 3-28 *The shelves behind the berths were enclosed with teak veneer, and the area immediately behind the berths were cut out so that shelving could be installed on top for books.*

to save the cutout pieces for doors, use a drill the same width as the saber saw blade and drill them continuously for a half inch or width of the saber saw blade. Use a sharp thin pocket knife to clean out the thin wall between holes. Measure carefully and, before making the cut, use a pencil to scribe the cut line.

Shock cord strung across the shelves keeps books and other items in place. Another way is to bend a length of brass rod as shown in Figure 3-29. Pad eyes screwed into the deck above hold the rod and make it easy to lift up to pull out books.

Fig. 3-29 *Another method of restraining books is to bend a length of brass rod and hinge them under the deck.*

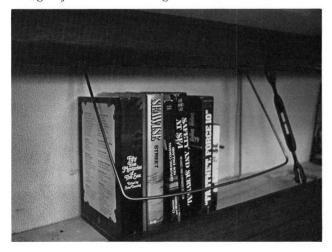

Recover All Cushions

Adriana's stock cushions were a burnt-orange-colored vinyl, easy to clean and waterproof, but sticky in hot weather and cold and clammy in the winter. The easiest solution was to make slip covers. There are lots of fabrics and colors, but to keep costs low, I used red corduroy. A local seamstress whipped them up at a very reasonable price. Velcro® was used to seal the back sides so they could be removed and washed periodically. Zippers, especially metal ones, invariably get sticky and, when tugged hard, begin ripping away from the fabric. Perhaps no other improvement made so much difference in the looks of the boat, making it warmer and more modern as well.

Replace Curtains and Rods

The original curtain rods were plastic-coated metal and were so tight that the curtain slides always hung up, eventually pulling away from the curtain. After years of resewing some of them each year, I took off the old rods and replaced them. The pop rivets into the inner liner were easily drilled out with a hand drill and new tracks screwed into the deck liner with ⅜-inch screws. Most chandleries sell curtain track and slides that work well, so there's really no need to fabricate your own.

For a time, I considered just using dowels fitted to wood blocks glued to the cabin sides, but these would have been bulky and probably weaker than tracks screwed flush to the cabin. Keep your old curtains for a pattern to make the new ones.

Relocate Stoves

With the small amount of counter space on *Adriana*, finding a place to put the cook stove was always a hassle. Usually, the portable two-burner alcohol stove was kept under the bridge with a piece of shock cord. Later I had a welder make a pivoting arm that could be screwed to the side of the galley. A swinging arm, with gimbals on top, permitted using the stove under way. When

Fig. 3-30 *A Sea-Swing stove, fitted with a kerosene burner, is used for cooking under way. The alcohol stove underneath the bridge deck is pulled out for cooking at anchor.*

not in use, the arm and stove could be swung outboard and more or less out of the way (see Chapter 11, Figure 11-3).

A better solution for this boat turned out to be installing a Sea Swing stove with a kerosene burner for use under way (Figure 3-30). Two mounting bases let me stow the stove in an out-of-the-way place when not in use. The two-burner alcohol stove is back under the bridge where it is easily pulled out on the new galley counter top for cooking at anchor. It would be nice to have a kerosene or gas stove/oven, but on the Triton this would necessitate shortening one of the bunks and reducing seating space. With pressure cookers and stove-top ovens, stove burners can do most of the things of a conventional oven.

These, then, were the major projects accomplished during my spring haulout. Figure 3-31 shows what *Adriana*'s main cabin looks like now. Another important job I undertook inside the hull was replacing gate valves and fiberglass tubes with sea cocks. This is described in Chapter 4.

FOR COMFORT AND SAFETY . . .

A Wood Ceiling

A wood ceiling can turn a dull-looking hull interior into a classy den. Mahogany, cypress, birch, maple, etc., all may be used. The later Tri-

tons had an inner liner for the main cabin only, and there only for the underside of the cabin, ending at the hull/deck joint. The head and forward cabin were left bare and spray painted with a horrible blue and grey speckled paint.

For a long time, I considered adding a ceiling (the term applies to wood paneling installed on the inside hull of a boat). To install a ceiling, strips of wood or hose must be glassed to the hull with fiberglass mat and resin. Use an adhesive putty or quick-setting glue to hold them in place while you glass over with a few layers of mat (see Chapter 2). Another handy method of holding them in place until the resin kicks is to use springloaded curtain rods that can be pushed against the wood and then propped against a bunk edge, or the other side of the hull (Figure 3-32). It may be necessary to cut kerfs on the wood strips (saw cuts across the back) if it won't easily conform to the hull. Sand away all paint from the hull and clean with acetone. Put an exhaust fan on the hatch to pull out dangerous fumes—styrene fumes can cause serious lung and brain damage and have been known to cause blackouts, heart attacks and even death.

This is a good time to consider gluing in foam insulation between the vertical strips. The cabin will retain warmth and coolness better, and help reduce condensation. See Chapter 14 for more details.

The horizontal wood paneling could be $5/16$-inch to $3/8$-inch thick and about $1\frac{1}{2}$ inches wide, and screwed to the vertical strips of wood,

Fig. 3-31   *These two photographs show Adriana's interior with all changes completed. Note the Alladin kerosene lamp on the bulkhead; this takes the chill off the air on cool nights and burns as bright as a 100-watt electrical bulb.*

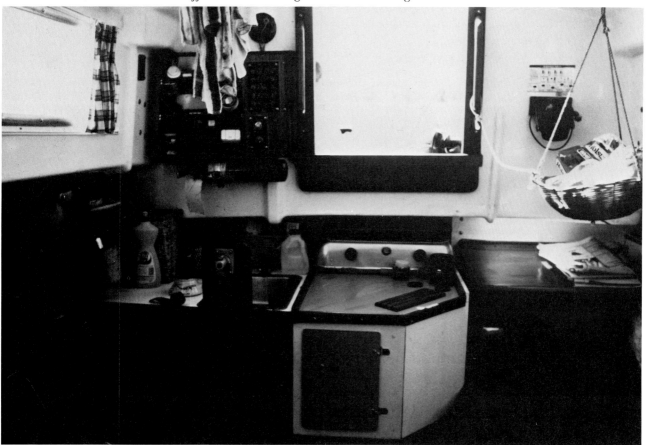

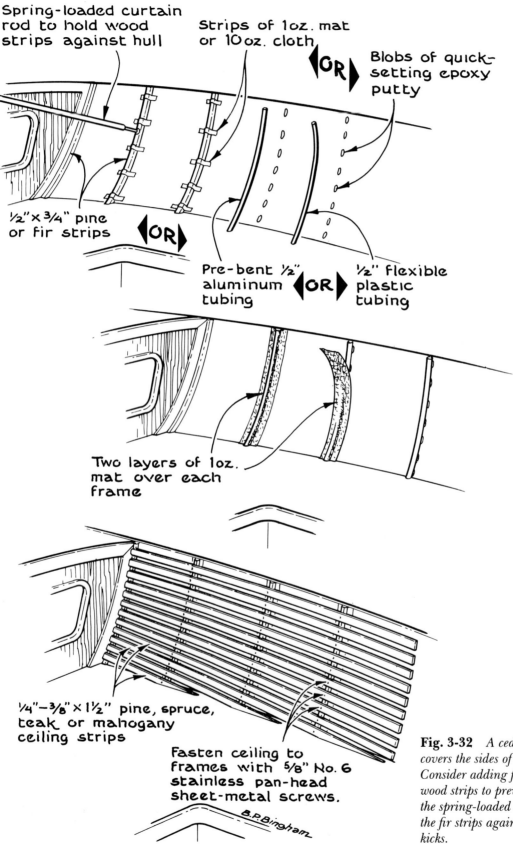

Spring-loaded curtain rod to hold wood strips against hull

Strips of 1oz. mat or 10oz. cloth

Blobs of quick-setting epoxy putty

½" × ¾" pine or fir strips

Pre-bent ½" aluminum tubing

½" flexible plastic tubing

Two layers of 1oz. mat over each frame

¼"–⅜" × 1½" pine, spruce, teak or mahogany ceiling strips

Fasten ceiling to frames with ⅝" No. 6 stainless pan-head sheet-metal screws.

B.P.Bingham

Fig. 3-32 *A cedar ceiling attractively covers the sides of bare fiberglass hulls. Consider adding foam insulation behind the wood strips to prevent condensation. Note the spring-loaded curtain rods, which keep the fir strips against the hull until the resin kicks.*

leaving a small amount of space between each for ventilation. (If you're screwing into wood use wood screws; use #6 sheet metal screws if screwing into hose and fiberglass.) The space between the ceiling strips doesn't need to be that wide, but it is important to let the hull breathe, and because hulls do twist under stress, it will keep the boards from buckling.

Covering the insides of a hull to make it look better presents a dilemma for the offshore sailor. If the hull cracks or is holed, it is vital to be able to get to that spot in order to effect some sort of repair—stuffing in towels, screwing plywood over the hole, draping a collision mat over it, using underwater epoxy, or whatever. The French monohull *Faram Seranissima* was lost in the North Atlantic in 1981 when she struck an object and the crew couldn't locate the hole. Fiberglass interior liners, commonly used on production sailboats to simplify the building of bunks and lockers, make it almost impossible to reach every inch of the hull. Often the only access is through hatches under berth cushions. Fiberglass is tough to cut or smash away with an ax. A plywood interior can be unscrewed if there is time, or knocked out with an ax in desperation. Also, when those inevitable leaks occur where deck hardware is thru-bolted through the deck, liners make it very hard to get at them. Nowadays, many builders are putting in removable vinyl panels that can be popped off to provide access. A wood ceiling does inhibit the speediness and ease of gaining access to the hull, but if it is screwed in, it can be removed without much difficulty, although slowly.

Ventilation

A last thought on interior modifications is ventilation. Dorades, mushroom vents and other types of on-deck ventilation will be discussed later. But for the moment, consider the problem of moving air about the cabin—through drawers, between cabins, and into lockers and cabinets to minimize the growth of mildew.

Plastic building vents, used in building construction to let eaves breathe, can be mounted on the sides of galley cabinets, berths, bins and anywhere else that air has a hard time circulating

Fig. 3-33 *Building vents, used on houses to ventilate eaves, can be installed in cabinetry to prevent mildew. This boat is a Kells 28.*

(Figure 3-33). A hole saw on a hand drill cuts the hole, and the vent pops in.

Bulkheads prevent the free flow of air between cabins, and many live-aboards, including Eric and Susan Hiscock, combat this by cutting large holes in them. When I visited them at their anchorage in New Zealand's Bay of Islands, their *Wanderer IV* had a one-square-foot hole cut in the bulkhead between the head and aft cabin. If you're worried about privacy, a small curtain can be hung on one side to close it off when the head is in use. You'll be surprised what a difference it makes.

Lastly, drawer fronts without finger holes let the air inside stagnate and mildew accumulate. Even with finger holes, drawers stuffed with clothing trap air. I once found my black dress shoes encrusted with yellow mustard-like powder after stowing them in a drawer. Yeech! Consider enlarging the hole or installing a building vent or two in the facing of the drawer, or replacing solid cabinet doors with louvered ones. Caning should be avoided on the door of any large locker full of heavy objects, as a can of tomatoes would have little difficulty busting through, en route to the cook's forehead.

Round Corners

An important consideration to keep in mind as you develop your plans is to avoid injury-causing pointed corners. Take a look at some new production boats; most boatbuilders are beginning to do wonderful things with curved lami-

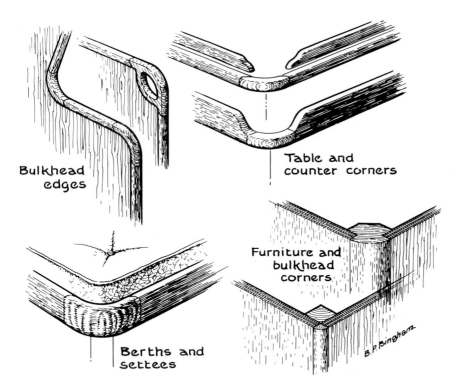

Bulkhead
edges

Table and
counter corners

Berths and
settees

Furniture and
bulkhead
corners

B.P.Bingham

Fig. 3-34 *All sharp or pointed corners inside the boat should be rounded to prevent injury.*

nated surfaces that are not only attractive, but safe.

Rounding pointed corners will require a bit more work on your part, but with a little thought, no special tools are needed and you'll be much more pleased with the result. Companies such as H & L Marine Woodwork make sectional moldings both straight and bent in several useful shapes. Figure 3-34 will give you some ideas.

Locking Hatches

Outside companionway locks are found on just about every boat. The standard padlock and hasp arrangement usually suffices to keep intruders out when you're gone. But what about the time when you're *in* the boat and someone comes aboard?

We've all heard horror stories about people being terrorized by burglars, rapists and the like. Suppose you see several men with machetes or guns climbing over the rail. Unless you're armed and prepared to blow them away, the safest course is to dart back inside and lock all the hatches. Then, assuming you have a VHF radio, call for help. If your hatches are well-con-

structed and securely locked, it'll take a lot of ax or firepower to roust you out.

Chapter 9 contains directions on how to reinforce your main companionway hatch. Here are a few suggestions on how to lock it from inside and out (Figure 3-35). They also emphasize watertightness, an important characteristic of any hatch, for safety as well as a dry cabin.

The simplest method is to use a dowel that can be wedged between the aft facing edge of the deck and the forward facing surface of the hatch. This does the same thing as dropping a stick on the track of a sliding glass patio door. It's simple and as strong as any lock, and unlike a hasp and lock, there isn't any slop to rattle around in the hopes of working screws loose.

Deadbolts can be screwed into the hatch and small aligning holes drilled into the side of the deck to secure the hatch. The exact configuration will depend on how your hatch is constructed.

And, of course, hasps and padlocks also can be used for this purpose. Thru-bolting the hasps and deadbolts is stronger than screwing them in because in most cases the thickness of wood and fiberglass aren't great enough to provide superior holding power.

Fig. 3-35 *A good security system on a boat includes some means of locking the hatches from the inside as well as outside. Also, weatherproofing adds to safety and comfort below.*

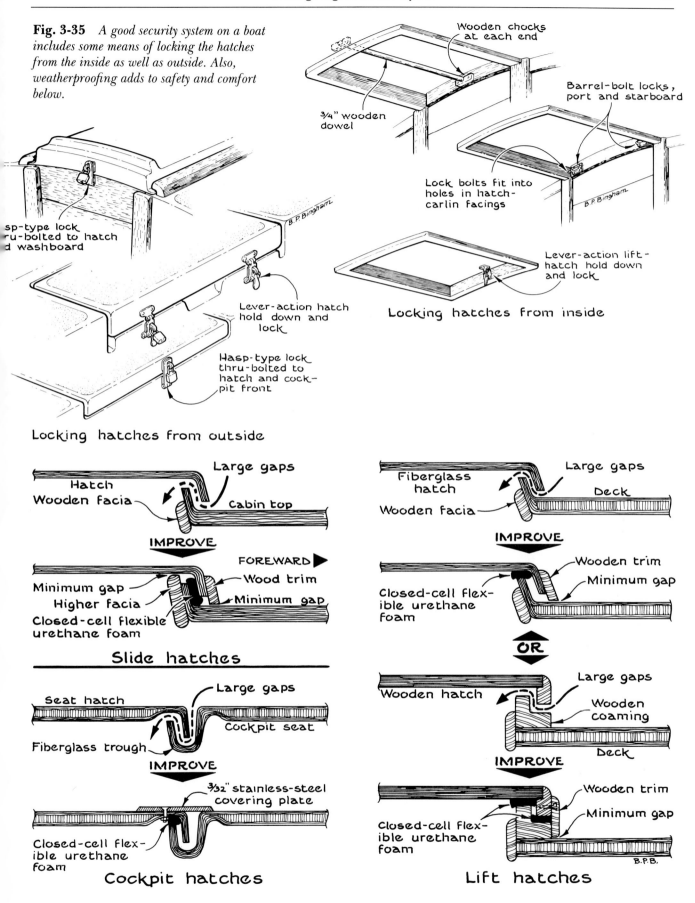

Wooden chocks at each end

¾" wooden dowel

Barrel-bolt locks, port and starboard

B.P. Bingham

Lock bolts fit into holes in hatch-carlin facings

Hasp-type lock thru-bolted to hatch and washboard

Lever-action lift-hatch hold down and lock

Locking hatches from inside

Lever-action hatch hold down and lock

Hasp-type lock thru-bolted to hatch and cock-pit front

Locking hatches from outside

Large gaps

Hatch
Wooden facia
Cabin top

IMPROVE

FOREWARD ▶

Minimum gap
Higher facia
Closed-cell flexible urethane foam

Wood trim
Minimum gap

Slide hatches

Seat hatch

Large gaps

Cockpit seat

Fiberglass trough

IMPROVE

³⁄₃₂" stainless-steel covering plate

Closed-cell flexible urethane foam

Cockpit hatches

Large gaps

Fiberglass hatch
Wooden facia
Deck

IMPROVE

Wooden trim
Minimum gap

Closed-cell flexible urethane foam

OR

Large gaps

Wooden hatch
Wooden coaming
Deck

IMPROVE

Wooden trim
Minimum gap

Closed-cell flexible urethane foam

B.P.B.

Lift hatches

Imagine the Worst

Living aboard for a time will surely point out any shortcomings in the layout of your interior, and odds are you'll make more changes as time goes by. You can't possibly think of everything at once, especially before you move aboard or take an extended cruise. Experience is the best teacher.

Before you shove off, however, have a seat in the cabin and look around. Imagine the boat knocked down with the spreaders in the water, or worse, turning over. What can come loose? Will the frying pan be launched across the cabin? Is the icebox lid hinged? (Those sharp corners could easily penetrate a skull.) Will all the books end up in the bilge? Is there a strainer on the bilge pump hose to prevent it from clogging up?

How about the crew? Can they be secured in their bunks where they won't be hurt? Are tools and emergency gear easily reached? Can you lock the hatch from the inside if there are intruders on deck or waves breaking over the boat? Don't set sail until you've considered every aspect of safety for yourself and your crew.

DISASTER CHECKLIST

- Strap batteries to hull or structural wood members with heavy canvas or polypropylene straps and large galvinized eyebolts or other strong fasteners.
- Devise a method of securing hatch boards in the cabin sole with piano hinges, deadbolts or any other method that will keep them in place with the boat upside down and gallons of bilge water pushing against them.
- Do the same for hatch boards underneath settees.
- Make heavy canvas lee cloths with boltropes on all four sides, or build sturdy bunk boards with secure mounts. Pad eyes to receive the wire cables or nylon rope that tightens them should be

thru-bolted to bulkheads or the deck or hull. (Figure 3-12).
- Lockers for pots and pans and canned goods should be made extra strong. Cabinet joints can be figerglassed. Doors should have hinges thru-bolted rather than screwed, and drawers should be notched so they don't fly open.
- Bilge pump intake hoses should have strainers, and if the bilge is deep and the hose hard to reach, strings should be attached to them so they can easily be fetched and cleared. At least one bilge pump should be operable from below.
- All hatches should be lockable from below with positive-action mechanisms.
- Safe storage for gimballed lamps should be provided in heavy weather—the glass chimneys break easily and are potentially dangerous.
- Engine beds should be securely bolted or glassed to the floors. The engine should be securely tightened to large-diameter mounts.
- All shelves should have high fiddles, covering boards or retaining lines to keep books and other items in place.
- All instruments should be securely thru-bolted to bulkheads or other strong structural members.
- Loose ballast should be fixed to the keel permanently before going to sea.

FURTHER READING

The Finely Fitted Yacht, Vols. I, II, by Ferenc Maté; Albatross Publishing House, 5934 Marine Drive, West Vancouver British Columbia, Canada V7W 2S2.

Yacht Joinery and Fitting by Mike Saunders; International Marine Publishing Co., Camden, Maine 04843.

Modern Wooden Yacht Construction by John Guzzwell; International Marine Publishing Co., Camden, Maine 04843.

The Boat Owner's Fitting Out Manual by Jeff Toghill; Van Nostrand and Reinhold Co., 135 West 50th St., New York, NY 10020.

The Perfect Box—39 Ways to Improve Your Boat's Ice Box; Spa Creek Instrument Co., 616 Third St., Annapolis, Maryland 21403.

CHAPTER 4

Installing and Maintaining Sea Cocks

Roll on, thou deep and dark blue ocean—roll!
Ten thousand fleets sweep over thee in vain;
Man marks the earth with ruin—his control
Stops with the shore.

GEORGE GORDON, LORD BYRON

Sea cocks are metal or plastic valves that are attached to thru-hull fittings wherever water enters or leaves the hull as part of the plumbing system. Sink drains, toilet discharge, engine sea water intake and bilge pump discharge are just some of the thru-hull fittings on a cruising boat. On many boats, gate valves are substituted for the more expensive sea cock, and in some cases, there is no valve at all. Before going to sea, all thru-hulls should be fitted with positive-action sea cocks.

Like many boats, the Triton had no sea cocks when I bought her. The cockpit scupper hoses were connected to eight-inch-long molded fiberglass tubes bonded to the bottom of the hull. Hose clamps kept the hoses fastened. But rubber does deteriorate over time, and if a hose ever burst, there'd be a real panic on board trying to pull apart the engine compartment boards to reach the tube and plug it with a softwood plug.

Softwood plugs should be kept handy no matter what sort of valve is fitted to the thru-hull, but a good quality sea cock is your best hedge against this calamity. I cut off the fiberglass tubes and installed R. C. Marine Zytel® ball valve-type sea cocks (Figure 4-1). They've worked perfectly,

Fig. 4-1 *Forespar's ball valve-type sea cock is manufactured in New Zealand from a DuPont glass-reinforced nylon product called Xytel®.*

Fig. 4-2 *Bronze gate valves are found on many new and used boats. The photo shows the gate partially open. They are inferior to sea cocks because debris can keep the gate from completely closing without the operator's knowledge.*

Fig. 4-3 *The most common type of sea cock is the tapered plug type. This one is made of bronze by Wilcox-Crittenden.*

require hardly any maintenance and are incredibly strong.

The engine intake had a gate valve (Figure 4-2), which looks like a garden faucet. This was removed and a small bronze sea cock fitted in its place. In the head, a large bronze Wilcox-Crittenden plug-type sea cock (Figure 4-3) was fitted to the discharge line, and a small Zytel sea cock fitted to the sea water intake/flush hose. This represents a significant upgrading in terms of safety and should be on everyone's list of "must" things to do. It's not hard, but it does require care and patience to do it right.

TYPES OF SEA VALVES

There are three major types of sea valves available today: 1) Traditional bronze tapered-plug sea cocks; 2) Bronze, stainless steel, and synthetic ball valve sea cocks, and; 3) Threaded gate valves.

The plug and ball valve-type sea cocks most often are cast in bronze, and may have some parts chromed. Whereas brass is an alloy of copper and zinc, bronze is an alloy of copper and tin, and obtains significant resistance to corrosion from the tin. Small amounts of aluminum, zinc, and silicon usually are added to increase strength and improve casting properties. Bronze is a good material for sea cocks; brass should *never* be used.

Stainless steel ball-valve sea cocks can be found with a bit of diligent searching. Humoric Metal Industries of Goderich, Ontario, is a builder of good-quality steel cruising sailboats, and they use an industrial stainless steel valve on all thru-hull fittings.

Technological advancements in the fabrication of synthetics have resulted in materials of far greater strength than those of just a few years ago. Plastic thru-hulls and sea cocks now are available in most chandleries. However, plastic is something of a misnomer, as most of these products are strong polymers such as DuPont's Xytel, which is a glass-reinforced nylon. Installation of plastic thru-hull fittings above the waterline is a common and acceptable practice. When they were first introduced, many yachtsmen were skeptical about their strength and reliability. Yet Xytel products have a tensile strength of 30,000 pounds per square inch. You can prove this to yourself by smashing a Xytel cleat or sea cock with a hammer—it hardly scratches! Those on my boat have worked great for several years. A little Vaseline applied to the ball every season keeps them turning freely (Figure 4-4). They can even be glassed to the hull, though I used the mounting base to thru-bolt

Fig. 4-4 *The ball valve of this Xytel sea cock requires only occasional lubrication with petroleum jelly to keep it operating smoothly. Unlike the tapered plug type, ball valves do not require lubrication to maintain watertightness.*

each one. For the steel boat owner concerned about corrosion caused by galvanic action between dissimilar metals, or anyone wanting to save weight and money, Xytel thru-hulls and sea cocks are a logical choice.

THE TROUBLE WITH GATE VALVES

There are several shortcomings commonly attributed to gate valves. First, they often are made of brass, which is not sufficiently corrosion-resistant for use in a marine environment. Second, they are not positive action; that is, rather than using a lever which is either clearly on or off, they employ threaded handles that must be turned several times before fully opening or closing the valve. It sometimes is difficult to know if the valve is closed all the way, or if it has stopped short of sealing due to the presence of a foreign object in the chamber. Third, gate valves typically do not have flanged bodies, as specified by the American Boat & Yacht Council (ABYC) *Standards and Recommended Practices for Small Craft*. Without a flanged body that can be directly thru-bolted to the hull, gate valves must be mounted on top of the thru-hull fitting. A hard, accidental knock or the use of force in turning the valve conceivably could crack the hull where the thru-hull enters.

INSTALLATING SEA COCKS

The ABYC small craft standards, Section H-27, specifies proper installation materials and procedures. In addition to using flange-bodied sea cocks that can be thru-fastened to the hull, each sea cock should be mounted with a backing block to distribute stress across a greater area of the hull (Figure 4-5). On wood or fiberglass hulls, wood or stainless steel make good backing blocks, though the latter can be difficult to work with. On steel or aluminum hulls, or in any installation where the sea cock and hull materials are galvanically incompatible, ABYC suggests an insulating block of micarta or similar durable insulating material (Figure 4-6).

While you should, of course, follow the manufacturer's instructions when installing a sea cock, the following steps generally will apply.

1. Select a sea cock with the appropriate diameter opening for the application at hand. Check that the tail piece makes a snug fit with the hose. When installing sea cocks for cockpit scuppers, use the largest size possible. In fact, it would be

Fig. 4-5 *Sea cocks of all types should be thru-bolted to the hull with a block of wood or other material between the hull and valve to distribute loads.*

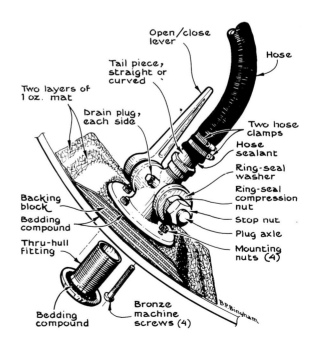

Open/close lever

Hose

Tail piece, straight or curved

Two layers of 1 oz. mat

Drain plug, each side

Two hose clamps

Hose sealant

Ring-seal washer

Ring-seal compression nut

Stop nut

Plug axle

Mounting nuts (4)

Backing block

Bedding compound

Thru-hull fitting

Bedding compound

Bronze machine screws (4)

B.P.Bingham

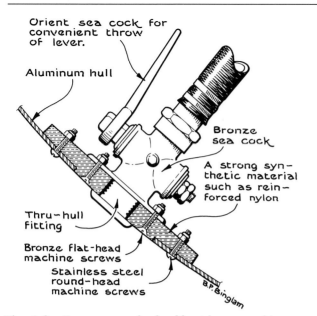

Fig. 4-6 *Bronze sea cocks should not be mounted in direct contact with steel and aluminum-hulled vessels, because the two metals are galvanically incompatible and corrosion will result. This drawing shows a layer of Micarta inserted between the valve and hull to insulate them. Xytel sea cocks avoid the problem of corrosion altogether, because they are synthetic.*

very smart to have at least 1½-inch scuppers, hoses and sea cocks. They are expensive, but it's important that the cockpit drain quickly when it's filled with water, as might occur from a breaking wave. Carrying hundreds of pounds of water in the cockpit makes the boat handle sluggishly, perhaps making handling so bad as to cause a broach.

2. Locate the spot for your thru-hull in a readily accessible place. If you cannot reach the sea cock in an emergency it is of little value. Orient sea cocks with drain plugs so that the drain plug can be reached for winterizing. And be certain there is enough space to conveniently throw the handle. Xytel sea cocks don't have drains, but the unobstructed throw of the handle is still a consideration.

3. Use a backing block of sufficient strength (strong enough so that the area occupied by the thru-hull will be as strong as any other area of the hull). Shape the block to fit the curvature of the hull.

4. Cut the size hole stipulated by the manufacturer of the thru-hull using a hole-saw attachment on your power drill. Start from inside the hull until the pilot drill bit pushes through. Then go outside and finish drilling the hole. On hulls that are cored, the core material must be

removed several inches around the hole for the thru-hull (a screwdriver of knife can be used to remove the core), and polyester or epoxy resin poured in to fill the void (Figure 4-7). The reason for this measure is that the compressive strength of core materials is comparatively less than solid fiberglass. Also, it is important to keep water away from the core material.

5. Drill the same size hole in the backing block, then mock-up the assembly by inserting the thru-hull from the outside and mounting the sea cock on top of it on the inside. Mark on the backing block where you should drill the bolt holes. (Some sea cocks do not have holes pre-drilled in the flange and will have to be drilled before this step can be completed.) Drill holes in the backing block, and through the hull.

   You may cause less chipping of the gel coat outside if you use a smaller bit for the first hole drilled from inside. Then put in the correct size bit and ream out the hole.

6. Apply bedding compound (such as polysulfide) to the underside of the thru-hull flange, sea cock mounting flange, bolt holes and between backing block and hull. Use liberal amounts of compound so that it oozes out all around.

7. Insert the bolts and tighten in the manner prescribed by the manufacturer's instructions.

Fig. 4-7 *When thru-hulls are installed on cored hulls, the core material must be cut away between the layers of fiberglass and the void filled with epoxy to provide greater hull compression strength when the thru-hull is tightened down.*

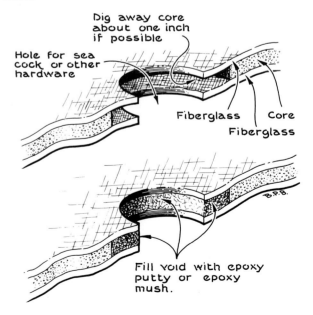

8. If countersinking flat-head bolts, fill in over the bolt heads with epoxy putty compound to achieve a smooth exterior surface. I've used round-head bolts, but these do protrude beyond the hull and might be vulnerable in a grounding.

ELECTRICAL BONDING

According to the ABYC small craft standards, electrically isolated thru-hull fittings do not need to be bonded (the electrical connecting of metal objects inside the boat to prevent electrolytic corrosion; see Chapter 13 for more details on bonding). However, you would be wise, especially if you have a metal hull, to consult these standards (see Appendix A) and other expert advice in determining whether or not to bond your sea cocks and thru-hull fittings to other metal and electrical devices on board.

ITT Jabsco, distributor of ball valve sea cocks, will neither endorse nor attack the practice of bonding sea cocks until more conclusive research on the subject is completed.

MAINTENANCE AND OPERATION

When hauled out, sea cocks should be winterized, and before launching they should be inspected and greased. Though they look benign enough sitting there beside your head, and may be operated with reassuring ease, testing is the only way to be certain they aren't corroded or leaking. They won't leak until the boat is launched, and then it's too late to repack the plug. Some skippers drill and tap the housing and insert a zerc fitting so that grease can be periodically pumped into the cavity and plug. This is an especially good idea if you spend six months or longer between haulouts.

In-the-water tests are as important as out-of-water inspections. Donald Street tells the story of a miscreant sea cock on *Iolaire*. In order to check for blockage in his sink drain, he closed the sea cock and removed the hose. Surprise!

Thinking that he had turned the handle to its open position, he threw the handle the other way and water still gushed in. It turned out that the plug had become waspwaisted through corrosion and admitted water in either open or closed positions.

Removing the hose from the sea cock tail piece, while in the water, is the acid test. But consider this: A 1½-inch thru-hull two feet below the waterline will admit 71 gallons of water per minute! A much safer way of checking is to wait until you're in the sling on launch day and then test each sea cock by closing it and pulling off the hose. You'll then be able to see if water is leaking in.

Once out of the water, on haul-out day, remove the drain plugs in the body of the sea cock and allow all water to drain. Frozen water could crack the casting. To be on the safe side, squirt antifreeze into each drain plug hole.

Before launching, include sea cocks on your checklist of things to do.

1. For tapered-plug types, follow manufacturer's instructions and remove nut and washer from the side of the sea cock. Two wrenches may be necessary. Using a wood mallet, tap out the tapered plug. The various parts are shown in Figure 4-8.
   Some ball valve-types will come apart, but generally it's not necessary.
2. Inspect plug for roughness or scratches. If scratches are light, smooth with emery cloth. If scratches are deep, apply a valve grinding compound to the plug and relap until the plug fits snugly inside the body (Figure 4-9).

Fig. 4-8 *This photo shows the various parts of a Wilcox-Crittenden sea cock disassembled. The tapered plug is just to the left of the housing; it must be periodically greased to remain watertight and to operate smoothly.*

Fig. 4-9 *If sand finds its way between the plug and housing, gouges may be found in the two surfaces. These should be smoothed using a valve grinding compound and lap cloth.*

3. Cover both the plug and internal wall of the cavity with a waterproof grease, such as you may use on your water pump. Apply liberally as the grease is an important factor in preventing leaks and in facilitating ease of operation. (I forgot to grease a plug-type sea cock on *Adriana* one spring, and leaks plagued me all that year.)
4. Reinsert plug and reassemble. Tighten nuts sufficiently to prevent loosening due to vibration. To be certain of the efficacy of your repair, you might again perform a test during launching.

Acording to Wilcox-Crittenden, manufacturer of plug-type sea cocks, annual maintenance, as described above, will lengthen the life of your sea cocks considerably.

Teflon Seals

A recent development in sea cock engineering is the use of a Teflon® seal, which does not re-quire lubrication and therefore is reputed to need no annual maintenance. While this indeed is good news, at least take the time to open and close the valve every so often—say once a month —to be sure it's working smoothly.

During the 10 years ITT Jabsco has been marketing Teflon seal ball-valve sea cocks, it has yet to sell a repair kit. If you do disassemble the sea cock, be sure to treat the Teflon seal kindly to prevent damage and possible leaking.

Softwood Plugs

An additional precaution associated with sea cocks is fashioning tapered soft wood plugs that can be pounded into the tailpiece of the sea cock in the event of hose or fitting failure (Figure 4-10). Attach one of the correct size to each sea cock, using a piece of line so they're never separated. Or, tape the plug to the hose just above the sea cock.

Opening and Closing Sea Cocks

The general rule about opening and closing sea cocks is to leave them closed unless in use. The obvious exception to this would be those attached to cockpit scuppers, which must be left open in order to drain any water, such as rain, from the cockpit. When the boat is left untended

Fig. 4-10 *Tapered softwood plugs should be kept on hand to insert into the tailpiece of a sea cock in the event a hose deteriorates and/or the sea cock fails to close.*

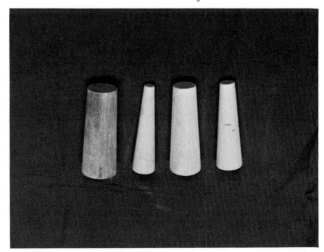

for any length of time, close all other sea cocks. With respect to those sea cocks attached to the toilet, some folks open and close them each time the head is used. Others simply leave them open, working the handle every once in a while to make sure the sea cock is still operating properly. Opening the cooling water sea cock is, of course, a part of your engine start-up procedure.

Maintaining sea cocks is a task every cruising sailor should learn to do himself. Know where every sea cock is located, how to get to it quickly, and how to maintain it.

SUMMARY

- All thru-hulls should be fitted with sea cocks.
- Sea cocks with 90-degree positive stop-to-stop action (handle can't go past a certain point) are better than ones that keep going past 90 degrees. With positive action, you *know* whether it's open or closed.
- Ball valve-type sea cocks leak less than the traditional plug-type, and require less maintenance.
- Grease plug-type sea cocks at least once each year.
- Thru-bolt sea cocks to the hull, using a backing block between the sea cock and hull. Apply liberal amounts of bedding compound.
- Use *two* stainless steel hose clamps to secure hose to the sea cock tailpiece.
- Use the largest possible sea cocks on cockpit scuppers.

FURTHER READING

The Handy Boatman; Time-Life Library of Boating, Alexandria, VA 22314.

CHAPTER 5

Basic Plumbing

Water, water everywhere,
and all the boards did shrink;
Water, water, everywhere,
Nor any drop to drink.

Samuel Taylor Coleridge

Fresh water is essential to the health and survival of man. In the northern Great Lakes the water is so pure that one is never in danger of dying from thirst. The consumption of salt water, however, is damaging to the kidneys in amounts of more than a pint or so. There are desalinators manufactured now for use on large yachts, but technology has yet to produce a viable unit for the 30 to 40-foot boat. Consequently, adequate water storage must be carried in tanks for the entire crew for the duration of a passage, plus a safety margin. And unless one is pouring water from a portable jerry jug, or ladling it from fixed tanks, a system of pumps, pipes and thru-hull discharge is necessary.

TANKS

Water tanks, like most other original-equipment tanks, are installed at the time of construction because they are generally located in the bilges and under cockpits and berths. Removing a tank is almost always a radical step, requiring dismantling floors and furniture. You are indeed lucky if your builder was clever enough to plan for their periodic removal. Installing a new tank is the reverse of removing one, and a major job, too.

Before throwing up your arms in despair, let's take a look at your requirements. One of the longest frequently made passages is from Southern California to the Marquesas, a distance of about 3,000 miles that takes most yachts from three to four weeks. A crew will consume, according to some estimates, between two and five gallons per person per day while cruising. Four persons on a 30-day cruise will need between 240 and 600 gallons of fresh water! This seems a bit high to me. Strict water conservation undoubtedly could bring this total down considerably.

Jon Sanders, an Australian who completed a double circumnavigation in October, 1982, says he restricted his freshwater usage to a half-gallon a day—a pretty stringent ration. This meant one wash a week for himself, and saltwater cleaning of clothes followed by a quick freshwater rinse. At this rate of consumption, a crew of four on a 30-day passage would need a minimum of 60 gallons. However, a person can supplement his liquid diet with soft drinks, which after all, are made with water. Cooking and washing requirements also need to be considered.

Roger Marshall, a Rhode Island naval architect, says he thinks a cruising boat's water supply should equal four to five percent of its total displacement. A 15,000-pound boat, therefore, would carry 600 to 750 pounds of water, or 75 to 93 gallons.

If you purchase a 35-foot boat with a 75-gallon water capacity, consider yourself lucky. Now, suppose you want to double that capacity to 150 gallons. Short of ripping out berth tops and installing a metal, wood or fiberglass tank, the simplest solution is to purchase a flexible nylon tank.

Tank Location

Because fresh water weighs eight pounds per gallon (62.5 pounds per cubic foot; saltwater is 64), it's not difficult to see that a large tank will be holding several hundred pounds of water and that its placement in the boat can be critical to trim.

Racers try to locate fuel and water tanks as close as possible to the boat's center of gravity to prevent hobbyhorsing. Tanks mounted in the extreme bow and stern place stress on the hull where it is unsupported by the water in which it rides.

Unfortunately, on most small cruising boats there is not a great deal of choice regarding tank location. In the main cabin, under-berth storage often is reserved for canned goods and other items that need to be readily accessible. Shallow-bilged boats have little room for tanks, though on larger boats or any boat with a deep enough bilge, this is an ideal location. Bilges are near the center of the boat, handy, yet out of the way. Two other probable locations in many boats are beneath the V-berths, beneath settees, or, on boats without quarter berths, just behind the bulkhead that separates the cabin from the under-cockpit area (Figure 5-1). Anytime tanks must be located to either side of the centerline (the engine and shaft are usually in the way), two tanks are necessary to counter one another, unless you can compensate for excess trim in some other way.

Building a Tank

The Gougeon Brothers of Bay City, Michigan, formulators of WEST System™ epoxy and

Fig. 5-1 *Possible water tank locations*

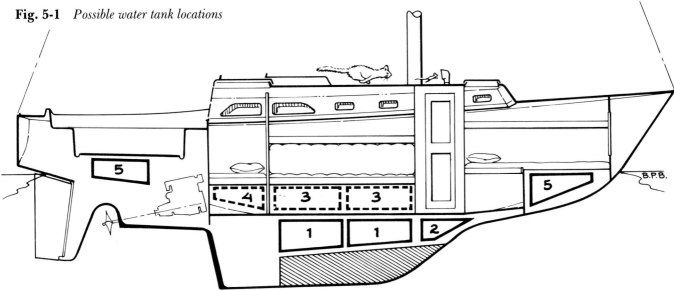

Tank numbers indicate preference of location for the sake of the vessel's performance and motion. Infringement on storage space has been discounted in this drawing.

builders of cold-molded sailboats, have had much experience building wood water and fuel tanks. Meade, the oldest brother, says that ¼-inch plywood is a sufficient thickness for a 40-gallon tank; ⅜-inch plywood gives an added margin of safety. Two baffles should be installed to keep water from gaining momentum as it sloshes around.

Obviously, the top of the berth must be removed to fit in the new tank. In this case, a steel tank of the right shape could just as easily be installed in place of wood, though the cost is substantially higher. Be certain that the tank will fit through the main hatch.

Some fiberglass production yards build tanks using the hull as one side. But as mentioned in Chapter 2, all hulls flex to a degree, and this occasionally places enough stress on the tank joints to crack them. In fact, a friend of mine recently was terribly disappointed when his long-awaited delivery of a C&C Landfall 43 from Newport, Rhode Island to St. Thomas fell through because the integral tanks started leaking when the boat was launched.

The Gougeon Brothers strongly suggest that water tanks be built separate from the hull so they can be removed to repair the hull, should that ever become necessary.

The shape of the tank will, of course, be dictated by the shape of the space available. If you want to maximize space utilization, thin sheets of plywood or veneer can be bent over a jig and laminated in several thicknesses (Figure 5-2). WEST System epoxy is a good bonding agent for this job. Of course, the tank also can be built from flat pieces of plywood, with joints angled to fit the hull.

The joints should be filleted (see Chapter 2) with some sort of resin or putty with a large enough radius so that the fiberglass mat or cloth will conform closely to the curve. Once you have taped all the seams and the resin has kicked, you can either glass a layer of fiberglass cloth to all the interior and exterior sides, or just finish with several coatings of WEST System epoxy or other brand. Warm resin will penetrate grain and allow air to escape better than cold, thick resin, so it is advisable to preheat the resin before applying it in cold temperatures. Also, best results are obtained when the boards are horizontal.

Securing Tanks

All tanks must be securely fastened to the hull and insides of furniture to keep them from moving around and possibly cracking open (Figure 5-3). Two methods are to glass strips of wood to the hull, or alternatively, to glass or bolt blocks of wood to the insides of furniture. Flat steel straps also can be run around the tank to hold it in place, using turnbuckles to tension the strap. Be sure to install a hard-size plastic deck plate in the top as an inspection port.

When fiberglassing inside the boat, be sure to mount an exhaust fan on one of the hatches to suck out dangerous styrene fumes, and don't spend more time than necessary breathing the fumes. Leave the boat while the resin cures—not only is the smell unpleasant and unhealthy, you could jiggle the bonding surfaces by walking around.

Flexible Tanks

With today's highly advanced synthetic materials, I'm much in favor of using flexible tanks when the boat's existing tank capacity is insufficient. They can be purchased for water, gasoline and diesel fuel, and used as waste holding tanks.

The French company, Pennel et Flipo, makes a high-quality line of flexible tanks that are marketed under the name Nauta. They are not inexpensive, but the 840-denier nylon coated with a nitrile compound is very rugged and should last a long time. Unlike inflatable dinghies, which deteriorate largely because of the ultraviolet rays of the sun, storage tanks are well protected inside the boat. And, if measures have been taken to prevent the abrasion of the tank against the hull and furniture, there's not a great deal to worry about.

The Nauta line includes all piping, deck fills and valves necessary for a complete installation. Figure 5-4 shows a flexible tank fitted beneath a berth, with a hose running to a deck fill. Again, consider the effect on trim before choosing a final site.

It is recommended that even flexible tanks be fitted to "berths" to prevent their movement under way. Bruce Bingham suggests a one-inch

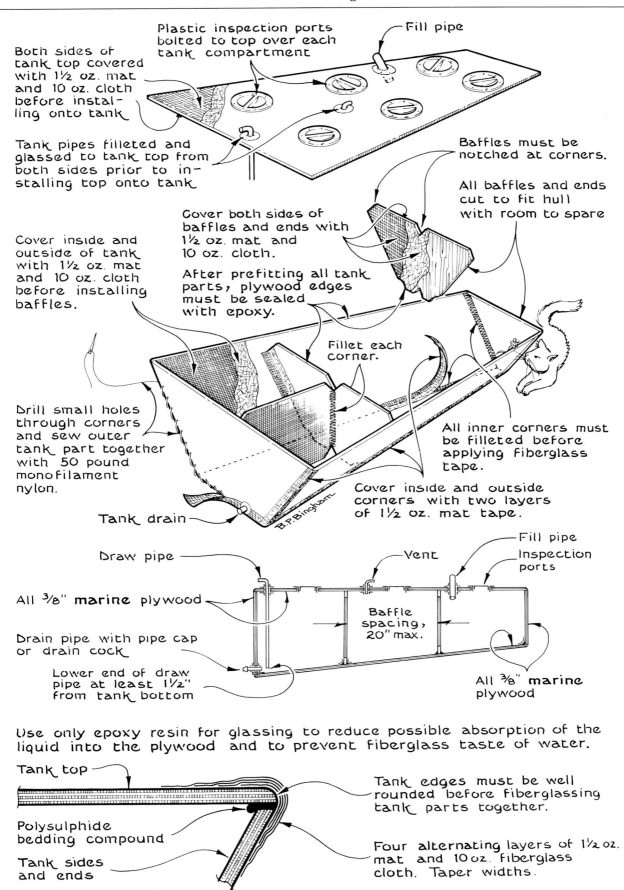

Plastic inspection ports bolted to top over each tank compartment

Fill pipe

Both sides of tank top covered with 1½ oz. mat and 10 oz. cloth before installing onto tank

Tank pipes filleted and glassed to tank top from both sides prior to installing top onto tank

Baffles must be notched at corners.

All baffles and ends cut to fit hull with room to spare

Cover both sides of baffles and ends with 1½ oz. mat and 10 oz. cloth.

Cover inside and outside of tank with 1½ oz. mat and 10 oz. cloth before installing baffles.

After prefitting all tank parts, plywood edges must be sealed with epoxy.

Fillet each corner.

Drill small holes through corners and sew outer tank part together with 50 pound monofilament nylon.

All inner corners must be filleted before applying fiberglass tape.

Tank drain

B.P.Bingham

Cover inside and outside corners with two layers of 1½ oz. mat tape.

Draw pipe

Vent

Fill pipe
Inspection ports

All ⅜" **marine** plywood

Baffle spacing, 20" max.

Drain pipe with pipe cap or drain cock

Lower end of draw pipe at least 1½" from tank bottom

All ⅜" **marine** plywood

Use only epoxy resin for glassing to reduce possible absorption of the liquid into the plywood and to prevent fiberglass taste of water.

Tank top

Tank edges must be well rounded before fiberglassing tank parts together.

Polysulphide bedding compound

Tank sides and ends

Four alternating layers of 1½ oz. mat and 10 oz. fiberglass cloth. Taper widths.

Fig. 5-2 *Quarter-inch plywood, taped on the seams and coated with epoxy resin, is sufficiently thick for a water tank up to about 40 gallons. Baffles and limber holes should also be figured in the construction.*

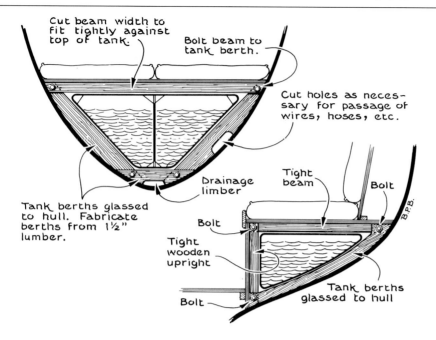

Fig. 5-3 *Water tanks should be glassed to the hull or held in place by strong boards bolted to furniture or bulkheads.*

urethane foam liner glued to the compartment. For large tanks, lightly glass over the foam, which may crush slightly as it conforms to the tank. Straps should hold the tank in place, but remember to adjust these to the full position. When the tank is deflated, the tie-downs should fit loosely. Elastic tie-downs can be used to hold the tank in place in any state of fullness.

PIPING

To move water to and from tanks, pipes are necessary. Copper, brass, and PVC are occasion-

Fig. 5-4 *Flexible water tanks can be stowed in hard-to-get-at areas, such as beneath bunks. Nauta, manufacturer of flexible water tanks, recommends making a "berth" for its tanks so they don't roll about.*

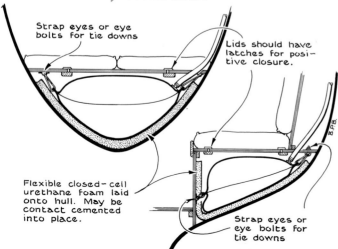

ally seen on older boats, but today the only real choice is vinyl. Most plumbing can be accomplished with various sizes of non-toxic clear vinyl hose, which is readily available in chandleries and hardware stores. Large-diameter hoses, such as are used for bilge pumps and head wastes, or hoses used for pressure water systems of 20 psi or greater, should have nylon or wire reinforcing incorporated into the hose to prevent collapse or explosion under pressure, especially around connectors.

Clear vinyl hose is easy to work with and can be routed just about anywhere. To pass a hose through a bulkhead or piece of cabinetry, drill a hole larger than the hose with a brace and bit or hole saw. When the pilot bit pokes through, go to the other side and finish the hole. Conceivably there could be some chafing if the hose rubs against a sharp piece of wood. So cut a six-inch length of larger diameter hose, slit one side, and slide it over the hose. In neat installations, all hoses are restrained with clamps screwed to the undersides of furniture.

Multiple Tank Plumbing

Water stored for long periods can grow foul, so it is important not to connect two tanks together to eliminate several feet of hose and a few fittings. Each tank should have its own outlet hose leading to the various pumps it services, but fitted to a Y-valve or T-valve to join with the other tank before it reaches the pump (Figure 5-5). In this way, when one tank is empty, the valve can be switched and the second tank used. Actually, it makes good sense to alternate tanks to minimize the amount of time water will stand in any one tank, and to keep the weight in each approximately equal.

Vents

Each rigid water tank must have its own vent in order for water to be drawn from the outlet hose. Vents are not required on flexible tanks because they deflate as water is drawn. Some boats have vent pipes exiting on deck or on the side of the hull, but this is an invitation to salt-spoiled water. If the vent must be on deck, be sure to bend a large U in the pipe and face it aft to make salt water entry more difficult (Figure 5-6).

Because there is plenty of air in the cabin, there is no reason why vents can't terminate in some obscure location, such as at the back of a

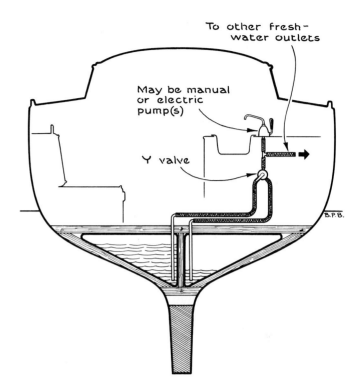

Fig. 5-5 *Tanks shouldn't be directly connected to one another to prevent a foul tank from tainting clean water. A diverter valve permits switching from one tank to the other.*

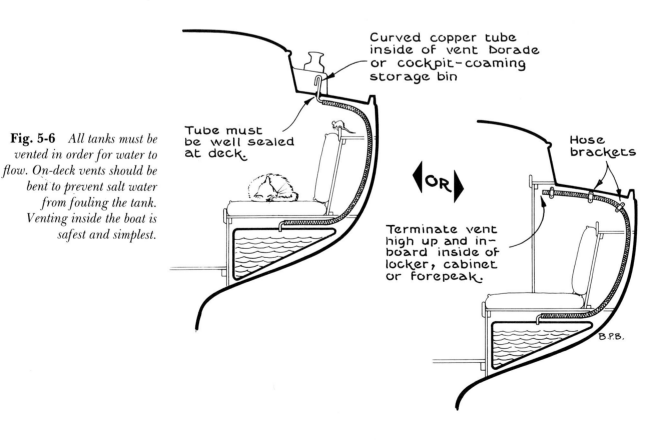

Fig. 5-6 *All tanks must be vented in order for water to flow. On-deck vents should be bent to prevent salt water from fouling the tank. Venting inside the boat is safest and simplest.*

cabinet. *Adriana*'s vent terminates in the forepeak; it is a copper pipe (vinyl can be used, too) that runs from the tank beneath the V-berths into the forepeak, where it simply lies against the side of the hull. I hardly know it's there.

Deck Fills

Most boats today are fitted with deck fills. Certainly this simplifies filling the tanks and avoids the problem of water dribbling from the hose inside the cabin. Deck fills usually are located on the side decks, which are frequently washed with salt water, dirt and other debris. Though I have seldom heard anyone complain about water fouled in this manner, many ocean cruising veterans maintain that tanks should be filled directly through the inspection ports in the tops of the tanks or through special tank-fill hardware. Deck fills can be hard to open if they aren't opened periodically and a light grease applied to the threads.

One advantage of deck fills is that a rain-water catchment system can be routed directly through them into the tank (see Chapter 9). Filling buckets adds an extra step. Whenever filling a tank through a deck fill, it should be your routine practice to wash down the deck around the deck fill before opening the cap. When filling the tanks with rain water, allow the rain to clean off the awnings or decks for a few minutes before routing the water into the tanks.

The rain itself is none too clean, either. Dust, soot, salt, bacteria and other invisible contaminants can be found in collected rain water. For this reason, a catchment system should incorporate a filter between the deck fill and tank. As a further precaution, a few drops of Clorox bleach or purifying tablets should be added to the tank with each fill.

Gauges

One of the advantages of large water tank inspection ports is that they enable you to estimate how full they are. A more accurate method is to install a clear vinyl hose on the exterior of the tank between the outlet and vent; mark it at quarter-full, half-full, and three-quarters full—or by the gallon if you want to be more precise. T-fittings installed in the lines make the job easy, unless you have trouble getting a tight fit at the connections (Figure 5-7).

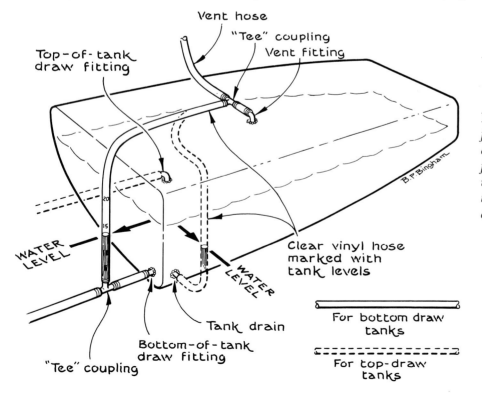

Fig. 5-7 *A simple gauge can be fashioned from two T-fittings and a length of clear vinyl hose. As you fill the tank, measure in graduated increments how much you put in the tank and mark the hose accordingly.*

Thru-hulls

When water is pumped out of a tank for use in a sink or shower, it ultimately must be disposed of somewhere. Rather than toss it overboard, the obvious solution is to route it through a thru-hull fitting in the bottom of the boat. They should be securely fastened to the hull and fitted with sea cocks to prevent water entering the boat in the event the hoses crack or come off the fitting.

This is such an important point that Chapter 4 is devoted solely to the subject of installing and maintaining thru-hull fittings and sea cocks. If you have decided to add a shower or second sink, it can be routed to an existing thru-hull by putting a Y or T-fitting in the existing line. Often this is preferable to drilling another hole in the boat and then investing in the expense of a thru-hull fitting and sea cock. Head sinks can discharge directly into the toilet bowl via a hose pushed under the backside of the seat.

Cockpit Scuppers

An exception to the above statement is cockpit scuppers, which have the important function of draining the cockpit of rain and sea water. It is advisable not to tap into these fittings to drain the water system. They should be as large as possible, two inches or larger would be nice, though on many boats they are dangerously smaller. The rules of the 1982/3 BOC Challenge, for example, stipulated a minimum 1½-inch diameter cockpit drains. Sea cocks large enough to handle this size hole are expensive, but it's a worthwhile investment.

The solution I prefer is seen on many racing boats nowadays. The cockpit scuppers empty into hoses that are led aft at a slight downward angle to the transom or under the counter, where they discharge above the waterline (Figure 5-8). If you're worried that water might come back up through the scuppers, reverse scoops or flappers can be fitted to the hull over the discharge hole. The floor of the cockpit must be higher than the waterline in order to angle the hoses downward and still exit above the waterline without the safety of sea cocks. The advantage is that you can eliminate two thru-hulls below the waterline; the disadvantage is that water in the cockpit might not drain as fast as through vertical scupper hoses.

If you're still worried about water backing through the hoses into the cockpit, then you're probably better off with the conventional scupper system that routes the water straight down to thru-hulls.

Some of the more radically designed racing boats avoid the problem altogether by opening up the after end of the cockpit well to the transom so that water merely washes itself aft and overboard—simplicity at its finest!

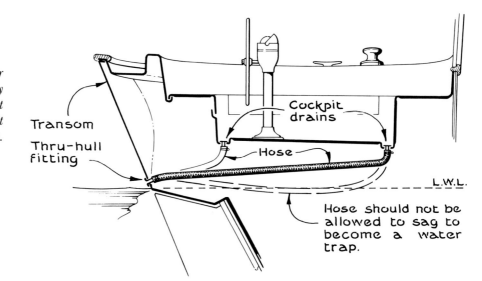

Fig. 5-8 *This scupper arrangement obviates sea cocks by discharging above the waterline at the transom. However, they won't drain as fast as vertical hoses.*

Transom
Thru-hull fitting

Cockpit drains

Hose

L.W.L.

Hose should not be allowed to sag to become a water trap.

PUMPS

A new or used sailboat probably has only some of the pumps you will want on board. Engine pumps, such as for raw water cooling, oil and fuel, come as part of the engine assembly. The average skipper only occasionally will have to familiarize himself with their location, replacement and maintenance. The head, sink and icebox may have pumps incorporated in their plumbing systems as well. But what about all those other pumps you may decide to add for safety and for additional comfort while living aboard? What's essential and what's a luxury? Manual or electric? Where to install? What maintenance is required? Let's fit out a typical cruiser with a sensible array of pumps.

Measuring Pump Capacity

There are several ways of measuring the capacity or amount of water that can be moved by any manual pump. Some are described as pumping so many gallons per minute. But this is not as accurate as measuring the number of gallons per stroke or throw, or number of strokes per gallon. When comparing the performance of two different pumps with different type ratings, convert one so that you're not comparing "apples and oranges."

For example, if one pump lists 16 gallons per minute, and another three strokes per gallon, convert the 16 gallons per minute into strokes per gallon. Guesswork is necessary, but you can come close. If you figure two seconds to raise the handle of a Navy piston pump, and a second to depress it, you'll be achieving one stroke every three seconds—fast work. But let's assume you can keep up this pace for a short while anyway. One stroke every three seconds equates to 20 strokes per minute. The pump's rated capacity is 16 gallons per minute. so dividing 16 by 20 we find that this pump will move 0.8 gallons of water per stroke. Obviously, a strong person will achieve better performance than a weaker one. The second pump moves a gallon every three strokes or ⅓ (0.33) of a gallon every one stroke.

The first pump has more than double the capacity of the second.

Some stores display their pumps fitted to large basins of water. The most accurate way to measure is to pump water into a measured container—how much water comes out with one stroke?

Remember, though, that pumping is hard work. In a matter of minutes, the person will tire and the amount of water being discharged will fall considerably below the pump's rated capacity.

The Manual Bilge Pump

The bilge pump is considered by some to be among the most important pieces of gear on the boat. Others contend that bilge pumps rarely are able to save a holed boat, and that their primary function is to clear small amounts of water from the bilge or sump. With the possible exception of a large crash pump driven by the ship's engine, it is true that most pumps simply won't be able to keep up with the amount of water flowing in through a crack or hole. If you recall from the previous chapter that a 1½-inch hole two feet below the waterline admits 71 gallons of water per minute, it's terrifying to imagine the amount of water that would enter a hole caused by striking a log, rock or another boat. To save a severely holed boat, it will be necessary to stem the flow with collision mats, mattresses and underwater epoxy, bailing as you go with sturdy buckets.

Most manufacturers install a bilge pump as standard or optional equipment. While they will no doubt choose a pump they think is appropriate for your vessel, their choice does not have to be yours.

Next to the proverbial bucket the simplest type of bilge pump is the Navy or piston pump. (Don't sneer at buckets. I was told a story by a physician who was caught in a gale sailing from Bermuda to Long Island. A wave smashed the main hatch weatherboards and partially filled the boat. The bilge pump couldn't empty water fast enough and the plastic bucket handles kept coming off. What saved them were two canvas buckets with wood bottoms.)

If, as a child, one of your chores was to pump

Fig. 5-9 *The Navy or piston-type bilge pump is tried and true, but its capacity is too small and it is too tiring to operate to qualify as the boat's main pump (ITT Jabsco Products).*

out the family dinghy or daysailer, you probably used a **Navy bilge pump** (Figure 5-9). This is basically a portable pump for moving small amounts of water, though some larger boats will have one permanently installed in the bilge as a backup to a manual diaphragm pump. The larger Navy pumps can actually move a great deal of water—a gallon every two or three strokes. However, when one has to pump many hours in order to save the boat—if that's possible —fatigue becomes a crucial factor. The difficulty with Navy pumps is that the throw or pull of the piston is quite long, often 24 inches or more, and is accomplished without mechanical advantage. Pulling a lever with vertical throw is more tiring than pushing a lever with horizontal throw.

By far the most common manual pump used on cruising sailboats is the **diaphragm pump.** In fact, you should install two—one that can be operated by the helmsman and another that can be operated by someone down below. This is what I've done on *Adriana.* A diaphragm pump has a large open chamber whose space is increased or decreased by a lever-controlled, rubber diaphragm. Rubber valves at either side of the chamber, where the intake and outlet hoses attach, alternately open and close as water is pumped through.

One of the largest diaphragm pumps is made by Edson and is rated at a gallon per stroke (Figure 5-10). This is the pump I will have on my next boat. Some are sold mounted on portable

Fig. 5-10 *Edson's diaphragm pump is capable of pushing a gallon per stroke, which is about the most you'll get from any diaphragm pump (Edson International).*

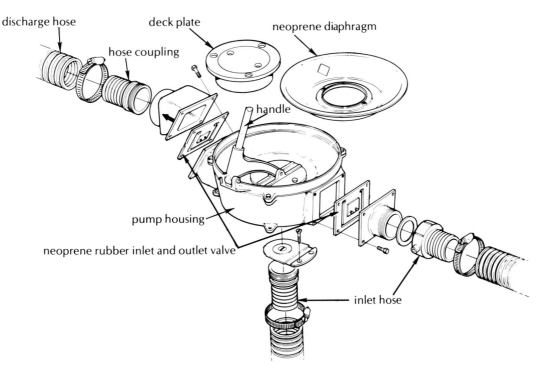

boards, others are installed beneath the cockpit or in the bilge. For smaller yachts, Whale, Gibb-Henderson, Plastimo and Guzzler all make diaphragm pumps that can handle about a gallon every three strokes, or 20 gallons per minute.

A good diaphragm pump will not easily clog and will be able to pass small bits of wood or other debris. Most diaphragm pumps jam when a foreign object sticks in the valve, keeping it open and preventing a watertight seal in the chamber. When this happens, either the hoses must be removed or the chamber opened—such as by removing the diaphragm—using a finger to clear away the debris. Jamming isn't supposed to occur in the diaphragm chamber unless a long narrow object, such as a stick, manages to pass through the valve and become wedged when the diaphragm is depressed. But I've found that dirt and sand lodged around the edges of the valves can prevent them from sealing properly.

To assist in preventing clogging, the end of the hose in the bilge should be fitted with a **strum box** or strainer (Figure 5-11). Many types are available. But be wary that even strainers can be sealed by a flat object such as a piece of paper. In fact, I've had more clogging troubles *with* strainers than without them. With centrifugal

Fig. 5-11   *Strum or strainer boxes can be fitted to the hose ends to prevent clogging. If located deep in the bilge, attach a string to the hose so you can easily retrieve the end and clear it.*

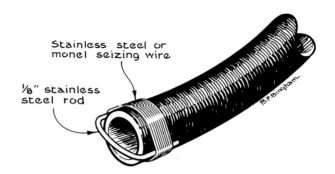

Fig. 5-12   *Because diaphragm pumps can pass small debris without clogging, a solution I prefer to the strum box is fastening a piece of bent rod over the end of the hose and lashing it with thin stainless steel or Monel wire.*

pumps, strainers are probably important, but diaphragm pumps can pass some debris. Another option is to bend a heavy piece of wire or rod over the opening to prevent an object from pressing up flat against the opening (Figure 5-12).

It sometimes is difficult to know when a pump is clogged as there still can be pressure felt when moving the lever. An easy way to make sure is to check for water coming out of the thru-hull discharge. But this can be done only if discharge is above the waterline. This will be a major factor in determining the best location of the pump and its thru-hull fititng.

Bilge Pump Location

There is no best place to discharge a bilge pump. But there are numerous options: A separate thru-hull with sea cock below the waterline; tapped into the cockpit scupper hose below the cockpit floor; through the transom (Figure 5-13); onto the cockpit floor; through the topsides; or through the coaming onto the deck. The main advantage of mounting it above the waterline is the reassurance of being able to see water pour out. However, locations that may be above water at the dock may disappear below the surface when heeled over under way. And, as bilge water often is oily, it's the last thing you want in the cockpit or on deck, when sure footing is of great importance. I favor a thru-hull

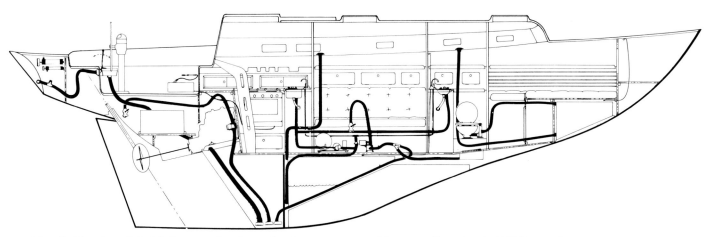

Fig. 5-13 *A well-fit 35-foot cruising boat often has as many as 10 pumps. Drawing by Bill Stanard.*

just under the stern or in the side of the hull several feet above the waterline.

Locating the pump is also a critical decision. A shorthanded crew at sea will want one pump easily operated by the helmsman. This means locating the pump either under the cockpit floor or under or beside cockpit seats. Before cutting any holes, pretend you're sitting at the wheel or tiller, braced for green seas. See where the lever handle would be most convenient. Take into account the amount of throw in the lever also, as you won't want to have to move too far from the helm. Another pump, mounted in the bilge and operated by a person sitting on a bunk or on the cabin sole, is good insurance.

Routing the Discharge Hose

Several factors should be considered in routing the hose. As water passes through a hose or pipe, the interior surface causes friction and retards the flow. To minimize friction, choose hose with a smooth interior wall (even though the exterior appears corrugated by spiral reinforcing wire to prevent collapse); keep the length as short as possible. Avoid sharp bends. Also, the higher the distance the water has to be lifted, the less efficient the pump. Hose routed to thru-hulls above the waterline that are not fitted with sea cocks should be routed as high as possible to prevent water from running back into the boat in the event the thru-hull becomes submerged. Some advocate looping the hose to prevent siphoning water back into the boat. But this cre-

ates unnecessary friction. A better solution is to install a sea cock or at least an in-line valve that can be opened and closed.

Electric Bilge Pumps

Electrically powered diaphragm pumps (Figure 5-14) are an alternative. But they are more expensive than their equivalently rated manual counterparts. Electrically powered centrifugal

Fig. 5-14 *ITT Jabsco manufactures a complete line of electric diaphragm pumps, suitable for many uses including deck washes and pressurized water systems. Capacity ranges from 180 to 250 gallons per hour.*

pumps (Figure 5-15), such as those made by Rule, Attwood and Mayfair, have been popular with yachtsmen due to their ease of installation, low cost, and the amount of water they can move. Centrifugal pumps are more efficient than diaphragm pumps and can handle more water (too much for some applications) at half the price. Before purchasing, check whether or not the pump is suited to its intended use. Is it self-priming? Submersible? Can it be run dry without damage? Centrifugal pumps often are fitted with bronze impellers and can be run dry for a period of time. However, they are not self-priming. This means that if the inlet hose is empty, the pump can't draw water from a source below. Pumps with flexible impellers that lap the inside wall of the chamber are self-priming and can lift water as much as 20 feet, but they cannot be run dry. ITT Jabsco's Par Dry Tank Switch will automatically cut off the pump when there's no water left.

Pumps with bronze impeller blades will not permit even small debris to pass through and thus can clog easily if not used with a fine-mesh strainer box. Flexible impellers can pass through small debris. All these pumps have their place aboard. But I, for one, don't want to depend solely on electrically operated bilge pumps during a disaster at sea—one has to assume that electricity and the ability to generate it will not always be available. A submersible pump (Figure

Fig. 5-16 *This "Bilge King" pump is submersible and will move 2,050 gallons per hour (Atwood Corporation).*

5-16) should be installed at the bottom of the bilge. A nonsubmersible electric centrifugal or diaphragm pump can be mounted under a settee, in the galley, in the engine room or any other location where its hose can be conveniently run into the bilge.

Engine-Driven Pumps

For getting rid of large volumes of water, it's hard to beat engine or generator-driven pumps. ITT Jabsco makes a line of these pumps that will remove from 26 to 83 gallons of water per minute at 1750 rpm (Figure 5-17). They are belt-driven and may be ordered with either manual or electromagnetic clutches. As long as the engine is running, these pumps will remove the most water with the least effort.

Fig. 5-15 *This centrifugal pump is not submersible, but its bronze impeller can be run dry without damage. It is not self-priming. Different models move from 600 to 6,000 gallons per hour (ITT Jabsco Products).*

Fig. 5-17 *Engine-driven bilge pumps are belt driven and can be ordered with manual or electromagnetic clutches. They push from 1,560 to 4,980 gallons per hour (ITT Jabsco Products).*

Fig. 5-18 *Wilcox-Crittenden's "Sea-Gal" is an easy-to-operate galley sink pump. The faucet and body are plastic. It is flanked by two Fynspray pumps, imported from New Zealand by South Pacific Associates.*

Using the Engine as a Bilge Pump

As a last-ditch effort, the engine's raw water intake hose can be removed from the thru-hull (after closing the sea cock) and rerouted into the bilge. When the engine is started, it draws water out of the bilge and runs it through the engine, discharging through the exhaust in the usual manner. This trick is not recommended except in an emergency, because bilge water is likely to be oily and full of debris and could clog the engine's water pump or damage other engine parts.

FRESHWATER SYSTEMS

Cruising in a cockleshell, you can pour water out of jerry cans or plastic milk containers. But it's obviously simpler to employ a pump for moving water from the tanks to the galley sink. Many pumps are available, manual or electric, with or without pressure tanks.

Manual Sink Pumps

The simplest galley pumps are those integral to the faucet and operated by a lever with vertical or horizontal throw. For small sinks, a pump such as Wilcox-Crittenden's "Sea-Gal" is compact and easy to use (Figure 5-18).

Manual foot-operated galley pumps are preferred by some cooks who want to keep both hands free while pumping. Whale makes two types of foot pumps, one operated by depressing a lever with the toe and another that is inset into the cabin floor and depressed by standing on it (Figure 5-19). On a moving boat it's not always easy to brace yourself comfortably to elevate one foot to operate the pump, but foot pumps do free your hands and are neat, out-of-the-way systems that have become quite popular.

Fig. 5-19 *Whale makes two types of foot-operated galley pumps, the lever-type left, and the "tip-toe" type right (Imtra Corporation).*

Pressure Water Systems

An easy way to electrify an existing manual pump is to install a small in-line electric pump. A switch on the faucet fixture is all that's necessary to bring water from the tank flowing out the faucet. Whale makes one that measures about two inches by six inches and draws two amps (Figure 5-20). To supply running water to more than one location, a larger capacity pump that can handle about three gallons per minute is suitable. A pressure switch activates the pump whenever pressure drops below a designated level, usually when the faucet is opened. This is called a "demand" system.

On larger boats, about 32 feet or more, pressure water systems are viable. There is some debate as to the wastefulness of pressurized water systems. Some claim it encourages needless running of the tap, say when doing dishes. Others suggest that regulating the water supply to a trickle conserves water and frees both hands from operating a manual pump.

In any case, it's hard to deny the hedonistic pleasure of a shower. And if you're going to install a pressure system, why not go the next step and fit a water heater as well—after all, you don't need anything more than a pail if a cold shower is all you're after.

ITT Jabsco, Raritan and Galley Maid make pressure water systems that can deliver up to 12 gallons of fresh water per minute. A system like these provides the accumulator tank, pump, motor and pressure gauge all in one assembly (Figure 5-21). However, if this unit is too bulky for existing installation sites, components can be purchased separately and tucked away in different locations (Figure 5-22).

The accumulator tank isn't really necessary, if space is a consideration. They work by pressurizing air in the tank; when the pressure reaches the designated level, it activates a pressure switch that turns on the pump. All it does is store a small amount of water under pressure so that the pump doesn't come on every time a faucet is opened. But with continuous use, like washing dishes, you get used to the sound of the pump racing to keep up. An accumulator tank also helps minimize pulsations in the lines, more frequently caused by diaphragm than centrifugal pumps. In any event, pulsations aren't really harmful.

Electric centrifugal and diaphragm pumps can both be used on pressure water systems. An automatic cycle or pressure switch will control the amount of pressure; Galley Maid's cuts in at 21 pounds per square inch (psi), cuts out at two psi (and at 10 psi if the main water tank runs dry). Running a pressure water system without water can result in damage to the equipment.

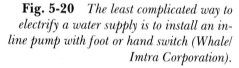

Fig. 5-20 *The least complicated way to electrify a water supply is to install an in-line pump with foot or hand switch (Whale/Imtra Corporation).*

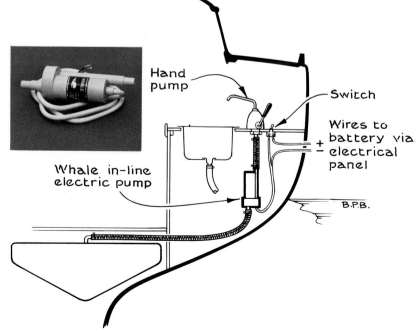

Fig. 5-21 *Galley Maid's pressure water system combines all the components in one unit, and it can deliver up to 12 gallons of fresh water per minute.*

Showers

One of the first questions many ask themselves when they contemplate the cruising life is, "How often will I be able to take showers?" Good question!

The answer depends on whether you have space aboard for a shower, and how much water you can carry in the ship's tanks. After all, if you've only 20 gallons of water, you can't very well afford to let the crew take five-gallon showers every day. Just a little space is required for a shower, but there are a few basic requirements: 1) cabin sole space, such as in the head, that can

Fig. 5-22 *A typical freshwater system with the components split up*

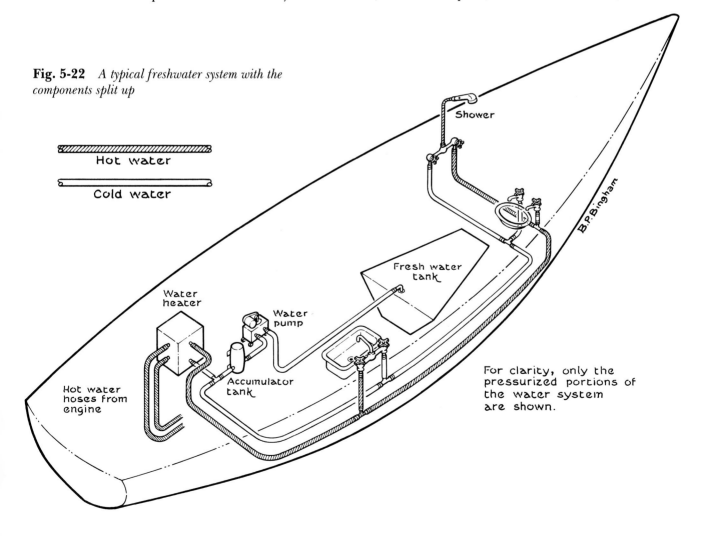

Hot water

Cold water

Shower

B.P.Bingham

Fresh water tank

Water heater

Water pump

Hot water hoses from engine

Accumulator tank

For clarity, only the pressurized portions of the water system are shown.

be fitted with a pan and drain for waste water, 2) a deep bilge or clearance under the sole for a waste discharge pump, 3) a pump to supply water to the shower head, and 4) enough room for you and your shower head to get to know one another. Standing headroom helps, too, though not essential. And if you want a *hot* shower, obviously some sort of heater also is necessary (Figure 5-23).

Study the shower arrangements on other boats to help you decide how to install yours. The drain is usually a fiberglass pan sunk into the sole covered with a teak grating (unless the pan is broad and flat enough so someone walking through the head won't trip). A pan can be made fairly simply by making a plywood box to the dimensions desired, coating it with a mold release agent (see Chapter 9, "Making a Sea-hood" for more details on making molds and laying in fiberglass), and then laying in alternate layers of 1½-ounce mat and 10-ounce cloth. If you intend to cover the pan with a teak grate, the fiberglass laminate won't need to be as great as if you intend to stand directly on it. A laminate thickness of ⅛ inch should be sufficient. If it will be walked on, consider using a core material to stiffen it. Use the sea hood lamination schedule in Chapter 9. Don't forget to make a flange on the pan so it can be screwed or bolted to the cabin sole.

Plastic drains can be purchased at chandleries or well-stocked hardware and building supply stores. A bit of Tuffy pad stuffed in the drain catches hair and other debris, preventing them from clogging the pump. Route the drain hose into the bilge or to a sump pump with a float switch that activates the pump when under water. The pump should discharge through the hull above the waterline. While a sea cock isn't always necessary in such installations, they should be used if the thru-hull is below the waterline when heeled, and at the very least you should have an in-line check valve so that the line can be closed when not in use.

The shower pump can be located just about any place convenient to the fresh water supply tank and head compartment. You can tap into an existing tank hose with a T-fitting to feed the pump and shower. On those sections supplying hot water, use heater hose instead of clear vinyl, as it will distort. A telephone-type shower nozzle that clips to the bulkhead doesn't take up much space. Wired with a pressure switch, the pump will turn on and off as you turn the handle at the mixer or push the shower head button. The pump should be wired to a circuit in the bus bar in which all member appliances or electronics are compatible. Don't overload the circuit (see Chapter 13).

Marine hot water heaters generally are designed to run off 115-volt AC (shore power or generator) and incorporate a heat exchanger

Fig. 5-23 *Adding a shower is not a simple job. The pan should be molded from fiberglass or laminated from thin veneers in a concave shape and coated with epoxy resin. The sump tank collects run-off and a pump moves it over the side when the float or manual switch is activated.*

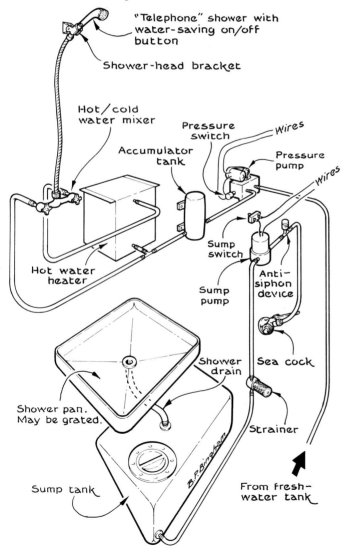

using hot water from the engine's cooling system to heat water that in turn is pumped to the shower or sink. Obviously, to have hot water under way without a generator, the engine must be run long enough to heat several gallons of water.

A CNG or LPG instantaneous bulkhead-mounted heater is another efficient method. The major difficulty with CNG is in obtaining it outside the states (see Chapter 11).

A simpler alternative to the pressure shower is a solar-heated gravity feed day tank mounted on the cabin top (Figure 5-24). The day tank is fed by a pump drawing on the main tank. Just enough water is kept in the tank to meet one day's needs, perhaps five gallons. Because of the weight of the water, it would be foolish to mount a large tank on deck.

To determine the dimensions of a solar-heated day tank, keep in mind that shallow tanks warm water fastest. In one gallon of water there are 231 cubic inches. Pat Rand Rose, author of the *Solar Boat Book*, suggests a depth of two inches. So a typical five-gallon day tank might measure two feet square and two inches deep (24" x 24" x 2" = 1,152 cu. in. ÷ 231 = 5 gal.). A day tank of these dimensions won't be very obtrusive on deck, and due to its low profile, it won't obstruct vision from the cockpit.

The next step is to weld a stainless steel or galvanized steel pan to the above dimensions. Also have the welder add two hose fittings to the bottom. They should be long enough to pass through the cabin top with enough left over to clamp on hoses. One fitting will be connected to the pump and main tank, the other to the warm water tap.

Make a plywood or hardwood box for the pan with enough space around the pan for two or more inches of insulating foam. If you decide on plywood, consider covering it with a sheathing of six or 10-ounce fiberglass cloth. Cut a piece of Plexiglas or Lexan to fit over the top of the pan. The pan itself should be painted with a flat black paint to absorb sunlight. An air vent must be drilled in the Plexiglas cover. Bed the cover with weather stripping to cushion it against the pan and to seal in moisture. Your pan should have a small flange with holes drilled in it to receive sheet metal screws holding the cover to the pan.

Or, you can drill through the Plexiglas into the wood housing. But this will complicate the fitting of a lid, which will be described shortly.

To hold the day tank to the deck, thru-bolt four pad eyes to the deck. Use stainless steel straps to secure the tank. Drill two holes in the

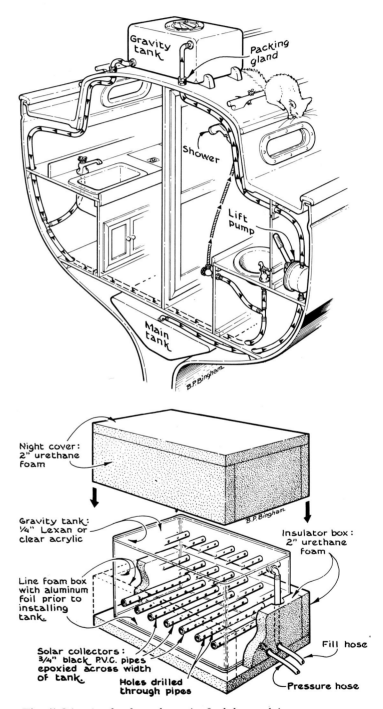

Fig. 5-24 *A solar-heated gravity feed day tank is an energy-conscious alternative to electrically heated or engine-heated showers.*

cabin top for the hose connectors; these, plus the pad eyes, must be well bedded with polysulfide or other suitable compound. The supply hose is connected to a small hand pump, such as a diaphragm mounted on a bulkhead in the head compartment. You can tap into an existing fresh water tank hose with a T-fitting. The warm water tap hose can be routed to the galley sink or head compartment for a shower.

While this arrangement will provide warm water after an hour or two of good sunlight, it won't keep water warm overnight. To do this, you must make a cover for the tank with two or more inches of insulating foam. The cover can be made of wood in two parts and hinged to either side of the day tank. Glue the foam to the inside of the lid using a compatible glue, cover with a layer of fiberglass cloth, and then glue a sheet of tinfoil or other reflective material to the inside. When the lid is open, the tinfoil will direct more light onto the water and speed the heating process.

If you haven't the inclination to install a pressure or gravity-feed shower on your boat, there is always the simple, inexpensive Sun Shower. It is just a simple variation on the solar heater just described—a lightweight plastic bag that is clear on one side, dark on the other. It is filled with

water, and tied to the deck with the clear side up. Before long the water inside is warmed by the sun. It is raised above deck on a halyard or tied to the boom, and water is drawn via a hose and nozzle attachment.

Regardless of which type of shower you decide to install, they all beat sponge baths in the cabin using water heated on the stove. And no shower at all leaves you feeling, as Valley girls say, "grodie to the max!"

SEAWATER SYSTEMS

For real luxury, a high-lift pump can be installed to provide deck wash, galley rinse, anchor wash and other useful functions. Without an accumulator tank, the system (Figure 5-25) will provide water only when the pump is running. If you plan to purchase an accumulator tank for salt water use, be sure to check that it's constructed of corrosion-resistant materials. These systems help keep the yacht clean and also help conserve fresh water by making it possible to rinse dishes in seawater first. For that matter, if the seawater is clean, fresh water rinsing is simply a waste of a limited resource. A filter in the seawater intake before the pump will remove

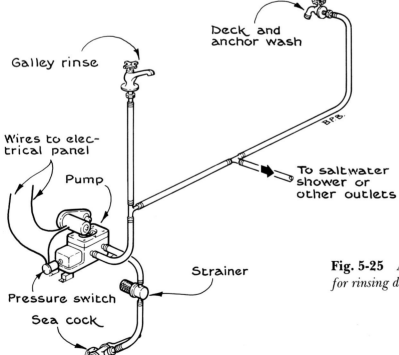

Fig. 5-25 *A typical seawater system such as this is ideal for rinsing dishes and washing down the deck.*

some salt and other junk you don't want in your sink or clogging the pump.

ODDS AND ENDS

Besides the basic use of pumps already mentioned, there's an almost limitless number of miscellaneous applications for small and sometimes odd special purpose pumps.

For transferring fuel, water or other liquids from one tank to another, use Beckson's "Siphon-Mate". It is a 11½-inch Navy-type pump fitted with a special valve that also enables it to be used as a siphon; as long as the source is higher in elevation than the receptacle, one can stroke it one time to initiate the flow, then stand back and drink a beer while the pump finishes the job. Depressing the handle cuts off the flow.

For toilets that use macerator action to grind wastes into small particles, ITT Jabsco manufactures small combination macerator/pump units that can be mounted either permanently or kept portable, and will empty a 30-gallon holding tank in less than five minutes. Even toilets without macerators require pumps to push wastes through the hull or into the holding tank.

The easiest way to retrofit a holding tank is by installing a flexible tank. Nauta tanks are available from 14 to 400 gallons. They fit neatly under bunks and should be mounted in "berths" the same way mentioned for flexible water tanks earlier in this chapter. A manual diaphragm pump for over-the-side discharge will be necessary (don't forget the sea cock) as well as a deck plate with hose to the tank for shoreside pumpout.

When it's time to change engine oil, getting the old oil out can be a slow, dirty and tedious operation, especially if your engine doesn't have a built-in sump pump. Small, manual Navy-type pumps are made specially for changing oil. One can be mounted permanently in the engine compartment with brackets, so that one hand is free to hold the container. Baggies fastened with rubber bands over the ends will catch the drips. Stick one hose end into the dipstick tube and the other hose end into a disposable container and start pumping.

INSTALLING PUMPS

In most instances, installing pumps aboard a yacht is a reasonably simple operation, and one that will give a feeling of satisfaction when done correctly. There's nothing quite so nice as upgrading a boat with a new piece of gear.

Pumps should be fastened securely, either screwed, or in the case of large or manual pumps, thru-bolted to a bulkhead or other strong surface. In some instances it is necessary to reinforce the bulkhead especially for receiving diaphragm bilge pumps—because long hours of hard pumping can weaken the mounting surface.

Cutting Holes

The most intimidating task involved in pump installations is cutting a hole in the hull for discharge, unless the discharge is routed to another hose and thru-hull with a Y or T-fitting. It is critical to think the procedure through carefully. But it needn't be intimidating. Besides, these are the sorts of things that make a person a more complete skipper, with the knowledge and confidence to make necessary repairs.

Select a thru-hull of a size compatible with your hose and, referring to manufacturer's instructions, use the appropriate size hole saw to cut through the hull (see Chapter 13, Figure 13-5). Bed the thru-hull inside and out with a generous amount of flexible bedding compound and tighten with a wrench. If installing a sea cock as well, be sure to thru-bolt it to the hull (see Chapter 4). Use two stainless steel hose clamps wherever a hose meets a fitting and periodically check for watertightness.

Sea Chest

Jim Kyle, an engineer at Cape Dory, showed me a method his company uses to reduce the number of thru-hulls on its boats. Discharge hoses from several sources, such as a shower drain and sink, are routed to a stainless steel box called a sea chest. Sometimes three and four dis-

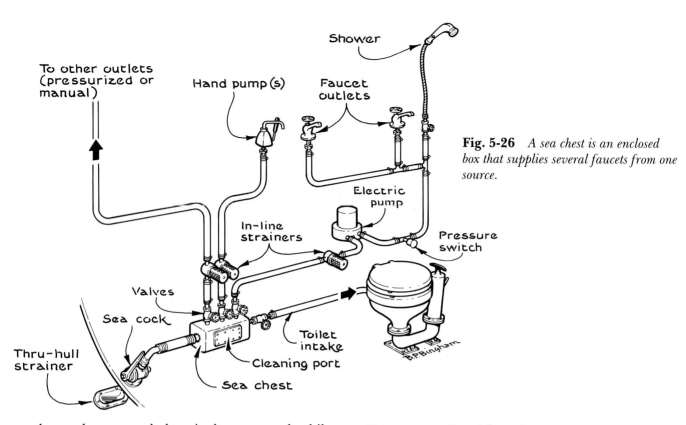

To other outlets (pressurized or manual)

Hand pump(s)

Faucet outlets

Shower

In-line strainers

Electric pump

Pressure switch

Valves

Sea cock

Thru-hull strainer

Toilet intake

Cleaning port

Sea chest

B.P.Bingham

Fig. 5-26 *A sea chest is an enclosed box that supplies several faucets from one source.*

charge hoses are led to it, but never the bilge pump, as it would restrict water discharge too much for this application. Sea chests can also be used to service multiple seawater pumps from one thru-hull fitting (Figure 5-26).

Hoses

When buying a hose be sure to buy the correct size. Vinyl hose should fit snugly, but it doesn't like being stretched too much. Sometimes the diameter of the discharge hose will be larger than the intake; in fact, a pump with a discharge opening 25 percent larger than its intake will be more efficient.

Hose for heads and pressure water systems exceeding about 20 psi should have reinforcing wires wound spirally into the wall. Clear nylon tubing isn't as thick-walled as nylon hose, and shouldn't be used on water systems unless for air vents or some other function that doesn't stress it very much. All hose should be non-toxic, and while this is the type generally sold by marine chandleries, if you buy elsewhere, be sure to ask. Garden hose changes the taste of water, so leave it home for the garden.

When connecting hose to connectors (sea cocks, pumps, sink drains, etc.) use a pipe sealant on the connector to ensure a watertight seal.

Emergency Considerations

Make sure every pump aboard is in an accessible location. If one stops—and the likelihood is that sometime during a pump's life it will—your life could depend upon how fast you can make repairs and resume operation. Diaphragms can tear. Electrical connections corrode and belts slip. Leave enough space around the pump to fit both your hands and necessary tools. Some pumps come apart without screwdrivers or wrenches. One would be wise to check the method of disassembly before purchasing a pump. Inside seat lockers, under galleys and in the bilge are common and usually convenient locations.

Diverter Valves

It's not uncommon to use one pump for two compartments, such as one fresh water pump for two tanks or a bilge pump for two separate parts of the bilge or cabin. A diverter valve allows you to close and open the passage to each compartment (Figure 5-27). Similarly, a Y-fitting enables two pumps to discharge through one outlet, which saves on hose and thru-hulls. Head wastes can be diverted to the holding tank or, by switching the diverter valve, directed overboard.

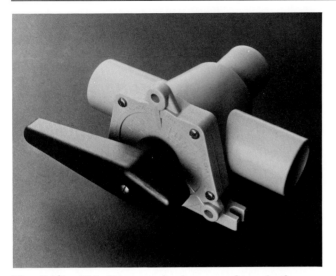

Fig. 5-27 *This diverter valve has several uses in the plumbing system: connecting two different water supplies and allowing the discharge of two sources through one thru-hull (Imtra Corporation).*

Float and Pressure Switches

Boats with a tendency to leak or those left untended for extended periods of time can be fitted with an automatic sensing device that will turn on the electric bilge pump when water reaches a certain level. Wood boat owners make frequent use of these units, often out of necessity. Be sure to buy a model that turns on at a higher water level than it turns off.

Float switches that turn on and off at the same height are constantly turning the pump on and off each time the water laps the sensing device. The next time you step aboard—that is if your boat is still afloat—you could find your battery totally discharged. Float switches also are used for automatic shower sump pumps.

In pressure water systems, pressure switches activate a pump when a faucet is opened. In some instances, check valves in the lines (devices that permit the flow of water in one direction only) prevent electric bilge pumps from accidentally siphoning water back into the boat.

PUMP MAINTENANCE

Most pumps require little or no maintenance. Check manufacturer's instructions to be sure.

The O-ring in Navy-type pumps eventually wears and squirts water up the piston. Donald Street, in *The Ocean Sailing Yacht Vol. II*, describes a means of replacing the O-ring on bronze-bodied pumps with a packing nut filled with greased flax and soldered to the top of the pump.

The most likely repair you'll have to make on other types of pumps is replacing the impeller or diaphragm. Again, carry spares, or, if available, the manufacturer's spare parts repair kit.

Jack Gault of Munster Simms Engineering Ltd. (Whale pumps), has some good suggestions on repairing torn or damaged diaphragms. A piece of sailcloth, foul weather gear, canvas, plastic food bag or other type of plastic-coated material that is strong and nonporous can be fitted over the old diaphragm to plug the hole (Figure 5-28). "First inclination," he says, "is to dispense with the damaged diaphragm but as the split is likely to be only a small part of the diaphragm area, it will provide excellent support for the substitute material." Use the makeshift

Fig. 5-28 *A ripped diaphragm can be repaired at sea by inserting a piece of sailcloth or foul weather gear over the diaphragm.*

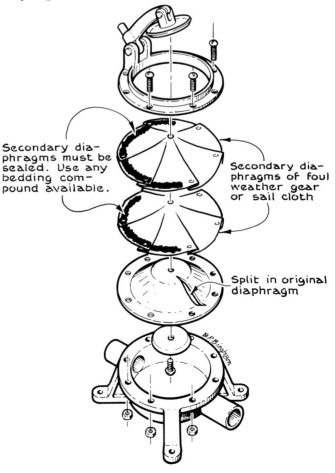

Secondary diaphragms must be sealed. Use any bedding compound available.

Secondary diaphragms of foul weather gear or sail cloth

Split in original diaphragm

diaphragm in two layers, one on either side of the old diaphragm, creating a sandwich.

A frightened man with a bucket in his hands still may be the most efficient pump. But in an emergency there are other chores for him to tend to, like steering the boat, which will reduce or eliminate his effectiveness as a bailer. Adequately sized and properly installed pumps are essential to any well-found yacht. And fresh and saltwater conveniences, which don't have to be extravagant, will certainly make life aboard more enjoyable.

SUMMARY

- Freshwater tanks should contain enough for entire crew for duration of longest passage, plus a safety margin.
- Water supply should be divided among two or more tanks and should not be directly connected.
- Locate tanks as near to the middle of the boat and as near to the centerline as possible.
- Vent tanks inside the boat.
- Fit sea cocks to all thru-hull fittings.

- Two diaphragm bilge pumps should be fitted; one operable from below, the other from the helm.
- An engine-driven pump and/or a large electric bilge pump should be fitted.
- Pressurized freshwater and seawater systems are optional; while convenient they are more subject to failure than manual pumps and may be difficult to repair in other countries.
- All pumps should be easily accessible, especially bilge pumps. Know how to clear the chambers.

FURTHER READING

The Complete Live-Aboard Book by Katy Burke; Seven Seas Press, 524 Thames Street, Newport, Rhode Island 02840.

The Ocean Sailing Yacht, Volumes I, II, by Donald M. Street, Jr.; W. W. Norton, 500 West Fifth Avenue, New York, New York 10110.

The Gougeon Brothers on Boat Construction by the Gougeon Brothers; 706 Martin Street, Bay City, Michigan 48706.

The Solar Boat Book by Pat Rand Rose; Ten Speed Press, Box 7123, Berkeley, California 94707.

CHAPTER 6

Steering Systems

Your true pilot cares nothing about anything on earth but the river, and his pride in his occupation surpasses the pride of kings.

MARK TWAIN

There are five basic types of steering systems: Tiller, cable, worm gear, hydraulic, and rack and pinion. Chances are, you'll stick with the type already on your boat, but there are advantages and disadvantages to each type, and you could decide to incur the expense of modifying or changing to another system altogether.

TILLER STEERING

Tiller steering is by far the simplest and easiest system to repair. Make a spare or emergency backup tiller either from solid wood (being careful to cut with the grain), laminate one over a form (Figure 6-1), or fashion one out of pipe. If

Fig. 6-1 *A new tiller can be cut from a piece of hardwood, such as oak, laminated up from thin pieces of hardwood over a form, or made from a piece of bent pipe. When cutting from a solid piece of wood, be sure to go with the grain as much as possible. When laminating, use a good waterproof glue, such as resorcinol, or epoxy resin in liberal amounts.*

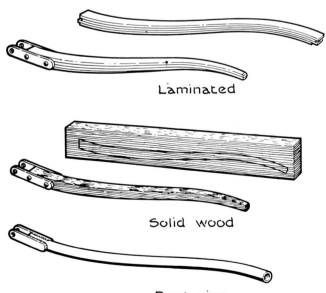

Laminated

Solid wood

Bent pipe

the main tiller breaks, dig into the lazarette and bolt on the spare. If the tiller head casting breaks, you'll need to jury rig some method of attaching the tiller to the rudderstock. In desperation, a pair of Vice-Grips or a crescent wrench might be clamped on. Perhaps a piece of pipe can be fitted over the handle to give greater leverage. But squeezing a round shaft with jury-rigged tools is futile in heavy weather; a stock squared at the end offers much surer attachment with an emergency tiller. However, this is a job for the machine shop, and removing the stock is often difficult. More sensible is to drill a hole through the stock to receive a bolt securing the tiller.

Most reasonably balanced boats up to about 45 feet can be steered with tillers. (Pelle Peterson designed the 1980 tiller-steered Swedish Twelve-Meter, *Sverige*, which was over 60 feet LOA. Balance is more a function of design than overall size.) With a self-steering wind vane, less time is spent at the helm, so the added convenience of wheel steering is diminished. Also, vanes that require control lines led to the helm are much easier to connect to a tiller than a wheel. A tiller gives more feedback to the helmsman than any type of wheel steering, a desirable feature on a small boat. However, on a large boat with excessive weather helm, tiller steering may be too punishing.

Fig. 6-2 *The most common cable system is the pedestal or quadrant-type pictured here. The steering wheel drives a chain fixed to a sprocket. The ends of the chain are attached to wire rope, usually 7 x 19, that runs through sheaves to the quadrant attached to the rudder shaft (Edson International).*

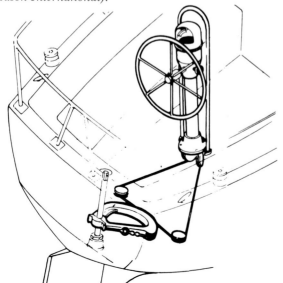

CABLE STEERING

Cable steering is perhaps the most common type seen on today's larger production boats (Figure 6-2). It is frequently fitted to boats that could just as well be steered by tiller. But it does serve the dubious function of making some skippers feel as though they are steering a bigger boat. On the plus side, wheels do give the helmsman more "feel" and quicker turning than any other system besides the tiller. The difficulty with any cable system is that sooner or later the cable, Nicopress terminals, cable clamps, roller chain or master link will fail.

Edson and Merriman/Yacht Specialties, two major manufacturers of steering systems in the U.S., offer many variations on the cable-quadrant type. These include dual-ratio quadrants for greater responsiveness, "radial" types that use a flat round plate fitted over the rudderstock rather than a quadrant, and radial and quadrant types with pull-pull cables run inside conduit (like throttle cables on lawnmowers and motorcycles). These steering systems, like most others, seem to have been developed not so much for their particular steering characteristics, but to adapt to a particular cockpit construction and its relationship to the rudderstock.

In the event of failure, it is essential to be able to fit an emergency tiller if you are not able to make repairs with a spare length of 7 x 19 wire clamps and master links. If this is not possible on your boat, determine if the rudderstock can be extended above the cockpit sole and squared or drilled to receive a tiller head.

Needless to say, an outboard rudder presents far fewer problems as the rudder head is more easily adapted to a spare tiller than an inboard rudderstock.

Some wheel steerers are located far aft in the cockpit, just forward of the rudderstock. Often this does not permit fixing an emergency tiller of any sufficient length to allow a helmsman to control the boat off the wind. Consider relocating the wheel farther forward in the cockpit with longer cables or more sheaves as necessary.

Installing cable steering systems is more difficult than, say, rack and pinion, but can be accomplished by the diligent worker. The first task

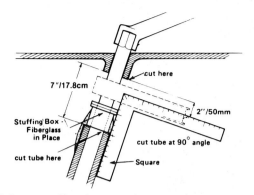

Fig. 6-3 *A stuffing box must be fitted to the rudderstock above the waterline and above it a section of stock exposed to fasten the quadrant or drive wheel (Edson International).*

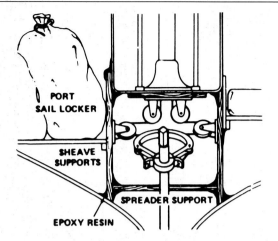

Fig. 6-5 *The outboard sheaves must be securely mounted under the cockpit floor. One method is to glass in plywood supports to the hull and outboard side of the cockpit seats (Edson International).*

is to determine where to mount the pedestal in the cockpit—are there obstructions underneath the cockpit floor? Can you crank winches comfortably? Is there enough sitting and/or standing room behind the wheel? If the cockpit floor oilcans, glass in a piece of plywood (½″ to ¾″ depending on how much stiffening is required) under the cockpit.

Drill the bolt holes for the pedestal, and a centering hole so you can locate it from underneath. The number and size of holes for the cable may vary with brand and model, so be sure to read the manufacturer's instructions carefully.

If your boat's rudderstock enters through a fiberglass tube, it will be necessary to cut a section away above the waterline to install a stuffing box (to keep water out) and expose a section of the stock so that the quadrant or drive wheel can be attached (Figure 6-3). The stuffing box should be strongly glassed to the tube with epoxy resin and a laminate of mat and cloth.

There are various ways to attach the quadrant to the rudderstock, including machining the

Fig. 6-4 *Of the many ways of attaching the quadrant to the stock, this drawing shows three: keyway machined in stock, thru-bolt, and drilled and tapped holes for cap screws (Edson International).*

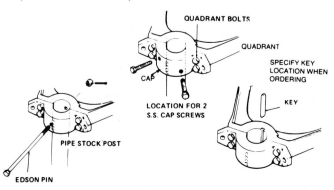

stock with a keyway, thru-bolting or drilling, and tapping for stainless steel cap screws (Figure 6-4).

With the pedestal in place and the quadrant mounted on the rudderstock, the idler must be mounted beneath it under the cockpit floor. Adjustment of the idler sheaves can wait until the other sheaves are fixed in place. These may be thru-bolted to plywood supports glassed to the hull and the outboard side of the cockpit seats (Figure 6-5). Mock up the installation using C-clamps to hold these sheaves in place. Then use a length of shock cord in place of wire to check for alignment. Lead the ends over the pedestal sprocket, through the cockpit floor, over the idler sheaves and outboard sheaves and tie them to the quadrant. When you are certain that all sheaves are properly positioned, thru-bolt the outboard sheaves, fasten the quadrant to the rudderstock and tighten the idler sheaves.

Now mount the roller chain and cut two lengths of 7x19 or 7x37 wire a foot or so longer than required. Use Nicopress terminal fittings and thimbles where the wire attaches to the roller chain, and cable clamps and thimbles to fasten the wire to the take-up eyes or other mechanism on the quadrant (Figure 6-6). This will enable shortening the wire if it stretches later on. When all is in place, turn the wheel hard over to hard over and have someone below check for misalignment, wracking or other distortion in the system.

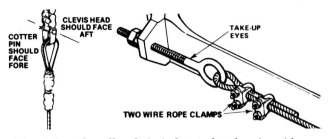

Fig. 6-6 *The roller chain is fastened to the wire with thimbles and Nicopress fittings and the wire to the quadrant with cable clamps (Edson International).*

Lastly, some method must be incorporated to prevent the quadrant from turning so far that the rudder is damaged. Rudder stops can be glassed to the underside of the cockpit floor and an arm fitted to the rudderstock that will hit the stops before the rudder turns too far to port or starboard. Or a pin can be bolted to the quadrant that will hit the stops. Or 2x4s can be glassed to the cockpit and hull with metal plates

Fig. 6-7 *Rudder stops should be securely fastened to some part of the hull or cockpit, independent of the steering system. This illustration shows several methods (Edson International).*

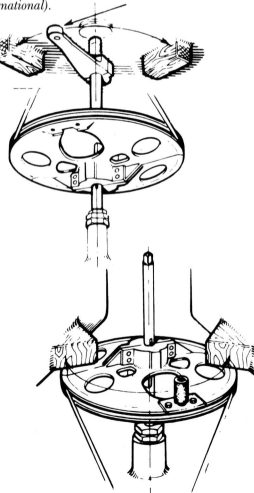

so that when the quadrant swings from side to side, it hits the metal plates before the rudder hits the hull (Figure 6-7).

Edson recommends lubricating the needle bearings in the pedestal bowl with Teflon while spinning the wheel, but don't over-grease as it can run onto the brake pads. Oil the chain with 30-weight motor oil—not grease—to penetrate the links. Wipe the wire with tissue soaked in oil. Broken or hooked strands will snag the tissue. Replace the wire every five years or less regardless of its condition. Check for play in the system by locking the wheel over and trying to move the quadrant; the wire should be tight enough so that it doesn't move, but not overly tight. Periodically check all screws, bolts and clevis and cotter pins. Under power, put a man below where he can view the quadrant and cable and put the helm hard over—look for any sign of bending, creaking or other indication of potential failure.

HYDRAULIC SYSTEMS

Hydraulic steering relies on a system of pumps and hoses through which a fluid is pushed under pressure to actuate a piston(s) that pushes a tiller arm attached to the rudderstock (Figure 6-8). Like the worm gear steerer, there is little feedback from the rudder to the helmsman. But, unlike the worm gear, the wheel reverses itself when you take your hands off. The principal advantage of hydraulic steering (and pull-pull cable) is that the hoses can be run just about anywhere under the cockpit regardless of configuration or obstacles. It also is quite a powerful steering system.

However, it is one of the more accident-prone types of steering systems, especially due to scarred piston walls and dirty seals where the hoses connect to the reservoir tank and piston. A crack in the nipples can cause a pressure loss in the system, which, of course, causes loss of steering. Dirt is the hydraulic system's worst enemy, and strict cleanliness must be observed when working on connectors or when bleeding the system (which involves pouring fluid into the reservoir while drawing off fluid—and air bubbles—from the highest point). Repairs are further complicated by the fact that many of the typical problems can't be seen and are difficult to trace. With cable, at least, you can grab the offending parts with your hand. Working on hydraulics in any kind of sea is not fun.

WORM GEAR AND RACK AND PINION STEERERS

Next to the tiller, the most foolproof steering systems are worm gear (Figure 6-9) and rack and pinion. Worm gear's almost total lack of feedback to the helmsman is disconcerting; however, on large boats it is a tolerable, if not sometimes desirable, quality. With high-quality gear and linkage, there is practically nothing that can break. However, because the rudderstock cannot freewheel with the gear attached, fitting an emergency tiller would take some time, unless there is enough room to install a long enough tiller to provide enough leverage to turn the stock with the gears attached. The recommended method is to remove the gear and bolt a specially welded plate and tiller to the stock.

Due to the inherent friction in the system it is possible to take your hands off the helm with worm gear and have the boat hold course. This

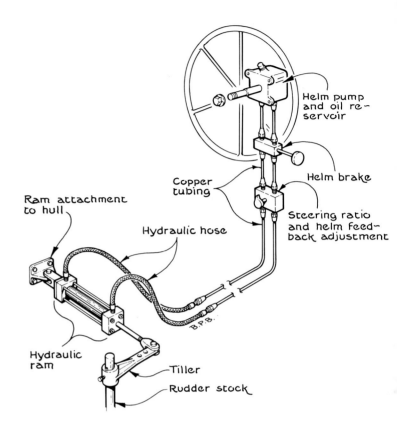

Fig. 6-8 *Hydraulic steering uses hoses and fluid much like the power steering fluid in your car. The weak link in this system is the connecting fittings, which if they leak, can cause a loss of power and attendant loss of steering. Feedback to the helmsman is relatively poor.*

Fig. 6-9 *Worm gear steering is one of the most foolproof, next to the simple tiller. There is little or no feedback to the helmsman, but the boat will hold course when you take your hands off the wheel (Edson International).*

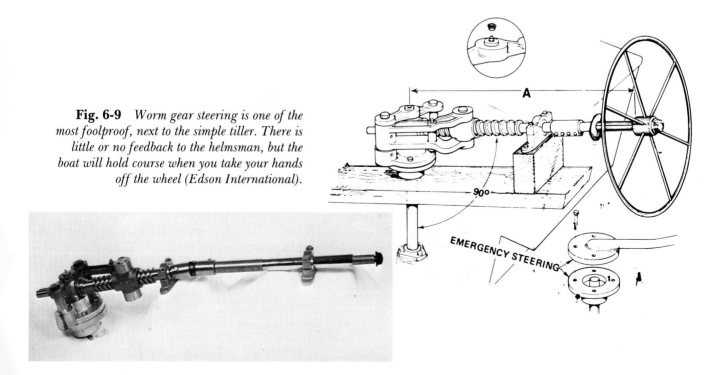

is why worm gear is also called "non-reversing."

This also means, however, that the rudder must be very strong, because the helm won't swing easily when forces are exerted on the rudder—odds are the rudder will break before the worm gear.

The limitation of worm gear and rack and pinion is that the wheel must be located close to the rudderstock, which on a center-cockpit boat is impossible. The worm gear generally is bolted inside a housing at the after end of the cockpit, either forward or aft of the rudder head (Figure 6-10). The housing is often constructed to form a helmsman's seat, with the wheel positioned virtually in his lap.

Edson's Simplex worm gear steerers range from 3.25 to six turns hardover to hardover in 90 degrees, which is about twice that of cable systems (e.g., for a 35-footer, the difference is about 3.25 to 1.8 turns). This is one reason why worm gears most often are fitted to heavy, full-keel boats. A lighter fin keel boat would lose its responsiveness with worm gear steering.

Rack and pinion steering is a geared system that incorporates a geared shaft (the pinion) rolling over a geared quadrant (the rack). They are suitable for boats up to about 40 feet and 30,000 pounds displacement. Versions are available for all types of rudders and stern shapes. Mounted aft in the cockpit similar to the worm gear steerer, it has similar wheel placement limitations because the rack must be fitted to the rudderstock. Figure 6-11 shows a typical installation. Simplicity of installation is one of its virtues. The gears must be securely thru-bolted to a sturdy surface (e.g., plywood glassed to the cockpit or a box—perhaps doubling as a helmsman's seat—covering the gear). The rack must be mounted 90 degrees to the rudderstock. A short section of the stock should be left to fit an emergency tiller.

Rack and pinion is a simple and robust steering system, and unlike worm steerers, there is complete feedback of the rudder to the helmsman. Lock-to-lock turns of Edson models are about 1.6 in 70 degrees and 1.8 in 80 degrees.

Fig. 6-10 *Both worm gear and rack and pinion steerers are mounted aft in the cockpit and a housing is generally fashioned to cover the mechanisms and provide seating for the helmsman. This boat has worm gear.*

Fig. 6-11 *Rack and pinion steerers incorporate a geared shaft (pinion) and flat, geared bar (rack). They are sturdy mechanisms and are located aft in the cockpit (Edson International).*

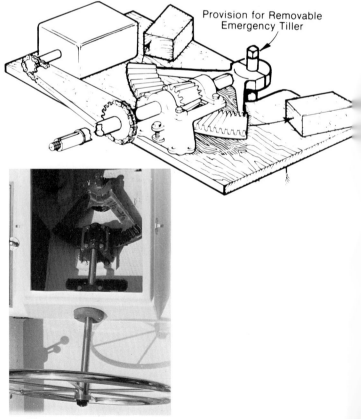

Maintenance of rack and pinion steering is straightforward—use 30-weight motor oil on the shaft bearing and a Teflon grease on the gear teeth. For worm gear, use 30-weight motor oil on the pivot points and water pump grease on the worm itself. If you have installed a universal joint in the wheel shaft to mount the wheel at a more comfortable angle (rack and pinion and worm gear steering must be fitted to the rudderstock at right angles), the universal joint should be periodically packed with grease and attention given to its protective rubber boot.

INSTALLATION

Wheel steering systems can be installed by the enterprising individual, though there is a need to consult closely with the manufacturer to be sure you have selected the right system and model to fit your boat. Some customizing of shaft lengths may be required, but if you have carefully measured the pertinent dimensions of your cockpit, rudder shaft angle, etc., most of this can be done by the manufacturer before it's delivered.

Perhaps the most important point in installing any wheel steering system is fastening parts to the hull, cockpit or housing. Tremendous forces are placed on steering systems, so every part should be thru-bolted, not screwed. Other parts, such as sheaves and idlers, may need glassing to the hull. Follow the guidelines for hull preparation and lamination techniques in Chapter 2. If a cockpit floor seems weak (it flexes when you stand on it), reinforce the floor by glassing at least ½-inch plywood underneath it before mounting a heavy pedestal.

AUTOPILOT ADAPTIONS

Cable, worm gear, hydraulic and rack and pinion steering systems all can be fitted with autopilots for self-steering. This is generally accomplished by a servo-drive motor connected to the steerer shaft by a roller chain and sprockets (Figure 6-12). With cable and hydraulic systems the autopilot may be located on a platform

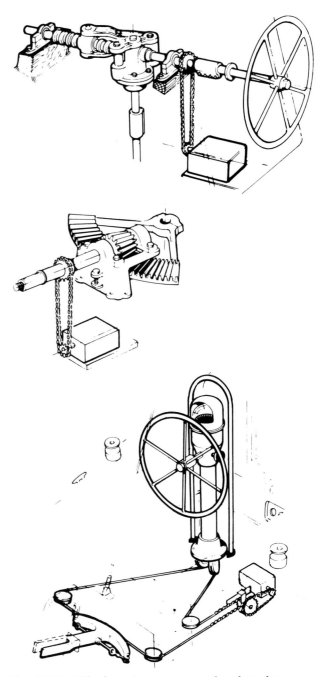

Fig. 6-12 *Wheel steering systems can be adapted to under-the-deck autopilots, usually by adding a sprocket to the steering shaft and connecting it to a motor by means of a chain (Edson International).*

in the lazarette or in a cockpit seat locker where the cable or hose may be routed near it. It also may be mounted in the steering box or under the cockpit near the rudderstock or steering gear. In any installation, the autopilot must be located somewhere adjacent to the rudderstock, steerer shaft, or, in the case of cable steering, near the cable. There are also autopilots, such as Autohelm's 3000 model, that mount in the cockpit and turn the steerer by means of a belt and drum (see Chapter 7). Mechanical and electromagnetic clutches can be fitted to engage and disengage the autopilot drive motor.

A thought to consider: Bob Verhaeghe, who manufactures Cruising Yacht Systems wind vanes says, "Save the money you would have spent on a wheel and invest it in an autopilot or wind vane. Then you won't need the wheel; in fact, you'll probably be glad you don't have it."

EMERGENCY STEERING SYSTEMS

When wheel steering fails, an emergency tiller that is easily shipped solves the problem. But, as mentioned earlier, there are common difficulties: With pedestal steerers, the pedestal is often too close to the rudderstock; with worm gear, the gear may need to be removed to allow the rudderstock to freewheel. And with worm gear and rack and pinion, access to the rudderstock may be difficult.

Figure 6-13 illustrates several methods of modifying the end of the rudderstock to accept a stout, emergency tiller. If you have converted from tiller to wheel steering, it may be possible to leave the tiller head attached to the stock, which will then make it possible to fit a modified tiller to the stock that will clear the wheel (Figure 6-14).

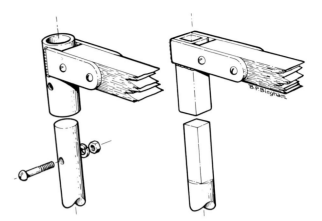

Fig. 6-13 *Provisions for emergency steering are a must. If the rudderhead cannot be modified to accept an emergency tiller, the top of the shaft can be squared or drilled for a pin to hold the tiller.*

As a last resort, with a more or less vertical rudderstock, it may be possible to reverse the tillerhead on the stock, and then mount the tiller facing aft—what the hell, it's worth a try. George Day, *Cruising World*'s executive editor, tells of the time he was aboard a 50-foot ketch in the Miami-Montego Bay Race. Speeding along at 1 a.m. on a quartering reach under full sail, the cable snapped just as they were passing between Cat Cay and Eleuthera. An emergency tiller could only be fitted facing aft. The crew took 15-minute turns sitting on the after deck using both feet to steer. As if this wasn't difficult enough, they had to keep remembering to push when they used to pull and vice versa!

Steering is an important enough function to

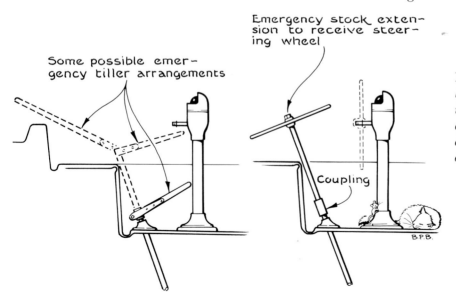

Some possible emergency tiller arrangements

Emergency stock extension to receive steering wheel

Coupling

Fig. 6-14 *Many wheel steerers are located so near to the rudderhead that it makes installing an emergency tiller quite difficult. One solution is to bend a piece of pipe so that it extends up and over the wheel.*

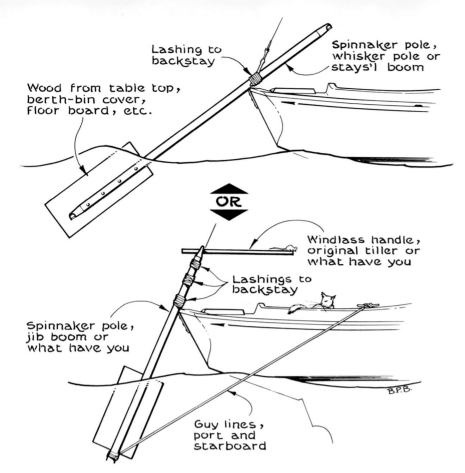

Lashing to backstay

Spinnaker pole, whisker pole or stays'l boom

Wood from table top, berth-bin cover, floor board, etc.

OR

Windlass handle, original tiller or what have you

Lashings to backstay

Spinnaker pole, jib boom or what have you

Guy lines, port and starboard

B.P.B.

Fig. 6-15 *An emergency makeshift rudder can be fashioned from pieces of plywood and 2 x 4s (carried aboard for this and other emergency purposes), or spinnaker pole and hatchboards. The best plan, however, is to prefabricate the rudder before you go cruising.*

justify saying: If an emergency back-up system cannot be fitted, buy another boat.

But what happens when the rudder itself fails? On some boats, the gudgeons and pintles aren't sufficiently strong. With fiberglass rudders, the rudderstock may break loose from the rudder blade, spinning freely.

There are at least three options. Steer with sails alone (pretty impractical); build a makeshift rudder (difficult and probably not very strong unless prefabricated) (Figure 6-15); or use the wind vane rudder (easy, if your boat is equipped with a vane that uses an auxiliary rudder). The most realistic way of preparing for this contingency on a majority of cruising boats, then, is to build an emergency rudder beforehand.

MAKING AN EMERGENCY RUDDER

Chapter 2, Figure 2-33 shows how to make a fiberglass rudder. Thru-bolt gudgeons to the transom and have pintles welded to the rudderstock so the rudder can be lifted from a seat locker or wherever else it's stowed and mounted without having to screw or bolt anything in some dubious, jury-rigged fashion. The rudderstock

should be drilled to receive an emergency tiller, also kept handy.

Ingenious sailors without prefabricated emergency rudders have reported marginal success using spinnaker poles lashed to hatch covers and ropes led from the rudder to port and starboard winches. But to accomplish this in storm conditions requires more luck than handy workmanship. You'll be well rewarded for planning ahead.

WIND VANE AUXILIARY RUDDERS

One type of wind vane utilizes an auxiliary rudder to steer the boat. The Hydrovane is one example, as is the Cruising Yacht Systems vane on *Adriana*. My CYS rudder is quite large, measuring about 40 inches by 12 inches, and it is more than powerful enough to steer the boat by itself (see Chapter 7). Should the main rudder become disabled or fall off, I would have no difficulty steering the boat to port with the vane rudder.

If the wind vane rudder can function as a primary rudder, conceive of a method to fit the tiller to its rudderstock. A weldment can be

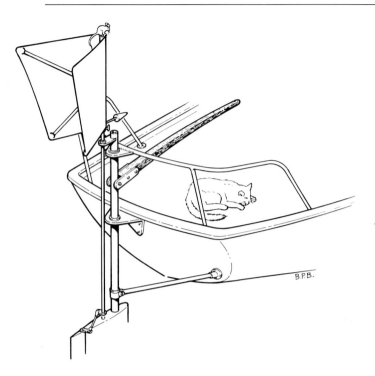

Fig. 6-16 *A wind vane self-steering device can be used for emergency steering if it uses an auxiliary rudder and if the stock incorporates welded plates inside the rudder as in Fig. 2-33.*

added to the rudderstock to receive a bolt-on tiller during an emergency (Figure 6-16).

WEAK LINKS IN THE STEERING SYSTEM

Because it is under water the rudder is subjected to considerable forces and is often a weak link. Over time, even the best engineered system can show signs of fatigue.

Check for potential problems in several places. An inboard rudder blade should be well secured to the stock. Good fiberglass designs incorporate metal arms welded to the stock that are encased by the rudder (see Chapter 2). Examples of things to look for are cracks in the gel coat and laminate, and play in the blade relative to the stock. Wood rudders may have bronze or stainless steel arms sandwiching the blade, or drifts driven through the planks. Look for splitting of the planks (not minor checking), corrosion around welds and discoloration of bronze fittings, indicating overstressing.

Stock supports inside the hull are potential problem areas (see Chapter 2), as is the tiller head. Aluminum castings can crack unexpectedly and there is virtually no way, short of X-rays, to foresee their development. Welded stainless steel or forged bronze is much stronger.

On outboard rudders and attached rudders, gudgeons and pintles carry the load. Screws are unsufficient to attach the hardware to the hull and rudder; thru-bolts must be used. If the dimensions of the hardware seem too small for the job, consider replacing them with more massive fittings.

Wood cheeks, or aluminum or stainless steel side plates, are important elements of outboard rudder strength. Often they are used to receive the tiller as well, and must be strong enough to resist twist. Thru-bolting the cheeks or plates to each other through the rudder head is the only acceptable attachment method (Figure 6-17).

Tillers, especially laminated ones, will break most often where they are bolted to the tiller head. Delamination is one sure sign that trouble is brewing, as is spongy wood around the bolt hole. Periodically remove the tiller from the fitting and inspect the bolt holes for signs of rot or delamination. Don't hesitate to replace the tiller when these signs are present. You know that when it does break, it'll happen when you are hard pressed in heavy weather. You can mortise stainless steel side plates to the tiller to take the strain, or in an emergency, cut off the end of the tiller and drill a new hole.

Cable systems fail most often where the wire, Nicopress or cable clamps come apart. Water may find its way into these parts and begin the diabolical, arcane process of corrosion. Tarnished or frayed wire strands are one sign, but as with the rigging, there's no certain way to determine what is going on inside the terminals. X-rays are the only sure method, but they are not always possible or practical. There is a two-part product called "Spot-Check", available at auto supply stores, which can be applied to a terminal, quadrant or other casting to help define cracks sort of like the stuff dentists use to pinpoint cavities. It is a good idea to replace the wire cable and connecting fittings every four or five years just to be on the safe side.

Worm gear and rack and pinion steering

Fig. 6-17 *Outboard rudders are in many ways the sturdiest and easiest to repair. Their one weak link is the rudderstock and cheek blocks, which should be sturdy and thru-bolted. Gudgeons and pintles should also be heavy duty and thru-bolted.*

might well outlast the boat and even yourself. I can envision scuba divers coming upon an old, sunken boat—the hull is disintegrating, a skeleton, and all that's left intact are a few heavy metal fittings, most notably the steering gears. Apply a Teflon grease every season and check the mounting bolts and you've probably done all that's necessary to protect the system.

Once you know that the steering system of your boat has been constructed as strongly as possible, and that you have an adequate back-up system, you've eliminated one of the major sources of worry in offshore cruising.

SUMMARY

- The most failsafe steering system is a well-built outboard rudder—with heavy stainless steel or bronze fittings—and a stout tiller.

- The most failsafe wheel steering systems are the worm gear and rack and pinion.
- Replace cable and Nicopress or cable clamps on cable systems periodically.
- Prefabricate an emergency rudder and tiller and stow on the boat in the event the main rudder is disabled.
- All fittings should be thru-bolted where possible because of the great stresses imposed on steering systems.

FURTHER READING

The Ocean Sailing Yacht, Vols. I, II, by Donald M. Street, Jr.; W. W. Norton & Company, 500 Fifth Avenue, New York, New York 10110.

Edson Catalog, The Edson Corporation, 460 Industrial Park Road, New Bedford, Massachusetts 02745.

CHAPTER 7

Self-Steering Systems

When our perils are past, shall our gratitude sleep?
No—here's to the pilot that weathered the storm.

GEORGE CANNING

Self-steering is not a requirement for good cruising. Many yachts have made their way around the world with the captain and crew steering every league of the way. Joshua Slocum balanced his sails to steer *Spray*, sometimes resorting to sheet-to-tiller arrangements. Robin Knox-Johnston sailed around the world alone in a ketch—with only the helm lashed.

In the past 10 years, sheet-to-tiller steering has become more popular, in large thanks to people like John Letcher and Lee Woas, who have spent years experimenting and writing about various arrangements. The necessary gear consists of a few small blocks, a few lengths of small line, and a piece of surgical tubing. The only installation is screwing in a few padeyes in the cockpit to attach the blocks, lines and tubing. (For additional information on this method of self-steering, see the reading list at the end of the chapter.)

The Age of the Microchip, however, has enormously simplified self-steering, and as expected in the ever-developing world of electronics, the cost of electronic autopilots has steadily decreased. It is now possible to purchase a quality autopilot for a 30 to 35-foot boat for about $600, and between $1,000 and $3,000 for 40 to 50-foot boats. This seems a small price to pay for hours of freedom at sea. Instead of steering and growing tired or bored the crew can navigate, read books, cook meals, sleep or work.

AUTOPILOTS VS. WIND VANES

Electronic autopilots operate differently than mechanical wind vanes. They use electrical power from the battery, and it is necessary to have some means of keeping the battery charged. Running the engine is one method, utilizing a solar panel, wind or water generator is another (see Chapter 12).

Autopilots steer magnetic compass courses whereas mechanical wind vanes steer courses relative to the wind direction. When the wind direction changes, an autopilot continues to steer the same course, even if the sails start slatting.

A wind vane continues to steer the same course relative to the wind even though the boat's heading has changed. In both cases, the watch is usually alerted by the new sounds or feel of the boat relative to the wind and water, and adjustments are made. Each has its advantage and disadvantage, and ideally I would own both.

Weekend sailors investing in self-steering frequently opt for the electronic autopilot, because it is less expensive, steers while motoring, and does not require adding a large, heavy and possibly ungainly looking support bracket on the transom. In contrast, cruisers planning to stay away from home for months or years usually invest in the wind vane. There is security in not having to rely on electrical power to make the boat steer herself. A good self-steering wind vane system will steer the boat even in gale conditions, when the crew may be exhausted and survival depends on keeping the boat on course a few more hours. If the boat is flooded, batteries cease working; corrosion can ruin the electronic circuits of the autopilot. On the other hand, a breaking wave may damage the wind vane. Even on the strongest units, the vane is usually lightweight (by necessity, to pick up wind shifts) and can be carried away by wind or water. Competitors in the 1982/83 BOC around the world race were plagued by self-steering failures, mostly in the violent Southern Ocean. The Australian Fleming gear (a servo-pendulum type) proved one of the most durable.

TILLER-MOUNTED AUTOPILOTS

The least expensive autopilots are designed for tillers (Figure 7-1). These portable units are mounted in the cockpit, often against the coaming, with the drive shaft coupled to a stud installed in the tiller. The location of the stud is

Fig. 7-1 *The Combi Autohelm 2000 autopilot is typical of other tiller-type units that mount in the cockpit and turn the helm by means of a push rod or jack screw fastened to the tiller (International Marine Instruments, Inc.).*

important because it determines the quickness of rudder response. Tiller Master recommends its unit be fixed to the tiller between 14 and 33 inches from the rudderstock or axis. For example, the stud should be mounted 18 inches from the rudderstock on Catalina 30s, and up to 33 inches on the Westsail 32, which has a large outboard rudder. Drive shaft extensions are available for installations in which the stud must be more than 33 inches from the rudderstock to compensate for the larger swing of the tiller.

Autohelm tiller-type autopilots separate the compass and electronic circuit board from the push rod, and like the Tiller Master, are easily detached. The Autohelm 2000 is advertised as capable of applying tiller loads in excess of 100 pounds, and on a "typical 30-footer," power consumption averages about 200 milliamps—less than a single navigation light. Gerry Spiess steered his 10-foot *Yankee Girl* across the Pacific with one of these units without ever recharging his batteries.

Installation is fairly simple (Figure 7-2). A gudgeon is provided with these units for mounting in the cockpit. The most preferred electrical hookup is a socket mounted out of the weather in the cockpit, perhaps in a seat locker, and wired to a circuit on the distribution panel. If there is a spare circuit, this would be preferable, though it could be wired to terminals already used for another piece of equipment, such as the VHF or depth sounder. The Tiller Master comes with a 1½-amp slow-blow fuse. If polarity

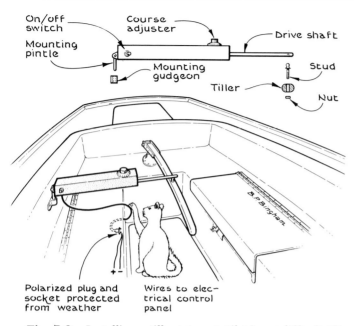

Fig. 7-2 *Installing a tiller-type autopilot is not difficult. The mounting brackets are screwed to the coaming or other part of the cockpit, and two wires are led via a connector to the positive and negative bus bars.*

Fig. 7-3 *Tiller-type autopilots, such as this Tiller Master, can be adapted to wheel steerers by means of a bar or sprocket.*

is reversed, the fuse will blow. All wire ends should be tinned with solder when making connections to prevent corrosion, and the ends leading to the circuit should have soldered crimp lug terminal eyes (see Chapter 12, Figure 12-27).

Many tiller-mounted autopilots also can be adapted to wheel steerers by means of a bracket bolted across the wheel (Figure 7-3).

Autohelm makes an economical autopilot (the Combi Autohelm 3000) for cable pedestal steerers that employs a ribbed rubber belt connecting the drive motor (mounted on the cockpit floor or pedestal base) to a drum that bolts to the spokes of the wheel steerer.

A useful accessory to most autopilots is a remote dodger (Figure 7-4). This hand-held device, which is connected to the autopilot by a long, flexible insulated wire, enables you to change course to avoid danger by just moving the toggle in your hand. When the toggle is released, the boat returns to its original course.

Fig. 7-4 *The Autohelm 5000 is available with a remote dodger that enables you to change course without disengaging the unit or returning to the helm (International Marine Instruments, Inc.).*

BELOW DECK AUTOPILOTS

For larger boats, which require greater power to turn the helm, more sophisticated systems are needed. Raytheon, Cetec Benmar and Cinkel are three major manufacturers of electronic autopilots adaptable to all types of wheel steering systems (see Chapter 6 for autopilot installations on various types of steering).

Electronic autopilots generally can be divided into three types: hunting, non-hunting proportional deadband, and non-hunting proportional rate. The hunting-type autopilot was developed in the 1930s and in comparison with the proportional rate autopilots sold today, is relatively simple. A *compass* detected the amount the rudder was to port or starboard of the desired heading and, via a *control unit*, activated a *motor drive* connected to the rudderstock to make corrections. (These three components are typical of all autopilots.) The system continually searched the correct heading, causing a zig-zag course. Power consumption and worn-out components were shortcomings of the hunting-type autopilots.

A decade later, the proportional deadband autopilot was developed to eliminate excessive hunting. In effect, a "deadband" was introduced into the system where the helm was not corected. When the error exceeded the limits of the dead-band, the helm was corrected proportional to the heading error.

Today, many of the more sophisticated autopilots have done away with the deadband, though they still operate on the proportional rate concept (Figure 7-5). The electronic control unit determines both the rate and amount of correction to be applied. To prevent relays from burning out (electro-mechanical switches that start the drive motor rotating clockwise or counterclockwise), these autopilots use transistors instead, which can be enclosed in a separate housing or inside the drive motor enclosure. This type of relay is of particular value to the hydraulic steering system due to its inherent slip (slop between the helm and the rudder), which can cause excessive corrections.

As everyone knows, the world of electronics is developing at a rapid pace, and the manufacturers of autopilots are making some interesting improvements in self-steering systems. For example, Wesmar uses a "saturable core sensor" in place of the traditional compass to electronically sense the electromagnetic field of the earth and instantly detect changes in course. The quicker a heading error is detected, the quicker a correction can be made. The Autohelm 5000 "Integrated Rate Pilot" is offered with an optional linear drive (Figure 7-6) that attaches directly to the rudderstock. Because it is independent of the steering system, it can be used as a backup if a cable or hose fails.

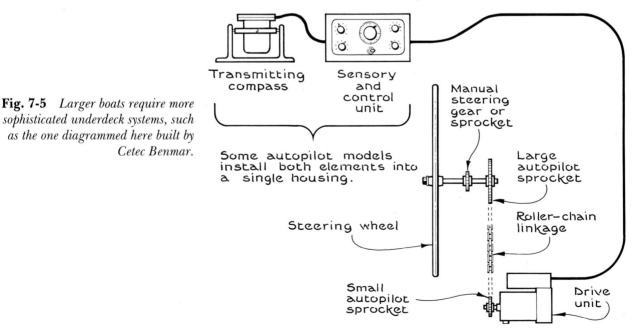

Fig. 7-5 *Larger boats require more sophisticated underdeck systems, such as the one diagrammed here built by Cetec Benmar.*

Transmitting compass

Sensory and control unit

Some autopilot models install both elements into a single housing.

Manual steering gear or sprocket

Large autopilot sprocket

Roller-chain linkage

Steering wheel

Small autopilot sprocket

Drive unit

Fig. 7-6 *Combi Autohelm's "Integrated Rate Pilot" features a linear drive that attaches directly to the rudderstock.*

Both the tiller type and more sophisticated below-deck autopilots can sometimes be fitted with accessory wind vanes so that the boat is electronically kept to a course relative to the wind instead of steering a strict compass course (Figure 7-7). Several BOC competitors, including Phillipe Jeantot and Richard Konkolski, made extensive use of their autopilots when their wind vanes were ineffective (such as in the troughs of high waves). That they never failed is further commendation.

Fig. 7-7 *Some autopilots can be purchased with a wind vane accessory that enables steering a course relative to the wind rather than a magnetic compass course.*

WIND VANES

Mechanical wind vanes do not rely on electrical power. This is a distinct advantage for world cruisers, particularly because in mid-ocean it is not so important to always steer a compass course. In fact, steering a course relative to the wind means fewer trips on deck to trim sails. If you've wandered a few miles south between position fixes, so what? You're still hundreds of miles from your destination.

There are several basic types of wind vanes (Figure 7-8):

A) Vane to rudder (direct to tiller or wheel)
B) Vane to trim tab on rudder
C) Vane to auxiliary rudder
D) Vane to trim tab on auxiliary rudder
E) Vane to servo-pendulum to rudder
F) Vane to servo-pendulum to auxiliary rudder

It is difficult to say that one system is far better than another because different boats vary considerably. Small boats (under 25 feet) for example, may successfully use type A, but owners of large boats find that it often lacks the necessary power.

In many ways, the trim tab attached to the main rudder (B) is excellent—there is no cumbersome and complicated gear mounted on the transom, and there is less water resistance than with the auxiliary rudder type. The problem for owners of old boats is that the trim tab is most easily fitted if it has been designed for the boat from the beginning—i.e., a custom boat. Outboard rudders can accept a trim tab with little difficulty, but inboard rudders present problems. A rudder with a straightline trailing edge can be fitted with a trim tab more easily than one with a round shape. Assuming the trim tab can be fitted, the trim tab shaft must be run up through the hull in a tube glassed inside the hull to the deck where it must link with the wind vane.

David White used such a system on his 56-foot Alan Gurney design, *Gladiator,* his entry in the 1982/3 BOC Challenge. In addition to the vane, he also had an Autohelm autopilot that was equipped with a vane (Figure 7-7).

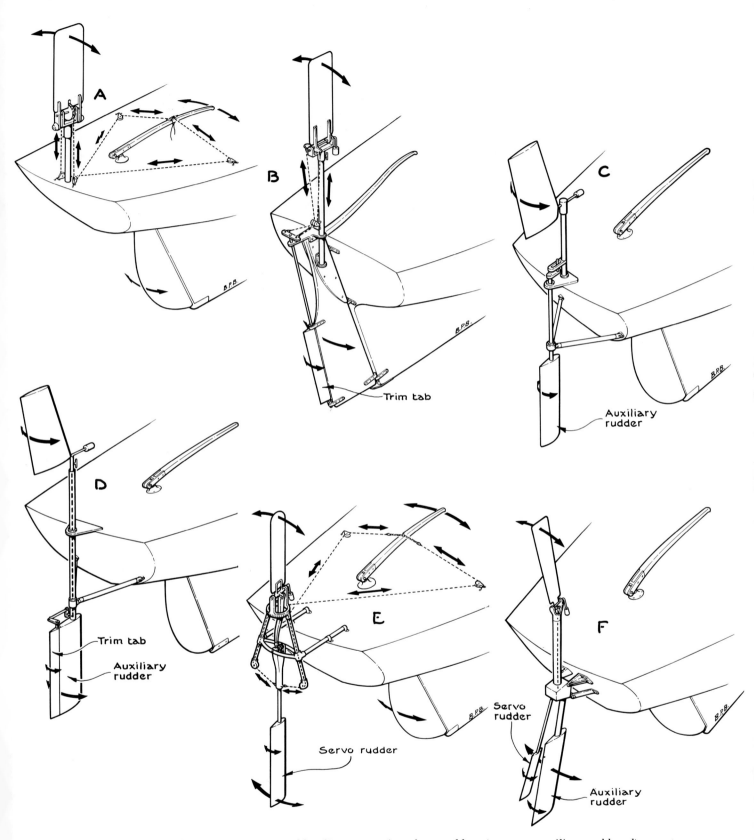

Fig. 7-8 *Types of wind vanes: a) vane to rudder, b) vane to trim tab on rudder, c) vane to auxiliary rudder, d) vane to trim tab on auxiliary rudder, e) vane to servo-pendulum to rudder, f) vane to servo-pendulum to auxiliary rudder.*

Vanes with auxiliary rudders (C,D,F) are quite powerful, especially the latter two, and can be used as backup steering systems (Chapter 6). Servo-pendulum vanes are powerful, too, though the mechanisms are more complicated and cannot be used for emergency steering unless incorporating an auxiliary rudder. Don't confuse the servo-blade for the rudder.

When shopping for an autopilot or wind vane, it is wise to consult with the various manufacturers, other people with similar size and shape boats (your sisterships would be best), and talk to people who have sailed with the vane you're considering.

Wheel steerers with few lock-to-lock turns can be fitted with large drums for those types of vanes connecting to the helm (Figure 7-9). The Atoms, for example, works on wheels with three or less full turns. The Aries (Figure 7-10), Hydrovane (Figure 7-11), and Sailomat (Figure 7-12) are three of the more popular self-steering vanes. More than half of the 1982/3 BOC Challenge entrants had Aries, though some changed to the Australian Fleming gear (also servo-pendulum) on reaching Sydney. Apparently, the heavy weather wreaked havoc with most self-steering gear and sent sailors scrambling for the most robust systems available. Frenchman Guy Bernardin used a Navik and Jacques de Roux had a Sailomat. De Roux ultimately lost his boat

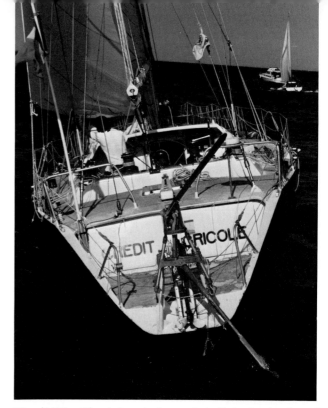

Fig. 7-10 *The Aries wind vane is built in England, and is one of the most popular. The boat is* Credit Agricole, *winner of the BOC Challenge. It is of the servo-pendulum variety with a horizontally pivoted vane (Herb McCormick photo).*

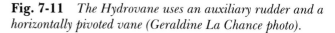

Fig. 7-11 *The Hydrovane uses an auxiliary rudder and a horizontally pivoted vane (Geraldine La Chance photo).*

Fig. 7-9 *The Atoms wind vane can be used with wheel steerers by means of a large pulley bolted to the wheel. It will work with wheels having three or less full turns from hard-to-port to hard-to-starboard.*

Fig. 7-12 *The Sailomat is a Swedish self-steering unit that is unique in that it employs both a servo-pendulum blade and auxiliary rudder.*

in the Southern Ocean, and his rescuer, Richard Broadhead, speculated that the Sailomat may have failed to control the boat as it slid down a large wave. In fairness to all these different models, each performed admirably until the fleet reached the wild and wooly Southern Ocean, where large confused seas imposed tremendous loads on the gear. Most cruisers aren't likely to take their boats within sight of icebergs off Antarctica!

For *Adriana*, I selected a vane of type D, which has an auxiliary rudder with attached trim tab. This Cruising Yacht Systems vane (Figure 7-13) could power a much larger sailboat than my 28-footer. One difference is that all mounting gear is available from local hardware stores, such as galvanized water pipe. Thus, should part of the assembly be damaged in a foreign land, chances are I could repair it myself. Of course, this is not true of the rudderstock and gearing system, but I probably could scrounge up a replacement for the rudder, vane and vane shaft.

Installation

The simplest type of wind vane to install is the vane to rudder (A), which is mounted on the after deck and turns the boat's tiller or wheel by means of lines led through blocks in the cockpit. As with other types, some special brackets may be necessary to securely mount the gear on the deck, which will vary, of course, according to the particular configuration of each boat. The cockpit blocks are straightforward and may be attached to pad eyes thru-bolted to the cockpit coaming.

If you're installing a trim tab on your boat's main rudder (B), be sure to thru-bolt the trim tab gudgeons and pintles or gudgeon hinges, especially if the fiberglass skin of the rudder is too thin to securely receive self-tapping screws.

With auxiliary rudders (C,D,F), the forces are much greater than with the aforementioned types. The auxiliary rudderstock is mounted on the hull by means of a bracket that must be thru-bolted to the transom, preferably with backing plates (plywood, stainless steel, aluminum) between each washer/nut and the hull. There is often some sort of deck support as well and these, too, should be thru-bolted. Bedding compound should be used to seal each bolt hole from moisture. Installation is somewhat simplified since no lines need to be led to the helm in the cockpit.

Servo-pendulum wind vanes (E,F) will mount in essentially the same manner as those with auxiliary rudders, as the servo-blade requires similar support on the transom.

While each manufacturer's installation instructions will vary, they will usually specify that the vane be located as close to the centerline as possible, though distances as much as six inches to one side or the other may be tolerable.

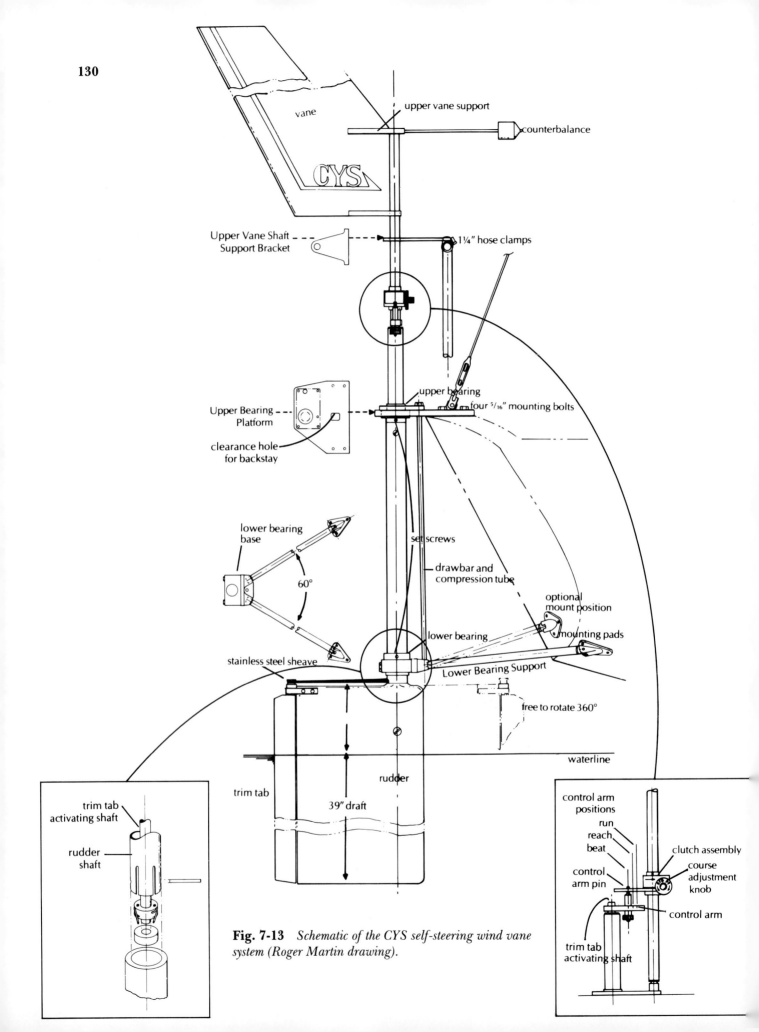

130

vane

CYS

upper vane support

counterbalance

Upper Vane Shaft
Support Bracket

1¼" hose clamps

upper bearing

four ⁵/₁₆" mounting bolts

Upper Bearing
Platform

clearance hole
for backstay

lower bearing
base

set screws

60°

drawbar and
compression tube

optional
mount position

mounting pads

stainless steel sheave

lower bearing

Lower Bearing Support

free to rotate 360°

waterline

trim tab

rudder

39" draft

trim tab
activating shaft

rudder
shaft

control arm
positions

run

reach

beat

control
arm pin

trim tab
activating shaft

clutch assembly

course
adjustment
knob

control arm

Fig. 7-13 *Schematic of the CYS self-steering wind vane
system (Roger Martin drawing).*

Similarly, the vane and auxiliary rudderstock (if there is one) should be as near vertical in the fore and aft axis as possible. If the boat is out of the water and sitting level in its cradle, a plumb can be used to determine the proper rudderstock position. If it is not level, the boot stripe can be extended aft past the transom with a string, and measuring 90 degrees from it, vertical can be established. Slight errors are not likely to be critical.

The vane shaft and rudderstock also should be vertical in the athwartship axis. This is easily determined using measurements from either side of the transom to the rudderstock. When the distance is equal on either side, measured at two separate places on the rudderstock—one higher than the other—the rudderstock is vertical.

WIND VANE ADJUSTMENTS

While wind vanes differ in design and operation, they have several features in common—a clutch to engage and disengage the vane from the steering, and a mechanism for adjustment so that the desired course is achieved. To fine tune the course heading, some units require adjusting the pilot sheets to the helm (Larwyck Monitor), changing the horizontal axis of the vane (Hydrovane), or turning some sort of wheel that changes the relationship of the vane and rudder (Sailomat).

The CYS vane is geared to a trim tab on the auxiliary rudder (Figure 7-14). The geared

Fig. 7-15 *The clutch mechanism on the CYS vane is contained in a Delrin box. When engaged, a geared knob changes the relationship between the vane and auxiliary rudder, and effects a course change.*

clutch changes the indexing of the fork and pin arrangement, ergo the trim tab as well (Figure 7-15).

SELF-STEERING EXPECTATIONS

Before buying, Bob Verhaeghe, builder of the CYS vane, urged me to write down a list of conceptions I had about vanes—how I thought a vane would change my sailing habits. Here's my list:

- Boat will steer the same with vane disengaged
- Vane will weigh down the stern of the boat (*Adriana* is rather fine in the stern)
- Drag will reduce speed
- Vane will get in the way when not in use
- Will take a lot of experience to learn how to use
- Must be disengaged when changing headsails
- Will not work when motoring
- Will have to lash helm
- Will have marginal performance downwind
- Will make even short passages easier

After a few seasons' use, here's what I've found about the accuracy of my list. The boat does not turn quite as easily with the vane disengaged. This is because the vane rudder is farther aft than the boat's rudder, and so a wider

Fig. 7-14 *Trim tab positions as vane corrects course (Roger Martin drawing).*

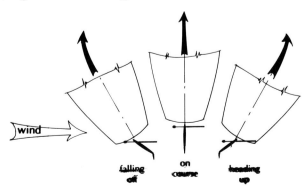

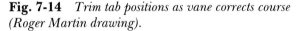

turning arc results. But with the trim tab pinned straight back, motoring is fairly easy.

The vane does not weigh the stern down at all. The rudder has positive buoyancy and the total weight of the entire unit in the water is less than 10 pounds. Boat speed does not seem to be affected. In fact, Bob firmly believes that a vane will require a skipper to better trim his sails, thereby making up for any fraction of a knot lost by increased drag.

The vane has been simple to learn to use and it is a pleasure to have aboard, even on short day sails. When changing headsails, a few turns on the knob in anticipation of the imbalance allows the vane to keep steering until the new sail is set. In tight quarters, it is simply disengaged.

When motoring, with the main up in light air, the vane is sometimes capable of holding a general course.

With my genoa, the tiller need not be lashed; but, with the working jib (*Adriana* has a fractional rig and the jib is quite small) she always has displayed some weather helm and lashing the helm to weather makes the vane steer better (Figure 7-16). Learning to use the vane off the wind is tricky, but it's mostly a matter of gaining experience.

Our first cruise with the CYS self-steering vane was from Newport to Martha's Vineyard (Figure 7-17). We logged about 100 miles over five days, and despite the fact that much of the sailing was between islands, all told we steered the boat by hand for only about 30 minutes. This left time to play games with the kids in the cockpit, go below for a change of clothes or raid the icebox.

Near shore, wind directions do change frequently so attention to course is necessary. But once we got the hang of the adjusting knob, it was a cinch to make course corrections. We found ourselves arriving in port far more rested than on earlier cruises when one person was always shackled to the helm. None of the joy of sailing was lost either; in fact, tweaking lines and playing with the vane satisfied the tinkerer in all of us.

BUYING A VANE

Mechanical wind vanes are not inexpensive, and though more costly than tiller-type autopilots, they may be about the same price as some more sophisticated below-deck autopilots.

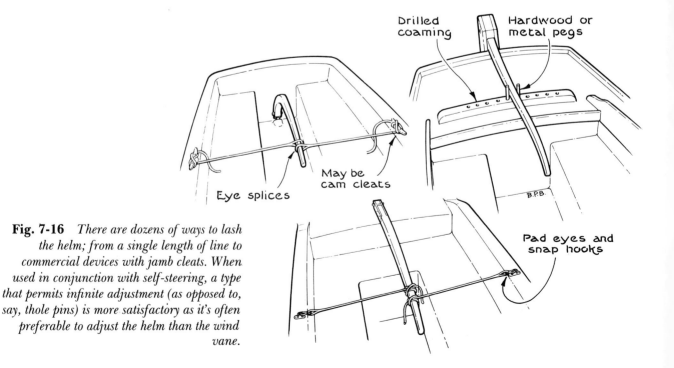

Fig. 7-16 *There are dozens of ways to lash the helm; from a single length of line to commercial devices with jamb cleats. When used in conjunction with self-steering, a type that permits infinite adjustment (as opposed to, say, thole pins) is more satisfactory as it's often preferable to adjust the helm than the wind vane.*

wind vane inoperable. Plus, there is a certain loss in power attributed to the friction of lines to the helm passing through blocks.

Auxiliary rudder wind vanes operate independent of the boat's steering system, and can even be used as an emergency backup steering system. Without a trim tab, however, the auxiliary vane rudder may experience difficulty generating the necessary power to turn the boat's larger main rudder.

With a trim tab on the auxiliary rudder, the vane is only being asked to turn a relatively small surface area, and the tab is only asked to turn a comparatively small auxiliary rudder. This type and the servo-pendulum seem to be the most powerful. Depending on your boat, however, other types may work satisfactorily. Again, consult owners and manufacturers for advice in matching your boat to a suitable steering system.

The unit should be intelligently engineered to withstand forces from any direction—and the sea *can* put a big load on steering gear! Most loads are in the horizontal axis, so sheer strength is more important than compressive strength. Materials should be strong and corrosion-resistant. The design, while seemingly complicated on first impression, should be understandable and repairable by the crew at sea.

Be wary of units with dissimilar metals in direct contact—some corrosion will surely develop.

Other points to consider:

• A removable vane and/or auxiliary rudder is preferable to prevent damage at the dock from other boats. And some models inhibit maneuverability, something you don't want when sailing in harbors.

• Underwater components should be strong and preferably connected to the bracket with sheer pins, or protected by some other means.

• Because different sea states have differing effects on steering, it is desirable to have some method of dampening the rate and amount of correction (a crude version of proportional rate correction in autopilots).

• The vane should disengage quickly so you can manually steer to avoid floating objects and collisions.

Fig. 7-17 *During a week's cruise to Martha's Vineyard, our new vane steered all but about the 30 minutes needed for dropping and hoisting the anchor.*

Therefore, you should carefully evaluate the models available and their suitability to your particular boat.

For moderate to heavy displacement boats, or those with considerable weather helm, it is necessary to fit a powerful vane. Servo-Pendulum types are quite powerful and have been highly favored by many long-distance sailors. The servo-blade amplifies the power of the gearing to the sheets connected to the helm. A disadvantage of the servo-pendulum type is that any failure of the boat's steering system renders the

SUMMARY

Self-steering is not essential, but once you have tried it, you may think it is. Both electronic autopilots and mechanical wind vanes are sophisticated pieces of gear and demand preventive maintenance. Electronic components must be kept dry, and drive motors and linkage should be lubricated per manufacturer's instructions. Under-deck installations should be readily accessible. Mechanical wind vanes should be robustly constructed, especially the mounting supports to the hull. Spare vanes should be carried, or a material such as plywood kept on hand for making new vanes. The well-fit cruiser may well have both electronic and mechanical systems ready for use.

FURTHER READING

Self-Steering for Sailboats by Gerard Dijkstra; Sail Books, 38 Commercial Wharf, Boston, Massachusetts 02110.

Self-Steering for Sailing Craft by John S. Letcher; International Marine Publishing Co., Camden, Maine 04843.

Wind-Vane Self-Steering: How to plan and make your own, by Bill Belcher; International Marine Publishing Co., Camden, Maine 04843.

Self-Steering Without A Windvane by Lee Woas; Seven Seas Press, 524 Thames St., Newport, Rhode Island 02840.

Electrical and Electronic Equipment for Yachts by John French; Dodd, Mead & Company, 79 Madison Ave., New York, New York 10016.

CHAPTER 8

Repowering With Diesel

My experience with engines is that if you depend on them they fail you, but if it just doesn't matter, they serve you.

FRANK WIGHTMAN

There remained only one area of real uncertainty . . . the engine . . . She was massive beyond belief, and intractable beyond bearing . . . According to mythology the virtue of these engines lies in the fact that they are simple and reliable. Although this myth is widely believed I am able to report that it is completely untrue. These engines are, in fact, vindictive, debased, black-minded ladies of no virtue and any non-Newfoundlander who goes shipmate with one is either a fool or a masochist, and is likely both.

FARLEY MOWAT

The powerplant is probably the most blessed and cursed piece of equipment on a small sailboat. Certainly it is the most expensive. It is a little strange that there are mechanically oriented persons who love analyzing how best to jury-rig the replacement of a broken gooseneck, but who can't tune an engine to save their lives. There are obvious advantages in being competent to perform basic maintenance functions—lower cost, freedom from the incompetencies of the local yard, and safety if and when your skills are called upon in a critical situation.

Engines are indeed wonderful when they work properly, and absolutely dreadful when they don't. My thinking is that if I'm going to rely on an engine, I'd better be able to *rely* on it. This requires performing routine maintenance and making basic repairs. And it means owning the simplest engine possible. A diesel is the answer. Before describing *Adriana's* conversion from gas to diesel, let's consider the alternatives.

GASOLINE ENGINES

Until recently, almost all mid-size yachts were fitted with gasoline engines. U.S. Coast Guard regulations required venting the bilge, bilge blowers, spark arrestors and so forth. The Atomic 4 in my boat was a good engine, and tuning it was no more difficult than changing the plugs, points, condensor and setting the timing of the family car. A few tools and an hour with a knowledgeable friend were all that was really needed to learn how.

Tales of yachts blowing up have a tendency to scare people into choosing diesel power rather than helping them make a rational choice. There are advantages to gas engines. They are less expensive; they accelerate faster; and it is sometimes easier to find a mechanic who will work on them.

EMERGENCE OF THE SMALL DIESEL

During the past five years or so, most boat-builders have switched to diesel. The reasons are twofold: New Coast Guard regulations added to the list of required safety gear and thus to the cost of the gas-powered boat; and the availability of smaller, lightweight, competitively priced diesels suitable for small sailboats (Figure 8-1).

The advantages of small diesels are many. Diesel fuel will not ignite even if a match is touched to it. Because diesels do not have spark plugs and points and distributors—compression, not electricity is used to combust the fuel—batteries are not required except for electric starting. A good number of diesels may be started by hand, including my 12-hp. BMW. The confidence this gives is considerable. An added bonus is diesels burn fuel at a slower rate than gas engines, so the equivalent tank of fuel will give extra hours of motoring. A curious fact about diesels is they burn 12,000 times more air than fuel—a much higher ratio than gasoline engines. In a poorly ventilated compartment, they can literally asphyxiate themselves, something to consider when switching power plants.

The decision to repower with diesel is certainly a significant one—it will cost time and money, but if you have great plans for your boat, you probably will be glad that you did so.

Fig. 8-1 *The BMW D-12 diesel is typical of many of the new lightweight, high-revving, inexpensive engines available on today's market. The D-12 weighs 229 pounds and can be hand-started (BMW of North America).*

ITEMIZATION OF MAN-HOURS AND EXPENSES

Man-Hours

Activity:	Hours:
Measurements	4
Remove old engine and clean area	14
Remove old bed and install new bed	30
Install and test new engine	48
Total	96

Expenses

Item:	Cost:
Yard bill (removing old engine from hull with tractor and lowering new engine into cockpit)	$36.00
Tools (crowbar, saber saw blades, copper wire, sanding belts and hacksaw)	33.95
Control cables	40.44
Battery cables and end fittings	19.24
Fuel tank fittings and fuel line hose	23.46
Waterline hose	8.50
Clamps for hoses and wires	7.49
Screws, bolts and washers	18.47
Fiberglass mat, resin, rags, brushes and acetone	50.04
Paint	7.65
Exhaust hose	40.38
Miscellaneous (bilge degreaser, caulking compound, etc.)	14.90
Total	$300.52

Engine Costs

Item:	Cost:
BMW D-12 engine	$3,089.00
Fiberglass engine bed	154.50
Controls (handle and mechanism)	46.05
Shut-off cable	28.92
Instrument wiring extension	21.64
Waterlock muffler	28.94
Vacuum valve	14.47
Seawater filter	31.06
Shaft coupling	66.15
Propeller shaft	78.44
Total	$3,559.17
Expenses	300.52
Total Costs	$3,859.69

GOING ENGINELESS

Engineless boats are not so uncommon as you might think (Figure 8-2). Garry Hoyt built the first Freedom 40 without an engine, and amazed observers in the Caribbean by tacking the cat ketch in and out of moorings under sail, alone, to prove the worthiness of his boat and rig.

Lin and Larry Pardey sailed around the world

Fig. 8-2 *The fellow pictured here I spotted while standing on the pier at Opua in New Zealand's Bay of Islands. The wind had died and he was determined to make the pier before dark. A sculling oar is an alternative to these sweeps.*

without an engine. They used sweeps from the cockpit or sculled with a stern oar when there was no wind and when they had to maneuver in tight quarters. Even in their new 30-footer, they say an engine will never dirty the hull.

Danny Greene, an associate editor of *Cruising World,* has lived aboard his 26-foot cutter, *Frolic,* for six years making migrational passages to the Caribbean and back to Newport each year— about 30,000 miles without an engine. The amount of additional storage space under the cockpit is considerable, which was enhanced by cutting out the footwell to avoid being swamped by breaking seas (see Chapter 9). Now the after end of the boat is like an extra room. On a small boat, there is never enough stowage space, especially for Danny, who carries numerous tools, a portable Honda generator, jerry jugs of water, etc.

On the down side, Danny is often forced to sail non-stop from Newport to some place like St. Martin, because most of the seaports along the East Coast have narrow channels, which he feels are too risky to try entering without auxiliary power. An outboard motor mounted on a transom bracket could be used for such occasions when there is little wind or foul tide. The Pardeys did just this with *Seraffyn* when they

transited the Panama Canal, where regulations require that vessels be able to sustain five knots.

Another alternative is to equip the boat's tender with an outboard and by lashing it alongside, maneuver the boat through channels and crowded moorings. This is the practice of some large sailing ships, such as the 125-foot *Bill of Rights,* which charters out of Newport and uses her yawl boat inside the harbor.

REPOWERING *ADRIANA*

My Atomic 4 gas engine, the same 30-hp. fire breather that has been fitted to thousands of other sailboats during the past two decades, was a trusty piece of machinery.

Parting with her was difficult.

But the day came when the end of her useful life was in sight. One of the new, lightweight, economical diesels was the logical choice for repowering *Adriana.*

European, Japanese and American engine manufacturers—Perkins, Westerbeke, Bukh, Volvo Penta, Yanmar and Universal to name a few—offer complete ranges of diesels, from 7-hp. one-lungers to powerful three, four and six-cylinder power plants for the large motorsailer. Eventually I settled on a 12-hp. BMW.

Tools required for installation are surprisingly few and only the drill, sander and saber saw are power. Screwdrivers, hammer, crowbar, hacksaw and others are of the kitchen-drawer variety. The BMW came with a small set of metric wrenches but so few are necessary that they wouldn't be expensive to purchase.

Completing the project, from the moment the first old wire was ripped out to the satisfying moment when the new engine turned over for the first time, required 96 man-hours of labor and about $300 in expenses over and above the cost of the engine and associated parts. A bruised knuckle produced a curse from time to time but on the whole it was a fun project, which gave me the satisfaction of knowing just how everything fits together.

On reflection, the complexity of the task was less than had been imagined, and it is a project within the skill levels of most household handymen.

Pulling the Old Engine

The first step in converting from gas to diesel power is to get rid of the old engine. Naively, I carefully unhooked each wire that led to the engine and labeled it accordingly, i.e., to solenoid, alternator, coil and so forth. This proved to be unnecessary as some of these items do not exist on diesels. On most of the new diesels, a wiring harness plugs into the back of the engine on one end, and into the back of the ignition panel on the other. This is simplicity itself, and one look at the apparatus will dispel any fears of having to rig a maze of new wires to make the engine run.

The engine compartment on the Triton is cramped (Figure 8-3). So, in order to lift the Atomic 4 from its bed, the alternator had to be removed, as well as the voltage regulator on the adjacent bulkhead. All hoses were removed, including the freshwater line to the exhaust, the return line to the thermostat and to the water pump. The transmission linkage, which on the Triton is an archaic contraption with a formidable shift lever inserted through a deck plate on the cockpit floor, also came out. It later would be replaced by a neat, single-lever control mounted on the starboard side of the cockpit footwell.

The copper, water-jacketed exhaust pipe was disconnected from the exhaust manifold at the back of the engine. Though it is one of the best

Fig. 8-3 *There wasn't much room to work on the Universal Atomic 4 gasoline engine in* Adriana. *Rebuilt once with a new short block and head, it was a good engine that required only periodic tuning and oil changes.*

systems available, it was now dispensible. Besides, it weighed about 40 pounds and placed too much weight in the stern of the boat. Its eight-foot length of curves and twists made it too ungainly to remove without first cutting it in half with a cold chisel. Bob Dobbins, a fellow Triton owner at the Bristol yard, also was repowering with a small Universal diesel. Together we carted off our old exhaust systems to a local metals dealer who paid 65¢ a pound for the copper. Every off-setting penny helps.

The throttle and choke cables unhooked from the engine with a few small bolts and the gas line and oil pressure gauge line came off with one nut each. All the existing instruments were located in the cockpit along with the throttle lever and, when these were removed, there were some unsightly holes. However, the new ignition and instrument panel, mounted on a teak board, nicely covered the lot.

The last item to be disconnected before the engine could be pulled was the propeller shaft coupling.

Here I made a messy mistake.

Peering in through the deck plate in the cockpit floor, it was difficult to see which set of bolts held the engine and shaft couplings together. One set was frozen so I removed four bolts closer to the engine. Later, when the mounting bolts had been removed and the engine still would not budge it became apparent that the frozen bolts would have to be dealt with. Brian Paiva, one of the yard hands, rotated the propeller to the most advantageous position so I could finagle a breaker bar in the cramped quarters behind the engine and beneath the cockpit. Soon, the shaft was disconnected in the proper place and the engine was ready to come out.

A six-inch by six-inch piece of oak used for making cradles was positioned horizontally over the companionway hatch and a chain fall led from the cross-bar to the lifting eye on top of the engine (Figure 8-4). Old blankets were placed along the sill of the bridge to prevent the chain from chewing up the teak. It all made the area look as though it were dressed for surgery. And indeed it was. The transplant was about to begin!

Brian, who handled the chain fall (Figure 8-5), asked if everything had been disconnected. I assured him that there was nothing left to do.

Fig. 8-4 *To lift the old engine out of the boat, we placed a fence post over the companionway hatch and used a chain fall to lift the 310 pounds of steel and iron high enough to swing into the cockpit.*

But a few pulls on the chain, which lifted the engine off its bed and allowed it to swing forward, revealed I had forgotten to unhook the water temperature gauge.

Then we decided that removing the starter motor and solenoid would increase clearance and prevent scraping the woodwork. The engine was hoisted high enough to clear the bridge, and with one person guiding the engine and two others lifting either end of the wood crossbar, the old Atomic 4 was set on the cockpit seat. The bolts I had incorrectly loosened were to the rear transmission housing, and a quart of tired grease slurped out onto the cockpit floor.

The chain was then transferred to the yard's

Fig. 8-5 *The Atomic 4, like most engines, has a lifting eye to connect the chain.*

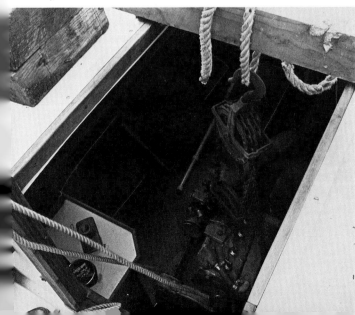

Fig. 8-6 *Brian Paiva used the yard's front-end loader to lift the Atomic 4 off* Adriana's *deck. The engine was later sold and word from the new owner is that it still runs smoothly.*

front-end loader (Figure 8-6), which lifted her off the boat.

It seemed a small and forlorn thing, this mighty mite that had powered *Adriana* through gales on Green Bay, into sheltered coves in Lake Huron's North Channel and had done most of the work in moving her through the Trent-Severn Waterway and the New York State Barge Canal en route from Lake Michigan to Newport, Rhode Island. After several days sitting on the floor of the yard's shed, she was cruelly sold for a sum sufficient to pay for yard bills and the cost of supplies to complete the installation of the new BMW diesel.

Fourteen years' worth of grease, oil, gunk and other bilge atrocities were ground into the hull in and around the engine compartment. The next task was to clean it up. A good quality bilge soap with the ability to emulsify helped greatly.

When the engine compartment is empty is an excellent time to install sea cocks for the cockpit scuppers and other thru-hull fittings if this hasn't already been done. You'll seldom have such good access to the under-cockpit area (see Chapter 4).

Installing the Bed

BMW offers a molded fiberglass engine bed that can be cut to fit almost any hull. It seemed to make more sense to use this than attempt to modify the old engine bed. Besides, the width of the old bed was too narrow to accept the new engine. Alternatively, stout wood beds can be glassed to the hull.

Bob Dobbins discovered that his new Universal diesel could be adapted to the old engine bed by bolting two pieces of custom-welded stainless steel plate on top of the bed flanges.

The Atomic 4 engine bed consisted of two vertical thick pieces of fiberglass glassed to the hull; a flange on top accepted the engine mounting bolts. Most of the two beds were easily cut away with a saber saw and what was left was hammered and pried off with a crowbar. This was perhaps the most physically demanding job of the entire project, but as one helper kept saying, "It's not a matter of *if* it will come, just when."

"When" turned out to be later than expected, but after a few hours the last globs of resin were ground off with a belt sander. The belt sander, equipped with aluminum oxide paper, was also the best tool to thoroughly clean up the area on the hull where the new bed would be glassed in. A good mask and goggles are required safety gear.

The most important part of any power plant conversion is making the new bed line up with the propeller shaft. Like most engines, the BMW diesel comes with heavy rubber mounts that adjust vertically about four inches. There also is some allowance to move the engine athwartships, but not much. Therefore, it's critical that the new engine bed be installed within the limits of these adjustments.

Fortunately, I was shown a simple method of accomplishing this seemingly impossible task. The engine bed is a glass box and the hull has numerous, complex curves. Making the two fit is, until I learned this trick, an intimidating proposition. Here's how it works:

Remove the propeller shaft. My shaft coupling was virtually amalgamated with the shaft, so it was necessary to remove the propeller first and then pull the shaft out inside the hull. Buy a coil of pliable copper or stainless steel wire and run it through the stuffing box, hull and cutlass bearing outside to the propeller aperture. Wrap the end around a screwdriver, stick or nail and by eye position the wire so that it is in the center of the cutlass bearing. The end of the wire coming inside the boat should then be made fast to

Fig. 8-7 *Once the Atomic 4 was removed, the old fiberglass engine beds were cut off with a saber saw and then ground flush with the hull using a belt sander. The alignment wire used to position the new bed is visible exiting from the stuffing box.*

some point in the cabin so that the wire is taut and in the center of the stuffing box (Figure 8-7). What you've done, in effect, is to extend the line of the propeller shaft over the engine bed. This becomes the all-important reference for lining up the engine bed.

The next step was to cut the fiberglass engine bed in such a manner that it would rest in the hull at the same angle as the wire, and at an elevation that would permit the engine-half coupling to be bolted to the shaft-half coupling. The critical measurement here, obtainable from the manufacturer's spec sheet (Figure 8-8), is the distance between the center of the engine-half coupling and the bottom of the rubber engine mount—2.44 inches on the BMW D-12. The top of the bed, then, should be 2.44 inches below the wire.

In taking my measurements, however, I planned to keep the bed an inch or so low, to achieve a perfect alignment by adjusting the engine mount bolts upward. Since the mount bolts had four inches of play, three inches of reserve space were left in the event of a measuring error.

This is an appropriate point to mention the Scatra CVA System (Figure 8-9), which connects the engine to the propeller shaft. Two constant velocity joints and a thrust bearing permit a misalignment of up to 16 degrees. Periodic realignment isn't necessary, and much softer than

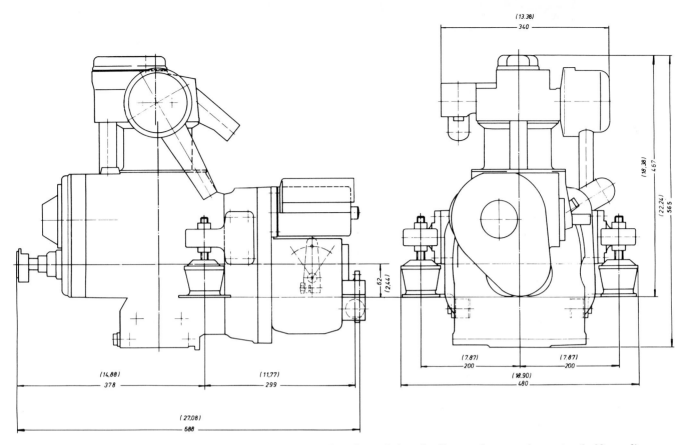

Fig. 8-8   *This spec sheet for the BMW D-12 was essential in determining the distance between the engine-half coupling and the bottom of the rubber engine mount—2.44 inches (BMW of North America).*

normal engine mounts can be used to reduce vibration and engine noise.

The BMW engine bed is essentially a rectangular fiberglass box and, normally, the easiest way to cut it to the shape of the hull is to put it in place and scribe a line along each side with a compass or pencil held to a piece of wood that

Fig. 8-9   *The Scatra CVA System incorporates two constant velocity joints (similar to those used on the front ends of cars with front-wheel drive) and a thrust bearing to provide a flexible coupling between the engine and prop shaft. Vibration and noise are reduced (Aqua Drive Inc.).*

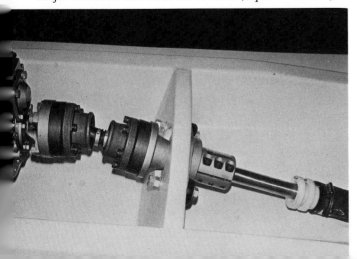

transfer the line of the hull onto the box. (See Chapter 9, "Making a Seahood", for details.) Unfortunately, the engine compartment in the Pearson Triton and many other boats is too narrow to do this accurately. The alternative is to cut and test, cut and test, until it's right.

Obviously, a conservative and patient approach will prevent whacking off too much, necessitating the purchase of another bed. Figures 8-10 and 8-11 show the final shape of the bed for the Triton. One will note that the side cuts are straighter than the lines of the hull. However, a small space between the two is not really that significant so long as it rests firmly on all four corners. The true strength of the installation relies upon fiberglassing the bed to the hull, which, of course, will cover any gaps.

Once the final shape was achieved, all surfaces on the bed that were to be bonded were sanded with a belt sander to remove the gel coat and any remaining dirt or oil.

The engine bed was now ready to be installed, but before doing so, the engine was placed on the bed in the cockpit in a mock-up installation

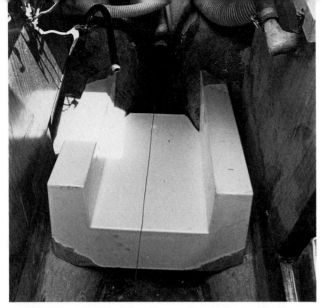

Fig. 8-10 *The new fiberglass engine bed, supplied by BMW, was set in place and carefully aligned with the wire. Cutting the box to the correct shape was a trial and error effort.*

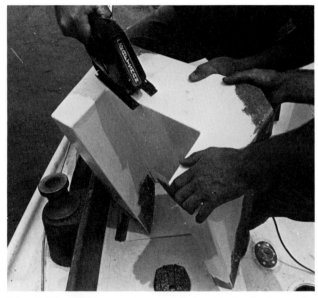

Fig. 8-11 *Here, an aperture is being cut in the front of the engine bed to permit inserting the mount bolts from inside.*

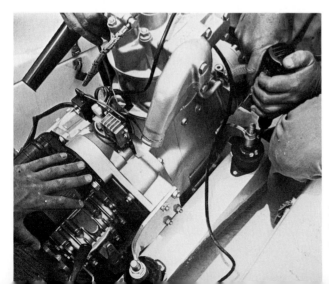

(Figure 8-12). This enabled me to drill the holes in the bed to accept the mounting bolts. Then, ⅜-inch bolts (the engine manufacturer will specify the correct size) were run through the holes from the underside and held in place with one nut on the topside. This made it unnecessary to drill the holes with the bed in the boat while holding the engine in place and with little room to work.

Again, measurement is the secret.

A careful study of the engine's dimensions and of the distance between the bed and reference wire on the vertical axis and engine bed and shaft coupling on the horizontal axis, should provide the figures needed to determine the proper location of the bolt holes.

One decision was made early on that saved a great deal of trouble, but which costs a bit more: a new propeller shaft whose length was determined by the final fore and aft location of the engine. Had I elected to keep the old shaft, it would have been critical to drill the mounting bolt holes the precise distance from the shaft-half coupling. The decision to buy a new shaft was prompted not only by the ease of installation, but also because the old shaft was worn around the stuffing box and packing gland, and this seemed the opportune replacement time.

So, only two measurements were of importance, rather than three: The bed and holes were positioned with attention to the centerline of the shaft, and with the vertical elevation of the shaft couplings; fore and aft distance was no longer an important consideration. As a result, we let the new engine protrude a few inches further into the cabin than the old one, but this meant only minor changes in the boards that cover the engine compartment. As it turned out, this prompted me to enlarge the counter space around the galley, something I had wanted to do for many years.

Now, the engine was set aside and the bed put in place inside the hull. Strips of fiberglass mat were cut, measuring about three inches by six inches, saturated with resin and placed over the four corners of the bed. It's helpful to have someone else around during this task—one person to prepare the mat and the other to tack them in place. We left the boat while these four

Fig. 8-12 *Before glassing the bed in place, the engine was set onto it in the cockpit so that holes for the mount bolts could be pre-drilled.*

Fig. 8-13 *With the bed glassed in place and the engine loosely bolted to it, the heavy work was completed.*

strips cured so as not to jiggle the bed out of alignment.

Sitting on the dock or in a local pub waiting for the resin to cure was the easiest part of this entire project and certainly the most fun. But after an hour or two I was anxious to get back to work.

The bed was glassed on all four sides, inside and out. Two square yards of mat and three quarts of resin were used, as well as half a dozen cheap, disposable brushes, stirring rods and a pair of scissors. A quart of acetone also was used to clean the hull and bed before fiberglassing and to remove the sticky resin from our hands.

That evening, before punching out, we placed the shiny, silver BMW onto its bed (Figure 8-13). The bolts, naturally, lined up perfectly with the engine mounts, and for the first time I could actually see how it looked in its new home. With a stick of wood and a little muscle, we lifted first the fore and then the aft engine mounts off the bolts, removed the nut on each (careful not to let a bolt drop into the bilge), and then set the engine down flush on the bed. Double nuts were then loosely fastened to each bolt.

Ancillary Hook-Ups

Once the engine is bolted to its beds, the ancillary hook-ups should be completed before launching. Final alignment of the engine to the shaft should be done in the water as all boats, even those constructed in heavy fiberglass, will change shape from the cradle to the water.

The immediate tasks are to install fuel lines, water hoses and exhaust, ignition wiring and throttle and transmission controls.

• Ignition and wiring harness—the new ignition panel can be mounted on a teak plate and placed over the holes left by the old instruments in the cockpit, or mounted inside the cabin in the main switchboard (Figure 8-14). Connecting the wiring harness on the BMW simply involved snapping one end into the back of the engine and the other into the rear side of the ignition and instrument panel. New battery cables may be necessary if the distance from the engine to the batteries is increased. Solder the terminal fittings to the ends of the cables—the same gauge terminals used on cars.

• Throttle and gear shift—Single-lever throttle and transmission controls can be mounted in the

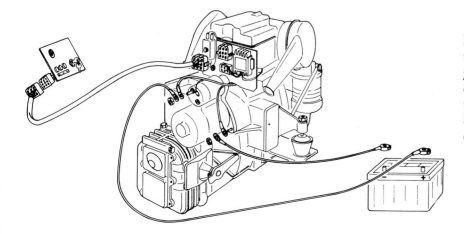

Fig. 8-14 *This schematic shows the wiring harness, which snaps into a panel on the backside of the engine, and includes the ignition and engine warning lights; and it shows where the battery cables lead. Very simple! (BMW of North America).*

Fig. 8-15 *The single-lever throttle and transmission controls mounted neatly in the footwell of the cockpit. A template provided by BMW made it easy to cut out the correct shape with a saber saw.*

same spot as the old throttle lever (Figures 8-15, 16), or a new site if it suits you better. Two control cables are fastened to the control plate linkage, led fair to the linkage on the engine, adjusted and fastened tight. One need only be certain that no sharp bends occur in the cables that might hamper movement of the inner wire in its sheath, and that the nut and barrel on each end be adjusted so that the gears, both forward, neutral and reverse, engage positively, and that full throttle on the lever corresponds with full open position on the engine throttle lever.

• Cooling system—The old seawater intake can be used to feed the new engine's cooling system.

Fig. 8-16 *The finished installation of the engine controls shows the teak plate, which covered the unsightly holes left by the old instruments.*

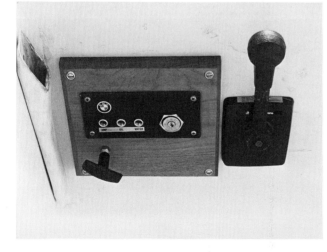

Even if the new engine is freshwater cooled, you'll still need seawater to cool the fresh water via the heat exchanger. You should take the trouble to replace the hose from the sea cock and thru-hull, as well as the hose clamps if they're at all corroded or difficult to loosen and tighten.

Run a length of reinforced heater hose from the intake sea cock to the suction side of the water pump. Then run a length from the other side of the pump to a vacuum release valve mounted well above the waterline, perhaps on the backside of a bulkhead, and then to a fitting on the exhaust manifold. This prevents water from siphoning through the line into the engine. On the BMW, water is introduced into the exhaust system inside the engine so no fancy or difficult plumbing is necessary. But some engines introduce the water into the exhaust at a fitting on the exhaust manifold, and extra hose and fittings may be required. Anchor all hoses with cable mounts to either existing bulkheads or tied off to existing wires or hosing in the engine compartment.

Small diesel exhaust systems (Figure 8-17) may consist of reinforced radiator-type hose run from the exhaust outlet on the engine to a plastic water lift muffler (mine was made by Vetus, a Dutch company), and then run to the exhaust tube in the transom.

The position of the water lift muffler is important; it should be mounted as low as possible to the rear of the engine so that when the engine is turned off, water in the hose extending from the muffler to the exhaust tube on the transom does not exceed the capacity of the muffler and thus enter the engine. Measure their respective capacities to be sure—an in-line valve (Figure 8-17) is smart insurance. With or without a valve, the hose should be looped as high as possible to the underside of the deck before coming down and fastening to the exhaust tube. An additional "silencer" further quiets the exhaust.

• Fuel lines—Diesels require a return fuel line (Figure 8-18) from the injection pump back to the tank. This line must not enter the tank too close to the feed line, as returning fuel is hot and should not be continually recycled. Also, drilling into an old tank to insert a fitting is a dangerous business, and even when the tank has been

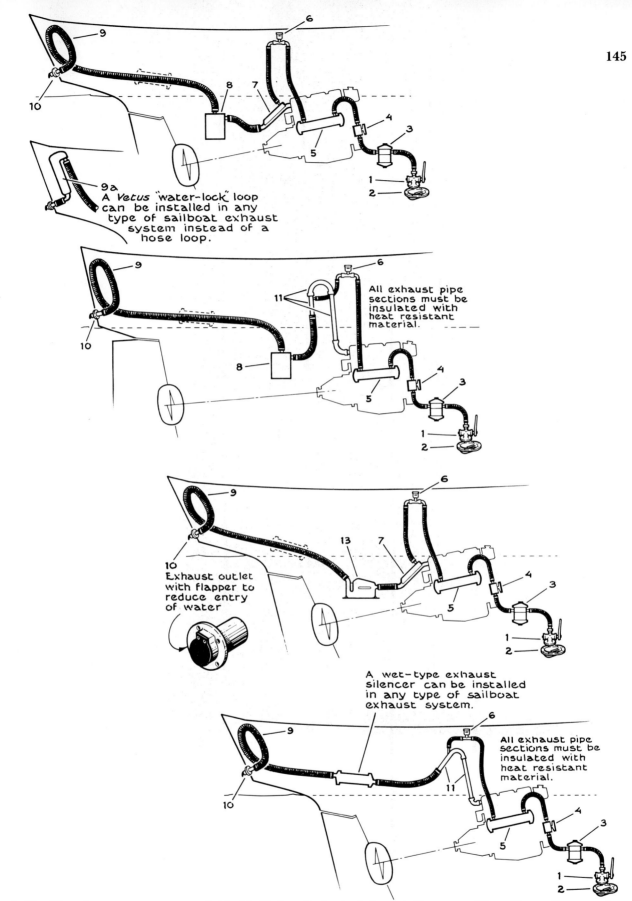

Fig. 8-17 *The exhaust system recommended by W. H. Den Ouden includes their Vetus waterlift muffler, a silencer and a waterlock goose neck at the transom to prevent water from entering the engine through the exhaust hose. Other systems also are shown for other types of engines. 1—thru-hull strainer, 2—sea cock, 3—in-line "clearable" strainer, 4—raw-water pump, 5—heat exchanger, 6—vented anti-siphon loop, 7—water injection exhaust elbow, 8—waterlift, 9—high loop in exhaust hose, 10—transom exhaust fitting, 11—high-dry metal exhaust pipe with insulated water injector on down side.*

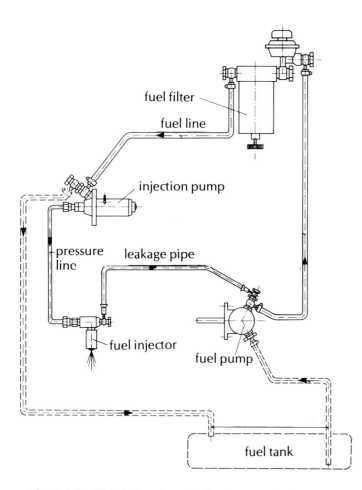

Fig. 8-19 *The old tank vent fitting was modified to accommodate the return fuel line from the engine, which enters from the left.*

Fig. 8-18 *This is the schematic for the D-12 fuel line system. Note that, unlike a gasoline engine, diesels require a return line to the tank for unused fuel (BMW of North America).*

professionally purged, many are loathe to risk a spark igniting any residual fumes. The easy solution is to replace the vent line fitting with a T-fitting using one end for the return fuel line and the other for the vent. If you can't find one that will fit the threads on your tank, a small radiator repair shop can drill a hole in one side of the old fitting and solder a barbed nipple to it (Figure 8-19).

• Shaft and propeller—Before launching, install the new shaft and propeller. The distance between the engine-half coupling and end of the cutlass bearing in the stern tube should be measured. Most prop shops use dimensions calculated to the SET or small end of taper.

Before installing the new shaft, it seems prudent to replace the cutlass bearing and flax in the packing nut at the stuffing box. One might also consider fitting a flexible synthetic coupling between the engine and shaft, such as the Drive Saver by Globe Rubber Works (figure 8-20).

Fig. 8-20 *The "Driver Saver" is a synthetic spacer inserted between the shaft and engine coupling to prevent stray electrical currents in the water from causing corrosion in the engine. It also smooths out any slight misalignment of the engine and shaft (Globe Rubber Works, Inc.).*

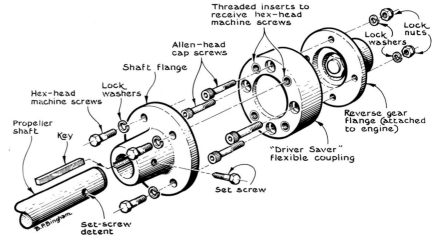

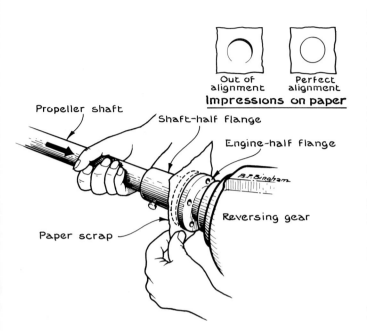

Impressions on paper

Out of alignment

Perfect alignment

Propeller shaft

Shaft-half flange

Engine-half flange

B.P.Bingham

Reversing gear

Paper scrap

Fig. 8-21 *The engine-half and shaft-half couplings should kiss simultaneously to assure proper alignment between engine and propeller shaft. Rotating the shaft by hand with a piece of paper in between will reveal if any part of the two surfaces are touching.*

This coupling reduces vibration and noise, and more importantly, prevents stray electrical currents in the water from causing corrosion in the engine. Most new diesels are fitted with sacrificial zincs, but it's nice knowing you have double security. Be sure to account for the width of this spacer when measuring the length of the shaft.

• Launch and alignment—With one person in the cabin adjusting the mounting bolts, another should position himself under the cockpit where he can see the coupling and call out instructions to raise or lower. By rotating the shaft with your hand, you can see where the two coupling halves begin to kiss one another. When all four coupling flanges barely touch is a near-perfect alignment. Hunker down on the engine mounting bolts so that nothing can vibrate out of place. While a feeler gauge is the traditional method, an easier way is to insert a piece of paper between the two couplings and study the imprints and grease markings for uniformity (Figure 8-21).

When the engine is started, check hoses for leaks and the engine bed for vibration.

HOW MANY HORSES?

Tom Colvin, a naval architect with a good many blue-water miles beneath his keel, suggests half a horsepower per long ton (2,240 pounds) for an ocean-cruising sailboat. The thinking here is that such a craft will use the engine primarily for recharging batteries, maneuvering among moorings, and occasionally motoring through doldrums. For a coastwise cruising sailboat, which may find itself powering against foul tides or racing darkness to make port, one horsepower per ton of displacement is recommended. Colvin's horsepower recommendations for various boats is given in Figure 8-22.

A contrasting opinion belongs to Ron Holland, a naval architect most noted for his racing

Fig. 8-22 *Tom Colvin's chart from* Cruising As A Way of Life *for maximum usable horsepower according to waterline length and displacement.*

| Waterline | Tons | Speed in Knots at | | | Maximum Usable | |
		10 HP	**15 HP**	**20 HP**	**Horsepower**	**Maximum Speed**
30 FT	5	6.70	7.30	—	16.2	7.3
	10	5.60	6.15	6.60	35	7.3
	15	5.00	5.50	5.90	58	7.3
35 FT	10	6.05	6.70	7.10	35	7.9
	15	5.35	5.90	6.40	58	7.9
	20	5.00	5.45	5.85	81	7.9
40 FT	15	5.75	6.35	6.80	58	8.45
	20	5.35	5.85	6.25	81	8.45
	25	5.05	5.55	5.85	105	8.45

designs. His ideal cruiser has a stronger engine, he said, because "it helps you achieve more because you aren't so reliant on the wind." While hull shape is certainly a factor, it's interesting that many production yards (presumably building coastal cruisers) fit engines with four to five horsepower per long ton.

FUEL CAPACITY

Colvin says 40 hours of smooth-water powering is adequate for most boats; 20 hours for ocean cruising craft. He further suggests purchasing a slow-revving diesel capable of being hand-started. Such an engine can be fitted with a large prop that will give the necessary push when the weather blows up. Of course, this causes more drag than a small propeller, but as he says, "choose an engine with a few big horses—not one with lots of little ponies."

Naval architect Roger Marshall suggests that fuel tankage hold an amount equal to three or four percent of total displacement—450 to 600 pounds for a 15,000-pound boat, or 60 to 80 gallons (7.5 gallons per pound).

PROPELLER SELECTION

Choosing the right propeller for a given boat and engine makes all the difference in performance and fuel efficiency. There are so many variables affecting correct pitch and size that scientific selection is difficult for the average person.

Propeller sizes are given in a pair of numbers, such as 13 x 9, or 12 x 8. The first number refers to the diameter of the blades in inches. The second refers to the pitch, or angle of the blades, and is the number of inches the prop theoretically should move forward with one revolution (Figure 8-23). The greater the pitch, the bigger the "bite" the prop takes.

Many engines have reduction gears to the propeller shaft. A 2:1 reduction gear means that the engine is always turning twice as fast as the prop shaft. An engine with 2:1 reduction gear would use a larger prop than one with direct drive. The

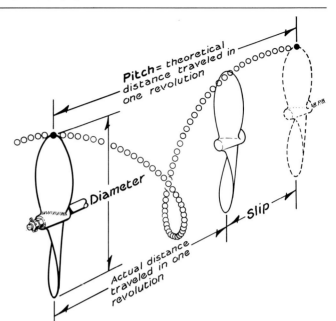

Fig. 8-23 *Propellers are referred to by two numbers. The first number indicates the diameter in inches; the second indicates the pitch, which is the theoretical number of inches the prop will move in one revolution through solid matter.*

smaller size for direct drive is necessary because, though the prop turns faster, there is less torque to keep it turning under load.

Racing sailboats use folding and feathering props to minimize drag while sailing. Folding props have blades that collapse backwards to form a small cone; feathering props have blades that change pitch to a horizontal position so that the least surface possible is exposed to the passing water. Studies by Michigan Wheel Company on drag tests indicate that fixed two-blade props locked in the vertical position offer about 15 to 20-percent more resistance than feathering two-blade props. While this evidence is compelling, sometimes these props don't like to open correctly. The cruising sailor who wishes to avoid as many repairs as possible may find the fixed-blade prop the wisest choice.

For the cruising sailor, it is less a decision and more a matter of personal inclination whether to power to windward or accept what Neptune delivers and do the best under sail alone. To effectively motorsail in heavy seas, a large propeller with high pitch coupled with reduction gear is the best combination. But the increased drag exacts a price in sailing performance.

There is a choice to be made between two and

Fig. 8-24 *A variable-pitch prop allows adjustment under way for varying sea states.*

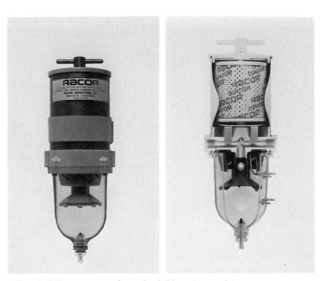

Fig. 8-25 *A secondary fuel filter is good insurance against dirty fuel clogging injectors. This one is made by Racor and features a glass bowl for visual inspection and a petcock to drain off water and other contaminants (Racor Industries).*

three-bladed props as well. The two-bladed prop will give about five to 10 percent more speed than the three-bladed prop under sail, though the latter is slightly more fuel efficient under power and vibrates less. When converting from three blades to two, it is unusual to increase the diameter.

Variable pitch propellers (Figure 8-24), have much to recommend them in that the pitch can be adjusted for different speeds and sea conditions, depending on the torque required.

When repowering with a new engine, it is probable that the old prop will work just fine. To find out, unfortunately, the boat must be in the water. Run with the engine in perfect running order, put it at full throttle with all gear on board and watch the tachometer. At full speed the tach should reach the engine's rated maximum rpm. If the engine fails to achieve the rated rpm, the prop may be too large or the pitch too great. Conversely, if the engine turns too fast, the prop is too small or the pitch too little. Most prop shops have "loaners" that they'll let you use to find the correct "wheel" for your boat. Their expertise will significantly decrease the time you spend in trial and error matchmaking.

FILTERS

The BMW D-12 came equipped with a top-quality fuel filter. This is one of the most important pieces of equipment on your diesel because dirty fuel clogs the injectors and is the most com-

mon cause of poor performance or engine failure.

It makes sense to add a secondary fuel filter. Fram makes excellent marine filters that remove all water and all solid contaminants down to one micron in diameter. Racor also makes an excellent filter (Figure 8-25), which has a glass bowl enabling visual inspection, and a petcock at the base to drain off water and contaminants.

Dale Nouse, *Cruising World*'s editor, is so fanatic about clean fuel that he not only has primary and secondary fuel filters in the system, but also uses a camp stove funnel-filter to strain the diesel fuel as it is pumped into the tank. The fact that he has never had any maintenance problems with his Perkins for 10 years must mean he's doing something right. Westerbeke recommends filtering diesel fuel with a 200-mesh screen.

MECHANICAL STARTERS

Larry Pardey once wrote an article for *Cruising World* in which he praised the hydraulic starters used on working water craft. Every diesel should have some alternative means of starting (besides electric). Because large engines are difficult to start by hand, he reasoned, why not use these hydraulic starters on cruising sailboats? American Bosch Diesel Products makes hydraulic start-

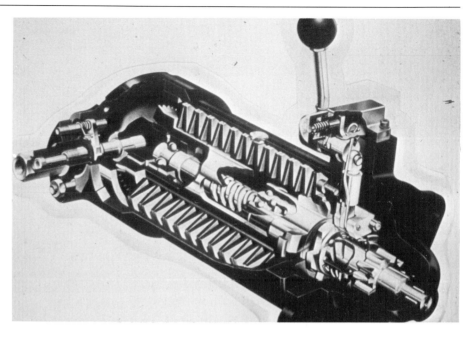

Fig. 8-26 *For engines that cannot be hand-cranked, a good back-up system is this Lucas spring starter.*

ers that cost between $1,000 and $4,000. Five to 10 minutes of hand pumping the accumulator tank will turn the engine over for up to two minutes.

One reader responded with news of a Lucas Marine spring starter (Fgure 8-26) that is wound up by hand in 12 turns, and when released, turns the flywheel just like your regular starter motor. It is powerful enough to start a six-cylinder, six-liter diesel engine.

In any event, if your diesel is too large to be started by hand, or isn't fitted with a manual crank, give serious consideration to installing a backup starting system. A wrench dropped across the terminals of your battery can short it instantaneously and leave you without starting power.

CUTLASS BEARINGS/STUFFING BOXES

Two pieces of engine-related gear that are all too often ignored are the cutlass bearing and the stuffing box (Figure 8-27). The cutlass bearing is a bronze tube with a grooved rubber liner that fits inside the fiberglass tube through which the prop shaft exits the hull. When I replaced *Adriana*'s engine and prop shaft, I discovered the

old cutlass bearing was worn smooth inside, which caused some wobble in the prop shaft. You don't see cutlass bearings in chandlery display cases, but a well-stocked store will have them in the back room.

Next time your boat is hauled, give a tug on the shaft to check for slop in the cutlass bearing. Replacing it is relatively simple. With the shaft out, pound out the cutlass bearing with a hammer using a section of wooden dowel of the right diameter. There may be a few set screws or Allen nuts to remove first, but that's it.

The stuffing box helps hold the shaft in align-

Fig. 8-27 *The cutlass bearing and stuffing box are critical to holding the shaft in alignment. They should be periodically inspected and serviced as necessary.*

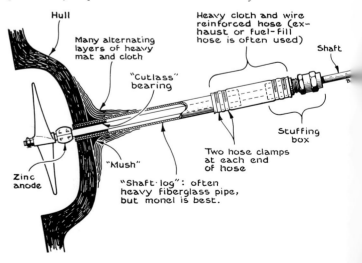

ment. A length of flax is "stuffed" inside the box between the first parts and is lubricated by seawater. The flax should be replaced every few years.

Tightening the stuffing box or packing gland decreases the amount of water permitted entry to the flax. The general rule is to tighten the box so that water periodically drips from the box. If you find the presence of any water in the bilge disconcerting, a new stuffing box seal called "Lasdrop" is supposed to prevent the drip-drip into the bilge.

SOUND INSULATION

Lining the engine box with one or two inches of lead-lined foam (Figure 8-28) significantly cuts down engine noise. Contact cement glues it to the box. But be sure it won't dissolve the foam. Seal exposed edges and seams with aluminum or Mylar tape. Enclose as much of the engine under the cockpit as possible by glassing boards to the underside of the cockpit (called curtains) and then gluing foam to them.

SUMMARY

- Diesel engines are safer (the fuel isn't explosive) and more economical but louder than gasoline engines.
- A backup starting system should be fitted, whether hand-cranked, hydraulic or spring.
- Secondary fuel filters are insurance against dirty fuel and water.
- Periodically check engine mounting bolts and shaft alignment.
- Regularly check stuffing box for proper amount of lubrication and change flax as required.
- When laying up the boat for a period of time, fill the tank (organisms that can live in diesel fuel find it hard to survive without air), and add a fuel-stabilizing chemical.

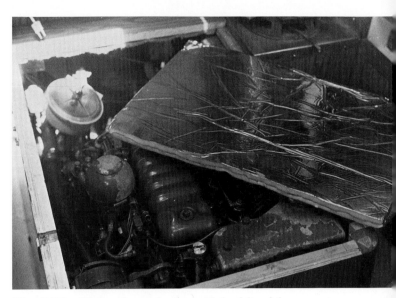

Fig. 8-28 *Lining the engine box with lead-lined foam one to two inches thick significantly reduces engine noise.*

- After running the engine under load, always throttle down to an idle for 10 to 20 minutes before shutting it off. This allows temperatures inside the engine to equalize before cooling.

FURTHER READING

The Care and Repair of Small Marine Diesels by Chris Thompson; International Marine Publishing, Camden, Maine.

The Care and Repair of Marine Gasoline Engines by Loris Goring; International Marine Publishing; Camden, Maine.

Engine Maintenance and Repair by David MacLean; Tab Books, Blue Ridge, Summit, Pennsylvania 17214.

Complete Guide to Outboard Motor Service & Repair by Paul Dempsey; Tab Books, Blue Ridge Summit, Pennsylvania 17214.

Sailboat Auxiliary Engine Maintenance, Clymer Publications, 222 North Virgil Avenue, Los Angeles, California 90004.

Engines for Sailboats by Conrad Miller; Yachting Books, Ziff-Davis Publishing Co., One Park Ave, New York, New York, 10016.

Diesel Engine Manual by Perry O. Black; Howard W. Sams & Co., Inc., Indianapolis, Indiana 46268.

CHAPTER 9

An Efficient Deck Layout

The third mate's boast about the decks, which were scrubbed night and morning, had come true. The racks of capstan bars, the rows of polished buckets, the rails with their long lines of pins and neatly coiled ropes, the tightly battened hatches and the glint of sunshine on the brasswork--all looked seamanlike and Bristol fashion.

REX CLEMENTS

So far we've talked about changes necessary to the interior and enclosed systems of a boat to make it a good, safe cruiser. The deck is no less rife with potential problems. Rig, sails and canvasmaking will be discussed in later chapters; in this chapter inspection of the boat is confined to the deck area, to weaknesses and possible solutions.

As with the boat's interior, the best deck layout is arrived at only after a season or two of sailing. You learn where it's most convenient to put your feet down, the places where people like to sit or sun bathe, and you begin to settle on how best to add equipment or make changes to existing features.

METALS AND WOOD

Just about everything on deck is made of wood, metal or some sort of fiber (as in rope). There is often more than one specific material suitable for a given job, and choosing wood for a winch base rather than metal is often a matter of personal preference. So, too, is the choice of mahogany over teak, or stainless steel over bronze.

The manufacturers of good quality gear have carefully chosen the material they think best for a specific item, but depending on your boat's hull and deck material—or other unique problems—you may wish to seek out gear made from less common materials. For example, if you have teak decks, you may prefer sheet blocks with wood shells rather than urethane synthetics. See Appendices B and C for more information on common woods and metals used in boatbuilding. Included is the galvanic series, which should be referred to whenever mating dissimilar metals.

152

BEDDING DECK FITTINGS

Using backing plates for thru-deck fittings is important (Figure 9-1). Cleats, winches, stanchions and any other item that is subject to strain should be installed with backing plates, or, if the stress is more moderate, with large washers. If the holes are close together, washers may do the job just as well. Either way, the idea is to distribute the stress on the bolts over as much area as possible. This point was made abundantly clear to me one spring day when *Adriana* was hit by a maladroit sailor on another boat and bolts holding the bow pulpit bases to the deck were nearly ripped right through the deck—the washers simply were too small.

Liberal amounts of good-quality bedding compound must be used to prevent leaks and rot in the deck core material. This is one of the easiest ways to ruin a boat, so do it right. Polysulfide compound, such as 3M's 5200 and Sikaflex 241 are excellent for this job, though all are adhesives as well and could make future removal difficult. Silicone rubber is also frequently used, though its not as durable as some other types. The best bedding job will seal wood cores with epoxy dabbed onto the inside of the hole; put masking tape over the hole from inside, pour a small amount of epoxy into the hole from the outside, let sit a few minutes, then go below again, remove the masking tape and catch the epoxy in a cup. A boss, which is a carved wood or formed metal plate flat on one side to receive the cleat or winch, and curved on the other to the shape of the deck or mounting surface, ensures a tight fit. Use bedding compound under the boss, on threads and under the heads of fasteners.

BOWSPRITS, PLATFORMS AND PULPITS

Possibly your boat has only a pulpit at the bow. Some boats are fitted with anchor rollers. And others, more traditionally styled, have bowsprits or platforms on which to neatly fit the anchor roller. If the pulpit is thru-bolted to the deck using large washers or backing plates on the un-

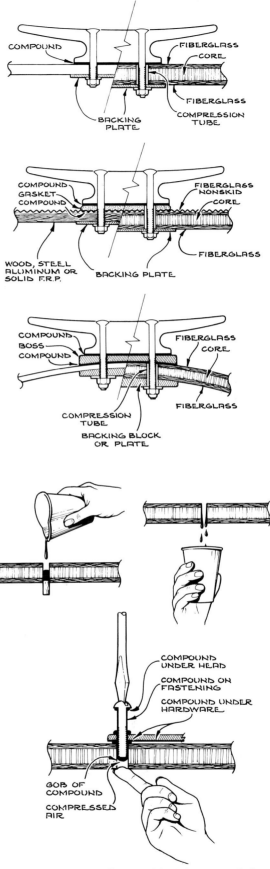

Fig. 9-1 *Proper installation of deck fittings includes thru-bolting, backing plates and liberal amounts of bedding compound.*

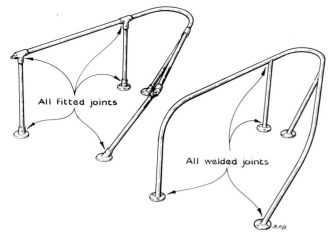

Fig. 9-2 *Welded pulpit joints are stronger than fitted joints.*

derside, you might as well be satisfied with it. Welded pulpits (Figure 9-2) are preferable to fitted ones (separate pieces held together with joints), but this isn't a major cause for concern, especially if you remember never to trust your life to pulpits and lifelines.

Bow Rollers

An anchor roller is, of course, very desirable in that it allows a plow-type or Bruce anchor to be stowed at the bow and ready, although in bad weather offshore it should be brought below and secured. Frank Mulville, an English single-hander with numerous ocean crossings, describes in his book *Singlehanded Cruising and Sailing*, a convenient anchoring system in which the rode is led back to the cockpit and tripped to run free when the decision is made to lower away. This, of course, would not be possible without some sort of roller at the bow.

Windline makes a full line of anchor rollers and supporting brackets that can be adapted to most any type of anchor and boat (Figure 9-3).

If your boat has a toe rail that extends to the

Fig. 9-3 *Windline Marine manufactures a complete line of bow rollers for all types of anchors and bow configurations. Note the locking pin to hold this CQR down on the roller.*

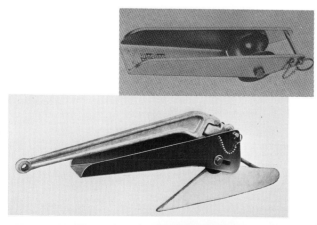

bow, it may be necessary to cut a piece out of the toe rail plank to fit the roller flush on deck, or add a piece of wood under the roller to elevate it above the toe rail. Be certain the point of the anchor flukes won't hit the hull when pulled in tight on the roller. Teak would be a good choice here, as would large backing washers or plates.

Bow Platforms

If your boat wasn't delivered to you with a bowsprit or bow platform, give serious thought to leaving it that way. They are expensive and difficult to make, are subject to damage at dockside or from bitchy seas, and it's not really the place you want to set an anchor or change a headsail in a gale. On the other hand, if your boat has a bowsprit or platform, they do look salty, so enjoy it.

One good reason to *add* a bowsprit is to move the headstay forward, thereby increasing the area of the foretriangle. This moves the center of effort of the sail plan forward and reduces weather helm. And, when the weather isn't too rough, anchors stowed beneath a bowsprit are kept well away from the hull.

On an outboard sloop or cutter rig, a downhaul on the jib might save going forward onto the sprit (Figure 9-4). A platform and rail on top

Fig. 9-4 *Gretel, a 90-foot, three-masted schooner, has the traditional netting underneath the bowsprit to provide footing.*

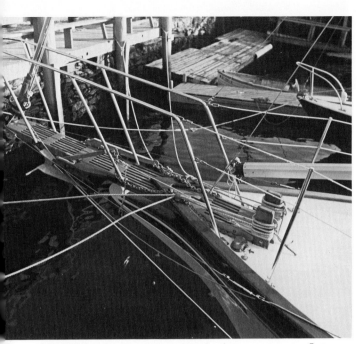

Fig. 9-5 *Contemporary practice is to construct a flat platform over the bowsprit, or leave out the bowsprit altogether. Note how neatly the Danforth and CQR anchors on this Krogen 38 are stowed, and how quickly they can be deployed.*

of the sprit gives additional security (Figure 9-5). If you have decided to add a sprit or platform for a bowroller and are using teak, don't bolt directly through the teak to the deck. Even with a good backing plate, the compression resistance of teak isn't good, and the bolt heads will crush the wood. A better choice is to clamp the inboard end of the sprit or platform to the deck with a metal strap (Figure 9-6).

ANCHOR WELLS, CHAINPIPES AND WINDLASSES

Some anchors don't stow well flat on deck, and this is one reason why plows and Bruce anchors mounted on outboard rollers are so popular. For securing lightweight (Danforth and fisherman types), chalks can be bolted to the deck to secure the Danforth; the fisherman can be unpinned and lashed to a stanchion as well as secured in chalks.

Anchor Wells

A trick in recent years has been to mold anchor wells into the foredeck. A well-designed one has a drain over the side that gets rid of water and lets you wash down the anchor in the well without getting the deck dirty. Also, it should have a locking mechanism to keep the lid from flying open if the boat is knocked down. Provisions should be made to lash the anchor inside the well to prevent it from flailing about or crashing against the lid in severe conditions.

Another anchor well is the vertical type, in which the anchor is lowered into a deep molding near the boat's rail. This type of well seems to be more secure in holding the anchor in place, though a strong lid with hasp and lock is still necessary. Both of these wells could be molded at home and fitted on the foredeck. Alterna-

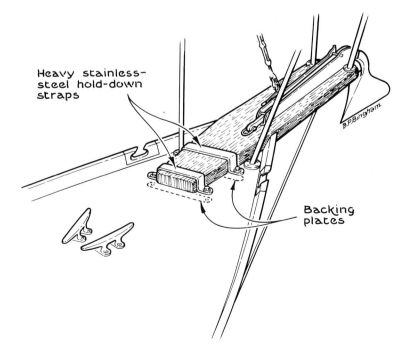

Heavy stainless-steel hold-down straps

Backing plates

Fig. 9-6 *Because teak's compressive strength is poor, large pieces subject to stress, such as bowsprit platforms, shouldn't be bolted directly to the deck. A metal strap is a better method.*

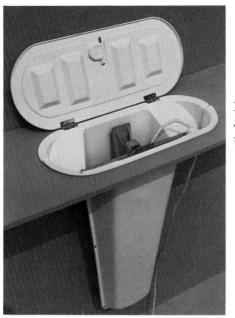

Fig. 9-7 *Sailing Specialties makes this vertical anchor well.*

increase strength for the compression loads that occur when bolting hinges and hasps, and to prevent moisture from reaching the core material.

Making An Anchor Well

An anchor well can be fabricated from plywood and glassed over with mat and polyester resin. Fair the outside edges and fillet the inside corners so the mat doesn't have to conform to sharp angles—it won't.

Windlasses

A windlass mounted between the bow roller and forward mooring cleat(s) is a useful piece of gear on any boat, and essential on most boats larger than 30 feet (Figure 9-8). It can take the strain out of shipping anchor in ordinary conditions, and is one of the best ways to break out an anchor fouled on the bottom.

One stormy October day on Lake Michigan, Gene Correll—an old sailing friend—and I hauled his boat off a beach after it had broken its mooring pendant. The 33-foot Pearson Vanguard lay in about 2½ feet of water; the hull

tively, you could buy one of these from a builder (just ask nicely!), or from a company such as Sailing Specialties, Inc. (Figure 9-7). But I imagine it will take a courageous person to cut such a large hole in his deck. If you do undertake the job, be certain to grout out the core material around the hole, and fill it with epoxy resin thickened with wood flour, chopped strand or microfibers (see Figure 4-7). This is necessary to

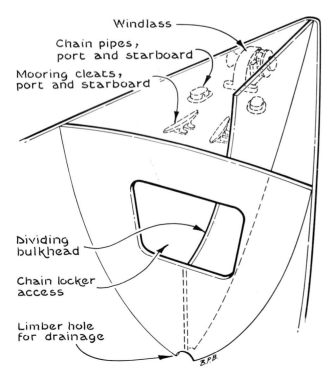

Fig. 9-8 *A safe and powerful anchoring system includes a large anchor locked to a bowroller, a samson post or large cleat for tying off nylon rode, a windlass, a watertight chain pipe or hatch, and a reinforced compartment for chain.*

drew 4½ feet. We took one long line off the masthead, attached to the main halyard, and leading it to an anchor several hundred feet abeam, we used a halyard winch to careen the boat as much as possible. The other anchor was led toward deep water with about 300 feet of line. With the small SL-200 Simpson-Lawrence windlass on the foredeck, we winched his seven-ton boat inch by inch toward deeper water, with only a 35-pound CQR dug into the sand to hold. Every time a knot attaching the two lines jammed in the bow chalk, it was necessary to lash a spare line to the rode outside the knot, pull the knot through, then unlash the extra line.

Larry Pardey points out that windlasses with aluminum cast bodies should be avoided in favor of bronze or iron bodies, for the very reason mentioned at the beginning of this chapter—an aluminum housing in direct contact with stainless steel bolts will corrode and make disassembly difficult.

A COMPLETE GROUND TACKLE SYSTEM

A preferred method of carrying anchor and ground tackle is a strong bow roller, thru-bolted to the deck, with the rode led aft to a large cleat or Samson post, and then into the forepeak floor by means of a chainpipe (Figure 9-9).

Many inexpensive chain pipes are on the market, but look for one that can be closed off tightly. Simpson-Lawrence makes a good bronze one available through Jay Stuart Haft in the U.S. On the inside of the lid is a clip to fasten the end of the rode so it doesn't drop all the way down the tube, making retrieval a pain. However, a watertight hatch is more easily sealed than even the best chain pipe.

Strong lashings should be used on the anchor; 35 or more pounds flopping around on the foredeck can only cause damage. On more than one occasion, I've seen people sailing with an anchor dangling over the side, only to come up short unexpectedly.

Generally, it is not considered wise to place too much weight in the ends of the boat because this increases the boat's tendency to hobbyhorse in seas. Keeping the weight amidships gives a

Fig. 9-9 *Manual and electric windlasses are expensive, but important for easy handling of ground tackle. They are more powerful than sheet winches for kedging off when aground.*

steadier motion. For this reason, chain, if possible, should be lead aft, perhaps under the forward berths. But don't impede its deployment with a poorly thought out installation; on many boats, chain stowage in the forepeak may be the best you can do. A strong plywood compartment reinforced with fiberglass, with limber holes drilled for drainage and fed chain by a wood trough, will keep this potentially unruly serpent tamed. If the chain isn't self-stowing, someone must go below to flake it, which is a nuisance. Hal Roth says tall, narrow storage is better than wide, flat compartments, and, as chain is smelly, wash it down as it comes aboard.

LIFELINES, STANCHIONS AND SAFETY LINES

In heavy weather, standard practice is to don a safety harness and fix it to some object on deck that is securely fastened. The fastening location should permit movement to all locations desired, such as the mast base—yet not allow the person to fall so far over the side that he cannot regain the deck. Lifelines, despite their apparent strength, are not the best choice for this purpose. The Fastnet disaster of 1979 and the Whitbread Round the World Race of 1973 recorded deaths due to failed lifelines. Perhaps no other description of death at sea is so chilling as the recollections of the crew of a French Whitbread boat who watched their skipper disappear overboard. He had his safety harness clipped to the lifeline when the boat was knocked down and he was sent flying along the deck. The harness hook snapped off the stanchion tops one by one. When he reached the end of the boat, the lifeline snapped, putting him in the water with no tie to the boat. Quickly, he was swept away, never to be seen again.

Use the largest diameter wire possible. The stanchion holes may require enlarging or the wire bought without a plastic covering to obtain a ⁵⁄₁₆-inch or larger diameter. Most often, 7 x 7 x 19 wire is used for lifelines, but as there's no real need for flexibility, 1 x 19 wire is a stronger choice.

Nevertheless, lifelines serve several important functions: A handhold when going forward, a brace for the legs, and to contain sails dropped on the deck. Most offshore races specify lifeline standards. The Offshore Racing Council (ORC) specifies double lifelines, and stanchions of at least 24 inches height (some sailors feel 27 to 30 inches is better), thru-bolted or welded to the deck. They should be spaced no more than seven feet apart. Custom-made stanchions of one-inch 316 stainless steel pipe (which has a thicker wall than tubing) will be stronger than most commercially available types. Weld them to ³⁄₁₆-inch bases with four bolt holes.

Some stanchion mounting methods are superior to others. On most production boats, the stanchion is bolted flush on deck (Figure 9-10).

If the boat has a toe rail of several inches height, or better yet, bulwarks of six inches or more, the stanchion also can be bolted in the vertical plane, which is much stronger.

Quality stanchions should be welded to their bases or fastened by bolts, not by Allen set screws, which only dimple the metal and let loose as soon as a strong force is exerted.

A Special Lifeline for Harnesses

Veteran singlehander Frank Mulville once showed me the lifeline system he uses on his Hillyard cutter, *Iskra*. He runs a length of wire from stem to stern, fastened at each end to pad eyes thru-bolted to the deck (Figure 9-11) and seized at the shrouds to keep it at waist level.

A good safety harness should have two attach-

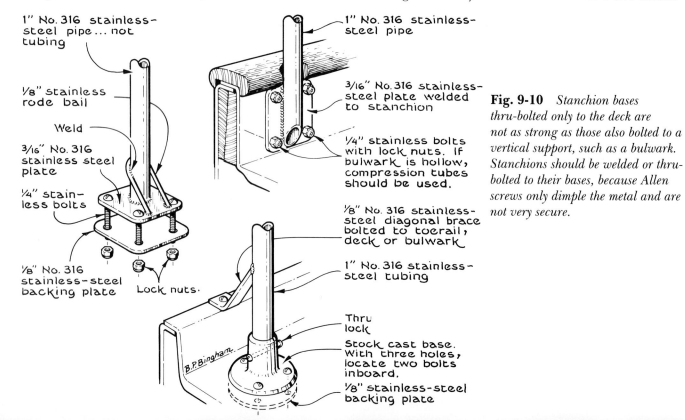

Fig. 9-10 *Stanchion bases thru-bolted only to the deck are not as strong as those also bolted to a vertical support, such as a bulwark. Stanchions should be welded or thru-bolted to their bases, because Allen screws only dimple the metal and are not very secure.*

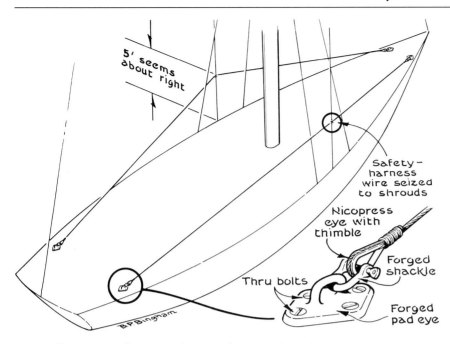

Fig. 9-11 *On his Hillyard-built* Iskra, *singlehander Frank Mulville uses a single length of large diameter wire run from stem to stern to attach his safety harness line. It is seized at the shrouds to hold it chest high, and requires unhooking only once on a trip up or down the deck.*

ment lines, one long and one short. With the long one, it may not be necessary to unhook it to reach the forestay on some small boats. The disadvantage of the short line is that if you're thrown overboard ahead of the shrouds or other point of interruption, you could be caught against the hull amidships without help from the crew. It is often easier to get back aboard by yourself from the stern, especially if you've installed a vane, handholds or ladder. If the wire is uninterrupted, use the short line. If it is lashed at the shrouds, use the long line when clipped forward of the shrouds.

If sailing alone, or alone on watch with an autopilot steering, it is very important to have some means, such as a tripline, of disengaging the autopilot or vane so that the boat will round up, slow down, and permit the man overboard to gain the deck. An easy means of climbing aboard also is essential.

The Latchway Safety System

An improved variation of this system is the Latchway Safety System (Figure 9-12) marketed

Fig. 9-12 *The Latchway Safety System by Henri-Lloyd uses an ingenious mechanism that allows the safety harness line to pass through stanchion fastenings without unhooking.*

by Henri-Lloyd, British manufacturers of foul weather gear. Again, a single wire is run from stem to stern, but attached to stanchions by special fasteners that are called "transfasteners". These unique devices permit the safety harness attachment lines to pass through them without disengaging, thereby obviating the need to unhook the line and reattach it on the other side.

The best lifeline system is worthless if the crew doesn't wear a harness and attach it religiously whenever alone on deck or whenever weather dictates. It, like the auto seatbelt, doesn't guarantee to save your life, but it vastly improves the odds. And that is what preparing a boat for sea is all about—stacking the cards as much in your favor as possible.

VENTILATION

Ventilating the cabin areas is vital to a dry, mildew-free living area that also is cool in hot weather—especially in the tropics. A closed boat soon develops condensation or retains humidity from breathing, cooking, lamps and wet clothing. And nothing dries out dampness like the movement of air, which causes the water to evaporate. Therefore, good cross-flow of air should be planned from the forepeak to the farthest accessible end of the boat. Fresh air also is of value in minimizing the effects of seasickness when holed up below.

Vents typically found on boats are cowls, sometimes mounted on Dorade boxes (Figure 9-13) and mushrooms. Some may be closed off

Fig. 9-14 *The plastic vent mounted on this hatch has an internal baffle to keep spray and rain out, while allowing air to enter. But immersed in a large boarding wave, or with the boat upside down, there is no way to prevent water entering. It should be possible to make every vent watertight.*

entirely when water is coming over the deck or a heavy rain finds its way through the vent. Other types cannot be closed off (Figure 9-14) and should either be modified or discarded in favor of a closable model. Mushroom vents can be closed from the inside, which is an appreciated convenience. Most cowl vents must be removed from the Dorade box and a deck plate screwed on in place of the cowl.

On *Adriana* we fitted a closable mushroom-type vent with a stainless steel cowling over it that prevents rain from getting under the vent cap (Figure 9-15). (Give plastic cowlings a miss, as they break easily when stepped on.) The mushroom works in all but the worst conditions, and does wonders in keeping air circulating below.

Cowl vents probably move more air than any other type, but they also present special problems. For one, lines are easily snagged on them. And, as mentioned, they cannot be closed from

Fig. 9-13 *This large dorade on the wood yawl Nirvana is protected by bronze pipes, which also prevent the fouling of sheets.*

Fig. 9-15 *This Beckson mushroom vent, which can be closed and locked, is covered by a stainless steel shield that will withstand someone standing on it.*

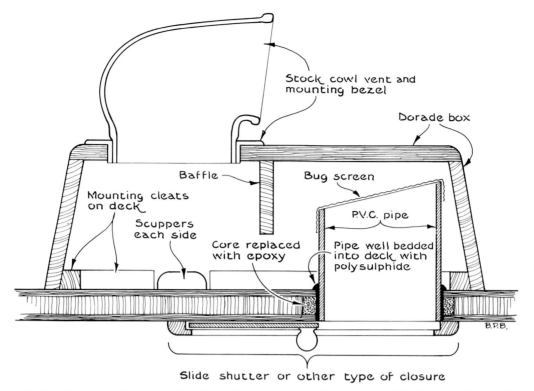

Stock cowl vent and
mounting bezel

Dorade box

Baffle

Bug screen

Mounting cleats
on deck

P.V.C. pipe

Scuppers
each side

Core replaced
with epoxy

Pipe well bedded
into deck with
polysulphide

B.P.B.

Slide shutter or other type of closure

Fig. 9-16 *This drawing shows how a standard Dorade-type vent and box can be modified to close from within the cabin. This saves a trip on deck to replace the Dorade with a deck plate. Also shown are a PVC rain trap and sliding shutter to control air flow in the cabin.*

below without modification (Figure 9-16). Stainless steel cages over the vent, bolted to the deck, are one solution to the line-snagging problem, and large PVC pipe, cut on one end at a diagonal and inserted into the vent, is another method of keeping out rain and spray. Shutters on the underside of the deck over the vent opening allow a degree of air flow control throughout the boat.

A primary source of ventilation, as well as access for persons, sails and stoves, are hatches. But the main companionway hatch is often a weak link in the boat's armament against boarding seas. On many boats they are too large, and if you're considering buying a boat with a large hatch and no bridge deck, give extra thought to the purchase—remedying this problem could be more trouble than it's worth. Large hatches do make going below easier, and do admit more air, but this is no place for compromise.

REQUIREMENTS OF A SEAWORTHY COMPANIONWAY

There are five basic requirements for a good main hatch—1) it should be small, not much more than shoulder width; 2) the weather boards should be solid hardwood or plywood, preferably ¾-inch thick, or Lexan; 3) as watertight as possible; 4) the retaining channels that hold the weather boards must be very strong; and 5) there should be devices to lock the hatch inside and outside.

Reinforcing the retaining channels is a good place to start beefing up the main hatch. Protection against vandals and thieves is an added bonus. If your channels aren't up to spec, remove them and follow the cross-sectional plan in Figure 9-17. Use ¾-inch thick hardwood. A strip of ⅛-inch stainless steel thru-bolted to the cabin wall, and locking mechanisms such as barrel bolts on the weather boards are extra insurance against boarding waves, crowbars or the forces that sometimes knock weather boards *out* when the boat is dropped hard off a wave. Inside, a piece of thick teak or other hardwood, several inches wide, should be thru-bolted to the cabin wall. If your boat doesn't have a flange, as pictured, then bolt through both the interior and exterior pieces.

Figure 9-17 also shows a storm shutter of ⅜-inch Plexiglas or Lexan that can be quickly screwed to the steel plate in the event of really nasty seas.

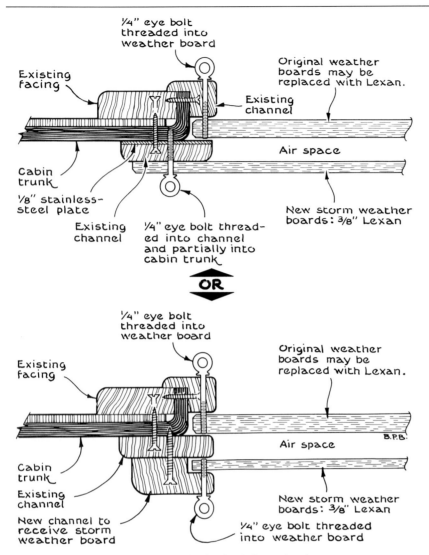

¼" eye bolt
threaded into
weather board

Existing
facing

Original weather
boards may be
replaced with Lexan.

Existing
channel

Cabin
trunk

Air space

⅛" stainless-
steel plate

Existing
channel

¼" eye bolt thread-
ed into channel
and partially into
cabin trunk

New storm weather
boards: ⅜" Lexan

OR

¼" eye bolt
threaded into
weather board

Existing
facing

Original weather
boards may be
replaced with Lexan.

Cabin
trunk

Air space

B.P.B.

Existing
channel

New channel to
receive storm
weather board

New storm weather
boards: ⅜" Lexan

¼" eye bolt threaded
into weather board

Fig. 9-17 *The retaining boards that hold the companionway slide (weather boards) can be beefed up by making provision for a storm shutter.*

Hatches should be able to be locked from both inside and outside, as should the weather boards themselves—even if the hatch is open. Deadbolt slides do the trick well for the weather boards and might work for the hatch. Chapter 3 suggests other locking hatches.

The forward hatch also should be lockable from inside and out, and it is smart to give some thought to having the hatch open either forward or aft (Figure 9-18). A rubber gasket around the perimeter of the hatch and a lever-action lock will increase its watertightness. Additionally, a locking mechanism such as a hasp thru-bolted to the deck on the outside gives extra strength against boarding waves.

Attractive smaller hatches made of smoked Lexan ventilate and light important areas of the boat—over the galley and overhead in the main cabin where heat from kerosene lamps accumu-

Fig. 9-18 *More air and less water gets below when the forward hatch can be opened in any direction. Bruce's clever drawing illustrates how this is possible.*

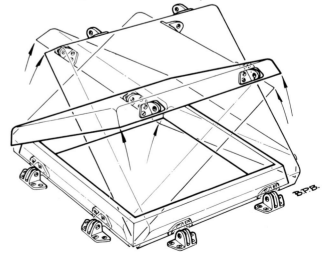

Fig. 9-19 *This Lewmar hatch can be dogged down tight and positively locked. It would be well suited as a ventilating hatch above the galley, or used for more watertight access to lazarettes than a molded lid.*

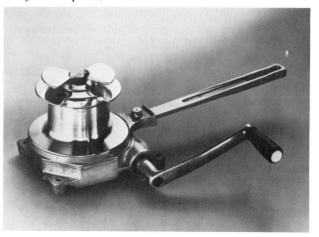

	Winch Power Ratios				
	10:1	20:1	30:1	40:1	50:1
			Maximum Sail Areas		
Main/Mizzen/Foresail/Self Trimming Headsail Sheets (Base on a 4 to 1 block purchase)	to 200	to 400	to 650	to 1,000	
Genoa/Jib/Working Staysail Sheets	to 100	to 200	to 300	to 400	to 600
Light Staysail Sheets (Secondary cockpit)	to 150	to 275	to 400	to 600	to 900
Spinnaker Sheets	to 200	to 400	to 900	to 2,000	to 4,000
Main/Mizzen/Foresail Halyards	to 200	to 300	to 400	to 600	to 1,000
Genoa/Jib/Working Staysail Halyards	to 200	to 275	to 350	to 500	to 800
Spinnaker Halyard	to 300	to 600	to 1,500	to 3,500	to 5,000
Light Staysail Halyards	to 300	to 400	to 500	to 700	to 1,000

Fig. 9-20 *Winch selection chart*

lates. Bomar, Goiot and Lewmar are leading manufacturers of these hatches; they are expensive, but worth the added investment (Figure 9-19).

A traditional skylight over the main cabin is attractive and certainly will improve the looks of the boat. However, they usually leak. Skylights are by no means cruising necessities, but if you decide you must have one, construct it strongly enough so the full weight of a man can fall on it without breaking. This means using a shatterproof material such as Lexan, and bolting brass rods or wood stringers over it.

WINCHES

These hefty little items are among the most expensive gear on your boat. The difference between good winches and poor or undersized ones is their quickness in trimming headsails and mainsails or hoisting men aloft, or breaking anchors out of Mother Earth. Figure 9-20 will help you size winches for your boat, and if you err, do so on the large side. They do require some maintenance each year, principally taking off the top part and greasing the gears. Waterpump or Teflon grease works well.

In recent years, self-tailing winches have become standard fare on many boats. Their labor-saving convenience cannot be denied, especially for the short-handed crew. However, they are quite expensive. One can do without them, but if you have the bucks, buy them. As a general rule, you can reduce winch size by 20 percent when converting to self-tailers.

Bottom-action winches, while rarely seen on racing boats, do make sense for the cruiser. The winch handle needn't be removed every time the sheet is led around the winch, but on the negative side, they are slower than top-action winches. Murray, a New Zealand company, manufactures handsome bottom-action winches in bronze (Figure 9-21). Eric and Susan Hiscock, plus Lin and Larry Pardey, swear by them.

Fig. 9-21 *Murray, a New Zealand company, makes a line of bronze bottom-action winches. The crank is geared low for extra power in trimming sheets just right (South Pacific Enterprises).*

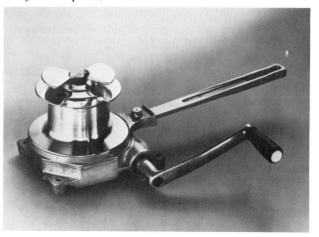

Fig. 9-22 *On* Frolic, *Danny Greene's 26-foot cutter, a large single winch is used amidships on the bridge deck, instead of two separate winches at the coamings.*

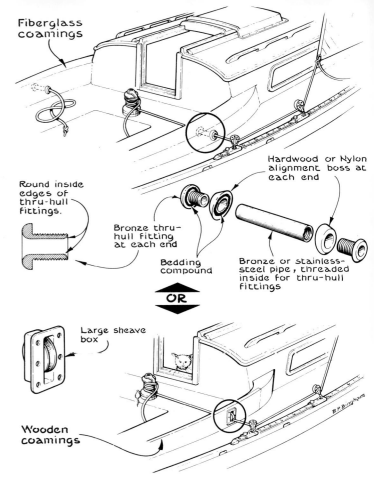

Single-Winch Sheeting

Because of the high cost of quality winches, there is much merit to using one winch for sheeting and another for halyards. A bridge deck makes a good central location for the sheet winch, which, because you've only bought one, can afford to be a bit bigger than required. Danny Greene has mounted a large winch here (see Figure 9-22) and, with both sheets long enough to reach the winch at all times, it is a simple matter to unwrap and wrap the other when tacking. If cockpit coamings obstruct a fair lead from the deck blocks, Barbarossa makes a roller that can be inserted into the coaming. Or you may be able to use flared stainless steel tubing through the coaming if the line doesn't turn sharp corners. The best part is that when the boat is heeled far over, no one has to go down on the leeward rail to trim the sails as it's all done from the security of the center cockpit area.

Single Halyard Winch

This same arrangement used for sheets can be used for halyard winches, with the use of cleats, turning sheaves and linestoppers (Figure 9-23). Many racing and cruising boats are now leading lines back to the cockpit, with winches mounted on the cabin top. They should be thru-bolted to the deck and well bedded.

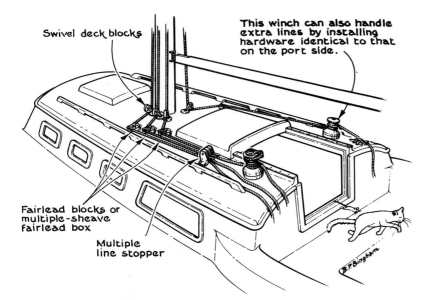

Fig. 9-23 *A single winch mounted next to the companionway hatch and a set of linestoppers can do the job of two or more mast-mounted halyard winches.*

HALYARD LEADS, CLEATS AND LINESTOPPERS

The single halyard winch concept requires that halyards be led aft via turning sheaves or fairleads at the base of the mast. Linestoppers are commonly used to snub them because it wouldn't be possible to cleat the halyard without removing it from the winch, and, since the winch must be cleared to make room for the next halyard, some method of securing the halyard in front of the winch is necessary—linestoppers, clam cleats or cam cleats.

I do not like them. Having sailed on numerous boats with them, it seems to me they are prone to slipping, and require considerable effort sometimes to jam the handle down hard enough to make it hold. But design improvements have been made, and their use on large racing yachts, including the 12-Meters, must say something in their defense.

As an alternative, extra winches and cleats can be installed on the cabin top though this is certainly more expensive and space-consuming.

The whole logic for leading halyards aft seems a bit suspect anyway. So what if you can raise and lower sails from the cockpit? You still have to go forward to unfurl the main when it's going up, and to gather it in when it comes down. Being able to drop sails from the cockpit may give you a few extra seconds of security, but in a blow (which is the only time this security is really necessary), a headsail loose on the foredeck won't stay there for long. Of course, nets on the lifelines and lazy jacks on the main do assist in keeping these sails under control, but again, it is only a delaying tactic.

CLEATS

The positioning of cleats is important. They should be angled about 15 to 20 degrees from the lead of the halyard or sheet to distribute the load on the bolts holding the cleat to the deck, and to make cleating and uncleating the line easier (Figure 9-24). Most cleats are much too small

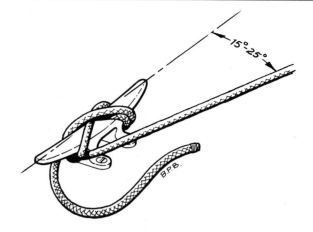

Fig. 9-24 *Cleats should be angled at about 15–25 degrees from the lead of the line for strength and ease of operation. For every 1/8 inch of line diameter, add one inch to cleat.*

for the size and number of lines the cruising sailor will want to use them for. Naval architect Ian Nicolson says that cleats on most boats can be enlarged 40 percent.

Breast cleats mounted on deck amidships are seldom seen on boats, but are of immense help when rafting to another vessel, furnishing a place to cleat off a fender or spring line at the dock, or to attach the rode of an anchor used to keep the boat off the dock. Select the largest cleat feasible for the location, and mount it clear of stanchions and shrouds. The cleat in Figure 9-25 is undersized and hidden behind the shrouds. This boat spent a winter next to me in

Fig. 9-25 *The breast cleat on this Krogen 38 is too small and is obscured behind the shrouds.*

Newport and when I asked the owner if I could tie a breast line to it, he said no, he'd let someone do that last year and the cleat was nearly pulled from the deck.

In addition to large cleats in the bow for anchoring and mooring, there should be large cleats on each quarter. Four-bolt cleats are stronger than two-bolt cleats. Be sure to buy good quality—you don't ever want to see snapped horns on your own boat!

This brings to mind again the business of using large thru-bolts and backing plates of plywood, stainless steel or aluminum. There is no excuse for having a flimsy piece of deck gear, because no matter how light the use you intend for it, sooner or later someone will inadvertently test it for you.

A note on cleating lines: Many persons seem to overdo it when cleating a line. Perhaps they believe the additional wraps and hitches lessen the chances of the line coming loose. In fact, one wrap around the base, followed by one figure eight, with the last part tucked under, is perfectly secure. Tying a Gordian knot on every cleat only increases the time required to uncleat the line. And nearly every line on a boat should be capable of being removed *instantly*.

MAST PULPITS

On larger boats, two pulpits to port and starboard of the mast provide a sense of safety and sure footing when working at the mast base in rolly seas. They often look to me a bit weak, as the stanchion bases are often more or less in a straight line. Placing them in a circle around the mast might obstruct access around the deck, but it will give them a stronger staying base.

The advantage of mast pulpits is that you can lean against them when working on the leeward side of the boat and if to windward and the boat rocks the other way, you have a brace to support yourself. But on smaller boats, say under 40 feet, there usually isn't sufficient deck space to justify their expense and labor.

If you do decide to install mast pulpits, place them far enough away from the mast so you can still crouch down inside them. There are times when we all want to get down on our knees, no matter what's behind us!

An alternative is to thru-bolt foot chalks at strategic spots around the mast to give better footing. A wedge-shaped length of teak cut two inches high will do the job.

DECK PRISMS

Deck prisms do a remarkable job of adding light below without the obstruction typical of hatches. Bomar and Jay Stuart Haft both sell deck prisms that have wide mounting flanges to conceal the hideous look of rough-cut fiberglass and deck core. You can also make your own from Lexan, and if you don't want to see through, wet sand the surfaces to make them translucent. Whenever cutting through the deck

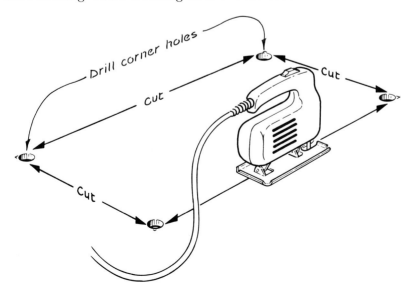

Fig. 9-26 *When cutting a hole in the deck for a prism or other fitting with square corners, drill pilot holes in each corner large enough to insert the saber saw blade.*

or cutting out a shape from inside a larger piece of material, first drill pilot holes *inside* the outline pattern (Figure 9-26). Then insert the saber saw blade and make the cut.

Use a polysulfide or equivalent bedding compound and apply liberally between the flange and deck. If it oozes out when the flanges are bolted down tight, then you know you've used enough. Excess compound can be cut away after it has hardened.

PROPANE TANKS

Propane is one of several fuels (diesel, kerosene, alcohol, and compressed natural gas are others) you might select for the galley stove/oven, cabin heater and possibly water heater. Chapter 12 discusses the pros and cons of each fuel and describes a gravity feed fuel system. But for the moment, assuming you have propane, you must also determine where on deck to locate the bottles. Because propane is heavier than air and can collect in the bilge if spilled, they must be located in an area isolated from the cabin—on deck or in a vented, vaportight locker.

Some of the newer boats built since propane has become more accepted (due in part to the use of automatic solenoid switches and leak detectors), have rather ingenious hiding places for tanks in and around the cockpit or sunk into the deck. The common characteristic of these installations is that each molded compartment has an overboard drain to rid the area of water and gas. With a vent on top, the danger of explosion at the bottle is almost nil. A trawler we once chartered had the propane tanks mounted under the flying bridge, a story above the main deck. This area was open on the aft side, and while the tanks were not the prettiest sight to behold, everyone felt more comfortable knowing the risk of explosion was minimized.

Locating the Locker

On boats without production propane storage, there are several options that permit a vented, drained locker. The first decision is whether the locker can best be mounted above

deck or below. If above, a spot on deck must be found where the locker will neither obstruct anyone nor foul lines. Like Lin and Larry Pardey's new 30-footer, David Markell's Pearson Vanguard has a propane tank deck box just forward of the cabin, in front of the forward hatch. There is an overboard drain drilled into the side of the box. The propane lines are led through a hole in the deck (you can buy commercial stuffing boxes for this purpose) under the box, which has been caulked well with bedding compound. They are led aft to the galley, and supported under the side decks. The box makes a nice spot to sit while motoring in and out of harbors, though it gets in the way of sunbathing. But, even though it is thru-bolted to the deck, it might not hold together under a large boarding wave. Of course, losing the tanks isn't really a matter of survival. Some things you just live with and hope for the best.

The deck box for the tank should be strong enough to jump on, built of plywood, plywood reinforced with fiberglass at the seams, or hardwood. The tanks should be secured inside the box with U-bolts and straps or wood framing (Figure 9-27). They should never be placed in direct sunlight. Even inside deck boxes, the temperature should be watched because heat causes the gas to expand, possibly enough to blow the relief valve.

Another method is to partition off part of a cockpit locker with plywood and fiberglass, mount the tanks inside, and drill a hole overboard above the waterline (Figure 9-28). (Also see Chapter 11, Figure 11-8.)

Marine Energy Systems manufactures a tank locker of molded fiberglass (Figure 9-29). At the very least, it would be suitable to lash this locker to a stanchion or other part of the boat. Or, it could be positioned in a seat locker with the drain vented overboard via a tube. If the drain is near the waterline heeled or level, a check valve in the line will prevent water from entering while allowing water to drain out.

Other Deck Tanks

Drip-feed diesel heaters and stoves require a tank elevated above the appliance. While they can be installed inside the cabin, the tank also

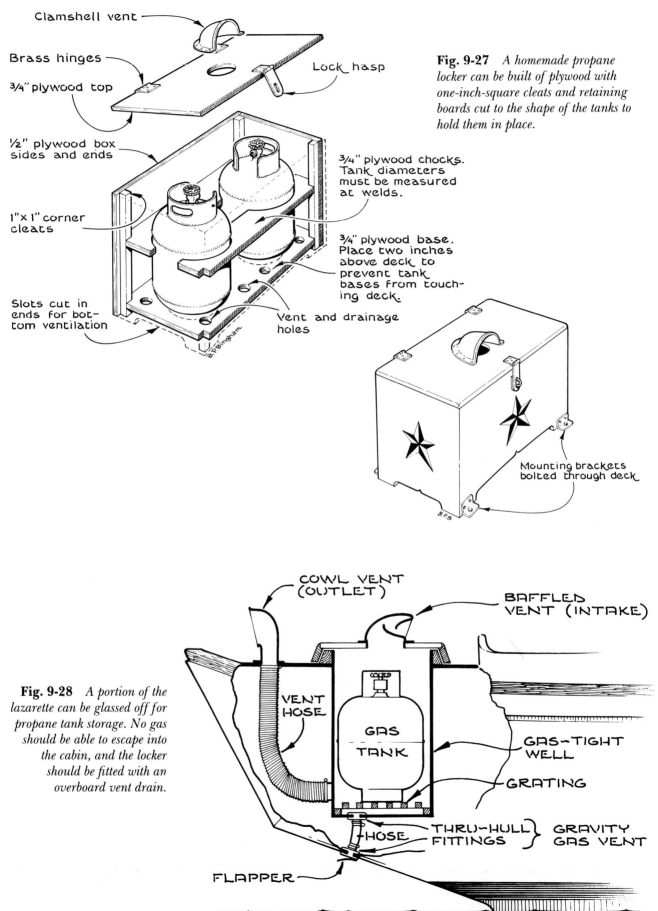

Clamshell vent

Brass hinges

3/4" plywood top

1/2" plywood box sides and ends

1"x 1" corner cleats

Slots cut in ends for bottom ventilation

Lock hasp

Fig. 9-27 *A homemade propane locker can be built of plywood with one-inch-square cleats and retaining boards cut to the shape of the tanks to hold them in place.*

3/4" plywood chocks. Tank diameters must be measured at welds.

3/4" plywood base. Place two inches above deck to prevent tank bases from touching deck.

Vent and drainage holes

Mounting brackets bolted through deck

Fig. 9-28 *A portion of the lazarette can be glassed off for propane tank storage. No gas should be able to escape into the cabin, and the locker should be fitted with an overboard vent drain.*

COWL VENT (OUTLET)

BAFFLED VENT (INTAKE)

VENT HOSE

GAS TANK

GAS-TIGHT WELL

GRATING

HOSE

THRU-HULL FITTINGS } GRAVITY GAS VENT

FLAPPER

Fig. 9-29 *Marine Energy Systems makes this molded fiberglass propane tank locker that could be adapted to many locations.*

can be located on deck. Again, it presents certain problems there, and it is vulnerable to the elements, but it is often no less awkward inside.

A water tank on deck for washing dishes and toiletries (see Chapter 5), means one less pump to break down. As an added bonus, if the tank is painted black, the sun will heat the water inside.

WATER FILLS AND RAIN CATCHMENTS

There is no little disagreement amongst sailors as to the best location for water fills. On many boats, the cap is situated on a side deck, forward or aft. A deck plate key or two-pronged spanner wrench is used to open the cap and a tube or hose channels water into the tank. One objection to this practice is the possibility of salt water seeping through the cap and fouling the fresh water in the tank, though the likelihood of this happening seems minimal. Applying Teflon or water pump grease to the cap threads will help. Some people like to fill tanks directly from below. The topside water-fill advocates object to the inevitable wetting of bunks and the rest of the cabin when a hose is taken below.

Deck fill fittings can be bought at a good chan-

dlery or ordered from a mail order catalog such as Goldberg's or Defender Industries. Use a tough reinforced hose of the correct diameter to fit snugly over the deck fill nipple inside and to the threaded pipe or elbow screwed into the tank top. Use a sealant and hose clamps on all connections.

One reason to locate the deck fill at the gunnel is that it can be opened during a rain storm to top off the tanks. To maximize the benefit, find the lowest point on deck. To calculate the surface of the deck area required to yield a given amount of water in the tank, let's assume the deck is crowned along the boat's centerline of the boat. We already know that 231 cubic inches equals one gallon of water.

From the calculations (Figure 9-30), a half-inch of rain will yield 52 gallons of water. This can be improved by increasing the surface area of the catchment area. Awnings that funnel water into a pipe and thence to a deck fill are another method (Figure 9-31).

Whenever filling tanks in this manner, wait for the rain to clean off the deck or canvas for a few minutes before opening the deck fill cap. Greasing the threads of the cap will help waterproof it so unwanted rain or sea water can't leak in. A filter in the line will remove residual dirt and other contaminants.

DECK DRAINS

The ability of a deck to clear itself of water—from rain or sea—is largely a function of its design. *Adriana* has a dead spot on either side of the deck just forward of the transom, which curves slightly upward. The gel coat here is stained from stagnant water, and the only easy remedy is constant sponging and applying rubbing compound or a polish such as Star-Brite. A more difficult remedy would be to build up the area so water runs off to a scupper or deck drain.

Because *Adriana* has a fiberglass toe rail, it is not possible to drill a hole through it to let the water run off. Were the toe rail teak, it would be a simple matter to make an overboard drain. If the deck is poorly designed, or if the trim (coam-

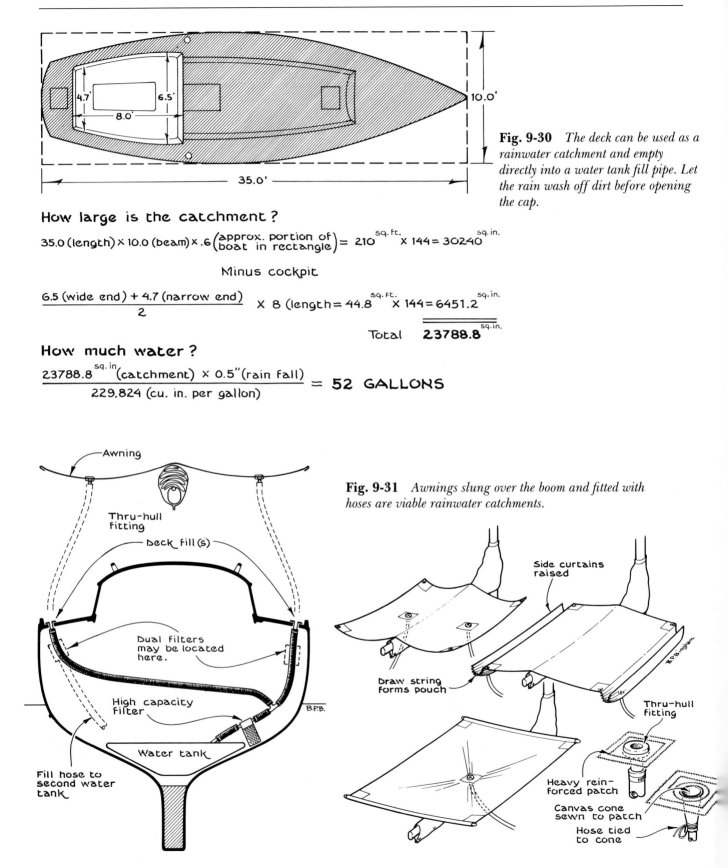

Fig. 9-30 *The deck can be used as a rainwater catchment and empty directly into a water tank fill pipe. Let the rain wash off dirt before opening the cap.*

How large is the catchment?

35.0 (length) × 10.0 (beam) × .6 $\binom{\text{approx. portion of}}{\text{boat in rectangle}}$ = 210 $^{\text{sq. ft.}}$ × 144 = 30240 $^{\text{sq. in.}}$

Minus cockpit

$$\frac{6.5 \text{ (wide end)} + 4.7 \text{ (narrow end)}}{2} \times 8 \text{ (length} = 44.8 ^{\text{sq. ft.}} \times 144 = 6451.2 ^{\text{sq. in.}}$$

Total **23788.8** $^{\text{sq. in.}}$

How much water?

$$\frac{23788.8 ^{\text{sq. in}} \text{(catchment)} \times 0.5'' \text{(rain fall)}}{229.824 \text{ (cu. in. per gallon)}} = \textbf{52 GALLONS}$$

Fig. 9-31 *Awnings slung over the boom and fitted with hoses are viable rainwater catchments.*

ings, toe rails, etc.) impedes the drainage of water on deck, first see if there is a way to route it directly overboard. If not, it's fairly easy to install a scupper with hose led to the cockpit scupper hose via a Y-fitting, or to any other thru-hull fitting in the hull. Granted, this is a lot of work for a minor irritation, but some may find it worthwhile, especially those who can't stand things out of order.

MAKING A SEA HOOD

For serious cruising, a sea hood (also called a storm hood or hatch turtle) mounted over the forward end of the main sliding hatch is almost essential. When water washes over the deck, as at some time it surely must, the vertical opening between the deck and the hatch allows it to stream inside the cabin. A sea hood provides the forward protection while the tracks of the hatch do their best to protect the flanks. Closing the hatch and inserting weather boards, with the possible addition of a Lexan storm shutter as mentioned earlier in this chapter, protects the top and aft sides. A sea hood also provides a place to snap on a cockpit dodger. Without it, the dodger must be designed with the complication of a sliding hatch in mind (e.g., one solution is to construct a low bridge over the sliding

hatch, similar to a traveler bridge, and snap the dodger to it).

A satisfactory sea hood can be fabricated out of solid hardwood or out of plywood with fiberglass and/or a wood such as teak covering it. The weakness of this construction is that flat surfaces are not as strong as rounded ones. Molding a crowned fiberglass sea hood in a female mold makes much sense.

To make your own, take approximate measurements of the area to be covered. Figure 9-32 will help.

Purchase some 1″ x 4″ furring strips, a piece of Masonite® and some screws. To take more precise measurements, mock up a sea hood over your hatch. Be sure the hatch can be pushed all the way open without hitting the sea hood. Similarly, don't extend the sea hood too far over the hatch opening, which would obstruct access below.

Transfer the curve of the deck by placing the 1″ x 6″ board horizontally on deck, just forward of the hatch. Use a compass (Figure 9-33) to follow the deck and scribe a line on the board. When this board has been sawn, it becomes the forward end of the mold. The back of the hood will be open to make room for the hatch, but it will be necessary to cut a second board to fit the back of the mold to hold it together during lamination and to keep the Masonite curve fair.

Build in a flange on the forward end and sides

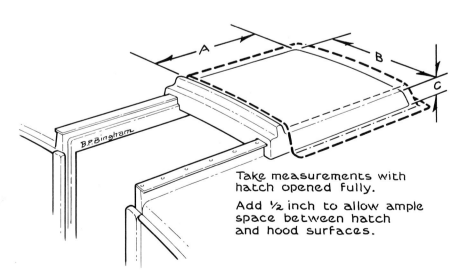

Take measurements with hatch opened fully.

Add ½ inch to allow ample space between hatch and hood surfaces.

Fig. 9-32 *Measure the size of your sea hood carefully, making certain it will be high enough to let the hatch slide underneath, and that the flanges won't interfere with other fittings.*

Fig. 9-33 *To transfer the deck to the mold frame, follow the deck line with a compass, scribing a mark on the board as you go.*

Fig. 9-34 *The corner of the mold shows the ¼-inch furring strip nailed to the mold frame side. The corner has been radiused so that the cloth, which will form the flange, will lie smoothly and not bunch up.*

of the mold so that the fiberglass cloth can be laid over it (Figure 9-34). The edges can be left ragged and trimmed later. This flange will be the place where the sea hood is later thru-bolted to the deck. Nail the Masonite over the four-sided frame (Figure 9-35).

Once the mold is tested to fit the deck, take it into the basement or some sheltered area where you can work with fiberglass. If working inside the boat, be sure it is well ventilated, as fiberglass gives off harmful styrene fumes.

Fiberglass cloth and mat does not bend well to sharp corners, so it is necessary to radius the corners with fillets of clay, epoxy putty or some other malleable material that will retain its shape when the cloth is pressed down on it (Figure 9-36).

I called the Baltek Corporation in Northvale, New Jersey, to order several sheets of Contourkore® end-grain balsa and spoke with Keith Walton, the chief engineer. After hearing my description of the project, he gave me the following lamination schedule:

    20 mils thickness of gel coat
    1½-ounce mat
    6–7-ounce cloth
    1½-ounce mat

    ½-inch Contourkore® end-grain balsa
    1½-ounce mat
    6–7-ounce cloth
    1½-ounce mat
    1½-ounce mat

An optional layer of 6–7-ounce cloth, Walton said, will leave a smoother finished surface than mat. He said this lamination schedule would give

Fig. 9-35 *Masonite is laid over the top of the frame and nailed. Note the curve in the end pieces and the radiused flanges.*

Fig. 9-36 *Fillets must be made with putty where the side pieces meet the Masonite. The gentle curves created by the fillets permit better conformance by the fiberglass cloth.*

Fig. 9-37 *Wax paper or a standard parting agent must be used to cover the mold before laying in the mat and cloth. This prevents the fiberglass from bonding to the mold.*

me a flange thickness of about ⅜-inch, sufficient for bearing loads and for bolting through to the deck. Figures 9-37 through 9-40 show how the precut and darted rolls of mat, cloth and balsa were glassed in. Ten-ounce cloth was used in place of 6-ounce and the gel coat dispensed with in favor of a simple paint job on completion. Or, I could have brushed on the gel coat after pulling the hood from the mold, rather than brushing it on inside the mold before the mat and cloth were laid in.

Cover the entire inside of the mold with wax paper or a parting agent. Then, with cheap disposable brushes, rubber surgical gloves and acetone solvent standing by, wet out the mold with resin. Then lay in a pre-cut piece of mat and wet it out with the brush. Saturate the strands of fiberglass so that no air bubbles exist. It's not as hard as it sounds. For small projects like a sea hood, a paint brush is suitable. Avoid too much brushing as the mat will begin to fall apart.

Polyester resin, like other two-part systems, requires a catalyst to make the resin cure. The speed with which curing occurs varies with temperature and with the amount of catalyst used. To be on the safe side, mix up a small amount in a clean container according to the ratios specified on the side of the can, and let sit. Observe how long it takes to go off. Poke it with a stick at various stages to see how it is hardening. When applying the resin to the mold, you'll want sufficient time to lay in and wet out mat and cloth before it hardens. The resin shouldn't harden in

Fig. 9-38 *Here, the first layer of 1½-ounce mat has been pre-cut and laid into the mold. Polyester resin is used to saturate the mat, and a cheap brush used to wet it out. Note the slits and darts in the far end to prevent bunching on the curve.*

Fig. 9-39 *After the mat is wetted out, a layer of 10-ounce cloth is pushed into place and also wetted out.*

Fig. 9-40 *With three layers of mat and cloth in the mold, ½-inch Baltek Contourkore® end-grain balsa is cut and placed in the mold.*

less than about 35 to 40 minutes; if it does, put less catalyst in the next time. There's nothing wrong with a slow cure, in fact, the longer the cure, the stronger it will be. Sometimes it takes overnight and you go to bed worrying that not enough catalyst was used. But by morning the resin is invariably rock hard.

While the first layer is still wet, lay in a precut piece of cloth and wet that out, too, followed by another piece of mat. You can now fit in the core material. It will probably be necessary to cut some pieces so that the core extends nearly to the edge of the mold, about a quarter to half-inch.

I discovered after I had pushed the balsa in place that the mat and cloth at the sides were sagging, and that it would have been better if I had designed in an outward angle greater than 90 degrees. To hold the layers of mat and cloth flush against the frame mold, I placed some strips of wax paper against it, then a board propped up by bricks (Figure 9-41). This worked satisfactorily.

When the resin kicked, I followed with the last four layers of mat and cloth, and let it cure for several days. Then I pried the sea hood from the mold, cut the rough edges with a saber saw and ground them down with a belt sander. A file and sanding block finished it off.

I discovered several voids and depressions in the surface of my sea hood, primarily because the wax paper bunched up in the corners. Had I to do it over, I would use a regular parting agent, or try paste wax. To fair out the surfaces, I used Interlux's 417 and 418 Epoxy Sanding Surfacer and Fairing Compound. It is a two-part putty that goes on smoothly with a wide putty knife, and sands easily after it has cured (Figure 9-42). For paint, I used a white topside enamel by Interlux. Two coats gave a nice lustre and covered up all the fiberglass.

Now, place the sea hood in position on deck and drill holes through the sea hood and deck. Drill one at a time, inserting a round head stainless steel bolt in the last hole before drilling the next. This will insure all bolts fitting in the end. Space bolts about six inches apart.

If there is a core in the deck (coachroof), you might consider coating the insides of the holes with epoxy glue or resin (Figure 9-1). Mix up a

Use polysulphide or other good bedding compound on the threads of each bolt, under the washer and under the head. Run the bolts through and have someone below put on a washer and nut. If you carefully measure the length of bolts needed, hexagonal acorn nuts can be used that will look better than regular nuts. Alternatively, you can sometimes buy plastic or vinyl finishing caps that fit over the nuts to conceal them and reduce the chance of injury if someone hits their head on the nut.

It also would be a good idea to bed the entire perimeter of the sea hood before placing it onto the deck for the last time. After all, the whole idea is to keep water out, and it is doubtful that a completely watertight seal can be had from just mating two bare surfaces of fiberglass.

A piece of teak stripping screwed or bolted to the forward edge of the sea hood will lend an attractive look to it, help conceal the raw edge of fiberglass, and also function as a splashboard. If you've done the job right, you should be able to stand on top of the sea hood and jump up and down without causing it to crack (Figure 9-43).

Fig. 9-41 *When the mat and cloth began sagging along the sides, I cut strips of wax paper and placed them between the wet resin and a board supported by bricks—it worked.*

batch, plug the bottom with tape, and pour into the hole. After a minute, remove the tape and catch the excess resin. This coating will seal off the grain of the core and prevent moisture from entering should the bedding compound later come loose and permit deck water to enter the hole. A rotten deck core is almost a complete write-off—very expensive to fix and disturbing to live with.

Fig. 9-42 *After the sea hood was popped from the mold, surface indentations were filled with Interlux 414 and 415 Epoxy Sanding Surfacer and Fairing Compound, then sanded.*

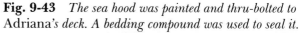

Fig. 9-43 *The sea hood was painted and thru-bolted to Adriana's deck. A bedding compound was used to seal it.*

COCKPITS

Along with the berths, the cockpit is the most-used locale on a sailboat. Here the boat is steered, and in it happens most of the navigation, lounging, and the many other daily activities that make up life on board a cruising boat.

It follows that the cockpit area design is of preeminent importance. What are the requirements of a good cockpit? Let's list some.

- Comfortable seating, level or heeled
- Small volume, to minimize amount of water that could fill it
- Large scuppers
- Good visibility over the cabin
- Surfaces to brace feet when heeled
- Easy to handle sheets and lines
- Convenient access to lockers and/or lazarettes
- Convenient helm
- Bridge deck or high companionway sill
- Long enough to lie down in

The list could go on ad infinitum. The basic theme, as repeated over and over in this book, is comfort, safety and utility. The stipulation of comfort is more than hedonism. An exhausted crew is a crew capable of placing the entire vessel in danger; a rested crew is stronger and makes better decisions.

Utility concerns the ability to efficiently carry out the multifarious functions necessary to keeping the ship going each day. The ease with which one can handle lines, find the jerry jug in the cockpit locker, toss a life ring to someone overboard, trim the mainsheet or lie down for a snooze are all factors to consider when selecting a boat. Unfortunately, many of these characteristics are not known until after you've sailed a number of miles. A sea trial helps, but you can't possibly answer all the questions.

If you're committed to your present boat, then you must live with it. Some things can be changed, however, and those are the ones we'll concentrate on. One way or another, depending on your ambition, almost any fault can be corrected.

Seating

Seating comfort depends to an extent on your individual body and how it fits the boat (Figure 9-44). The seats are more than likely molded into the deck, and changing them is a drastic measure.

Backrests can be moved inboard more easily than outboard. False backrests can be fashioned from wood (or plywood covered with fiberglass) to shorten the distance between the back and the boat's centerline. If the distance to the nearest foot brace is too long (Figure 9-45), this might be considered. Of course, the width of the seat

Fig. 9-44 *Comfortable seating depends on the match between an individual's body and the distance between backrests and foot supports. Poor seating causes unnecessary fatigue, the enemy of good judgment at sea.*

Too wide

Too narrow

Too narrow

Just right

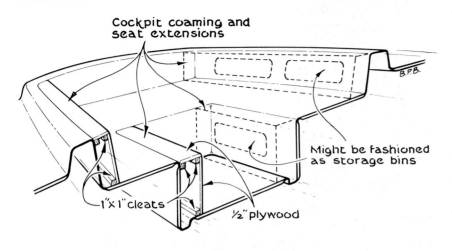

Cockpit coaming and seat extensions

1″x1″ cleats

½″ plywood

Might be fashioned as storage bins

B.P.B.

Fig. 9-45 *Here's one way to shorten the distance between the backrests and footrests. Cleats are screwed to the seat and backrest, the area is enclosed with ½-inch plywood and covered with several layers of fiberglass mat and cloth. Sand and paint. Side cutouts could make storage room for winch handles, line and the like.*

also will be shortened, unless the seat is extended over the footwell. Then, space for legs and feet is a consideration. Most people are most comfortable and least tired if their legs can extend straight to the footrest so that leg muscles don't need to be flexed. Sitting for long periods with knees bent is very tiring.

Cockpit Size

Dealing with too large a cockpit is more serious a problem than the relative discomfort of an ill-designed cockpit. A boat at sea can and more than likely will be pooped sooner or later. We were pooped on *Adriana* one summer while sailing in Green Bay. Thirty-knot winds were whipping up steep, breaking six to eight-foot seas in the shallow bay. As the wind increased, the main was furled with roller furling gear up to the numbers. Suddenly, a wave larger than the rest reared up and broke over the cockpit. The next instant we were sitting up to our chests in water. As the boat rolled, half the water rushed overboard. Now the water was only filling the footwell and we were no longer quite so anxious. The scuppers required several minutes to drain the remaining water. (As a footnote, Carl Alberg, designer of the Triton, calculated that a flooded cockpit would lower the stern just six inches.)

This sort of spine-tingling soaking can happen most anytime when seas are steep. Boats with large footwells, no bridge deck or with a low companionway sill invite disaster. A footwell that measures five feet long by 2½ feet wide by two

feet deep can hold 25 cubic feet of water. Since each cubic foot weighs about 60 pounds, the footwell can hold 1,500 pounds of water. Add to this the amount of water that could be held between coamings above the seats, and the figures are even more staggering.

The Offshore Racing Council limits cockpit volume to six percent LOA times maximum beam times freeboard aft. For example, a 32-foot boat with 9½ foot beam and 3-foot freeboard aft—32 x .06 x 9.5 x 3—is limited by this rule to a 54.72 cubic foot cockpit. Also, the cockpit floor under these rules must be 0.02 x LWL above the waterline.

Hal Roth, a blue-water sailor who has published several books on how to outfit cruising boats, modified his Spencer 35, *Whisper*, by radically extending the cabin several feet aft. He did this not to increase living space below, but to minimize cockpit size.

From one point of view, a cockpit can never be too small. Naval architect and boatbuilder Tom Colvin told me once he has built just three boats with cockpits. He said he simply doesn't believe in them for offshore sailing. But comfort is its own dictum. If you're going to spend 50 percent of your time in the cockpit, it really should have a comfortable length and width—at least enough to lie down in.

Frolic's Shallow Footwell

Aside from having no footwell at all (very safe, but no place to stand up in without hitting your head on the boom), the best arrangement is the

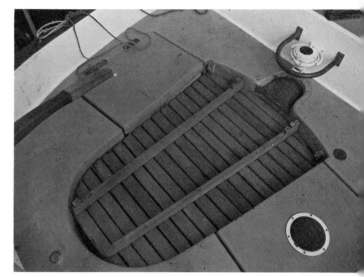

Fig. 9-46 *Frolic's cockpit has been modified for safety offshore. The footwell was cut off from underneath with a saber saw, and a new floor glassed in just several inches deep. Seat lockers also were glassed shut.*

Fig. 9-48 *With the grating upside down, the longitudinal supports provide footrests when heeling.*

shallowest. Danny Greene fabricated a cockpit that is as safe as any I've seen. After several years sailing his Mystic 10–3 to the Caribbean from Newport each fall, he decided that even a conventionally sized footwell was too large. He cut off the footwell from below and fiberglassed in a new floor only four inches below the seats. He used plywood and fiberglass mat with polyester resin. Figures 9-46 and 9-49 illustrate the various permutations of his cockpit arrangement. The floor grating can be mounted flush for

sleeping, inverted to provide a foot brace, and elevated for dining—a safe and functional arrangement, though it takes getting used to.

Shortening the Cockpit

Excessively large footwells can be made smaller in several ways. Depending on the tiller or wheel location, part of the footwell can be boxed off either permanently or temporarily

Fig. 9-47 *A teak-planked grating was made to fit the footwell. In this configuration, it is flush with the seats— an excellent idea for sleeping outside in the tropics.*

Fig. 9-49 *With a box or some other flat object underneath, the grating elevates for use as a dining table.*

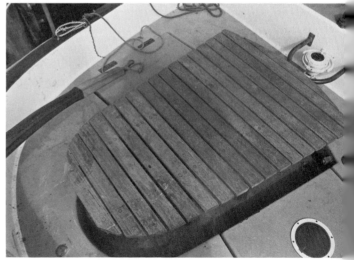

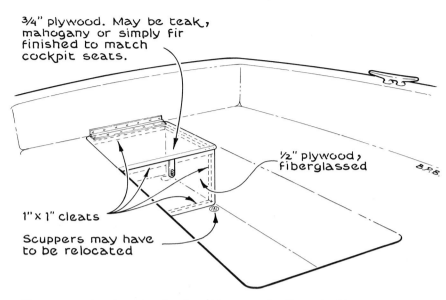

3/4" plywood. May be teak, mahogany or simply fir finished to match cockpit seats.

1/2" plywood, fiberglassed

1" x 1" cleats

Scuppers may have to be relocated

Box may be located at either end of cockpit.

Fig. 9-50 *To minimize the volume of the footwell, one end can be closed off with plywoood and fiberglass. A watertight, lockable lid gives access to new storage. Scuppers might need to be relocated.*

during offshore passages (Figure 9-50). The area could also be used for storage, accessible from the cockpit or down below.

Plywood fiberglassed to the sides of the footwell also can work well. Don't forget to sand the gel coat off the footwell surfaces and to wash with a solvent like acetone before laying in glass. Gel coats contain mold release agents that will prevent good adhesion unless removed.

On *Iskra*, Frank Mulville shortens the cockpit by dropping in a bottomless wood box that is securely fastened to the footwell sides. A canvas is stretched taut over the rest in bad weather. While this might not withstand a real blast, it would slow down and perhaps deflect some incoming water over the side.

Seat Lockers

Seat lockers should have deep gutters molded in to allow water to run off. These should be deep enough so they won't overflow into the locker when a wave breaks. If the gutters aren't deep enough, glue a rubber gasket around the inside perimeter of the lid and install a lever-action type lock that compresses the gasket lid tightly. Other solutions are to run scupper hoses from the gutters into the cockpit or screw a thin wood or Plexiglas strip over the crack between

the lid and seat (don't screw to both or you won't be able to open it!) A method of locking the lid should also be arranged, using locks and hasps or other secure locking mechanism. Murray-Clevco makes an unusual hinge that works like a spring-loaded clevis pin. (See Chapter 3, Figure 3-24). These can be mounted where the lock and hasp normally are and prevent the lid from opening unless the pin is popped.

A drastic measure is to seal the lid off altogether and gain access to the locker area from below. This means going below to fetch fenders and lines, and admittedly might be impractical on some boats. But there is security in knowing there are no openings on deck in the hull except for the hatches and vents.

Ideally, I'd leave one seat locker that could be opened from the cockpit, but it would only be about six inches deep, so even if it did fill with water, there would be no great danger. In it I would store winch handles, bilge pump handles, small bits of line, the ship's horn, sail ties and all those other odds and ends that are needed on deck, sometimes at a moment's notice.

Blower Openings

The U.S. Coast Guard requires bilge blowers for gas engines. On *Adriana,* the blower was mounted on the footwell wall. If the cockpit filled up with water, it ran through this hole into the locker and then into the bilge. With the new diesel installed, the blower was no longer required; I removed it and sealed the hole—one less weak link to worry about!

The blower hose led to a vent on the after deck where air from the bilge was expelled. Next to it was another vent to introduce air into the bilge, also required by the U.S. Coast Guard. Although the blower was no longer required, the vents should be retained to remove unpleasant fumes and to provide the engine with air. In heavy weather, these cowls should be removed and deck plates screwed in.

Engine Controls

Engine controls mounted in the footwell wall, if not recessed or protected by a bar (Figure 9-51) are susceptible to damage from an errant foot or dropped winch handle. I've had the ignition key broken off inside the lock in this way.

Another method of protecting the engine instruments is a Plexiglas cover that is hinged above the panel. To start the engine or kill it, simply lift the plate up, and lower it when done.

Compass Location

Placing the compass in a convenient location so that it can be read from anyplace in the cockpit shouldn't pose any significant problem. On the centerline is preferable, but sometimes this is too much in the way and makes it vulnerable to breakage. With good, visible lubber lines, the compass can be mounted on the aft side of the cabin, either to port or starboard of the companionway hatch, or one on both sides if need be. Pedestal wheel steerers, of course, lick the problem by placing the compass on top of the pedestal. On some older wood boats with tiller steering, a binnacle was mounted in the middle of the cockpit just to place the compass on centerline and in an easily viewed location. What's important is that the compass lubberline be parallel to the ship's keel, and free from the magnetic influence of metal objects.

Surplus Seating

A last thought on cockpits is provision for seating at coaming level. You can now purchase small, portable seats that fit over winches, but I think the teak step arrangement in Figure 9-52 is more sensible.

Fig. 9-51 *The throttle on this boat has been protected with a simple piece of bent aluminum bolted to the footwell side. A stop has been seized to the bar to prevent the throttle from being backed off below idling speed.*

Fig. 9-52 *A nifty seat and step was made of teak to mount flush with the top of the coaming. It is supported on the other side with braces.*

LIFE RAFTS, MAN-OVERBOARD POLES AND OTHER SAFETY EQUIPMENT

Life rafts are expensive—several thousand dollars for a good one. Many cannot afford them and rely on their hard or rubber dinghy to serve this hopefully-never-needed function.

Life rafts are difficult to deploy in a gale with steep, breaking waves. If possible, a life raft cannister should be mounted somewhere on deck or near the cockpit where it can be opened, inflated and launched successfully.

An ideal spot is in the cockpit footwell, covered by a fabricated enclosure that not only contains the life raft, but reduces the volume of the footwell at the same time.

On deck forward or on the after deck are two other possible sites, but here they are as vulnerable as the deck boxes discussed earlier in this chapter. Some new boats are built with cavities molded into the cockpit specifically to house the life raft. This could be accomplished on an older boat, perhaps using a seat locker in the same manner as was described for propane bottle lockers.

Man-overboard poles are generally mounted in a tube fixed to the stern pulpit, sometimes with the tip run through a piece of PVC tube lashed to the backstay. Life rings and horseshoes can be easily mounted in the special holders sold by manufacturers, which are clamped to stanchions or the stern pulpit. There is a degree of comfort in storing life jackets somewhere near the cockpit, such as in a seat locker, but there's no real reason why they can't be stored just as safely down below in a readily accessible place. Flares should be kept dry and are best stored in airtight pouches in a well-ventilated locker in the cabin. A gasketed munitions box works well. Except for the life raft, most safety and emergency equipment can be brought on board with little construction of special housings or holders. Finding the best storage places is more a matter of studying the peculiarities of your boat than unraveling some arcane secret that only master mariners know.

LIGHTS

U.S. Coast Guard requirements specify certain navigational lights for certain size boats. According to the most recent amendments to the International Regulations for Preventing Collisions at Sea (COLREGS), sailing vessels under 20 meters (65 feet), are required to carry red and green sidelights and a white stern light. Under 20 meters, these lights may be combined in a single lantern carried at the top of the mast, popularly known as the masthead tricolor. Under power, even with sails raised, the tricolor is not legal and the regular sidelights and stern light must be shown along with a white bow (mast) light.

Almost all cruising sailboats are sold with this lighting system already installed. The ship's 12-volt battery is the power source. Oil lamps may be carried as back-ups. Sidelight lamps can be fastened to boards on the shrouds and the stern lamp carried on the stern rail.

The lamps should be removable from the mounting boards for refilling and bringing below in rough weather. Properly sealed electric lights are easier to deal with and certainly less expensive. But if it's the salty look you desire, consider adding oil lamps.

BOOM GALLOWS

One of the most important, handiest and sometimes most bothersome additions to the deck are boom gallows. This heavy-duty crutch for the boom can be used to lash the boom in heavy weather, thus preventing the boom from swinging even the slightest distance. When all hell breaks loose, you don't want to risk the boom and furled or reefed mainsail banging back and forth—the blocks and boom bails could break, or if the topping lift snaps, the whole mess could come crashing down into the cockpit.

While custom bronze corner fittings can be purchased to join the vertical supports and gallows pipe or board for about $150, a very serviceable set of gallows can be built with hardware store materials.

Determining where and how to mount the vertical poles to the deck is the most important consideration. Figures 9-53 to 9-55 illustrate one method. Stainless steel pipe (galvanized also could be used) is cut at the right length, and preferably long enough for someone to stand in the cockpit without hitting his head on the gallows. Of course, if the gallows are mounted over the cabin, this wouldn't be a problem. The ends can be mounted in hardwood blocks fixed to the deck, and the pipe strapped to the coaming or cabin side.

The top member can be another length of pipe welded or joined with right angle pipe con-

Fig. 9-53 *Boom gallows support the boom in gale conditions. This one was made from one-inch stainless steel pipe and teak.*

Fig. 9-54 *This gallows detail shows how stanchion bases and pipe fittings were used to hold the sections of pipe together and to the gallows. They also could have been welded.*

nections to the vertical pipes. A more attractive method is to select an attractive piece of wood and bolt it to the pipe. If using stainless steel pipe, save your drill bits and have your local metal smith drill them for you.

Most boom gallows have three stations for resting the boom, one on centerline and one each side of center. Cut these from the hardwood and cover with leather tacked in with bronze tacks or boatnails.

Boom gallows are handy places to dry out bathing suits or tie a bunch of bananas, fasten

Fig. 9-55 *Stanchion bases were used to anchor the vertical sections that also were held in alignment by teak blocks thru-bolted to the coaming.*

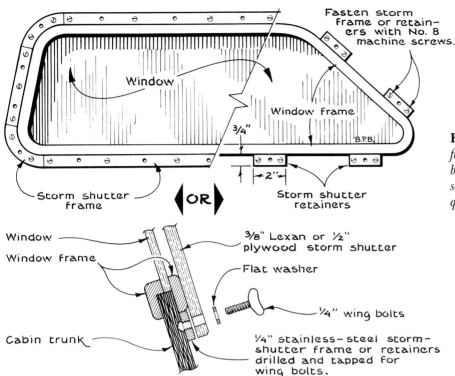

Fig. 9-56 *Storm shutters should be fitted to all large ports. Steel plates bolted to the cabin sides with machine screws and wing nuts make the quickest and easiest installation.*

one end of a cockpit awning or function as a handhold when leaning over the side to pee. Well made, they also contribute a rugged good looks.

STORM SHUTTERS

Ports are one of the most vulnerable points of a yacht. They are the thinnest material between the inside of the boat and the sea, and often the weakest. Large ports are especially dangerous, and all too common on many boats. In his classic analysis of damage to boats in *Heavy Weather Sailing,* Adlard Coles asserts that more ports are broken on the lee side by the cabin slamming against the water than those broken by waves hitting against them on the weather side. In late 1982, the 58-foot *Trashman* sank, with loss of life, primarily because storm shutters only were fitted to the weather-side ports. In either case, storm shutters should be on hand to protect any port larger than six or eight inches across.

Storm shutters can be made from many materials. Edward S. Brewer writes that 3/8 to 1/2-inch plywood, 1/8-inch aluminum and 5/16 to 3/8-inch Lexan are suitable. Because few production boats have provisions for storm shutters, it may

be necessary to machine the hardware. The shutters should overlap the port by an inch or more, and be fastened by a wing bolt screwed into a plate thru-bolted to the cabin side around the circumference of the port (Figure 9-56). A 1″ x 2″ stainless steel plate drilled and tapped for 5/16-inch machine screws will make putting up the shutters a quick and easy job when heavy weather threatens. Another way is to bolt wood channels to the cabin side and slide in a Lexan shutter held in place with retaining pins.

BULWARKS

Sure footing at the perimeter of the deck is essential. Low, molded toe rails are better than nothing, but could be supplemented by bolting a length of 1″ x 2″ teak on top. An even better plan is adding six-inch-high bulwarks (Figure 9-57). New Found Metals of Port Townsend, Washington, makes handsome cast bronze fittings for hardwood bulwark ends that accept 3 5/16-inch boards. Elevating the boards an inch off deck allows water to run off. If you have molded in toe rails, installation will be complicated, unless there is a flat surface for the hardware. Here custom fabrications may work better.

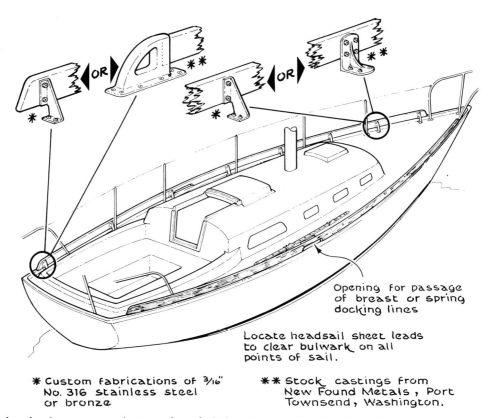

* Custom fabrications of 3/16"
No. 316 stainless steel
or bronze

** Stock castings from
New Found Metals, Port
Townsend, Washington.

Opening for passage
of breast or spring
docking lines

Locate headsail sheet leads
to clear bulwark on all
points of sail.

Fig. 9-57 *Bulwarks give more security to work on deck than low toe rails. New Found Metals makes handsome end fittings of bronze for this purpose, as well as gallow corners and other items.*

Also plan for hawse-holes so you can still use your breast cleats. One can't begin to appreciate the sense of security good bulwarks provide until sitting on the foredeck in a gale, trying to change jibs.

DINGHY STOWAGE

Offshore, dinghies cannot be towed behind the boat. Eventually, the strain on the painter will cause it to chafe and break. Similarly, stowing dinghies in davits hung over the stern invites disaster—one large wave washing over the transom could tear it away. And, in a rolly anchorage they are difficult to launch, especially by a single person. At the least, dinghies in davits should have strong canvas covers to keep them from filling with water.

Stowing dinghies on deck is safest, using thru-bolted padeyes with strong lashings over the up-turned hull. On small boats, even a seven-foot dinghy is too large to stow on deck. And even if it can be wedged in somewhere, it could pose a danger to crew working on deck. Two-part nesting dinghies are the answer. Danny Greene de-

signed one of the first nesting dinghies (Figure 9-58). His *Two Bits* is a 9'6" dinghy that breaks down into two sections, each capable of floating on its own. To launch, he ties a painter to each end, throws both halves over the side, jumps into the larger, pulls the two halves together, and inserts three large stainless steel bolts with wing nuts to secure them.

On *Frolic*, Danny stows the two halves, one inside the other, upside down on the foredeck. Heavy lashings keep it in place. Slotted toe rails and deck pad eyes can be used for anchoring the lines. Try, as much as possible, to leave the side-decks and foredeck unobstructed. Plans are available for $30, and to date more than 700 sets have been sold—testimony to the cleverness and wisdom of this idea. Many other nesting dinghies appear in the classified pages of boating magazines.

SUMMARY

Most boat handling jobs take place on deck and in the cockpit—setting sails, dropping ground tackle, launching the dinghy—and for

Fig. 9-58 *Danny Greene (inset) designed and built Two-Bits as a two-part nesting dinghy for stowage on deck of small boats. Here Two-Bits is shown on the coachroof of a Contessa 26. (Danny Greene photo).*

this reason the deck plan must be intelligently conceived to facilitate these tasks.

- All deck fittings should be well bedded and thru-bolted and all vents and hatches capable of being made watertight.
- Everything on deck must be strong enough to stand on, jump on, and withstand a strong blow.
- Ground tackle must be able to be securely stowed above and below deck, yet ready for deployment in minimum time.
- Lifelines should be 30 inches high, stanchions thru-bolted, preferably both horizontally and vertically. They should not be used for safety harness lines unless you are absolutely certain of their strength and attachment to the pulpits or deck.
- Stanchions should be thru-bolted or welded to their bases.
- Hatches must be able to be locked from inside and outside, and held open at various heights to provide ventilation.
- Oversize winches are less taxing on the crew, especially if they are self-tailing.
- Oversize cleats are stronger, can receive multiple lines, and are easier to use. Large breast cleats located amidships are recommended.

- Propane tank lockers should be sealed off from the interior and vented overboard.
- A rainwater catchment system minimizes reliance on shore water.
- A sea hood protects the vulnerable and non-watertight main hatch and makes possible secure fastening of dodgers.
- Cockpits should be long enough to lie down in, but the footwells should be as small as possible without sacrificing comfort.
- Scuppers should be at least 1½ inches in diameter or larger.
- Cockpit footrests and backrests should be placed at comfortable distances to mimimize fatigue.
- Seat lockers should have deep gutters and be lockable.
- Life rafts, man-overboard poles and other safety gear must be mounted on deck where they are safe from large boarding waves, yet quickly deployable.
- There must be some method of lashing the boom without movement, preferably to a strong set of gallows.
- Large ports must have storm shutters that can be screwed in with relative ease.
- Provision should be made for stowing a hard or inflatable dinghy on deck.

FURTHER READING

Customizing Your Boat by Ian Nicolson; Van Nostrand Reinhold: 135 West 50th Street, New York, New York 10020.

The Ocean Sailing Yacht, Vols. I and II, by Donald M. Street, Jr.; W. W. Norton & Company, 500 Fifth Avenue, New York, New York 10110.

The Self-Sufficient Sailor by Lin and Larry Pardey; W. W. Norton & Company, 500 Fifth Avenue, New York, New York 10110.

Cruising Under Sail by Eric Hiscock; Oxford University Press, Walton St., Oxford 0X2 6DP, England.

Single-handed Cruising and Sailing by Frank Mulville; Nautical, Macmillan London Ltd., 4 Little Essex St., London, WC2 3LF England.

Heavy Weather Sailing by Adlard Coles; Grenada Publishing Ltd., Frogmore, St. Albans, Hertfordshire AL22NF, England.

Metal Corrosion in Boats by Nigel Warren; International Marine Publishing Co., Camden, Maine 04843.

CHAPTER 10

Rigs and Sails

There lies the port; the vessel puffs her sail:
There gloom the dark broad seas.

ALFRED LORD TENNYSON

The sailboat's rig and sails are its means of propulsion and the features that most distinguish it from other types of watercraft. Like the auxiliary engine, they have many moving parts, all working in concert in their job of making the boat move. The loads on the rig and sails are considerable and so it is not surprising that torn sails and dismastings are not uncommon.

The weekend sailor can afford to take a few chances—waiting an extra year to replace standing rigging, limiting inspections for corrosion to a walk around the mast, and sailing with torn batten pockets until season's end. Not so the cruiser. Replacement parts and repair services are not so easily obtained away from home port, nor affordable if cruising on a limited budget. In some countries, parts and services may be nonexistent. And if these aren't reasons enough to invest in a good rig and a large sail inventory, the cruiser should remember his boat and his life may depend upon their functioning.

TYPES OF RIGS

Determining the best rig for cruising is an argument so seldom resolved that this in itself admits the utility of all different types. However, coastal cruisers generally favor the more weatherly rigs, as a greater percentage of their sailing time is spent beating to windward. Blue-water passage makers more often choose a good reaching rig, such as the ketch or schooner, because the distances they cover enable them to plan trade wind routes and the more comfortable, off-the-wind points of sail.

It seems that everyone has a favorite rig. Certainly there is no lack of widely divergent opinions in the cruising literature, so it is not my

Fig. 10-1 *These drawings illustrate how similarly sized sloops, cutters, ketches and yawls might add and shorten sail in varying wind conditions. Definitions: Sloop—single mast with main and jib; may be fractional rig. Cutter—single mast with main, jib and staysail. Mast is stepped near center of boat, distinguishing it from a double-headsail sloop, which has the mast stepped farther forward. Ketch—two masts with main, jib and mizzen; may have double headsails. Mizzenmast is about two-thirds height of mainmast and is stepped forward of the rudderstock. Yawl—two masts with main, jib and mizzen; mizzen is shorter than ketch mizzen and is stepped aft of the rudderstock. May have double headsails. On ketches and yawls with outboard rudders, the size of the mizzen is more telling.*

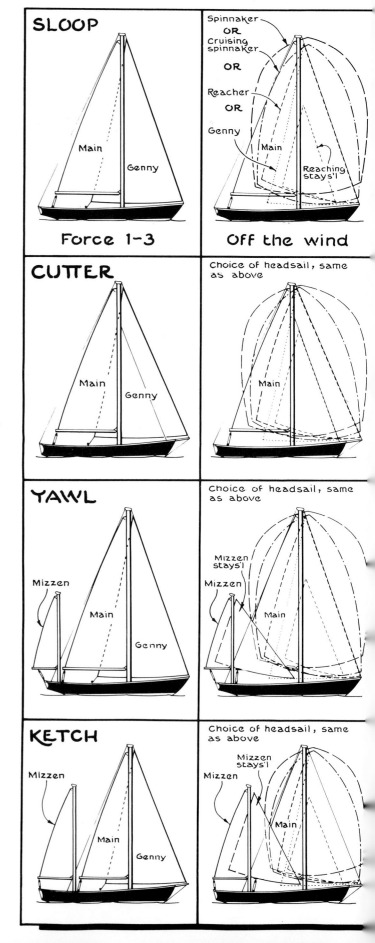

purpose here to summarize the pros and cons of each rig. However, like everyone else, I too have some opinions and observations on the subject, and these are contained in the following section.

Sloop, Cutter, Ketch and Yawl

Determining how to strengthen the rig and obtain well-made sails is partly contingent on the type of rig, and how it will handle both heavy and light weather. A ketch or yawl, with two masts, has a few more options than the single-masted sloop and cutter. Figure 10-1 illustrates how similar size sloops, cutters, ketches and yawls add and shorten sail.

The mizzen on the yawl is only used in light to moderate winds when the course is off the wind; going to windward it is often furled on the boom. Because the yawl's mizzenmast is shorter than the ketch's, it isn't used as often to fly a mizzen staysail. Yet the yawl's mainmast is taller than the ketch's. In fact, it may be about the same height as a similarly sized sloop, only the boom may be shorter to make room for the mizzen.

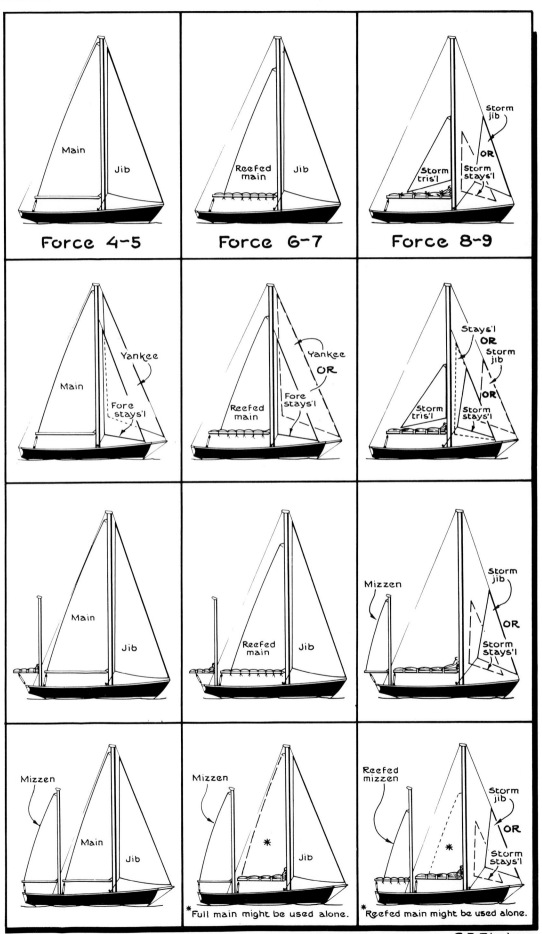

Force 4-5

Force 6-7

Force 8-9

B.B.Bingham

Yawl and ketch mizzens are used somewhat similarly to the staysail on the cutter, namely keeping the center of effort near the middle of the boat. When the wind reaches about Force 6, the 35-foot ketch handles nicely with mizzen and jib alone. Because these two sails are located at equidistant ends of the boat, they balance nicely and the boat will steer herself quite happily.

In the same conditions, the cutter will drop the jib, partly because it is farther forward, often on a bowsprit. The closer one confines sail handling near to the mast, the safer it is. No one wants to go out on a long sprit in a gale and try to bring down even a small jib. Also, keeping the staysail set and dropping the jib has the effect of moving the center of effort aft; reefing the main moves it forward. The two changes cancel each other and the boat continues to balance well. Without the staysail, a smaller jib would have to be set, and in combination with even a reefed main, the center of effort is often too far forward, possibly causing a neutral or lee helm.

Contrast this to the sloop. When the sail area carried in the foretriangle is reduced, it has the effect of moving the center of effort aft. With a full main, weather helm increases. Reefing the main pushes the center of effort forward—sometimes too far. A storm trysail and storm jib should be designed for the sloop to complement one another, achieving a degree of balance that is manageable under every condition. In severe conditions the boat should be able to lie ahull, run under bare poles, lie to a sea anchor, or fly just a storm trysail to keep the bow to the wind.

The more combinations possible, the better. If this sounds like a condemnation of sloops, it isn't. Sloops are often the fastest of the four rigs. They certainly go to weather best and are the least expensive to buy and maintain.

Tristan Jones prefers the yawl because the mainmast is tall enough to carry lots of sail in light air; the boat can balance under mizzen and jib alone; the mizzen is not so huge as to blanket the main the way a ketch's mizzen does downwind; and in light air a mizzen staysail is an alternative to the large headsail—blooper, reacher, gollywobbler, cruising chute, etc.

Eric Hiscock, on the other hand, praises the virtues of the ketch for blue-water sailing, because most sailing is done reaching, and the size of each individual sail is smaller.

The Cat Ketch

The cat ketch rig popularized by Garry Hoyt's line of Freedom boats is one of the most radical developments ever to hit the mass-production market. True, there are other oddball rigs such as the Lungstrom (butterfly), Chinese lug, and Gallant, but despite the efforts of their supporters, they really haven't been accepted by the average cruising man as well as the Freedom rig. One reason is Hoyt's marketing skills, and another is the sheer logic and simplicity of the cat ketch rig.

The rig is not new. In the late 1800's and early 1900's a number of working and recreational craft were rigged with free-standing spars of equal or near-equal height. The New Haven Sharpie, for example, was a common sight on Long Island Sound and also used by oystermen in the Carolinas. The rig was introduced to Florida waters by R. M. Monroe in the 1870's.

More recently, in 1973, Jerry Milgram's *Cascade* tore up the Southern Ocean Racing Conference (S.O.R.C.) prompting rule changes penalizing the rig. What Hoyt did was to bring together several "old" ideas and meld them into a new concept: Freestanding spars, sleeved sails and wishbone booms. Today there are a number of variations on this theme—fully battened sails, rotating wing spars tapering into a trailing edge with a conventional sail track, deck-mounted booms, single-masted freestanding rigs, and so on.

Of most interest to the cruising sailor is the freestanding spar that eliminates literally dozens of wires and fittings—any one of which could give out and threaten the entire rig. With the freestanding spar, there is only one part—the mast itself—and if it is engineered strongly enough, why worry?

Initially, Hoyt and the Freedom builders, Tillotson-Pearson, tried fiberglass spars, but they tended to whip and bend. They found the answer in the expensive, but very strong high-tech material carbon fiber. As mentioned in Chapter 1, when Tony Lush pitchpoled his 54-foot *Lady Pepperell* (Figure 10-2) in the Southern Ocean, the spars were still standing when the boat righted. Until then, no one had taken a freestanding cat ketch, carbon fiber rig below the great capes and through the Roaring Forties.

Fig. 10-2 *Tony Lush sailed* Lady Pepperell *in the 1982/3 BOC round the world race. She was a modified Hunter 54, with freestanding carbon fiber spars. The rig survived pitchpoling in the Southern Ocean, though the boat later sank (Barbara Lloyd photo).*

Double Headsails

As length and displacement increase, there is a temptation to add a staysail to divide up the foretriangle and give more options in making up sail combinations. You would need to do a number of things (Figure 10-3):

1) Install a new stay from the mast to the foredeck —wire, terminals, tang, turnbuckle, deck plate.
2) Install running backstays or lower aft shrouds that attach at the same height as the new inner forestay to equalize the load on the mast.
3) Make or purchase a sail, perhaps with a set of reef points sewn in.
4) Rig the sail with sheets, blocks, fairleads, pad eyes, cleats, traveler and car.
5) Recut the jib or make a Yankee, high-cut lapper or small genoa.

Sloops as small as about 32 feet can still benefit from the advantages of double headsails even though their masts are several feet farther forward than a cutter of the same size. Adding a bowsprit to smaller boats spreads out the sail plan and leaves more room for a staysail of honest size. It would be wise to consult a naval architect or sailmaker to determine the effect of any sail plan change on overall balance.

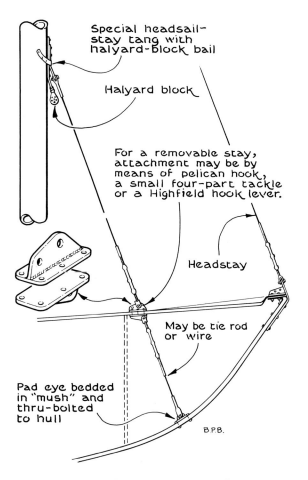

Fig. 10-3 *A removable inner forestay can be added to a sloop for flying a self-tending staysail in crowded anchorages or in storm conditions.*

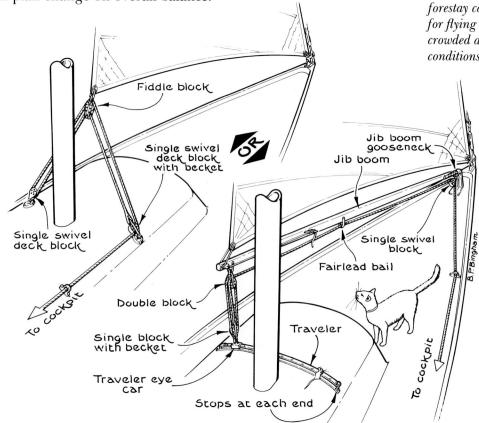

A few summers ago, I was sitting at my mooring in Newport Harbor watching a singlehander on a new Pearson 323. Before approaching the harbor entrance, he dropped the jib, set an inner forestay (it had been lashed back at the mast), set a clubless staysail, and sailed into the harbor looking for a mooring. Later he rowed by and stopped to chat. Besides using the staysail for storm weather, he said that it was most useful when singlehanding in close quarters because it is self-tending, not so large as to obscure his view, and quick to drop. Though the Pearson 323 wasn't designed for double headsails, adding a staysail gave his sloop greater versatility for handling a variety of conditions. And—here is the important part—it also provides a back-up to the forestay.

Conversions

Just as the addition of an inner forestay converts a sloop to a double-headsail sloop, it is possible to convert a sloop to a yawl, or vice versa. A number of maxi ocean racers built 10 to 15 years ago were originally rigged as yawls and ketches, in part because at that time sail cloth and winches were inadequate to handle the larger sail areas required on a 70 to 80-foot sloop. With developments in sails and winches, such boats as *Kialoa*, *Ondine*, *Tempest* and *Windward Passage* are now sloop-rigged.

It is doubtful that the cruising sailor would wish to trade his yawl rig for a sloop; more likely he would elect to go in the other direction— from sloop to yawl (Figure 10-4).

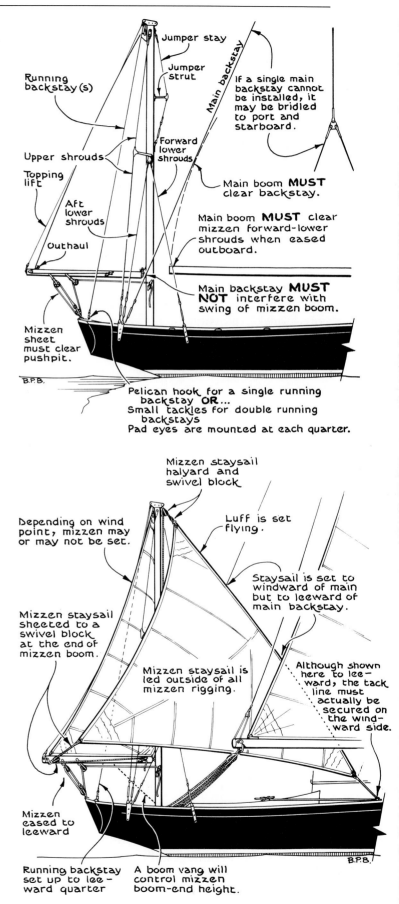

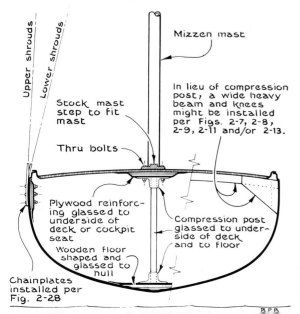

Fig. 10-4 *Sloops can be converted to yawls by adding a mizzenmast. The main boom may need shortening.*

Before making such a conversion, it would be a good idea to consult a naval architect or at least a very experienced sailmaker. A thorough study of the hull and sail plan are necessary to calculate the position of the new mizzenmast, sail area of the mizzen, and possible shortening of the main boom and mainsail.

Chainplates will have to be added to take the stays of the new mizzen. These can be the thru-deck type, but chainplates bolted through the sides of the hull are strong and give a wider staying base. There is also less potential for leaking and ultimately these will be easier to install.

The step for the mizzenmast must be precisely located, probably on the cockpit sole or after-deck, and support of this area should be given much thought. On fiberglass boats without cored decks, glassing in plywood (better compressive strength than foam or balsa to resist thru-bolting loads of the step) underneath is important. It may not be necessary to insert a compression post between the bottom of the cockpit sole or afterdeck and hull, but if it is, be certain to distribute the loads of the post over as wide an area as possible. Unlike beneath the mainmast, there is no keel under the mizzen to take the load. Actually, on boats under 40 feet, the mizzenmast is probably small enough that reinforcing the fiberglass panel with plywood or adding an athwartship beam (see Chapter 2) is probably sufficient.

Triatic stays connecting the mastheads of the main and mizzen should be avoided, if at all possible. If the mainmast goes over the side, there is no point in sending the mizzen mast with it, as the mizzenmast can be jury-rigged on the mainmast step. Thus the mainmast backstay will have to be split forward of the mizzenmast, or twin backstays installed, making sure they don't interfere with the swing of the mizzen boom.

Mizzen shrouds can be led forward—if they don't obstruct the mainmast's boom—and a set of shrouds led aft for support. Forestays are obviously out of the question, as are backstays unless there is a very large boomkin. If upper forward shrouds are not used, jumper struts and stays resist the aft bending moment caused by aft-leading spreaders and shrouds.

In sum, the advantages of a yawl are its ability to use the mizzenmast as a jury-rigged main-

mast, set a riding sail for heaving-to or at anchor, set a balancing sail on a reach, and furnishing a point from which to set a mizzen staysail on a reach. The mainsail and foretriangle remain large enough for good windward and downwind performance.

SPARS

Regardless of the rig material chosen, the thickness of its mast or aspect ratio, the guiding principle for the cruiser must be a rig's ability to stand up to years of hard use. The conventionally stayed rig must be held rigidly enough to survive a knockdown, whereas it is expected that the freestanding mast will deflect under load. Carbon fiber and other "exotic" new materials are the strongest, followed by steel, aluminum, hollow wood and solid wood. Used properly, each material can make a viable spar.

Materials

Extruded aluminum spar sections are by far the most common today, though certainly not the only viable material. Solid wood spars are satisfactory on short, gaff-rigged boats, but are not as strong as hollow wood spars such as the Herreshoff box method of construction. An attractive feature of the box section is that a serviceable replacement spar can be made just about anywhere in the world. In his book, *One Hand For Yourself, One For The Ship*, Tristan Jones describes the materials and glues required to do this (a 36-foot spar can be made from twelve 14-foot prescarfed, seasoned lengths of spruce, glued with resorcinol). He suggests storing them under the deck in the cabin, passing through bulkheads if necessary. Hollow spars are vulnerable to dry rot and require periodic varnishing and inspection. Where the gooseneck, tangs and spreaders are attached, the hollow wood spar should be filled with blocks of solid wood.

As mentioned earlier, fiberglass and carbon fiber have been successfully used to make free-standing spars and it is not inconceivable that

Yacht Size Approx. Waterline Length	Typical Mast Section	Wall Thickness	Approx. Mast Weight
feet	inches	inches	lb/ft
18	4·5 x 3	0·08	1·15
19	4·8 x 3·2	0·08	1·21
21	5·2 x 3·9	0·09	1·51
22	5·5 x 3·6	0·10	1·81
22	6 x 3·6	0·10	1·97
24	5·5 x 4·25	0·13	2·3
26	6·3 x 4·8	0·13	2·47
28	8 x 4·5	0·13	2·94
30	7·8 x 5·5	0·16	3·67
33	8 x 6·6	0·16	4·35
35	9·5 x 6·5	0·16	4·9
45	10·5 x 7·5	0·21	6·7
50	12 x 8	0·25	9·7
80	14 x 10	0·25	11·5

Fig. 10-5 *A general guide to sizing aluminum alloy masts (Proctor Masts)*

someday they might be sufficiently developed for stayed rigs. Carbon fibers, for instance, can be laminated to wood spars to increase stiffness.

I once sailed in the annual Carriacou workboat regatta in the Grenadines aboard a 68-foot Swedish schooner with tapered steel spars, but for most smaller cruising boats, the weight of steel is prohibitive.

Determining the dimensions and wall thickness of aluminum spars is best left to an experienced sparmaker, though Figure 10-5 gives rough estimates. Considerations include the height of the spar, fractional or masthead rig, method of staying, boat stability, type of aluminum used, and whether the spar is to be stepped at the keel or on deck. A cruising spar should be as thick as is feasible, with consideration given to weight aloft and the ability of the stays and shrouds to hold it in column with a given staying base.

Repairs

Once an aluminum spar is buckled or even slightly dimpled, it is probably unsalvageable. However, I have seen aluminum spars cut in half

near deck level and a sleeve inserted, along with fancy gearing to raise and lower the spar to get under bridges. A similar repair can be made to damaged spars.

Most aluminum masts, however, seem to break at the spreaders, and if one is able to bring it back aboard, lash it and make port, he would be well advised to consult a sparmaker before trying to fix it with a sleeve. A new mast, perhaps of thicker wall section, probably will give more confidence.

I once owned a 17'3" Silhouette Mark I that had a solid spruce spar. One day, sailing in a fresh breeze, a shroud swaging cracked sending the spar over the side. I found a skilled woodworker who was able to scarf in a new section, tapering the V-shaped scarf almost three feet. This saved the considerable delay and expense of making a new mast. A hollow wood spar might also be repaired in a similar method.

Maintenance

Anodizing is an electrolytic process that helps prevent corrosion and yields a harder finish than standard, unfinished aluminum. Many new boats are offered with painted spars (two-part linear or aliphatic polyurethanes such as Awlgrip are commonly used—see Chapter 15), though Bristol sparmaker Eric Hall says that paint is largely for cosmetic purposes and that no significant gain in corrosion resistance is obtained over anodizing.

The fewer holes drilled in an aluminum extrusion the better. Of course it is necessary to drill holes or weld on plates for mounting bosses, tangs, winches and cleats, and these should be placed with some knowledge of how holes and welds can weaken a section. Small holes are of no great concern, but larger holes, such as for inspection or internal halyard exits, should be staggered to minimize weakening of the mast (Figure 10-6).

Stainless steel fasteners are not 100-percent galvanically compatible with aluminum, and can cause corrosion over a period of time. While it is common practice in New England and elsewhere to leave spars standing during winter haulout (a dubious practice), they should be unstepped

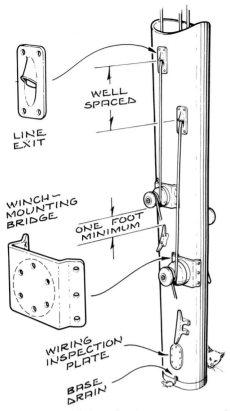

Fig. 10-6 *Fittings added to aluminum masts must be spaced above and below each other to prevent weakening.*

every few years and major fittings such as spreader bases and tangs removed to inspect for corrosion. Similarly, cracks should be dealt with promptly. A stop-gap measure is to drill a hole at each end of the crack to prevent it from spreading. Have the crack welded at the earliest opportunity. Periodically check all weldments for cracking, lubricate all moveable parts such as blocks and sheaves, and look for signs of wear, such as where wire halyards pass over sheaves. Rough edges should be filed to prevent chafe.

Deck-stepped spars should have drain holes at the base to allow water inside the spar to drain out. It is quite likely that the base of the mast frequently will be wet, and thus it is important that the mast step or heel plate be of the same material as the mast to prevent corrosion. Drain holes at the base actually may introduce water inside. For this reason, Ross Norgrove, in his book *Cruising Rigs And Rigging*, recommends inserting a tapered plug bedded with Thiokol just below where the lowest halyard exits (assuming internal halyards, which introduce more water

inside the spar than external halyards). This solution makes even more sense on keel-stepped masts, because water draining inside the boat only adds to the condensation, and being in an enclosed area also increases the potential for corrosion and dry rot. Tight fitting deck collars on keel-stepped spars are a must, too, if water is to be kept outside, where it belongs.

Deck-Stepped and Keel-Stepped Masts

For the ultimate in strength, the ocean cruising boat should have a keel-stepped mast, because if a shroud or stay lets go, the deck helps support the mast, hopefully long enough to bring the boat about on another tack and ease the load. In the same situation, a deck-stepped mast is already gone. Tom Colvin points out that following a dismasting, the keel-stepped mast may well leave a stub long enough to be brought up to deck level and jury rigged to carry a small sail. On the other hand, a deck-stepped mast is more likely to come down in one piece, (if the cause is a broken rigging) and is less likely to damage the deck.

Coastal cruisers, especially those anticipating sailing in canals and under low bridges, must admit the advantages of the deck-stepped mast, especially one mounted on a tabernacle. A tabernacle (Figure 10-7) with a large thru-bolt provides a fulcrum to raise and lower the spar by removing just the lower bolt. See Figure 10-8 for a system of raising and lowering the mast.

Spreaders

Spreader failures, along with wire terminal failures, are probably the most common cause of dismastings, and so must be strong and properly installed. Most rigs have single or double spreaders (Figure 10-9), though occasionally you see a large boat with three. Because the wider the shroud angle the less load exerted on the spar, the cruising boat should have the widest spreaders possible, without extending to the rail of the boat. (Spreaders are notorious for locking with your neighbor's during raftups, or damaging themselves when the boat is tied to a high pier.)

Fig. 10-7 *Murray Davis' Turtle, an Ushant 40 motorsailer built in England, has large tabernacles for lowering the spars.*

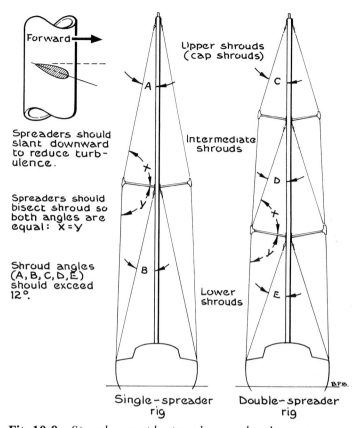

Forward ➡

Spreaders should slant downward to reduce turbulence.

Spreaders should bisect shroud so both angles are equal: X = Y

Shroud angles (A, B, C, D, E) should exceed 12°.

Upper shrouds (cap shrouds)

Intermediate shrouds

Lower shrouds

Single-spreader rig

Double-spreader rig

B.P.B.

Fit. 10-9 *Spreaders must be strongly secured to the mast, and bisect the shroud angles.*

Fig. 10-8 *With a large tabernacle and a little brainpower, the spinnaker pole or boom can be used to raise and lower a deck-stepped spar.*

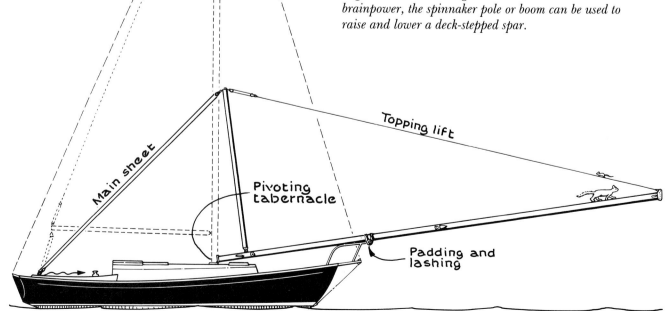

Main sheet

Topping lift

Pivoting tabernacle

Padding and lashing

B.P.B.

Racers have brought their shrouds more inboard during recent years to narrow the sheeting angle of headsails, giving them better windward ability. But this is of less concern to the cruiser, who is more interested in keeping his rig than pointing a few degrees higher. Chainplates installed through the sides of the hull achieve a wider staying base than chainplates located on the side decks or cabin top. It is annoying when walking forward to have to step around shrouds mounted inboard. Outboard chainplate installations can get in the way too, however, if the lower shrouds are angled too low over the side decks.

For the cruising boat, the shroud angle from the masthead should be no less than about 12 degrees out from the perpendicular line of the mast. The angle can be increased by shortening the spar (not very realistic), widening the spreaders, or adding another set of spreaders, enabling the first set to be moved higher up. The second set also reduces the load on the first set. While double spreaders strengthen any rig, (the load on upper shrouds is reduced by about 15 percent), they are particularly advisable on boats over about 45 feet, where the spar height is such that the shroud angle becomes too narrow.

Fixed and articulating spreaders are both viable choices, with the latter getting the edge because of its ability to move fore and after under stress, such as when the mainsail is let out on a downwind run. Neither fixed nor articulating spreaders must be allowed to shift position up or down. All spreaders should bisect the shroud angle at the spreader tip (Figure 10-9) so as not to create uneven forces on the spreader, and to prevent the spreader from moving up and down.

On aluminum masts, the spreader bases should be welded or thru-bolted to the mast with compression tubes over the bolt inside to distribute loads to both sides of the mast. On wood spars, they should be fastened with wood screws into pilot holes whose diameters have been carefully calculated to ensure a tight fit. The holes should be proportionately shorter than the length of the screws and narrower in diameter by at least the thickness of the screw threads.

Airfoil section spreaders with tapered leading and trailing edges are commonplace on racing boats now because they offer less wind resistance. They should be angled down on the leading edge 10 to 15 degrees so they offer less wind resistance when the boat is heeled (Figure 10-9).

Regardless of spreader tip configuration, they should not allow the shrouds to jump out when sudden loads are exerted on the rig, such as when slamming into head seas, or jibing (Figure 10-10). Rubber spreader boots, leather or other anti-chafe material should be taped to the spreader tips to prevent chafing overlapping headsails or eased mainsails.

STANDING RIGGING

Standing rigging is the system of wires, terminals and fittings that hold a stayed spar upright. In determining the size and strength of its various parts, the wire is generally regarded as the necessary weak link, meaning that every other part—bulkhead, chainplate, tang, terminal, turnbuckle pin, etc., should be stronger than the wire. If the terminals are engineered to 110 percent the breaking strength of the wire, little is gained by engineering the chainplates or tangs to 150 percent.

Types of Wire and Rod

Galvanized wire was once the standard standing rigging material, but now stainless steel is found on most boats. Stainless steel 1 x 19 wire rope is generally used for standing rigging, and 7 x 19 wire rope, because of its greater flexibility, is used for running rigging. There are numerous variations of these two, such as 7 x 7 and 6 x 37. The first number refers to the number of strands in any given length of rigging, the second to the number of wires in each strand (Figure 10-11). Fiber cores are sometimes added to increase flexibility, which is important for running rigging where wire rope passes through sheaves and blocks under tremendous strain. The fiber core, however, lessens the strength of the wire compared to wire-core rigging.

In preparing a boat for cruising, common sense advice is to replace all standing rigging

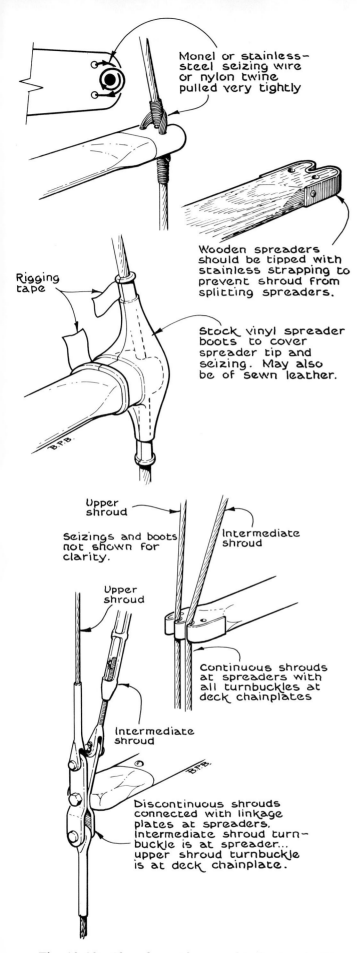

Monel or stainless-steel seizing wire or nylon twine pulled very tightly

Wooden spreaders should be tipped with stainless strapping to prevent shroud from splitting spreaders.

Rigging tape

Stock vinyl spreader boots to cover spreader tip and seizing. May also be of sewn leather.

Upper shroud

Intermediate shroud

Seizings and boots not shown for clarity.

Upper shroud

Continuous shrouds at spreaders with all turnbuckles at deck chainplates

Intermediate shroud

Discontinuous shrouds connected with linkage plates at spreaders. Intermediate shroud turnbuckle is at spreader... upper shroud turnbuckle is at deck chainplate.

Fig. 10-10 *Shrouds must be secured to the spreader tips to prevent them from jumping out. Sail chafe protection, such as rubber boots, should be fixed to the spreader tips.*

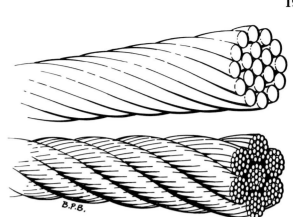

B.P.B.

Fig. 10-11 *1 x 19 wire is generally used for standing rigging, and 7 x 19 for running rigging.*

with wire rope one size larger—for example, 7/16-inch diameter for 3/8-inch diameter, which increases breaking strength by 5,000 pounds for 1 x 19 wire (Figure 10-12a). Larger turnbuckles, clevis pins, chainplates and tangs will probably need to be fitted so that each part is stronger

Fig. 10-12a *Breaking strength and weight of different size and type wires*

	Breaking Strength of Wire (pounds)					
Diam.	1 x 19 Stainless steel	7 x 7 Stainless steel	7 x 19 Stainless steel	Dacron	Nylon	Manila
1/16	500	480	500			
3/32	1200	920	1050			
1/8	2100	1700	1760			
5/32	3300	2600	2400			
3/16	4700	3700	3700			
7/32	6300	4800	5000			
1/4	8200	6100	6400	1650	1650	600
9/32	10300	7600	7800			
5/16	12500	9100	9000	2500	2500	1000
3/8	17500	12600	12000	3700	3700	1350
7/16	22500	16500	16300	5000	5000	1750
1/2	30000	21300	22800	6400	6400	2650
9/16	36200	26600	28500			
5/8	47000	32500	35000	10000	10000	4400
3/4	67500	45500	49600	12500	14000	5400
7/8	91400	60200	66500			

than the wire. If a fitting has a lower breaking strength than the wire, no advantage is gained. Ross Norgrove's formula is to multiply ballast by two to determine the breaking strength of the wire. For example, 7,000 pounds ballast times two equals 14,000 pounds breaking strength of the wire. From Figure 10-12, either 5/16 or 3/8-inch wire should do the job, with the latter giving a substantial safety margin. However, hull form and size also affect stability, and therefore the desired wire size. See *Skene's Elements of Yacht Design* by Francis Kinney for more scientific formulas, or better yet, consult a naval architect.

Weight and windage aloft are considerations, but less so for the cruiser than racer. For the cruiser, the ultimate goal is to keep the rig standing. Using the same size turnbuckles and wire for all standing rigging simplifies the spare parts inventory.

Rod rigging, originally developed for biplane rigging in World War I, was introduced to the sailing world on several boats of note, including the J-boat *Ranger,* and later when Navtec rigged the 12-Meter *Heritage* for the 1970 America's Cup races. The principal advantage of rod is that it stretches about 35 percent less than wire, and so forestay sag is less and sail shape more efficient. Further, the elastic limit (the amount a material can be stretched and still return to its former dimension) of wire is about 40 percent of its breaking strength. For rod it is about 80

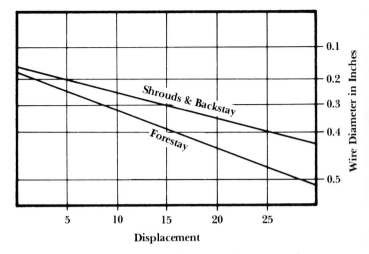

Fig. 10-12b *Suggested wire diameters for cruising boats* (Boat Data Book; *Ian Nicolson*)

percent. And, because headstays are tensioned to about 50 percent of breaking strength, this can result in permanent stretch of wire forestays. Another advantage is that because rod is solid, smaller diameter rod can be manufactured to the same breaking strength as larger diameter wire (Figure 10-13). This means less windage at about the same weight.

Navtec rod rigging and some brands of wire rope, such as Universal's "Super Stainless", are made from Armco Steel Company's product, Nitronic 50. It is more corrosion resistant than 302 and 304 stainless, and stronger than 316 stainless. Nitronic 50 is an alloy including carbon,

Fig. 10-13 *This table compares the properties of Navtec rod rigging with 1x19 wire of equivalent breaking strength.*

Size	Breaking Strength (lbs.)	Diameter (ins.)	Stretch[b]	Weight/100 ft. (lbs.)	Drag[c]
−12 Navtec standard	12,500	.281	2.11	21.3	4.1
5/16 1 x 19 wire	12,500	.323	3.00	21.0	6.3
5/16 diameter rod[a]	13,000	.312	1.75	26.2	4.7
−12 Navtec HP rod[d]	11,600	.250	2.11	18.0	3.8
−17 Navtec standard	17,500	.330	2.11	29.3	4.9
3/8 1 x 19 wire	17,500	.385	3.00	29.4	7.5
3/8 diameter rod[a]	18,100	.375	1.68	37.8	5.6

[a] This rod is same nominal diameter as wire.

[b] Stretch is measured in inches/100 feet at load equal to 25% of breaking strength.

[c] Drag is measured in pounds/100 feet of rigging at 22 knots. Based on Stevens Institute data.

[d] Manufactured from MP35N.

manganese, phosphorous, sulfur, chromium, nickel, molybdenum, nitrogen, columbium and vanadium, and has many industrial applications in addition to sailboat rigging. Of course, it is much more expensive than 302/304 stainless steel wire rope, but its greater corrosion resistance means longer life (See Appendix C).

While rod rigging has been controversial in cruising circles due to occasional reports of it breaking without warning, even at dockside, most failures can be traced to improper installation. This has been most common at the spreader tips, where tubes are bent over the spreader tip to duplicate the angle of the shroud —an error of more than two to three percent causes fatigue of the rod. Discontinuous rigging, in which each shroud terminates at a link plate attached to the spreader tip, provides full articulation and reduces problems of fatigue at the spreader tip. However, rod rigging's greatest disadvantage to the world cruiser is the difficulty in carrying spare shrouds and stays—minimum coil size is 200 times rod diameter, or 50 inches for ¼-inch rod. This is an important consideration because a length of wire slightly longer than the longest stay should be carried in reserve, with a means of fastening terminal fittings.

Adding Shrouds and Stays

The general rule to be observed aboard the cruising boat is that every wire should have a backup in the event of a rigging failure. This does not necessarily mean two parallel wires running from the same chainplate to the same tang on the mast, but simply another wire that can absorb a large share of the load if the primary wire breaks.

Twin forestays enable hanking on twin jibs for downwind sailing (Figure 10-14), but unless they are anchored by separate fittings, the alternate loading on one stay and then the other can cause fatigue of tangs and possibly stemhead fittings. An inner forestay, such as the one shown in Figure 10-3, can be set in heavy weather to help keep the mast in column, and hopefully keep the spar standing if the forestay goes—at least long enough to ease the load and make repairs.

Single backstays are easily replaced with twins,

one to each quarter. This requires fitting chainplates (see Figure 10-4) either on the hull sides or to knees glassed inside at the hull/deck joint (Figure 2-6). At the masthead, two tangs must be fitted. Alternatively, the single backstay can be left and running backstays added port and starboard (Figure 10-15). Running backstays are frequently seen on gaff-rigged boats in which the gaff prevent rigging a single backstay on centerline, and on double-headsail boats in which the running backstays support the mast where the inner forestay attaches. This leads us to another important principle—for every mast support, there should be an equal and opposite support to keep the mast rigidly stayed in column.

Double lower shrouds are better than single lowers because not only do they provide support athwartships, but also slightly fore and aft of the upper shroud. Double spreader rigs should have

Fig. 10-14 *Twin forestays not only provide the rig with backup strength, but they enable setting twin jibs for downwind sailing.*

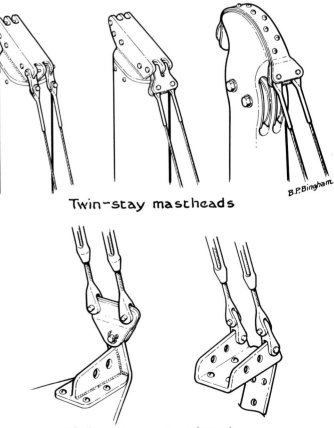

Twin-stay mastheads

Twin-stay stemheads

intermediates and upper shrouds either continuously run from masthead to deck, or discontinuously run to link plates at each spreader tip.

Terminals

Warm salt water poses the greatest danger to standing rigging, and the point of attack is frequently the terminal fittings connecting the wire to the turnbuckle, tang or chainplate. Almost every type of terminal encloses the wire and prevents quick evaporation of water, which eventually begins to corrode the wire.

Terminal fittings should be sufficiently strong

Fig. 10-15 *Running backstays, while cumbersome, back up the backstay and oppose the inner forestay's forces to keep the spar in column.*

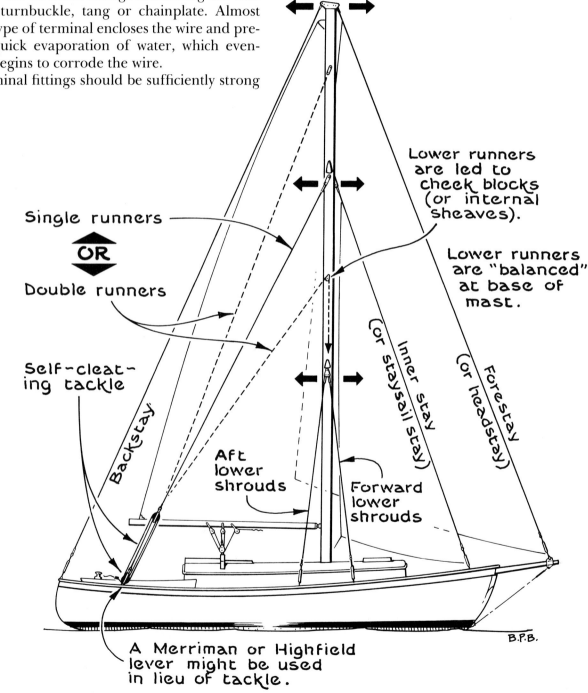

Single runners

OR

Double runners

Self-cleating tackle

Backstay

Aft lower shrouds

Forward lower shrouds

Inner stay (or staysail stay)

Forestay (or headstay)

Lower runners are led to cheek blocks (or internal sheaves).

Lower runners are "balanced" at base of mast.

A Merriman or Highfield lever might be used in lieu of tackle.

B.P.B.

that if the entire stay or shroud is subjected to a bench test, the wire will break before the terminal lets go. Typical terminals are shown in Figure 10-16.

The least expensive method, and one of the strongest, is the splice. With practice, a hand-spliced eye can last for years and certainly exceeds the breaking strength of the wire. The only difficulty is that splicing 1 x 19 wire is very difficult; 7 x 7 wire is generally favored, but then the extra stretch of 7 x 7 must be lived with. Toggles can be inserted between the turnbuckle and chainplate if at some point the latter cannot take up the slack.

Poured sockets are used on elevators and cranes, which should say all that's necessary about their strength. Zinc is heated up with a torch and poured into the cone of the socket to form a metalurgical bond. Ross Norgrove gives good step-by-step instructions for making poured sockets in his book, *Cruising Rigs and Rigging*.

In contrast to the metalurgical bond of poured sockets, and the friction bond of hand-splicing, most other terminals types rely on mechanical bonds, that is, by squeezing the terminal onto the wire. Properly executed, mechanical bonds can be quite strong, but there is always the risk of excessively or unevenly distorting the wire. In the case of swaging there is danger in failing to achieve uniform loading on the wires inside. Here is one area in which rod rigging excells. The end of the wire is flattened by a process called "cold heading". The cold-formed head is made by inserting the end of a length of rod in a vice. The end is then smashed with a hydraulic piston. The head then is inserted into a specially machined rod seat at the end of the turnbuckle (Figure 10-17)—the assembly is partially articulated to alleviate stress, and is incredibly strong.

The greatest virtue of the Norseman and Sta-Lok terminals is the ease with which an ordinary person can fasten them to wire. Wrenches, pliers, wire cutters and seizing twine are the only tools and parts necessary. Properly done, they are strong and even reusable, with the exception of the cone, several of which should be carried as spares. Figure 10-18 shows how these terminals are fitted.

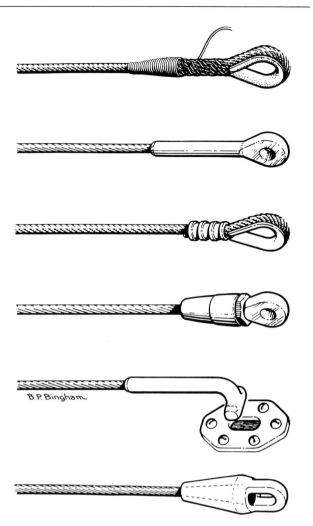

Fig. 10-16 *These six terminal fittings are typical of those found on most sailboats today. From top to bottom: hand-spliced eye, roller-swaged terminal, Nicopress terminal, Norseman terminal, hook-in T terminal, and poured socket terminal.*

Fig. 10-17 *Navtec's internal stemball tang, showing the cold-formed head at the end of the rod.*

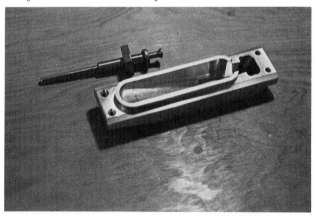

Fig. 10-18 *Installation sequence for fitting a Sta-Lok terminal to wire: 1) Parts of a terminal—end, cap, cone, body, and tools required, 2) slide body over wire, 3) unlay wire by turning with pliers, 4) slide on cone; distance from top of core wire should be same as the core diameter, about $\frac{3}{32}"$, 5) either drop cap into end fitting, or 6) fit on top of all the wire strands, 7) screw on end fitting to body, 8) take off end fitting and inspect the wires—do they overlap? Is one caught in the slit of the cone? Are they making indentations on the top of the cone? Reassemble with Lok-Tite on threads and silicone caulk on wire ends.*

1

2

3

4

5

6

7

8

Talurit and Nicopress terminals both have the advantage of wrapping the wire around a thimble, and a bit of extra strength is gained by the additional friction of the wire against the thimble. Nicopress fittings can be installed by the skipper with the help of the wire cutter-type Nicopress tool, which should be carried abroad.

Turnbuckles, Tangs, Thimbles and Chainplates

Turnbuckles, tangs and chainplates (Figure 10-19) should be matched in size with the wire and terminal fittings to which they're attached. The breaking strength of any fitting should exceed the breaking strength of the wire—up to two times as much for blocks and sheaves with wires pulling parallel to themselves. Check the specifications of any fitting you buy for working and ultimate tensile strength.

Forestays tend to sag off more than any other stay, and if an unfair load is placed on any fitting, such as the terminal, turnbuckle or tang (Figure 10-20), consider adding a toggle to provide greater articulation of the wire and terminal and to prevent twisting. This will lengthen the life of the wire.

Turnbuckles and clevis pins will not unscrew

STAINLESS STEEL CHAINPLATE SIZES

Wire Dia.	A Pin Dia.	B Radius	C Offset	D* Maximum Thickness
1/8"	1/4"	3/8"	1/16"	3/16"
5/32"	5/16"	7/16"	1/16"	1/4"
3/16"	3/8"	1/2"	1/8"	5/16"
1/4"	1/2"	11/16"	1/8"	3/8"
9/32"	1/2"	11/16"	1/8"	3/8"
5/16"	5/8"	13/16"	3/16"	1/2"
3/8"	5/8"	7/8"	3/16"	1/2"
7/16"	3/4"	1"	3/16"	9/16"
1/2"	7/8"	1 3/16"	1/4"	11/16"
9/16"	7/8"	1 1/4"	1/4"	11/16"
5/8"	1"	1 3/8"	1/4"	3/4"

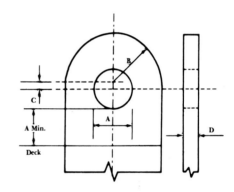

Fig. 10-19 *Table for determining chainplate size*

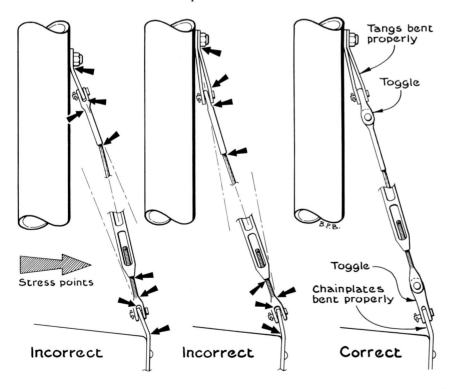

Tangs bent properly

Toggle

Fig. 10-20 *Turnbuckles, terminals and tangs must lead fair to prevent stress loading. Toggles help the wire articulate, and prevent unnecessary stress on the wire and terminals.*

Stress points

Incorrect   Incorrect

Toggle

Chainplates bent properly

Correct

Fig. 10-21 *William Compton's reinforced thimble prevents collapse under load (William Compton photo).*

or pop out if you insert cotter pins or wire through the barrel and end parts. A few turns of sailmakers tape over the barrel and sharp ends of wire and cotter pins will protect sheets and sails from chafe, as will turnbuckle boots.

One way to measure the strength of a turnbuckle is by examining the size of the pin at the ends that hold the terminal eye or chainplate. Make sure it is sufficiently large to be of greater breaking strength than the wire.

Thimbles should be correctly sized to the wire used. A fellow in Florida, William Compton, is making a reinforced thimble that includes a small weldment inside the eye (Figure 10-21), that prevents the thimble from collapsing under load.

Fasteners

Rivets, machine screws, self-tapping machine screws and self-tapping sheet metal screws (Figure 10-22) are used for fastening fittings to spars —cleats, blocks, bails and winches. Where possible, secure highly stressed hardware—such as spreader sockets, winches and tangs—with machine screws bolted through the width of the spar with compression tubes and locknuts, into the spar itself if the wall is thick enough, or to a plate welded to the spar. When using dissimilar metal fastenings on an aluminum spar, you can prevent corrosion by inserting a gasket of Micarta, surgical rubber, sheet nylon or Formica, and by wrapping vinyl tape over the threads. Use a seizing compound such as Loktite or fit

locknuts to prevent them from vibrating loose.

Elsewhere on the spar, where a fitting is not duplicated on the other side to facilitate bolting through its width—or where access up inside the spar is not possible—self-tapping machine or sheet metal screws are the most practical. Good results can be had with rivets, too. Sail track, small blocks and other light hardware can be fastened with rivets or screws. Boom bails for vangs should be thru-bolted with compression tubes. The critical factor in using self-tapping sheet metal screws is the diameter of the pilot hole — too small and the screw won't thread all the way snugly, too large and the threads of the screw won't bite deep enough into the spar wall. A rule of thumb is to drill the pilot hole abut 75 percent of the diameter of the screw size. For example, for a ¼-inch screw, use a ³⁄₁₆-inch drill bit. A lubricating wax (an auto paste wax will do) smeared over the threads will help it drive in and prevent snapping the head off the screw if it jams.

Blind drive rivets are installed either with a special tool or by hitting the expanding pin with a hammer. Pilot holes should be the same diameter as the rivet for a snug fit. To remove old pop rivets, grind the head down or drill it out with a larger diameter bit. Then drive any remainder of the rivet through with a punch and hammer.

Self-tapping sheet metal screws and pop rivets can be purchased in stainless steel or aluminum. The former is stronger, but will corrode slightly in contact with aluminum. Using the seizing compound mentioned earlier will help minimize

Fig. 10-22 *Machine screws, self-tapping screws and pop rivets are the three fasteners typically used for fastening fittings to aluminum spars.*

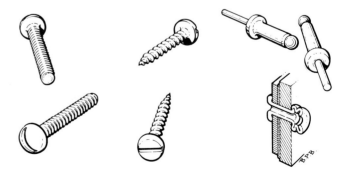

galvanic action and make later removal much easier.

RUNNING RIGGING

Running rigging consists of all the fiber and wire ropes used to raise, lower and trim sails. Breaking a halyard is not usually a catastrophe, though if it happens when hove-to with storm sails, quick action is required to regain control of the boat. Because the breaking strength of running rigging is seldom tested under straight loads, most problems are caused by chafe—unfair leads, rough-edged sheaves and rubbing against standard rigging.

Types of Line

Manilla rope is seldom seen on boats nowadays, and there is really no reason it should, considering the very real advantages of modern synthetic ropes such as nylon and Dacron. These two products, available in three-strand, braid and plaited versions, can do most of the line jobs required on a modern cruising boat.

Nylon is slightly stronger than Dacron, and has more stretch—about 17 percent of its length under load. Because of its elasticity, nylon is most suitable for applications where one wants the line to function as a shock absorber—anchor rodes, docklines and dinghy painters.

Dacron has about half the stretch of nylon and so is preferred for halyards, sheets, guys and vangs; pre-stretched rope has, of course, even less stretch.

Polypropylene is sometimes used for dinghy painters because it floats and will not foul the mother ship's propeller when the line is slack. However, it is difficult for tying knots, wanting as it does to continually spring back. And it won't coil to save your life. It is not as strong as nylon and Dacron, which prejudices its use as a painter.

Halyards are commonly made with 7x19 wire spliced to Dacron rope tails, though all-wire and all-rope halyards are feasible. 7x19 wire is used because of its flexibility, which enables it to bend around relatively small-diameter sheaves without distorting the lay of the strands.

Blocks and Sheaves

Blocks are used in abundance on any boat, to gain purchase power and to fairly direct the lead of the line. Just a few of their applications are jib sheets, mainsheets, travelers, halyards, boom vangs and handy billies. The size of the block should be sufficiently large to withstand the loads exerted on it by line under load. An old rule of thumb is that for every $\frac{1}{8}$-inch line of diameter, the block should be increased one inch. With stronger modern materials, however, adhering to this formula results in overkill (Figure 10-23). Check the manufacturer's specifications for safe working loads, making sure the block is stronger than the line on it.

Sheaves for wire, such as those at the masthead for wire halyards, should have deep grooves to keep the wire from jumping out. The sheave diameter should be about 20 to 30 times the wire diameter. For example, a $\frac{3}{16}$-inch wire should have a sheave between $3\frac{3}{4}$ and $5\frac{1}{2}$ inches in diameter, and every block should have some

SHEAVE SIZES FOR ROPE CORDAGE

Rope Size *inches*	Recommended Sheave Diameter *inches*	Minimum Sheave Diameter *inches*
$\frac{1}{16}$ & $\frac{1}{8}$	1	$\frac{5}{8}$
$\frac{3}{16}$	$1\frac{1}{2}$	1
$\frac{1}{4}$	$1\frac{3}{4}$	1
$\frac{5}{16}$	2	$1\frac{1}{8}$
$\frac{3}{8}$	$2\frac{1}{4}$	$1\frac{1}{4}$
$\frac{7}{16}$	$2\frac{1}{2}$	$1\frac{3}{4}$
$\frac{1}{2}$	$2\frac{3}{4}$	$2\frac{1}{4}$
$\frac{9}{16}$	$3\frac{1}{4}$	$2\frac{5}{8}$
$\frac{5}{8}$	$3\frac{1}{2}$	$2\frac{7}{8}$

Note: Rope sizes are diameters.

Fig. 10-23 *Table for determining block size* (Boat Data Book; *Ian Nicolson*)

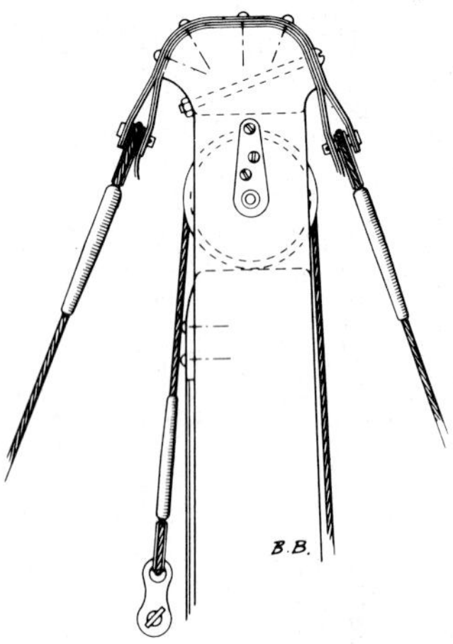

Fig. 10-24 *Masthead sheave diameters should be about 20 to 30 times the diameter of the wire. A U-strap should be fitted to the top to prevent the wire from jumping out.*

sort of retainer over the top to guarantee the wire stays put (Figure 10-24).

Mainsheet

The closer to the mast the mainsheet is attached to the boom, the more power is required to trim the main. Mainsheets can be attached to the deck anywhere from a traveler over the main

companionway hatch to the bridge deck, to a traveler mounted on a beam across the cockpit, to a traveler thru-bolted to the afterdeck and attached to a boom bail or a swiveling tang at the end of the boom (Figure 10-25). The more power required to trim the mainsail, the more blocks are required to provide the necessary purchase power, and the greater the likelihood of needing a winch for assistance.

Travelers give better control of the mainsail's shape and are standard fare on racers. The cruiser can obtain satisfactory sail shape through using vangs and preventers, and so dispense with the mainsheet traveler. With a double block at the boom end, and single blocks thru-bolted to the aft end of the cockpit and to either side of the boom, there is usually sufficient purchase power to control the mainsail and boom (if not, increase the purchase ratio). An advantage or disadvantage of this arrangement is that the mainsheet is kept aft of the cockpit and out of everyone's way, but one does have to turn around to handle it. On a racer, this might have the crew tripping over the helmsman. But the value of an unobstructed cockpit may be of more worth to the cruising sailor—it's really a matter of personal preference.

Fig. 10-25 *Various mainsheet arrangements*

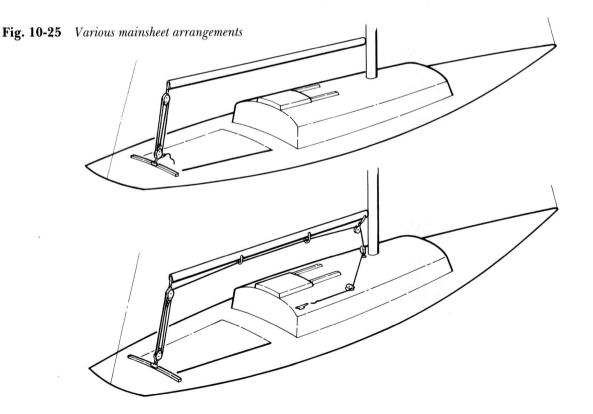

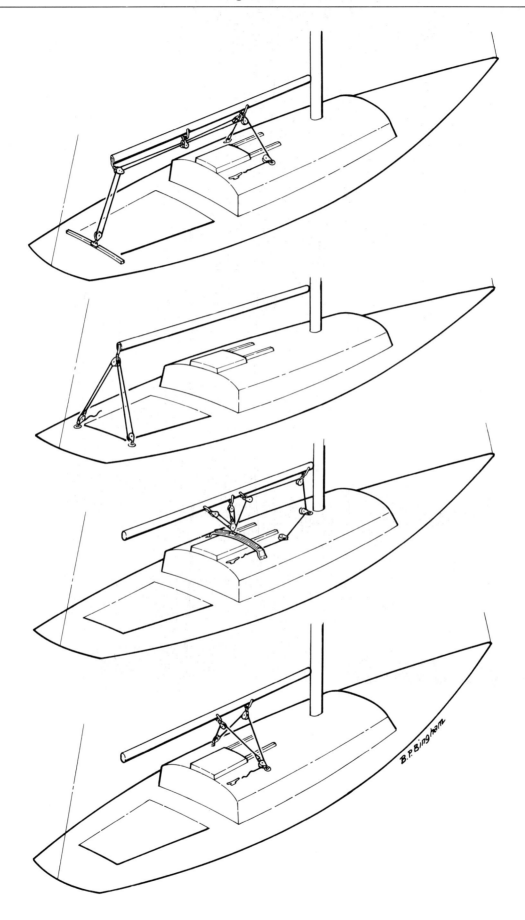

B.P. Bingham

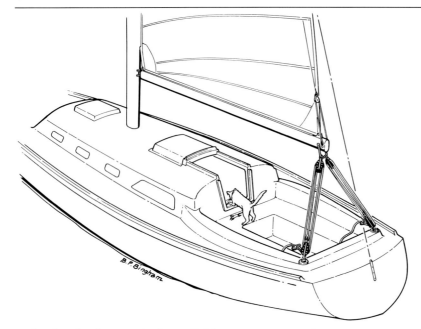

Fig. 10-26 *Twin mainsheets is a rather novel arrangement. While more cumbersome during tacking, the leeward tackle can function as a close reaching vang.*

An intriguing variation of this arrangement is to rig two independent mainsheet tackles, one to port and one to starboard (Figure 10-26). Obviously, tacking would require judicious timing in the release of one mainsheet as the other is being trimmed. Yet when close reaching, the leeward mainsheet functions as a boom vang, while the weather mainsheet controls trim. Not only does this system obviate the clutter of a vang at the mast base, which often interferes with dinghy stowage, it also eliminates uncontrolled jibes.

Halyards

As mentioned earlier, most halyards today are 7x19 stainless steel wire with rope tails. All-wire halyards (Figure 10-27) have the least stretch, and wind up on reel winches, but the brakes require maintenance and if they let go, the spinning winch handle could bust an arm or skull. It is also difficult to control the braking of the winch when letting wire out. All-rope halyards are anathema to the racer because of stretch problems. But for the small-boat cruiser, they have much to recommend them, especially when a self-tailing winch is used. The halyard will stretch after you're underway, but all this requires is a few more turns on the winch. Pre-stretched line minimizes the number of times the halyard will have to be taken up.

All-rope halyards used in conjunction with

HALYARD SIZES

Mainsail Luff or Headsail Leech	Main Halyard	Jib Halyard	Spinnaker Halyard	Topping Lift
20'	1/8"	5/32"	3/16"	1/8"
25'	1/8"	5/32"	3/16"	1/8"
30'	5/32"	3/16"	7/32"	5/32"
35'	5/32"	3/16"	7/32"	5/32"
40'	3/16"	7/32"	1/4"	3/16"
45'	3/16"	7/32"	1/4"	3/16"
50'	7/32"	1/4"	9/32"	7/32"
55'	7/32"	1/4"	9/32"	7/32"
60'	7/32"	1/4"	9/32"	7/32"
65'	1/4"	9/32"	5/16"	1/4"
70'	1/4"	9/32"	5/16"	1/4"
75'	1/4"	9/32"	5/16"	1/4"
80'	1/4"	9/32"	5/16"	1/4"
85'	9/32"	5/16"	3/8"	9/32"
90'	9/32"	5/16"	3/8"	9/32"
95'	9/32"	5/16"	3/8"	9/32"
100'	9/32"	5/16"	3/8"	9/32"

Note: For rope spinnaker halyards and rope topping lifts, use rope diameter twice wire diameter shown.

Fig. 10-27 *Table for halyard sizes (Nicro-Fico)*

blocks shackled to the masthead, or masthead sheaves, are the epitome of simplicity. They are the easiest to replace if a halyard breaks. Kevlar rope is incredibly strong and has little stretch. Internal halyards, in contrast, reduce noise and windage, but are more difficult to fish through the spar and exit hole. Wire-rope halyards are more difficult to replace if you have to make the splice under way. Carry a Nicopress tool and spare sleeves just in case. With all-rope halyards, a ready-made backup consists of a coil of spare line kept in a locker, cut to length ahead of time and spliced at one end with an eye. Carry enough line to replace every halyard and sheet at least once.

Obviously, the choice between wire and rope is a matter of individual preference, as is leading them internally or externally. Each system has its virtues and vices, but simplicity and ease of repair or replacement are worthy considerations.

Jib Sheets

Dacron jib sheets should be sized not so much for strength as for comfort in handling (Figure 10-28). Smaller line cuts into the palms. If each sheet is long enough for a knot about five to six feet from the tail, you won't need to reach out on deck for the tail when preparing to come about.

Snap shackles should not be used to attach the sheets to the clew. When the boat is headed up or in irons, the flapping of the sail makes the shackle a dancing murder weapon. Better to tie bowlines in the sheets; they won't let go (like snap shackles), won't hurt your noggin and are easily untied. If each sail has its own set of sheets permanently tied on the business of changing sails is simplified, especially when switching to very light or heavy sails with correspondingly different diameter sheets.

Downhauls

When it's blowing hard and the boat is tossing about in a seaway, being able to drop the jib from the cockpit saves a trip to the bow, (Figure 10-29). With double lifelines and criss-crossed lines or netting between them, the sail will stay on deck long enough to reach smooth water or change point of sail to achieve a steadier motion before moving forward to bag the sail.

Fig. 10-29 *Downhauls should be attached to the top jib hank, either by a snap shackle or bowline. It is then led to a block at the bow and aft to the mast or cockpit.*

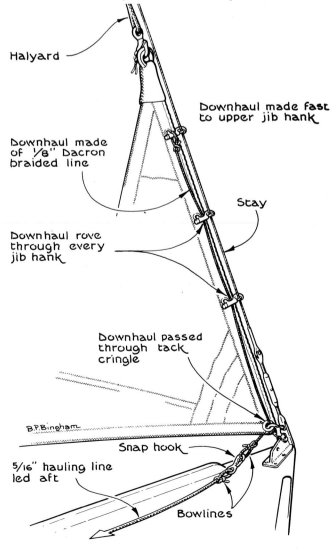

JIBSHEET SIZING	
Headsail Leech	**Jib Sheet Diameter**
20'	¼"
25'	5⁄16"
30'	5⁄16"
35'	⅜"
40'	7⁄16"
45'	½"
50'	9⁄16"
55'	⅝"
60'	⅝"
65'	¾"
70'	¾"
75'	1"

Fig. 10-28 *Table for jibsheet sizing (Nicro-Fico)*

Each sail should have its own downhaul.

Splice an eye in the end of a ¼-inch or ⅜-inch line through the top jib hank (not to the head, as this will fall below the top hank once the halyard is slack and may jam). Or a shackle can be used if you want to unclip it from the sail. The downhaul is then led through a block at the bow and aft. An eye splice at the tack end clips to a permanently rigged line on deck, run through fairleads to the cockpit or mast, depending on where the halyard is cleated off. The splice and shackle can be dispensed with if you decide instead to simply tie a bowline to the jib hank. To keep the downhaul from flying about, it can be run up through all the other hanks if there's enough space. At the very least, there should be a cleat to secure the other end of the downhaul back at the mast or cockpit.

Boom Vangs and Preventers

The purposes of boom vangs and preventers are two-fold: a) to flatten the sail and remove twist, and; b) to prevent jibing. Unless boom vangs are led to the boat's rail, they won't prevent a jibe when the mainsail is set aback (Figure 10-30). Attaching the boom vang at the base of the mast is most useful when sailing to windward, but it also interferes with stowing a dinghy

on deck. But then, of course, there is no danger of jibing. Off the wind, it may still help flatten the sail, though it won't have the strength or "preventer" quality it does when there is a pad-eye or stanchion base and sufficient line in the vang to lead it to either rail. Not only is sail shape and speed improved, and the danger of jibing minimized, but sail chafe can be minimized by holding the sail away from spreaders. Also, that annoying slatting is reduced in calm conditions.

There are a wide variety of methods to attach boom vangs to the boom: with specially designed clips that fit into the sail track, claws that surround the boom (mostly for roller reefing), bails bolted to the boom, or pad eyes welded to the underside of the boom. If you use roller reefing, be sure you can unhook the vang so it doesn't prevent the boom from rotating, or leave any large, sharp objects on the boom that might rip the sail. These are some of the reasons why slab or jiffy reefing is often considered preferable. Better sail shape is another.

A preventer is not always as effective as a boom vang in controlling mainsail shape, but it is superior in preventing the boom from jibing. A stout line is led from the end of the boom forward to a cleat, padeye or block on deck (Figure 10-31). These should be well reinforced with backing blocks to distribute loads. The greater the angle between the boom and preventer, the stronger it will be.

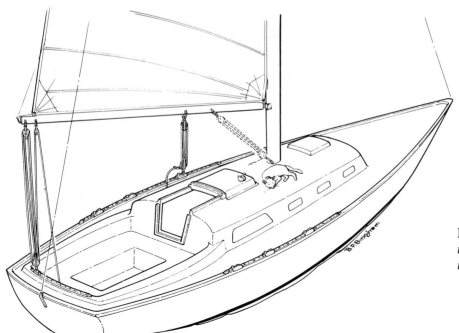

Fig. 10-30 *Attach boom vangs to the rail when running downwind if they also are used to prevent jibes.*

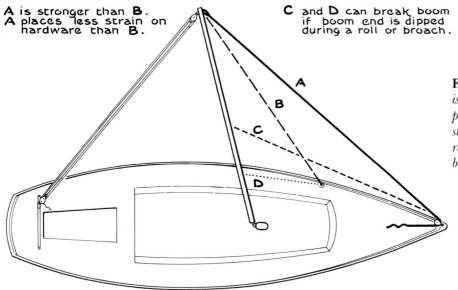

A is stronger than B.
A places less strain on hardware than B.

C and D can break boom if boom end is dipped during a roll or broach.

Fig. 10-31 *A simple jibe preventer is run from the end of the boom to a point forward on deck. This point—a stanchion base or pad eye—must be reinforced under the deck with a backing block.*

Lazy Jacks

One of the best ways to control sails being lowered is by way of lazy jacks (Figure 10-32). These are lines led from the boom to a point on the mast; they run on both sides of the sail so when it is lowered it naturally flakes on top of the boom and doesn't tumble down over the deck. As you may want to control their tension, they should be led to a single line—perhaps to the topping lift—that runs through a block on the mast and down to a cleat. The other lines can be run under the boom or terminated to strap eyes screwed into the boom. The number of lines depends on the size of the sail.

Whipping Lines

All line, whether running rigging, anchor rodes, painters, outhauls, etc., should have their ends whipped to prevent ugly mare's tails. Not only are they unseamanlike, they snag cleats and eat away good (and expensive) line like a cancer. There are several methods of whipping, and the simplest can be mastered by a young child—so there's no excuse for not learning how to do it properly. If you can't or won't master whipping, at least dunk the ends in that dip-whip stuff!

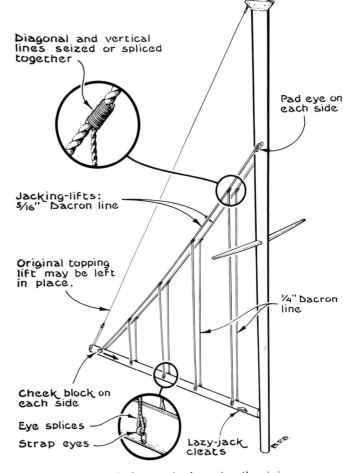

Diagonal and vertical lines seized or spliced together

Jacking-lifts: 5/16" Dacron line

Original topping lift may be left in place.

Pad eye on each side

¼" Dacron line

Cheek block on each side

Eye splices

Strap eyes

Lazy-jack cleats

Fig. 10-32 *Lazy jacks contain the mainsail as it is lowered.*

SAILS

A good inventory of sails represents a substantial investment. It only makes sense to give serious thought to their type, material, weight, special features and number. Because even a modestly sized cruising boat will have literally thousands of dollars tied up in sails, they should be cared for with equal thought and attention.

Most of us make lists of things we'd like to add to our boats. Some of these items are bound to cross over the line between what's essential and what would "be nice to have"—a Loran with more functions, a better quality stereo, new tableware. Sails, it often seem, take a second seat to these and other gear. But filling a gap in the sail inventory (for instance, buying a 130-percent genoa to add to the working jib and #1 genoa headsail inventory), can make all the difference between an enjoyable sail and one in which the boat just won't move because the right combination of sails can't be found.

Types of Sailcloth and Weights

Howe & Bainbridge is probably the largest sailcloth manufacturer in the United States, and supplies most major lofts, excluding Hood, which makes its own cloth and is regarded, in some circles at least, as the best available. Certainly, Hood has been responsible for much of the developmental work done in the past 10 years in sails and rigging.

The day of the cotton sail has long since passed. Nowadays, mainsails and headsails are almost universally made of Dacron or Terylene (a product similar to Dacron made in England). Spinnakers and very light off-the-wind headsails are made of nylon. High-priced racing boats, including the America's Cup 12-Meters, are now using space-age clothes such as Kevlar and Mylar to reinforce certain parts of their sails. But these cloths are expensive and require extra care in handling because they can be damaged by improper furling or folding. While they have remarkable abilities to hold shape, their frailities make them unsuitable for the cruising man. After more developmental work is done, perhaps materials such as these will be viable for the cruising boat.

Sailcloth is woven from two sets of threads: Those that run the length of the bolt are called the warp threads, and those that run at right angles along the width of the bolt are called the weft, or filler threads. If the warp and weft threads are of the same size, strength and stretch, the cloth is called "balanced." If one set of threads is stronger than the other, the construction is called "unbalanced." Because sailcloth is woven from threads passing over and under one another at right angles, a load on the bias (Figure 10-33) elongates the cloth by forcing the individual threads to fill the tiny spaces between them. When there's no space left, stretch stops.

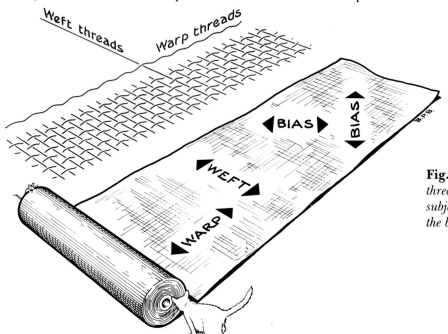

Fig. 10-33 *Sailcloth is woven with threads running at right angles. It is most subject to stretch when loads are placed on the bias.*

The strain on the edge of a sail is proportionate to its length, especially the unsupported edge from the clew to the head. On a high-aspect mainsail, for example, the strain is greatest along the leech. The cloth used for this type of sail (high-aspect is defined as any sail whose luff is at least 2½ times longer than the foot), is woven with weft threads larger than the warp, and pulled tighter. Low-aspect mainsails are made from cloth that is more balanced, and therefore lower in bias stretch.

To inhibit stretch, sails are "stabilized" by washing and heat-processing the cloth to induce shrinkage—sort of like pre-shrunk jeans. Then a filler and/or finish is added, often a polymer resin, that minimizes porosity and helps protect the threads from fatigue and ultraviolet deterioration. Special cloths are woven for the charter industry and for leech protection on roller furling headsails that have been treated with additional ultraviolet inhibitors. But this process makes the cloth heavier, quite stiff, and unsuitable for across-the-board application. Sails should *always* be covered or bagged when not in use to prevent unnecessary exposure to ultraviolet rays.

Sailcloths are distinguished by their weight in ounces for a given area. In the United States, the American Bureau of Standards stipulates the area as 28½ inches by 36 inches, and in the United Kingdom, a square yard (36"x36") is used. There is also a metric system that weighs cloth in grams per square meter. If ordering sails in another country, it is important to know which system is being used; Figure 10-34 is a conversion chart.

There are many factors involved in determining the correct weight cloth for a given sail. These include: typical wind force, area, aspect ratio and displacement of the boat. While your sailmaker is the best advisor, a bit of knowledge on your part will help you talk more intelligently with him, and give you a basis for overruling him if you see your needs differently than he does.

A sail made from cloth that is too light will stretch out of shape prematurely, and a cloth too heavy for its application won't achieve a very good shape, especially in light air. On the other hand, light cloth achieves a better shape and reduces weight aloft, while heavier cloth, with its

EQUIVALENT CLOTH WEIGHTS

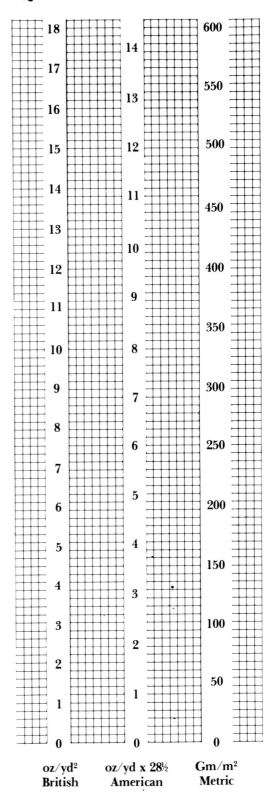

oz/yd²	oz/yd x 28½	Gm/m²
British	American	Metric

Fig. 10-34 *Table of equivalent cloth weights*

necessarily heavier thread, has greater tear strength.

Mainsails and working headsails are often made from the same weight cloth. Light, intermediate and heavy genoas are made from progressively heavier cloths below and above the weights of working sails. Racing sailors carry different weight genoas of the same size for different wind conditions. This enables them to maximize speed at all times. But the cruising sailor may not have the room or cash to indulge in this luxury. Also, cloth weights recommended by most sail lofts, in my experience, tend to be the weights used by the majority of their clientele, that is, the weekend racer/cruiser. Figure 10-35 incorporates the recommendations of cloth manufacturers, such as Howe & Bainbridge, and modified by the advice of experienced sailmakers for the cruising sailor. They are, for the most part, an ounce or two heavier than those weights recommended for the weekend racer/cruiser.

A rough formula suggested by Jeremy Howard-Williams, in his book *Sails*, derives the weight (oz./yd.²) for working sails by dividing the waterline length of the boat by three, and subtracting 10 percent. Add 10 percent for coastal cruising, 20 percent for occasional offshore passages, and as much as 30 percent for a stiff, heavy displacement offshore cruising boat. Consult your sailmaker for his advice and make it quite clear just what sort of cruising you intend to do.

Sail Reinforcements

To stand up to the wear and tear of everyday use, good cruising sails need reinforcement. The corners of each sail—tack, clew and head—should have several layers of cloth heavier than the sail itself sewn on top of each other, and extending at least several feet into the sail. The more layers the better. The size of reinforcing patches at the tack and clew of the sail should be about 1/12 the length of the luff and leech respectively, and 1/8 the length of the foot. A two-ply leech adds strength to this critical area, as does tabling the raw edges all around. Not only is the leech unsupported for the most part, but the

RECOMMENDED CLOTH WEIGHTS

Yacht	Mainsail and Working Headsail	Genoa	Light Genoa
L.W.L.:			
20 ft	5½	5	3–4½
21–25 ft	7–8	6–7	3–5
26–30 ft	8–9	6–7½	4–5½
31–35 ft	9–10½	7½–8½	4–6
36–40 ft	10½–12	8–9½	4–6
41–45 ft	12–13½	9½–10½	5–6½
46–50 ft	13½–14½	*	*
51–60 ft	14½–16	*	*
61–70 ft	16–18	*	*

* requires special assessment.

Fig. 10-35 *Table of recommended cloth weights for different size boats*

placement of batten pockets is likely to subject it to a certain amount of chafe. Batten pockets should be sewn of several layers and nylon protectors sewn into the inside end to prevent chafe. Triple stitching is a worthwhile additional expense.

Similarly, those panels where reef points are sewn in should at least be reinforced with heavier weight patches, or be sewn with two-ply cloth and patches on top. Follow the rule of thumb above for the size of these patches.

Aaron Jasper, who runs the North Sails loft in Newport, Rhode Island, says that he doesn't recommend hand-sewn cringles on large boats, because they tend to distort under load. Navy bronze or plastic cringles with stainless steel nails to grip the cloth are now standard in his loft; a hydraulic press is used to secure the two halves together, and takes the skill and risk out of making a cringle.

Seams are particularly susceptible to chafe and ultraviolet deterioration because of the exposure of the threads used to sew panels together. Tape can be applied over seams, or, as is more common in many lofts, a liquid plastic such as Howe & Bainbridge's Seam-Kote is brushed over the seams, doubling their resistance to chafe and ultra-violet deterioration.

Boltropes, headboards and sail slides or jib hanks must be properly sewn to the sail, using the correct size thread for the job and with the correct stitches. Sail slides and jib hanks are probably the items most subject to failure, and the ones you should be able to replace yourself under way.

Battens can be made from wood or fiberglass, though the latter is much more common today, partly because they are easier for the manufacturer to taper, and partly because they bend easier and are stronger. Corners should be well rounded and a cap or tape applied to the ends to prevent chafing the batten pocket and sail.

The Battenless, Roachless Mainsail

Some cruising sailors, no doubt distraught over the number of hours spent repairing batten pockets, advocate the use of battenless, roachless mainsails. On the plus side, battens and batten pockets are eliminated, which may be the single largest cause of sail repairs. And, on boats with excessive weather helm, the reduction in sail area can make the boat balance better.

An interesting example is Gene and Anne Correll, who sail a Pearson Vanguard out of Wyandotte, Michigan. The Vanguard has always displayed rather heavy weather helm in high winds, and this can really wear out a crew in a hurry. Some owners have installed wheel steering to ease the strain on the helmsman (worm gear is probably best in this instance), while others have tried moving the center of effort forward by installing a short bowsprit and moving the forestay a few feet forward (raking the mast forward apparently is insufficient on the Vanguard, though reefing the main before shortening the headsail does help).

After reading Hal Roth's book, *After 50,000 Miles*, Gene was convinced that a battenless, roachless mainsail was the answer for him, little suspecting the effect it would have on *Huntress'* center of effort.

Some sailmakers discouraged Gene from making the sail, insisting that the speed lost wouldn't be worth the advantage of eliminating torn batten pockets. Gene persisted, however, had the sail made, and discovered, much to his joy, that the boat balanced better than with the older main with a full roach.

Jane DeRidder wrote an article for *Cruising*

World titled, "Get Rid of that Roach", which wasn't an admonishment about trafficking in marijuana, but an appeal for the roachless main. She and her husband Shelley, blue-water sailors for many years, say it is well worth the slight loss in speed.

On the negative side, a battenless, roachless sail will never achieve the same desirable shape of a conventional sail. The reduction in sail area does cause a loss of speed, and while some justify it by saying sailboats are so slow anyway, what's another ½-knot drop in speed, I'm inclined to think that that ½-knot is extra important *because* sailboats are so slow. Using a roachless main on a well-balanced boat could cause neutral or slight lee helm, which would not be desirable. In the end, however, it is a matter of priorities and individual preference.

As a footnote on Gene Correll's experience, those of you with old sails should be aware that *they* may be the cause of any unusual weather helm you are experiencing. As a sail loses shape over the years (often caused by using the sail in winds that are too strong), the position of maximum draft is moved aft, which in turn pushes the aft end of the boat sideways and the bow higher. You might be surprised what a difference a new, properly cut sail will do to improve balance, speed and windward ability.

Sail Inventories

The well-found cruising boat should carry sails for all types of weather, ranging from ghosting conditions, to full-blown gales. Of course, much of the inventory will apply to those middle and more normal conditions. But short-changing yourself by skipping storm sails or drifters means endangering the boat and crew at worst, and subjecting them to excessive heel or irritating slatting at least.

Naturally, there is the problem of stowing a large inventory of sails, especially on smaller boats. Too frequently, the interior layout of modern production boats ignores sail stowage space—forepeaks are small and inaccessible, cockpit seat lockers are infringed by large aft quarter cabins, and lazarettes disappear with cockpits pushed all the way to the stern to make

more room below. This can be partially over-
come if the working sails can be furled and
stowed on deck. Club-footed jibs and staysails,
while posing a certain danger on the foredeck
(clobbering crew if the wind backs), do have the
advantage of making it easy to furl and stow the
sail. Roller furling genoas keep the sail off the
deck entirely, but even without them, headsails
can be furled along the deck, protected with specially sewn canvas covers and lashed to the stanchions. Other sails will have to find a home
below.

The following are suggested minimum sail inventories for sloops, cutters, ketches and yawls,
including optional sails.

Sloop with single headsail (Figure 10-36)

> Mainsail
> Working jib
> No. 1 genoa (150 percent)
> No. 2 genoa (110–130 percent)
> Drifter, reacher or cruising spinnaker
> Trysail
> Storm jib
> (Optional)
> No. 2 jib
> Second mainsail

Fig. 10-36 *Suggested sail inventory*
for a sloop

Note: a genoa designated as #1 or #2, does not refer to a
specific percentage of foretriangle size (the LP measurement,
which is a perpendicular from the luff intersecting the clew, is
used in determining 130 percent, 150 percent, etc.). Rather,
#1 or #2 refers to the largest headsail carried on board, next
largest, and so on.

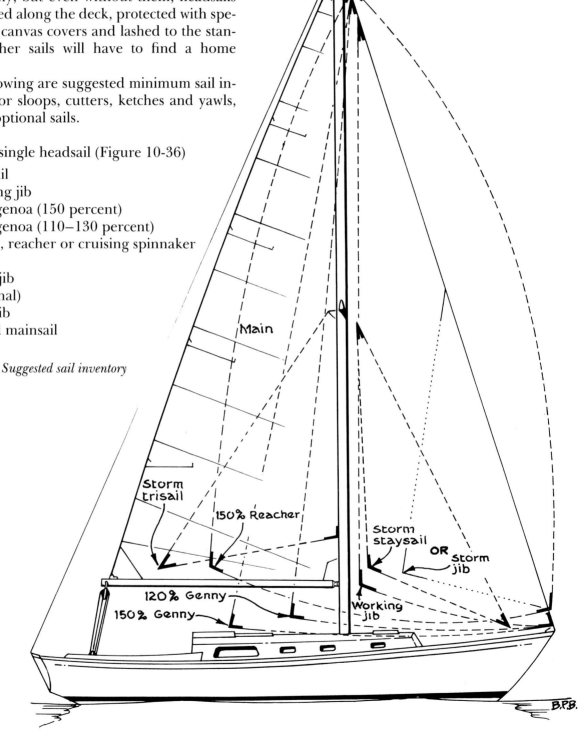
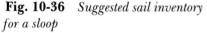

Cutter and double headsail sloops (Figure 10-37)

Mainsail
Yankee jib
Staysail with reef points
Trysail
Storm jib
Drifter, reacher or cruising spinnaker
(Optional)
No. 1 Yankee jib
No. 3 Yankee jib
Small or storm staysail

Fig. 10-37 *Suggested sail inventory for a cutter*

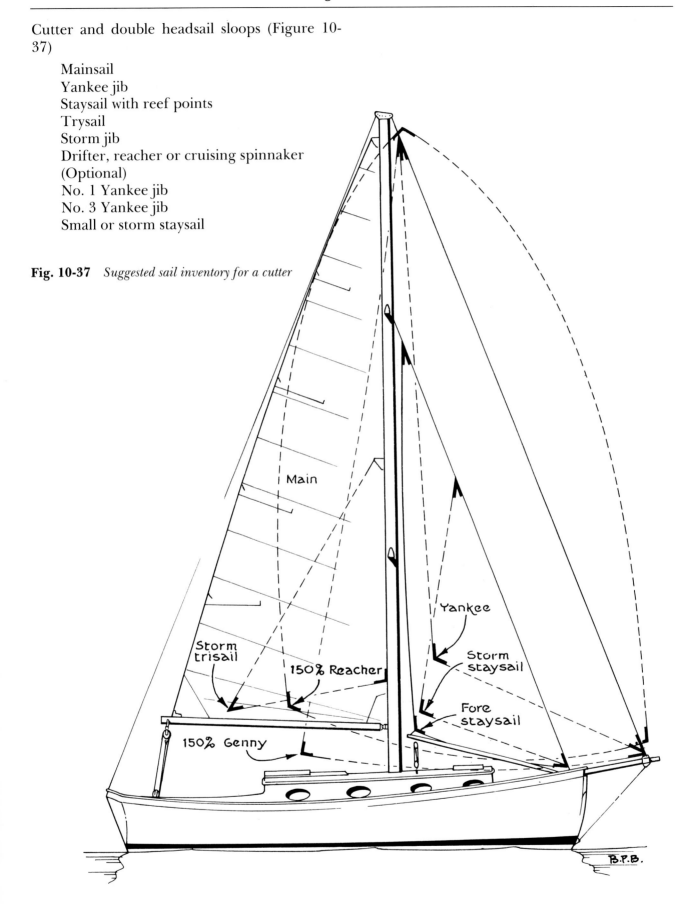

Ketch and Yawl (Figure 10-38)

    Mainsail
    Mizzen
    Working jib
    No. 1 genoa (150 percent)
    No. 2 genoa (110–130 percent)
    Drifter, reacher or cruising spinnaker
    Trysail
    Storm jib
    (Optional)
    No. 2 jib
    Mizzen staysail

When cruising with a limited sail inventory, the light air genoa is often not included. The weight of the sail and sheets keep the heavier cloth genoa from filling. A trick to reduce weight is to take off the standard sheets and use a smaller diameter line. The diameter of most sheets is chosen more for handling, not for strength, and in extreme light airs, moving down a size or two won't hurt.

Fig. 10-38   *Suggested sail inventory for a ketch or yawl*

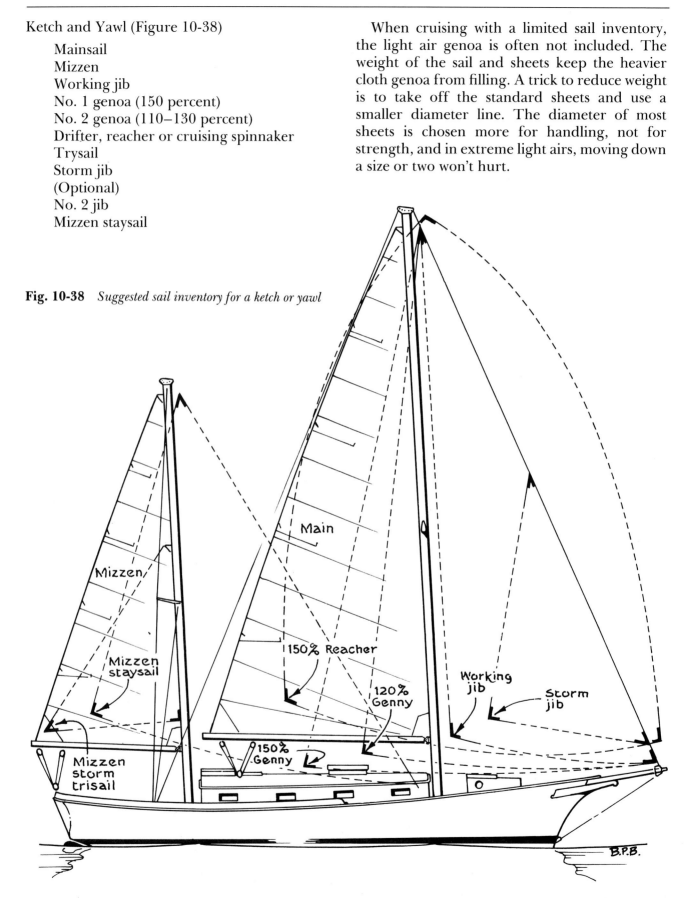

Making Your Own

Should you decide to sew your own sails, you will need four things: 1) a heavy-duty sewing machine, such as a Reeds, 2) a large floor area to lay out cloth, 3) cloth, thread and other hardware, and 4) some instruction on how to do it. There are a number of good books on how to make sails and these should be read thoroughly. Considering the cost of sailcoth, it would be wise to take a course in sailmaking, such as the correspondence courses offered by Sailrite Enterprises of Columbus City, Indiana. Everyone I know who has dealt with Sailrite has nothing but good things to say. It offers all the different types and weights of cloth, thread and hardware, even the preferred sewing machine. The savings one can achieve by building his own sails is substantial, not to mention the independence it gives the cruiser.

In Spring 1983, Danny Greene finished a passage from Puerto Rico to Haiti with a new suit of sails he made on a hilltop above a friend's house in Puerto Rico. He wrote that the sails performed beautifully, despite the insects, cockroaches, lizards, cats and dogs that hampered his work. "There are still a few unidentified tails sewn into the seams," he later wrote, but, considering their performance, obviously he got his money's worth from Sailrite.

Getting the Sails Made

When I went shopping for a new mainsail for *Adriana* at the Annapolis Boat Show, I visited as many sailmakers' booths as possible and asked for quotes. Here's what I found:

Amazing, isn't it? With boat show discounts, the final price quoted ranged all the way from $431 to $823. Sails U.S.A. and Rockall are "discount" sailmakers, which accounts for their lower prices. While the same quality and weight cloth may be used as the higher priced lofts, savings are often obtained by using less stitching, and smaller patches. Plus, there are optional extras such as spring-loading batten pockets, sail slides on shackles, triple stitching and fancy batten pocket enclosures. The point is that prices of sails vary, and are sometimes negotiable. This is most often true in the fall and winter when sail lofts aren't very busy; they need the work to keep staff earning their salaries over the dark, cold months of winter. Try to negotiate in April, the same price you were quoted at the fall boat show however, and chances are they'll tell you they don't even have the time to make the sail until July.

The best advice may be to get a referral from someone you know and trust—if he or she has had a good experience with a loft, perhaps you will, too. If your friend is familiar with the sailmaker, an introduction never hurts. Like everything else, including the automated Detroit assemblylines, some days the products are good, other days they're bad. There is a human element that cannot be entirely controlled. Take confidence in the fact, however, that if unsatisfied, you can always take the sail back and ask for alterations. On large racing boats, alterations are routine. This alone recommends using a local loft.

It is not uncommon, especially when taking big orders, for the head sailmaker to go sailing with the client for an hour or so to observe the

MANUFACTURER	MAINSAIL*	REEF POINTS	CUNNINGHAM	NUMBERS	TOTAL	WITH BOAT SHOW DISCOUNT
Sails U.S.A.	$591	58	15	15	679	$509.25
Rockall	575	80			655	431.00
Hood	653	139			792	792.00
Shore	792	94	20		906	815.00
Ratsey & Lapthorn	940	70			1010	823.00
Haarstick	677	110			787	585.60

* All 6½ oz. Dacron (September 1981)

existing sails and learn more intimately what the client expects. If your boat isn't close enough to the loft for the sailmaker to measure the pertinent dimensions, ask for a custom measurement form and do it yourself. There are occasional differences in rigs and fittings even among different hull numbers of the same product on boat. A racing sail differs from a cruising sail, as often does the sophistication of skippers. Rod Stephens says that cruising sailors should sail their boats at 95 percent efficiency of the racing skipper. Whether or not you agree, the point is that the cruising skipper should know something about the theory of sails, trim, and what will best meet his needs.

Reefing Systems

Perhaps no other alteration to your sails is as important as the sewing of reef points. Whether you use roller reefing or slab (jiffy) reefing (Figure 10-39), it is important to achieve a flat set on

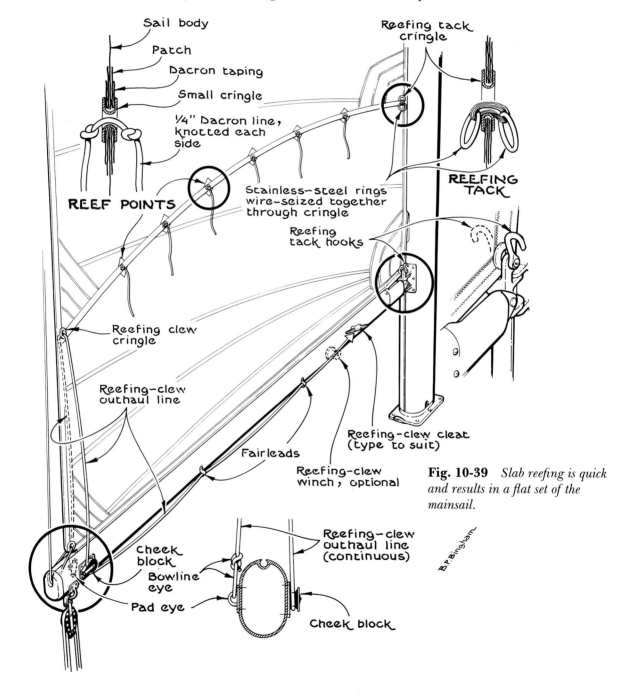

Fig. 10-39 *Slab reefing is quick and results in a flat set of the mainsail.*

the main. Failure to achieve this can impair your ability to handle the boat. *Adriana* once was pooped in Green Bay because the roller reefing left such a belly in the sail that she wouldn't point —a beam reach was about the best she'd do. Not even stuffing towels into the foot of the sail, nor pulling the boom as far to windward as possible made any difference. The next year I installed slab reefing and experienced no more problems.

The ability to reef down in a blow is vital. Heel is reduced, speed is seldom lost (and actually may be increased if the boat excels at lower angles of heel), and the crew will certainly feel safer.

To install slab reefing, the mainsail must have one or more sets of reef points sewn in. These are cringles pressed or sewn over reinforced patches on the sail, and because the sail is not made entirely flat, the line of points will not be straight. Your sailmaker will know where to place them. Two or three sets are desirable if you are to get maximum use from your mainsail in worsening conditions.

Once the reef points are sewn in, take a length of ³⁄₁₆ to ¼-inch Dacron line and cut it into three-foot lengths (longer if your mainsail exceeds about 300 square feet). Run the line through a cringle and tie knots on either side so that it hangs evenly on either side.

You'll also need a cheek block bolted or screwed to the boom for each set of points, and a cleat forward near the gooseneck so you can pull in the leech after slackening the halyard. A reefing hook should be fixed to the gooseneck to secure the cringle at the luff of the sail. And lastly, a length of line must be led from a padeye on one side of the boom, up through the cringle at the leech, down through the cheek block, and forward to the cleat. Fairleads keep this line from sagging off the boom.

To use slab reefing, 1) ease the mainsheet, 2) take up the topping lift, 3) slacken the main halyard, 4) fit the luff cringle over the reefing hook at the gooseneck, 5) take up the halyard, 6) pull in on the reefing line until the clew is tight to the boom, then cleat it, 7) ease the topping lift, 8) sheet in the sail, and tie the lines in the reef points under the boom using a reef knot. This whole process takes very little time—a minute or two with practice.

SUMMARY

The rig and sails are the sailboat's primary means of propulsion, and every means possible must be taken to keep it standing. Regular inspection of spars, fittings, wires, and lines should be undertaken, and replacements made where necessary.

- Avoid triatic stays on ketches and yawls, if possible.
- When adding fittings to spars, correctly size pilot holes according to the size of screw, rivet or bolt.
- Aluminum spars should have drain holes above the deck.
- Spreaders preferably should be rigidly fixed, but should bisect the shroud, and be as wide as possible without extending over the boat's rail.
- Shrouds must be secured to the spreader tip to prevent them from popping out.
- Discontinuous rigging has less chance of exerting uneven loads on spreaders; link plates should be used, especially on double spreader rigs with intermediate shrouds.
- Shrouds should be angled no less than 12 degrees out from the perpendicular line of the mast.
- Install oversize standing rigging, tangs, chainplates and blocks so each part is stronger than the wire.
- Every shroud and stay should have a backup that stands a chance of holding up the spar should the primary shroud or stay break.
- Poured socket terminals are strongest, followed by Nicopress and possibly a good splice. Terminals and bands should be stronger than the breaking strength of the wire.
- Halyards and sheets should be sized for comfort in handling; if they are large enough to pull hard on without hurting your hand, they probably are more than strong enough for the job.
- Headsail downhauls can prevent or at least postpone a trip to the bow.
- Boom vangs and preventers should always be used when running downwind.
- Sails should be sewn from the correct weight cloth for maximum performance and lifespan. Reinforcements should be made to all corners and areas of stress.
- Sail inventories should include sails for weather ranging from light to storm conditions.
- Mainsails, and sometimes staysails and jibs, should have reef points sewn in, and a handy method of shortening sail.

FURTHER READING

Cruising Rigs and Rigging by Ross Norgrove; International Marine Publishing Co., Camden, Maine 04843.

Sail Power by Wallace Ross; Alfred A. Knopf, 201 E. 50 St., New York, New York 10022.

Advanced Sailboat Cruising by Colin Mudie, Geoff Hales and Michael Handford; Nautical, Macmillan London Ltd., 4 Little Essex St., London WC2R 3LF, England.

Sails by Jeremy Howard-Williams; John de Graff, Inc., Clinton Corners, New York, 12514.

The Ocean Sailing Yacht, Vols I and II, by Donald M. Street, Jr.; W. W. Norton & Co., 500 Fifth, New York, New York 10110.

The Amateur Sailmaker's Library by James L. Grant; Sailrite Enterprises, Route 1, Columbia City, Indiana 46725.

Make Your Own Sails by R. M. Bowker and S. A. Budd; St. Martin's Press, 175 Fifth Ave., New York, New York 10010.

The Care of Alloy Spars and Rigging by David Potter; Granada Publishing Ltd., Frogmore, St. Albans, Hertfordshire AL2 2NF England.

PART TWO

Ancillary Systems

CHAPTER 11

Galley Systems

So we lived on cold bacon, tinned herrings and beer, and relieved our feelings by punching the barometer.

ARTHUR RANSOME

Eating well at sea, or at the dock, is a pleasure to be regarded as highly as fine weather, a sound boat and a compatible crew. When everyone is pleased with the food, inclement weather and other annoyances don't seem so serious. But when the food is lousy, it exacerbates every other problem, making more sensitive crewmembers whine and gripe, and taking the edge off even the most optimistic.

Health and safety is involved in cooking, too. Albeit some singlehanded passage-makers live on beans and sardines for weeks at a time, they are by and large a hardy lot who know themselves and what it takes to be comfortable. For some, the prospect of cooking *anything* is more insufferable than a boring diet. Not so for most of us, especially when we aren't moved to stoicism by the competitiveness of a race with other sailors, or aren't trying to prove something to ourselves.

Choosing a balanced diet for each member of the crew is not within the scope of this book. But providing the space and major equipment to prepare food certainly is. One can survive with a few ounces of water each day for several weeks, longer by adding a few ounces of food. For the man in a life raft, cooking is impossible, unless drying fish filets in the sun is a form of baking. Under normal circumstances, however, the crew will want tasty meals, and the ease with which these can be prepared will go a long way in making a cruise happy and memorable.

REQUIREMENTS OF A GOOD GALLEY

The well-thought-out galley will have sufficient storage space for foodstuffs: cans, boxes, jars, bottles. Cutlery and plates and pans should be stowed in a secure place where they won't fall out when the boat heels, yet be within arm's reach when the cook wants them.

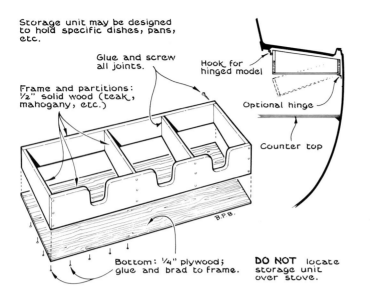

Storage unit may be designed to hold specific dishes, pans, etc.

Glue and screw all joints.

Hook for hinged model

Frame and partitions: ½" solid wood (teak, mahogany, etc.)

Optional hinge

Counter top

B.P.B.

Bottom: ¼" plywood; glue and brad to frame.

DO NOT locate storage unit over stove.

Fig. 11-1 *Plates and glasses can be stored in plywood cabinets you can make yourself. Under deck areas adjacent to the galley are convenient and don't take up otherwise usable space.*

Under-deck areas are often wasted space, and near the galley they can be converted to convenient storage for plates and glasses. Quarter-inch plywood can be cut with a saber saw, framed with cleats, glued and nailed to form holders for these items (Figure 11-1).

Cutlery is best left inside drawers that are notched inside the facing to keep them from spewing their contents when the boat heels (Figure 11-2). Plywood spacers or plastic Rubbermaid cutlery dividers inside drawers maintain a semblance of order.

Pots and pans, especially the heavy cast-iron variety, are best kept low, for better weight distribution and for safety. Underneath the galley or in a padded bin against the hull is ideal. On

Adriana I stow these items behind the starboard bunk, next to the galley. It's not perfect, but it does work. A few of my less-used pans are kept in a galley bin under the bridge deck and behind the galley sink. Essentially, the area is dead storage, which may have its own usefulness, but it would be better if the compartment were more readily accessible.

The galley sink should be deep and, if possible, a double model. With two sink compartments, dishes can be washed in one and rinsed in the other. They should be wide and deep enough, say 10 inches, so that a dish can be passed beneath the spigot—a high one helps. *Adriana*'s galley is too small for a deep double sink, so I use a plastic basin to wash dishes with

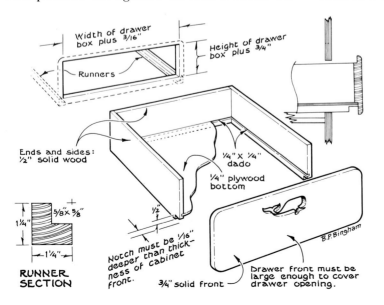

Width of drawer box plus 3/16"

Height of drawer box plus ¾"

Runners

Ends and sides: ½" solid wood

¼" X ¼" dado

¼" plywood bottom

5/8 X 5/8"

1¼"

½"

1¼"

RUNNER SECTION

Notch must be 1/16" deeper than thickness of cabinet front.

¾" solid front

Drawer front must be large enough to cover drawer opening.

B.P.Bingham

Fig. 11-2 *Cutlery should be placed in divided drawers with notches to prevent them from spilling out when the boat heels. Make finger holes for ventilation.*

salt water and soap (Prell shampoo and Joy detergent suds well in salt water), then transfer them to the sink for a fresh-water rinse. A sea water pump at the galley sink helps conserve fresh water. For pumps, see Chapter 5, and to install a seacock at the intake thru-hull see Chapter 4.

The resulting conservation of fresh water cannot be appreciated until you've carried water to your boat in jerry jugs, or tried to drain off water from awning or deck catchment systems. Living aboard at the dock with the luxury of unlimited fresh water from a nearby hose and faucet definitely dulls your appreciation for this precious commodity.

The stove is as important as any other element of the galley, and selection of fuel type no less so. The first decision is whether to have stove-top burners or a stove/oven combination. With pressure cookers and hayboxes, turkeys and roasts can be satisfactorily cooked on a stove top, but the end result is a little less certain. Fresh bread, a tough product to come by at sea or in secluded anchorages, is most easily baked in an oven. So, if there's space in your galley, give extra thought to an oven.

A stove top can be mounted on removable gimbals for cooking, and stowed elsewhere when not in use. Figure 11-3 shows a contraption I had made by a handy welder who understood the problem I presented him. It was made from galvanized pipe bent to a gentle curve. A flat piece of metal was welded on top, to which I screw the stove gimbals. The assembly is held to the galley side by two pipe joints welded to a flat piece of metal that in turn screws to the galley. A thumb screw allows the whole thing to be fastened in place when cooking, or to swing outboard out of the way when dinner is done. Weights (thin pieces of lead, for example), should be secured to the drip pan to counteract the weight of heavy pots and to dampen the stove's motion as it swings. When I get sick of having the stove obstructing access to the sink I remove it from the gimbals and stow it on the galley counter under the bridge deck. Two screw eyes in the bulkhead and a length of shock cord hold it in place.

A stove/oven, however, must be fitted to one spot permanently by virtue of its size alone. Al-

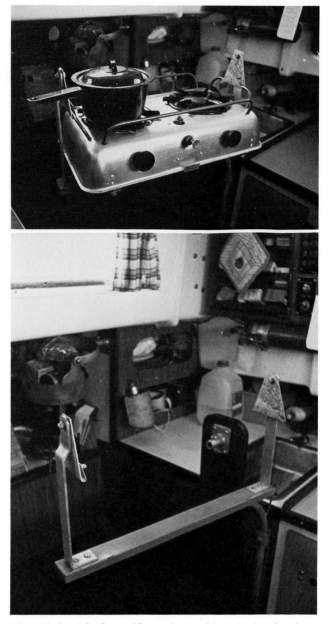

Fig. 11-3 *I had a welder make up this swinging bracket to hold my alcohol stove. It was later abandoned in favor of storing the stove under the bridge deck and using the Sea Swing stove (seen under the deck) on a second mount next to the sink when sailing.*

most always, it will be mounted to face athwartship and gimballed so that it swings as the boat rocks, minimizing the chance of dumping pots full of hot stew over the cook's bare legs. (Burns are extremely serious injuries and must be avoided in every possible way. Always carry a good supply of burn cream like Silvadene to treat burns until professional medical care can be obtained.)

Gimballing is not absolutely necessary when cooking, and always a nuisance when you're not. A deadbolt that locks the stove to the bulkheads on either side is a wise installation.

High stove fiddles—three to four inches—will keep most pots on the burner even if the stove isn't gimballed. Free-thinking Tom Colvin challenges conventional thought by advocating un-gimballed stoves mounted to face fore and aft in the galley. The gimbals, he says, only increase the likelihood of scalding the cook, and facing fore or aft means that if the boat is suddenly rocked the pots will fly sideways, athwartship, while the cook will probably fall away from the stove, forward or aft, at the same time he or she goes sideways. In other words, cook and stew won't meet. And the best place for a galley, according to Tom? In the forward cabin! Most motion is athwartships, he reasons, which affects the bow no more than the midships area. And if the boat is beating into seas, yes the motion forward is worse, but who wants to cook then, anyway? Tom says he has built three boats for clients with the galley forward, and though each was at first skeptical, after months of cruising, none of them wanted any changes.

As Tom points out, there is an obvious danger cooking in a seaway, where the cook may be thrown against the stove and burn him or herself on the burner or, more likely, with the contents of the pot or pan. A strong bar thru-bolted to the counter, across the front of the stove is a partial preventive measure (Figure 11-4). And recessing the stove six or eight inches from the bar helps equally well.

The reverse of this problem is when the stove is to windward or uphill and the cook must brace on some surface to leeward to stay near the stove. A canvas belt with a sliding shackle on one end can be used to brace the cook's back, but be careful that it doesn't hold the cook too close to the stove. If a hot pot starts sliding toward the cook, the brace just about eliminates the cook's chances of getting out of the way (Figure 11-5). For this reason, Tom Colvin doesn't approve of galley straps, either.

Fig. 11-4 *Ideally, the stove should be recessed from the front of the galley counter and a strong stainless steel bar bolted across the opening to prevent the cook from being thrown onto the stove.*

Fig. 11-5 *Galley straps give the cook something to brace against when the boat is heeled, but if it lurches the other way, it could prevent the cook from escaping.*

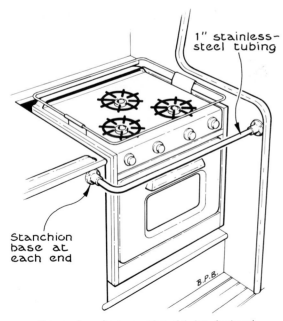

Base hardware should be bolted to surfaces...not screwed.

TYPES OF FUELS

There are at least a half-dozen types of fuels for marine stoves. Rate them according to: safety, availability, cost and BTU output.

Alcohol (CH₂O)

About 75 percent of all new boats sold in the United States are equipped with alcohol stoves. The reasons are twofold: it is the cheapest type of stove available to the manufacturer, and for years it was about the only fuel people felt was safe. Boating literature, abetted by the U.S. Coast Guard, proclaimed that because alcohol and water mix, a fire could easily be extinguished. Of course, anyone who has experienced a galley fire knows that finding a bucket of water while the curtains go up in flames is not all that simple. And oftentimes, water just displaces the alcohol, which continues to burn.

It is ironic that alcohol, once considered the safest fuel, is now being regarded as one of the most dangerous. Sailing publications have carried a number of stories in recent years describing horrible burns resulting from alcohol stove spills. The most common cause is failing on first try to heat the burner sufficiently to vaporize the fuel. While the burner is still hot, someone opens the throttle, sending more alcohol into the cup. While the burner isn't hot enough to vaporize the alcohol and burn safely (a temperature of 689° F is required), it is hot enough to ignite the liquid alcohol, sending flames spewing upward. If the throttle is still open, the entire contents of the tank can fuel the fire, and, if the stove is gimballed, it can even spill over onto one's legs. The moral of these stories is that if the burner isn't hot enough to vaporize the alcohol the first time, WAIT for at least several minutes before trying that burner again.

Other reasons to treat alcohol stoves gingerly are that the flame is very pale and in sunlight is often impossible to see. Dark-colored burners help distinguish the flame. I put a pan over the burner when priming. Not only does this contain the flames somewhat, it also darkens the burner area, making the flames easier to see.

Alcohol vapors are heavier than air and do not blow away as readily as one might think. If alcohol vapor in the air exceeds 3.3 percent, and a heat source is applied, ignition could result, another reason for caution.

Alcohol's heat output is only 2,500 to 3,000 BTUs (British Thermal Units—the amount of heat required to raise the temperature of one pound of pure water 1°F). This is about half the output of LPG or CNG. Boiling a pot of water takes about eight to 10 minutes. Non-pressurized alcohol stoves are said to take a bit longer, but the several I have owned seemed to work about as well as the pressurized types. The advantage of a non-pressurized model is that if an accident does occur, fuel will not continue to be pushed through the burners and into the cup, nor is there a danger of flare-ups because no priming is required.

Origo recently introduced a new type of non-pressurized alcohol stove that does away with the Primus-type burner altogether (Figure 11-6). It works something like a Sterno stove, but much better.

Fig. 11-6 *The Origo 3000 alcohol two burner stove is non-pressurized. Alcohol is poured into the two fiber-filled cannisters, and a Sterno-type cover is slid over the top to extinguish flames.*

The tank, which is essentially the entire inside body of the stove, is packed with a non-flammable pulp which in turn is soaked with alcohol. A wire mesh holds the pulp down in place. A fondue-type plate slides over the opening to extinguish the flame.

A last reason not to buy an alcohol stove is the cost of fuel. Alcohol, costly enough in the U.S., is prohibitively expensive in other areas of the world—sometimes $10 a gallon and more. In yet other countries, it is not even available.

Kerosene

Like alcohol, kerosene vapors make some crew members seasick in short order. Unlike alcohol, it burns much hotter (3,500 to 4,000 BTUs), boiling water in about five minutes, though I have yet to achieve this performance with my Sea Swing fitted with an Optimus kerosene burner.

Kerosene is almost universally available and it is comparatively cheap. Tristan Jones has written that kerosene is the only fuel to consider for global passage-making.

On the down side, the priming operation of kerosene stoves can be dangerous, mainly because alcohol is required to preheat the burners. Substitute primers, such as mineral spirits, produce hotter flames and can ruin the burners. Kerosene, derived from diesel oil, does not evaporate like alcohol. It must be watched carefully to prevent it from soaking into insulation or other absorbent materials where it could pose a future danger—let alone a nasty smell. More highly refined grades of kerosene are frequently available through chandleries; they smell better and burn cleaner, but are correspondingly more expensive.

Nevertheless, kerosene remains the choice of many cruising people. (See Chapter 14 for a permanent kerosene tank-and-plumbing system.)

Diesel

Diesel oil is a safe cooking fuel, and if the boat has a diesel auxiliary, there is the added advantage of not having to add an extra tank for the

Fig. 11-7 *A Dickinson diesel stove eliminates carrying a different type of fuel if the auxiliary engine is also diesel.*

stove. A separate fuel line can be run from the fuel tank to the stove.

Diesel burns quite hot and precautions must be taken to install tiles or stainless steel around the stove area to protect the hull and woodwork from overheating.

In his book, *After 50,000 Miles*, Hal Roth makes a strong case for the diesel stove, which also can be used for heating in cold climates such as his native Pacific Northwest. Roth writes that he almost always uses it on low setting, and claims that at full power it could melt scrap iron. The desirability of such a stove is unquestionable on a sail to Iceland, but for the cruiser in tropical climes, it's dubious at best.

Diesel stoves must be vented through the coachroof of the boat. This requires some bending of the stovepipe to keep it clear of the boat—and the people in it. In cold weather, they need electric fans to aid ignition. And, as many of these stoves are quite heavy, installation is often difficult. Dickinson makes a fine range of diesel cookers (Figure 11-7) as does Taylor in England.

Liquid Propane Gas (LPG)

Butane (C_2H_{10}) and Propane (C_3H_8) are gases turned liquid under pressure in special bottles.

When released from the bottle in the stove burner, liquid returns to its gaseous form. Both are very explosive, burn hot and clean, and because they are heavier than air they can collect in the bilge if a leak occurs.

Propane poses a vexing choice. On one hand, it is dangerous. On the other, it burns hot and clean and is available in most countries. When cruising outside the U.S., metric fittings should be carried to fill the tanks ashore. More and more LPG stoves are appearing on new yachts, and those persons that have used them successfully swear by them. LPG has an output of between 5,000 and 6,000 BTUs, about twice that of alcohol. Food and water are heated more quickly.

Two of the major dangers with odorless LPG —asphyxiation and explosion—are now minimized because the law requires that chemicals be added to make the gas easily detected by smell. These chemicals are non-toxic. Also, solenoid switches in the fuel lines at the tank shut off the line when activated by a manual switch in the cabin near the stove. Thermal couples located in the burner flame automatically shut off the line if the flame goes out. Without these, and with the burner still open, fuel would continue to pour into the cabin. Religiously closing fuel lines at the tank via the manual solenoid switch, and at the stove after each use also lessens the chances of disaster. (See "Installing an LPG system" later in this chapter for more details.) In fact, the safest practice is to shut off the fuel at the tank while the burner is still lit. When all the fuel in the line has burned, the flame will go out; then the stove burners can be shut off. Ron Barr, a former charter captain and now co-owner of the Armchair Sailor Bookstore in Newport, suggests keeping on hand a short piece of mechanical plumbing with a petcock to bypass the solenoid in the event of electrical failure on board. "When your batteries go flat," he says, "you might want to put on a cup of tea to console yourself!"

Compressed Natural Gas (CNG)

Critics of LPG are frequently more impressed with the attributes of CNG, because it is lighter than air and will rise and dissipate into the atmosphere, given some overhead ventilation. Like LPG, it is relatively non-toxic, meaning that breathing the vapors will not cause injury or death. What is potentially dangerous is that a leak in an enclosed cabin displaces the air and can cause suffocation. CNG, of course, is also explosive, but with only a quarter the force of LPG. CNG's ignition temperature is 1100°, LPG's 800°, and the percent of gas in the air by volume required for ignition is about twice as much for CNG (5% to 15%) than for LPG (2% to 9.5%). Nevertheless, one should regard CNG with the same caution as LPG—it is a combustible gas and it is dangerous. Chemicals are added to CNG to make them easy to detect by smelling.

The American Boat and Yacht Council (ABYC) recommends copper tubing for LPG installations, though high-pressure flexible hose can be used. Bruce Bingham says the ABYC standards are a carry-over from the trailer industry and not necessarily consistent with current safety practices. He prefers flexible hose throughout. CNG is incompatible with copper, so flexible hose must be used with it. Of course, flexible hose with push-on type connectors makes routing the hose and making connections much simpler.

Trying to gimbal a stove with copper tubing, however, is impossible. So short flexible hoses are used with LPG where it connects with the stove. But it's one more joint to worry about. With CNG or LPG, a flexible fuel line system reduces possible leaks due to vibration of flared copper fittings. Where the hosing passes through bulkheads or any other barrier, rubber ferrules (short tube or bushing) should be used to prevent abrasion. Alternatively, a six-inch length of clear vinyl hose can be slit open on one side and slid over the fuel line where it passes through a bulkhead.

It is interesting to note that more and more racing boats are using CNG in this country because the tanks can be installed in the bilge, thus keeping weight out of the ends of the boat.

A further attraction of CNG is that the bottle opening is so small, an accidentally damaged regulator will let so little gas escape there would be no danger of the bottle launching itself into your face. With LPG this is a possibility, though not necessarily a likely one. The amount of pressure in a CNG burner is less than half that of LPG and about $\frac{1}{100}$ that of alcohol or kerosene. And because CNG is the cleanest fuel of all, burner clogging is minimal. However, CNG fuel consumption is greater than propane or kerosene, though less than alcohol.

The major drawbacks with CNG are that it not only burns quickly, but it is only available on the U.S. seaboards—and then, only at certain authorized dealers. The bottles, which by Federal law are "purchased" on a permanent lease-back arrangement to ensure periodic inspection, can be mailed to one of several distributors by U.P.S. In the past year or so, however, Gas Systems in California and the Corp Brothers in Providence, Rhode Island, have increased their number of dealers dramatically. Plans are in the works to include the Caribbean soon. This would be good news indeed. Obviously, the distributors realize they have a good thing on their hands, and it's only a matter of time before CNG significantly erodes the propane market. However, it will be many years before CNG is distributed worldwide.

Electricity

Large motorsailers and powerboats may have electric ranges that operate just like the ones in your home. But these are vessels with enormous generators to provide sufficient electrical power for cooking and dozens of other functions. On a 25 to 45-foot sailboat, electric stoves are hardly worth considering. Not only is it difficult to generate enough juice without shore power—even with wind, water and solar generators—but because everything in a small boat sooner or later falls prey to salt air, electrical appliances should always be viewed with suspicion.

Sterno

This is the canned fuel used on some camp stoves and fondue sets. A match lights the solid fuel inside, which burns quite harmlessly. Unfortunately, it doesn't burn hot enough to do much good for cooking. I carry a few cans to use in my Sea Swing stove just in case I can't get the kerosene burner to work, a contingency yet to arise.

Summing up, the consensus amongst *many* (note the care in avoiding *most*—this is a controversial subject!) cruisers is that CNG is probably the best all-around fuel for cruising the waters of the United States. For worldwide cruising, kerosene is tough to beat, though propane is certainly in wide use. Alcohol and diesel are in the minority.

INSTALLING AN LPG SYSTEM

Determining stove and tank locations is the first step in installing your own LPG System. As mentioned in Chapter 9 (Figures 9-27 to 9-29), propane tanks must be stored on deck or in a vapor-proof locker where the gas cannot possibly enter the cabin.

The ABYC requires that the tank housing have "at least two vents having an aggregate free area equal to one square inch for each seven pounds of the total LPG capacity of the cylinders, the vent area being equally divided top and bottom." The bottom vent should be at floor level, and the housing should be at least two feet from any semi-enclosure including the cockpit.

For additional safety information consult the National Fire Protection Association's (NFPA) recommendations in Appendix D.

Most marine tanks are made of aluminum as they are more corrosion-resistant than steel, and range in size from about five to 20 pounds of gas. Each cylinder is fitted with a manual shut-off valve and a safety relief valve. Vertically installed cylinders are most common, though there are some that can be mounted horizontally. Never mount a vertical cylinder on its side, because it does not have the special J-shaped tube to prevent liquid gas from reaching the outlet valve.

It makes sense to join two cylinders with a valve that permits switching from the empty tank to the full one. Not so much extra space is required for the second tank, and there's an obvious advantage in having more fuel and less frequent refillings. Two small tanks are easier to carry than one large tank, and while one is ashore being filled, you still have the other for cooking. Open only one cylinder valve at a time.

Inside the deck box each cylinder should be well chocked with wood and held in place with straps to prevent any movement, especially when copper tubing is used for fuel lines.

Fuel lines should be suitable for LPG gas. (Note that copper tubing is not compatible with CNG.) ABYC recommends annealed copper tubing of Grade K or L type, as specified by the American Society of Testing and Materials. Katy Burke writes in *The Complete Live-Aboard Book* that she and Bruce Bingham used flexible high-pressure hose purchased from a trailer-supply store, because they were afraid that copper tubing might work loose at the connectors due to vibration and the general working of the boat. Where it passed through bulkheads, clear plastic hose was slipped over to prevent chafe.

The tubing diameter will vary with the amount of fuel carried, generally between ¼ inch and ⅜ inch. The latter can service appliances burning up to 75,000 BTUs, much more than the typical marine stove. Secure the copper tubing or flexible hose with non-ferrous clips that will not bite or crimp the fuel line—plastic electrical clips work well.

An electrically operated solenoid shut-off valve should be installed in the fuel line immediately after the tank and outside the cabin. A light tells whether the switch is activated or not. Locate the solenoid panel where it is easily seen and operated from the galley.

Thermo-couple heat sensors installed at every burner and in the oven add another measure of safety by automatically shutting off the system when the flame goes out. Lastly, a gas detector or "sniffer" will sound an alarm if a leak develops. The sniffer will draw some juice, but not much. (Chapter 12 discusses ways of keeping the batteries topped off without an engine.) Your LPG installation should resemble that in Figure 11-8.

In the eventuality of a leak, it is helpful to have an approved blower installed in the bilge to rid the area of fumes. Gasoline auxiliaries require such a blower, but diesels do not. I removed the blower on *Adriana* when I converted to diesel, but would probably reinstall it if I decided to install a LPG stove system.

Test the system by pressurizing it to a minimum of five pounds per square inch (a pressure gauge in the line will give you a reading). Dab each connector with a solution of water and liquid detergent to see if bubbles appear. If they do, a leak is occurring. Another method is to

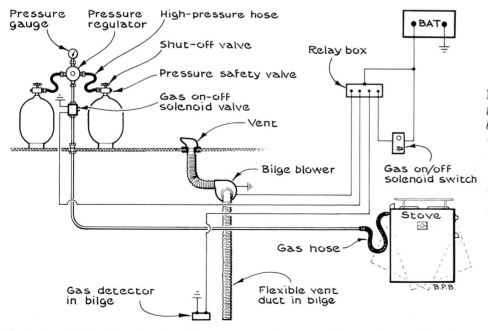

Pressure gauge
Pressure regulator
High-pressure hose
Shut-off valve
Pressure safety valve
Gas on-off solenoid valve
Vent
Relay box
BAT
Bilge blower
Gas on/off solenoid switch
Stove
Gas hose
Gas detector in bilge
Flexible vent duct in bilge
B.P.B.

Fig. 11-8 *A proper LPG installation features a ventilated bottle locker, vapor-tight ferrules where lines pass through bulkheads, solenoid switches to shut off gas, and bilge blowers and sniffers as safety precautions.*

Gas solenoid off and bilge-blower on relays may be activated by the gas detector or by the flame-out thermocouples.

install an in-line leak detector, available from trailer supply stores. If no leaks appear, close off the appliance valves, open the cylinder valve and note the pressure. Then close the cylinder shut-off valve and observe the pressure gauge. It should not change for at least 15 minutes. If no change occurs within this time period, the installation is sound and you can begin using the stove. If the pressure drops, go back and recheck each connection and the burners. Never check for leaks by applying an open flame to the suspected site. Periodically check the system about once each month.

If you don't have a pressure gauge, open the gas line to the stove, with the valve at the tank shut off. After 15 minutes, open the valve at the stove burner (keeping the tank valve closed) and strike a match. If the burner lights, the lines are able to retain pressure. If it doesn't light, the gas has leaked out and you must check all connections for the leak source.

REFRIGERATION

There is little doubt that most of us are happier with cold beers, frozen steaks and crisp lettuce than with warm drinks, tinned meats and wilted greens. Obtaining ice once a week—or even more—is an ordeal we all tire of quickly. After a year or two of this, you may decide either to forget ice altogether and adapt your eating/drinking habits, or to install some sort of mechanical refrigeration.

The icebox is of critical importance to the effectiveness of any refrigeration system. Chapter 3 details the construction features of an effective icebox—four inches or more insulation, staggered joints, taped seams, tinfoil reflective barrier and Mylar moisture barrier, gasketed lid, etc. Here we'll concern ourselves with how to keep the box cold with mechanical refrigeration.

Basic Types of Refrigeration

Many refrigeration units on medium to large sailboats use engine-driven *compressors* to compress gas from an *evaporator,* which becomes hot,

and push it into a *condenser* where it is cooled and condensed to a liquid. An evaporator changes it back to a gas and to a much colder temperature, before sending it on its way through another cycle. R-12 is a commonly used gas, which is non-toxic and non-flammable. Major marine refrigeration manufacturers are Grunert, Crosby, Spa Creek, Faire Harbour and Technautics.

The development of hermetically sealed compressors made possible small, quiet, and maintenance-free portable units. The latest refrigeration systems, such as Adler-Barbour's ColdMachine™, run off 115-volts AC and 12-volts DC instead of belts driven by the auxiliary engine. A small electric motor drives the compressor, so you only need to run the engine periodically to keep the batteries charged. Still, engine-driven compressors probably require less engine running time.

Both engine and battery-driven systems have compressors, evaporators and condensers. They also have some sort of metering device, ranging from a simple capillary tube to an expansion valve, which determines how much gas is reaching the evaporator. A capillary tube is nothing more than a length of tubing with a small pin hole whose diameter and length is carefully determined to regulate the amount of gas passing through. An expansion valve is, more accurately, a needle valve that opens and closes in response to pressure and temperature, thereby regulating the refrigerant gas.

There are two ways of cooling the condenser: air and water. In air-cooled types, the refrigerant gas is cooled by passing through coils of tubing inside an array of cooling fins, the same sort of thing you see on motorcycle and lawnmower engine heads. The fins absorb the heat and dissipate it into the outside air with the help of a small electric fan. It is a simple system that requires little maintenance. Its only disadvantage is that the condenser must be located in a well-ventilated spot. The engine room is likely too hot and poorly ventilated; underneath bunks is a possible site, but some sort of caning or other vent should be installed in the bunk face to let air in and out.

Water-cooled condensers function like heat exchangers. The gas passes through a tube that is surrounded by a water jacket full of circulating cold sea water. The sea water can be obtained by tapping into the engine cooling system so that raw water drawn in by the engine's water pump passes through the refrigerator's water jacket before it reaches the engine. The water temperature is not increased much, but because any malfunction jeopardizes the all-important engine, some refrigeration systems use separate pumps and thru-hull fitting to obtain their cooling sea water.

Let's take a brief look at both a typical engine-driven system and a popular battery-powered system.

THE SEA FROST®

The Sea Frost is a small, easily installed engine-driven refrigeration unit made by the C. F. Horton Company of Dover, New Hampshire. Total operating weight is about 75 pounds, and parts consist of a block, compressor, condenser and valve/control unit (Figure 11-9). The block is actually a holding or eutetic plate that is full of brine. When frozen, it "holds over" the cold just like a block of ice. The difference between this system and an icebox is that instead of rowing ashore for more ice, you just turn on the engine —for as little as 30 to 45 minutes a day. Not bad.

I was first acquainted with the Sea Frost during a visit to Arthur Martin in Kittery, Maine. Arthur, who once helped Ray Hunt design the Concordia yawl, now is a bug about energy efficiency. He designed a 48-foot power boat by tripling the dimensions of his Appledore rowing/sailing pod. We took a ride aboard the Energy 48, and one of the first things Arthur mentioned was the Sea Frost refrigerator. "It does just what they say it will," he said. In a well-insulated box, very little running time is required.

Three different block sizes are available—the half block for iceboxes smaller than four cubic feet, the regular single block, and the double block for boxes exceeding 10 pounds of ice-melt per day (the company says that because up to 45 percent more engine running time is needed for the double block, it is recommended only for "an extremely large or poorly insulated box").

The single block mounts high up in the icebox and occupies about the same amount of space as 20 to 25 pounds of ice. The belt-driven compressor mounts on or close to the engine (such as an adjacent bulkhead). An eight-position bracket with swing arm allows some flexibility in mounting the compressor. The condenser is inserted in the engine's raw water cooling line, and the valve/control unit is usually mounted outside the icebox somewhere. The parts are connected by copper refrigerant lines and Swagelok® double ferrule fittings.

The most difficult task will be mounting the compressor in the engine compartment, especially if there is little clearance around the engine, or if the engine is small and doesn't have an external alternator and pulley (for example, the alternator on my BMW D-12 is internally geared). Of course, if clearance is the only problem, some modification to the engine compartment usually can be made by moving one side a few inches farther away from the engine.

Two ice cube trays put into a 70°F box will freeze after 20 minutes of engine running time —provided the icebox is well insulated. The temperature will drop to about 21°F after an hour of running time. Less than one hour of daily engine running time is required to keep the icebox at 45°F or less.

Fig. 11-9 *The Sea Frost refrigeration unit, made by C. F. Horton Co., is engine-driven, requiring about 30 to 45 minutes of daily engine running time.*

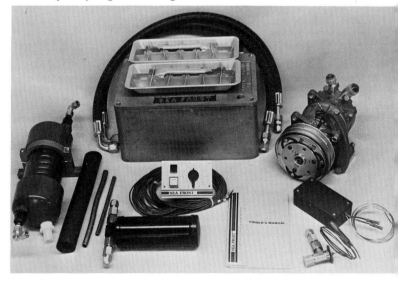

The ColdMachine™

For years, the Adler-Barbour Marine Systems of Pelham, New York, has been manufacturing ColdPump engine-driven refrigeration units, which are widely used industrially and on cruising sailboats. With the development of hermetic compressors, Adler-Barbour began producing a small, inexpensive 115-volt and 12-volt unit that cycles (runs intermittently) off shore power or off the ship's batteries. The ColdMachine (Figure 11-10) will fit any box up to 9½ cubic feet and is divided into two basic installation components: the freezer compartment with ice trays that goes inside the icebox (vertical and horizontal models are available), and the compressor/ evaporator/condenser package that can be installed in any well-ventilated (it's air-cooled) site up to 15 feet from the icebox. This site can be anywhere temperatures don't exceed 130°F and that has at least two separate openings of at least 10 square inches each.

The compressor draws 5.6 amps and cycles about 20 to 30 minutes each hour, so daily consumption is about 45 to 67 amp-hours. At the dock, there is obviously no difficulty in supplying this amount of power. But at anchor or under way, that's a lot of amps to come up with. No matter how many amp-hours are in your battery bank, if you aren't realistic about the ColdMachine's power needs, you could be disappointed.

You probably will find that if you rely on the

Fig. 11-10 *Adler-Barbour's ColdMachine uses a compressor run by an electric motor that cycles off the ship's battery.*

engine for charging the batteries you'll need to run it several hours a day. I think that's too much for the cruising boat. A better solution is to use an alternative energy source (Chapter 12). John Campbell, a free-lance writer cruising the Caribbean, has two 30-watt solar panels permanently mounted on a hard bimini over the cockpit. These, he reports, are sufficient to keep the batteries topped off and his ColdMachine working efficiently. Even though he has a well insulated box, however, it is difficult to understand how two 30-watt panels, providing at best about 30 amp-hours a day, can keep up with the refrigerator. As always, much depends on the ability of the icebox to retain cold, what the contents are, and how often it is opened.

Installing the ColdMachine is very simple, requiring only a hand drill, screwdriver and wrenches. A platform for the compressor package will probably have to be fashioned—perhaps from plywood—mounted beneath a berth or in a cockpit seat locker. The wires to the battery can be led directly to the terminals or to the battery selector switch, but not to the distribution panel or charger, if there is one.

CONTEMPLATING CHANGES

The galley is one place worth splurging on. But on small boats there often isn't room to spend much money, even if you have it. When I sit on my settee in the main cabin surveying my meager galley, I often contemplate enlarging the galley to include a stove/oven and deep double sink. To do this, I would have to rob the starboard settee of several feet, which would make it too short to sleep on. Then I think of all those times that we've been under way at night and by far the most comfortable place to sleep was the leeward bunk. Sure, I could sleep in the weather bunk with a sturdy lee cloth or board, but I doubt that sleeping there would be as restful as sleeping on the low side.

I scan the cabin for solutions. Perhaps the starboard bunk could be extended into the old hanging locker area beneath the sink and vanity. A footwell could be cut in the bulkhead separating the main cabin from the hanging locker/vanity. In fact, the footwell might even be fashioned to run under the sink, thereby preserving both the vanity and a full-length bunk. So why not just get out the saber saw and do it? Good question. I just might! But like every other change I've made to *Adriana,* I need time to consider the implications.

As much as I like to eat, experience shows that I spend relatively little time at the stove. The same logic that says keep the head tiny because it is used only minutes each day, also says don't encroach on living and lounging space for the convenience of boiling water several times a day —especially when water can be boiled quite satisfactorily in the existing stove/galley arrangement. So, for the moment, I'll live with my small galley.

The real proof that a change is necessary is when you simply can't live with the present arrangement any longer. When you find yourself clutching a crowbar with white knuckles, don't resist the urge! Do it! Until then, make the best with what you've got. In my circumstance, I'd rather have cabin seating space for three friends to enjoy a brandy, a smoke and good stories, than have a full-service galley and no place to sit. Food is great, but friends are better. In the final analysis, the soul rules the stomach.

SUMMARY

A balanced diet is essential to the health and vigor of the crew, and the galley systems must facilitate food preparation by preserving fresh foods as long as possible, making cooking a safe and easy task, and dishwashing as fast and least bothersome a chore as possible.

• Dishes and glasses should be stored adjacent to the galley in bins that prevent them from sliding out; cutlery should be placed in divided drawers, notched to prevent them from dump-

ing on the floor; and heavy pots should be secured some place low in the boat.

• Cooking under way is always a potentially dangerous proposition. Considerable thought must be given to the type of stove or oven, its fore and aft or athwartship mount, and whether it should be gimballed or not. A strong bar across a recessed stove minimizes the cook's chances of being thrown onto the stove when the boat lurches.

• Select your cooking fuel with care. Alcohol is inefficient and expensive, and not as safe as popularly thought. Diesel stoves make a lot of sense, but frequently cause excessive heat in the cabin, especially if you're sailing in the tropics. In the States, CNG is becoming a preferred fuel, but propane, if installed correctly, can be a safe and more efficient fuel.

• The effectiveness of a refrigeration system depends largely on the icebox's insulation. For long-range cruising, engine-driven compressors probably require less engine running time than compressors run by electric motors cycling off the engine's batteries.

FURTHER READING

One Hand For Yourself, One For The Ship, by Tristan Jones; Macmillan Publishing Company, 866 Third Avenue, New York, New York 10022.

The Ocean Sailing Yacht, Vols I, and II Donald M. Street, Jr.; W.W. Norton & Company, 500 Fifth Avenue, New York, New York 10110.

Marine Refrigeration Guidebook by Howard M. Crosby; Crosby Marine Refrigeration Systems, 204 Second Avenue South, St. Petersburg, Florida 33701.

Marine Refrigeration For The Do It Yourself Sailor by Art Smith; P.O. Box 6538, Fort Lauderdale, Florida.

The Box Book by Adler-Barbour; 43 Lawton Street, New Rochelle, New York 10801.

The Perfect Box—39 Ways to Improve Your Boat's Ice Box, by Spa Creek Instrument Co; 616 Third St., Annapolis, Maryland 21403.

CHAPTER 12

Generating Electrical Power

"Look aloft!" cried Starbuck. "The corpusants! the corpusants!"

All the yard-arms were tipped with a pallid fire; and touched at each tri-pointed lightning-rod-end with three tapering white flames, each of the three tall masts was silently burning in that sulphurous air, like three gigantic wax tapers before an altar.

HERMAN MELVILLE

Picture this: A cruising sailboat flies into English Harbor in Antigua after a long day's sail. The couple on board drop sails, ready the ground tackle, and find themselves a nice spot away from the other yachts. Customs and immigrations can wait for morning; they're too tired now to deal with the paperwork and hassle.

When everything is tidy, they settle back in the cockpit to watch the sun go down. A couple of beers are brought up from the icebox, the tabs are popped—and guess what? They're warm!

Perhaps an Englishman wouldn't mind that the ice melted days ago, but Americans are used to drinking their beers cold—anything else just doesn't make it. What to do?

Independence afloat means different things to different people, and certainly it is a goal of people who cruise—almost a non-negotiable fact of cruising life.

Whether you equip your boat with a powerful diesel-fueled generator to run the refrigerator, microwave oven and hot water heater, or choose to simplify your energy needs by using oil running lamps and eating nonperishable foods, the basic fact of cruising is that at sea, the boat must be able to provide all its energy requirements. Self-reliance is further enhanced by minimizing the amount of energy-producing fuels that must be brought on board.

Traditionally, fossil fuels have furnished man with his chief source of energy—to propel his many vehicles, cook his food and heat his home. Yet we have learned we can no longer expect these fuels to last forever—the Earth, our home, is of finite size, and the fuels within her of limited supply. Even while they are still available, the cruising sailor may find it difficult to pay premium prices for these fuels, assuming he can even find them in the remote outposts of the world to which he travels. Because electrical power is the most important type of energy used on boats—with the possible exception, or addition, of liquid fuels for stoves and engines—this chapter focuses on the many ways of generating electricity efficiently and economically.

During the past decade, a heightened energy-consciousness among scientists, businessmen and politicians has introduced to the layman new ways of generating the electrical power necessary to live our lives in the manner to which we have so easily become accustomed. The sun, water and wind—three of the four fundamental elements thought by ancient Greek philosophers to comprise all matter (the fourth was Earth)—are the sources of power for most of the generating devices in use today aboard boats. Because the cost of research and development is so high, it was predictable that most research efforts have been centered in industrial circles, with practical application spinoffs trickling down to the consumer much later. Such was the case with the microcomputer chip, Teflon and the much-acclaimed Tang drink used by the astronauts. Enough has happened in the business of alternative energy that it is appropriate today to take stock of developments and assess their usefulness to the cruising sailor.

BATTERIES

Most forms of generating electrical power aboard boats depend on storing that energy in one or more batteries. This marvelous invention enables you to draw upon the battery when you need electricity. Without batteries you would be able to use the lights and instruments only when the charging device (be it a wind-, water- or engine-driven generator, or solar panel) was in operation.

Selecting an appropriate battery for this task is a more important choice than many persons are aware. The deep-cycle, lead-acid storage battery with its heavy plates, as opposed to the standard automotive type, is the best type of battery to run most sailboat accessories. A heavy-duty or deep-cycle battery should be reserved for the engine, so that running appliances won't wear down your engine-starting battery. A three-way switch isolates each battery for use and charging,

and permits using both when they are weak and you need all the power you can get.

Each time a battery is drawn down and recharged, tiny amounts of unwanted material build up on the plates. This process is called sulfation. Some of it flakes off and drops to the bottom of the battery case. Eventually, there is so little lead left in the plates that a small discharge current exhausts them, or so many sulfation flakes build up that they connect negative and positive plates and short-circuit the battery. In either case, the battery must then be rebuilt or replaced.

Good batteries, such as those built by Surrette aren't cheap. But they are a very important investment for the cruising person. It is not uncommon nowadays for 40-foot cruising boats to carry a battery bank of 600 to 800 amphours. With this amount of current capacity, one battery can be used strictly for starting the engine, and the others used for running lights, electronics and other on-board appliances. And, unlike having just one 80-amp-hour car battery, you won't be in constant danger of seriously depleting your electrical supply.

Some electrical generating devices often do little more than trickle-charge the battery, even if they are capable of higher charging rates during periods of high wind, fast speed or direct sunlight. Trickle-charging supplies about 0.1 amp (100 milliamps), and tends to damage battery plates. In a deep-cycle battery, the plates are stronger than in standard marine or automotive batteries, and thus are able to stand up longer to the deleterious effects of trickle-charging. Overcharging also can be a problem and to prevent this, many generator makers also sell optional voltage limiters, if their product isn't already equipped with a regulator.

MEASURING ELECTRICITY

Before looking at the various means of generating electrical power, let's review some basic terms (Figure 12-1) and a table for measuring the amount of electricity used on board. This way, you can determine more accurately how

ELECTRICAL MEASUREMENTS

| AMPS X VOLTS = WATTS |
| WATTS ÷ VOLTS = AMPS |
| WATTS ÷ AMPS = VOLTS |

| AMPS X HOURS OF USE = AMPHOURS |
| MA = 1/1,000 AMPS |

DEFINITIONS

AMP   amount of current flowing (like water through a pipe)
VOLT   pressure or push of electricity (like amount of water pressure in a pipe)
WATT   a measure of electrical power (746 watts = 1 horsepower)
GENERATOR any machine that generates electricity. More specifically, a machine that generates direct current (DC).
ALTERNATOR a machine that generates alternating current (AC). In battery-charging alternators, AC is internally changed to DC before reaching the battery.
INVERTER   turns applied signal upside down (reverses its phase). Changes DC to AC.

Fig. 12-1 *A brief glossary of electrical terms and equations*

much electricity you'll need to run the various electrical gadgets on your boats.

Let's assume you have a 12-volt electrical system and a 12-volt battery.

"Volts" refers to the electrical potential of your battery. Put another way, it is the potential difference between two points in a conducting wire—in this case, your battery.

"Amps" is the amount of electrical current that flows from your battery. Because your battery's voltage is nearly constant, the current drawn by most appliances also will be nearly constant. Current is a rate of flow, and therefore it is incorrect to say "amperes per hour". This is like saying "knots per hour".

"Watts" is a term used to rate some electrical items, such as light bulbs. Amps X volts = watts. Watts ÷ volts = amps. So, if you run a 15-watt fluorescent bulb on a 12-volt system, you are drawing 1.25 amps (15W ÷ 12V = 1.25A). Amps X hours of operation = total ampere-hours. By listing all your electrical appliances, along with their amps and hours of operation, you can estimate your daily usage of electricity (Figure 12-2).

Remember that a milliamp is one-thousandth of an amp. Thus, 50 milliamps equals 0.05 amps.

A solar panel advertised as producing, say, 30 to 35 amp-hours per week, is only producing about 600 milliamps (8 hours of sunshine x 7 days = 56 sunlit hours; 56 x 600 ma = 33,600 ma, or 33.6 amp-hours each week). Also, panels are usually rated at peak efficiency, 90 degrees to a bright sun, and obviously such a condition is likely the exception rather than the rule.

As you compare data on generator output, keep in mind that resistance (level of battery charge) affects generator output. As a battery charges, generator output decreases. So, if an advertisement claims that Brand X puts out six amps, try to determine if this measurement was obtained with a dead battery, half-charged battery, etc. There is no standard for such measurements that I'm aware of. Don't expect always to get the same output the manufacturer claims—you may keep your batteries charged higher than the level used during testing, or the manufacturer may have taken statistical liberties that distorted the unit's performance.

The wind, of course, is more fickle than the predictable fall of night, but no less so than the possibility of cloud cover. While a wind generator may produce more amps when it's blowing 15 mph, there will be occasions of no wind at all.

AUXILIARY GENERATOR WORKSHEET

Current Used

Load/Appliance	Current/Amps	Hours of Operation	Total Amp-Hours
Stereo			
Bilge Pump			
Cabin Lights			
VHF-Receive			
-Transmit			
Running Lights			
Autopilot			
Refrigerator			
Totals:	_____ 1		_____ 2

Current Generated

Generator #1 _____ : Avg Amps _____ X Expected Hrs Opr _____ = _____ Amp-Hours

Generator #2 _____ : Avg Amps _____ X Expected Hrs Opr _____ = _____ Amp-Hours

Total: _____   Total: _____
   　　　　3

Total Amps Needed _____ ÷ Generator Output _____ = _____ Number of Hours
   　　　　　　　　　2　　　　　　　　　　　　　　3

Required to Recharge Batteries. (Resistance Affects Charge Rate).

Battery Size

Avg Current Drawn _____ X 24 Hours = _____ Total Minimum Battery Amp-Hours
   　　　　　　　　1

Fig. 12-2 *Use this worksheet to determine the amount of electricity used on board. The formula for determining total battery amp-hours is a minimum; many cruising boats carry a bank of batteries with far greater capacity.*

The amps produced by a water-driven generator can be accurately calculated if you know how much time you'll spend sailing and at what speed. But since speed is predicated on the wind available, water-driven generators, too, offer no guaranteed amount of energy. The percentage of clear days can help you determine the practicality of solar panels, and this, of course, varies around the world.

Evaluate your sailing patterns, consider the geographical regions through which you'll be sailing and then assess the different products

OUTPUT OF DIFFERENT GENERATORS

Generator	Cost	Output	Hours of Operation	Total Amp-Hours
Water Generator	$1,400	5.25 amps @ 5 knots	12 hours	63.00 AH
Solar Panels (2)	$1,300	2.64 amps avg. skies	12 hours	31.75 AH
Wind Generator (Fixed)	$ 600	1.5 amps @ 15 mph wind	12 hours	18.00 AH
Wind Generator (Portable)	$ 600	6.0 amps @ 15 mph wind	12 hours	72.00 AH

Fig. 12-3 *This table is a rough comparison of four different alternative energy generators. Prices are approximate, and the outputs have been taken from manufacturers' literature.*

(Figure 12-3). Different persons may well come up with different answers.

FUEL/POWERED GENERATORS AND INVERTERS

Any boat with an inboard engine or large outboard has, or is capable of, being fitted with a generator or alternator to recharge batteries. This permits use of electric starters and allows the battery to be tapped for lights, electronic navigation instruments and some small 12-volt appliances, such as cabin fans. For weekend sailors, this is often a sufficient and reliable method of obtaining electrical power. However, for extended use, noise and the cost of engine fuel are mitigating factors.

Most ship's electrical systems are 12-volt direct current (DC) (boats over 45 feet frequently also use 24 and/or 36-VDC systems). Thus the cruising sailor is limited in the type of appliances that can be powered from his 12 VDC system.

Power tools, microwave ovens, blenders, coffee makers and washing machines can make life aboard easier, but almost all require 110-volt alternating current (AC). If these are required items on your boat, you have essentially four choices: 1) carry an auxiliary or portable AC generator that is run by gasoline or diesel fuel, 2) install an inverter to make AC out of your DC engine battery, 3) install an engine-driven AC alternator or 4) install an AC electric generator that runs off a battery or DC power source.

Large vessels may install in the engine compartment a diesel- or gasoline-fueled generator, such as those manufactured by Onan (Figure 12-4). In addition to providing almost unlimited electrical power, some models also may be rigged with a belt and clutch to the propeller shaft and thereby serve as a backup means of propulsion.

Danny Greene carries a portable Honda generator (Figure 12-5) with him on his 26-foot cutter. When the impulse strikes him, in the cockpit or on the beach, he can knock together a new dinghy design with the aid of a power drill and saber saw powered by his hand-carried generator.

An inverter, while small compared to a fuel-powered generator, can do some of the same things, but not all. Hooked up to the batteries it can convert their DC voltage to 110-volt AC—the net result is the same as the AC fuel-powered generator—it's simply a different means to the same end. However, an inverter won't recharge your battery, and at least 20 percent of the avail-

Fig. 12-4 *A 20-kw diesel auxiliary generator by Onan has a water-cooled exhaust for quiet operation.*

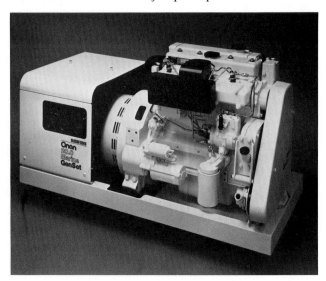

Fig. 12-5 *Danny Greene has cruised with this Honda generator for seven years, and it still starts every time.*

able power is lost between the source and appliance.

Of the many companies making inverters, Radio Shack, Heath and Dynamote (Figure 12-6) are among the better known. For those sailors wishing to learn something of the intricacies of inverters, the Heath Company offers a do-it-yourself kit (Figure 12-7). Dynamote manufactures two types of inverters, the "static" type that works directly off the battery (meaning that at

anchor, there's no need to start the engine), and the "dynamic" type, that works off the engine alternator only when running.

Some household tools and appliances are not designed for operation with the square wave generated by inverters. Check appliances to determine whether they will work on square waves as well as conventional sine waves. The Heath Company advises customers that incandescent lamps, electric shavers, soldering irons and "other devices that present a resistive or small inductive load" work well with inverters. Prob-

Fig. 12-6 *This Dynamote inverter takes up to 200 amps of 14-volt current and changes it to 120-volts AC power, 60 Hz.*

Fig. 12-7 *The Heath Company makes this do-it-yourself inverter kit.*

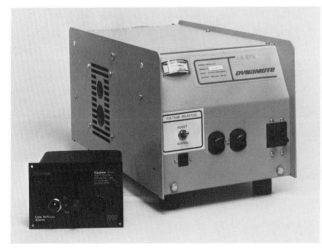

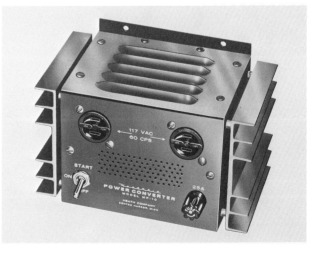

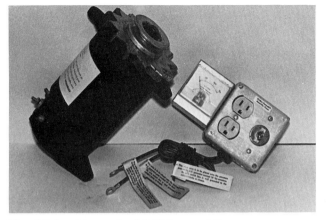

Fig. 12-8 *Alternatives' 3,000-watt AC generator produces 110-120 volts, 60 cycles at 3,600 rpm, and is excited by the ship's 12-volt battery.*

lems may be experienced with radios, T.V.s (which may hum or buzz), C.B.s, tape recorders and electric drills (which may fail to start).

The third solution to providing AC power is to install an engine-driven AC alternator. This looks much like the DC generator or alternator already on your engine and works the same way, that is, by pulley and belt. A company called Alternatives (Figure 12-8) offers an inexpensive 3,000-watt AC generator that produces 110 to 120 volts. The unit, designed to operate with a fixed engine rpm, is excited by the ship's 12-volt battery and draws 18 amps, which in turn is replenished by the engine's DC generator. The Mercantile Manufacturing Company also makes an AC generator, called "Auto-Gen" (Figure 12-9), that produces 120 or 240 volts and, depending on model, from 2,500 to 5,500 watts. They automatically maintain proper voltage and frequency over a wide range of engine speeds, and

Fig. 12-9 *Mercantile Manufacturing Company offers the Auto-Gen, which can produce either 120 volts or 240 volts at 3,600 rpm.*

are priced accordingly for this worthwhile feature. Microwaves, blenders and other major appliances can be run off these alternators.

A drawback to fuel-powered generators and inverters is that one must listen to the noise of an internal combustion engine in order to reap the benefits. AC generators can recharge batteries if wired to a battery charger or built with integral converters. Inverters won't recharge your batteries, but then they're only used when the engine is running and the batteries will be recharged by the engine's own alternator. Cost and peace of mind—yours and your neighbor's—are important considerations.

The fourth and last type is an electric generator that produces AC from a 12-volt DC power source. Honeywell makes two models ranging from 500 to 1,600 watts with full sine wave. Minimum battery size recommended is 85 amp-hours.

MANUAL GENERATORS

For those who want to recharge their 12-volt batteries and get a little exercise at the same time, there is the Wesson Pedal Power generator (Figure 12-10). It measures only 10″ x 15″ x 17″, weighs 22 pounds and is modestly priced. Using fluorescent lights (which use less electricity than

Fig. 12-10 *The Wesson Pedal Power machine is an inexpensive and healthy way to top off batteries. It produces 5 amps at 60 rpm.*

incandescent bulbs), the inventor says he can get six hours of light from one hour of pedaling. Maybe his legs look like Alley Oop's, but because the device can be stored inside and doesn't rely on any other power source than his own legs, it's a nifty way to keep the batteries topped off.

WATER-DRIVEN GENERATORS

When assessing the various means of charging it is important to consider how much time will be spent sailing and how much time will be spent at anchor. While some wind-driven generators will work when the boat is either in motion or at rest, water-driven generators only produce electricity when moving. Tapping the ocean for power is, however, a natural solution.

Motorola builds a 14-volt, 20-amp alternator that is run off the propeller shaft by a pulley and belt. The unit recharges batteries while the boat is sailing by harnessing the energy potential of the freewheeling propeller. It is specially designed to work at low rpm. The same company also builds a transom-mounted "Hydro-alternator" that looks like a small electric outboard. At seven knots it will produce 12 amps. Phillipe Jeantot used a similar model, made by Wattas (Figure 12-11) in the BOC Challenge.

On the face of it, alternators designed to be pulley-driven by the freewheeling propeller sound nearly ideal, because the shaft is there

Fig. 12-11 *This Wattas water generator was used by Phillipe Jeantot in the BOC Challenge.*

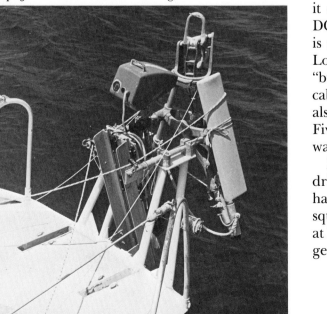

anyway, doing nothing while you sail. Its potential energy might as well be harnessed. The Deerfoot 62, designed for Steve Daschew and built in South Africa, incorporates an auxiliary propeller and shaft just for this purpose. I think this is a better idea than using the engine prop shaft, because the cutlass bearing usually makes some noise if the prop is left to freewheel with the engine off. Also, it causes that much more wear and tear on the transmission, which is a costly piece of equipment. Sailing hundreds or thousands of miles with the prop freewheeling is adding unnecessary hours of wear to your transmission.

On the other hand, there is probably less drag using the engine prop shaft than using an auxiliary prop shaft—be it hung off the stern or run through the hull. Studies have shown that there is little difference in drag between freewheeling propellers and those locked in place, though if the prop is vertically aligned behind the keel when locked, drag may be less.

One of the best known water-driven generators is the "Aquair 50" alternator made by Ampair Products of Surrey, England. This water turbine is trailed behind the boat on 60 feet of braided rope. The 12-volt model will generate three amps at six knots while producing 25 pounds of drag. At anchor, the Aquair 50 may be converted to a wind-driven generator by fitting the stern pulpit-mounted generator unit with a 26-inch-diameter set of wind blades.

The Greenwich Corporation of Nokesville, Virginia, manufactures the "Power Log" (Figure 12-12), a self-contained, water-driven alternator it claims can provide up to 12 amps of 12-volt DC power. Unlike the Aquair, whose alternator is separate from the turbine blades, the Power Log combines both in a 4½-inch by 12-inch "bulb" that is trailed behind the boat by a 25-foot cable. Hamilton Ferris of Dover, Massachusetts, also makes excellent water and wind generators. Five amps at six knots is "guaranteed" for his water-driven model.

Drag is a factor in deciding to use a water-driven generator. At six knots, the Power Log has 35 pounds of drag. And, because drag squares with velocity, it's not difficult to see that at high speeds, it would be advisable to hand the generator and stow it below.

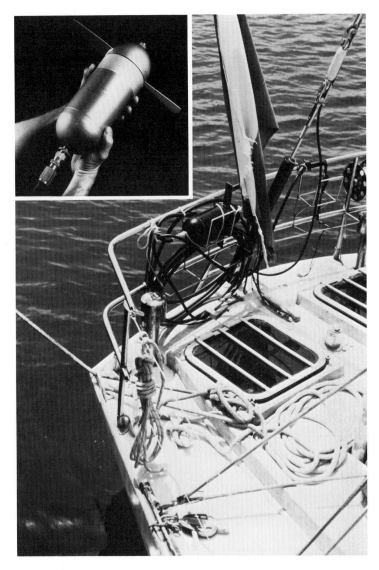

Fig. 12-12 *The Greenwich Power Log is a state-of-the-art water-driven generator that is towed behind the boat and produces up to 12 amps. Richard Konkolski used one on* Nike III *in the BOC Challenge.*

WIND-DRIVEN GENERATORS

There are a rapidly growing number of wind-driven generators available on today's market—some of which can be used both under way and at anchor, and some only at anchor.

Aubrey Raus of Provincetown, Massachusetts (Figure 12-13), set about designing a wind generator with the goal of producing four to six amps in 10 to 15 mph of wind. Because he believes that most cruising sailors spend most of their time at anchor, he developed the "Web Charger", a magnet-type generator coupled with a 5′4″ propeller. The unit is hoisted off the deck

by the jib halyard and secured by two guys. It begins with one-amp output in six to eight-mph winds.

The cousin of the Aquair 50 used to be the Ampair 50, but it has now been superseded by the Ampair 75 permanent magnet wind generator (Figure 12-14). It features a six blade wind turbine measuring three feet in diameter, the largest the company feels is safe for use on yachts. It is still more compact than the Web Charger (as it is intended to be in continuous operation) and produces correspondingly less power. The Ampair 75 delivers about two amps in 12-knot winds, and can give up to seven amps in 20 to 25 knots of wind.

Both the Web Charger and Ampair 75 use permanent magnet rotors to minimize losses in energizing the magnetic field.

A contrasting approach is represented by the Łodyn wind-driven generator (Figure 12-15). It is made of lightweight aluminum, weighs only

Fig. 12-13 *Aubrey Raus of Provincetown, Massachusetts, designed and builds the Web Charger, a portable wind-driven generator capable of producing up to 10 amps in 22-mph winds.*

Fig. 12-14 *An offshoot of one of the first commercially produced wind-driven generators for small boats, the Ampair 75 (inset) produces about 5 amps in 18 mph of wind.*

Fig. 12-15 *The Eodyn wind-driven generator has low windage and produces about 90 ma in 15-mph winds (Viscom International).*

milliamps is really only trickle-charging the battery, and probably won't be powerful enough to keep the icebox cold—the goal of many cruisers.

A major decision in choosing a wind-driven generator is selecting between a permanent (Ampair-type) and portable (Web Charger-type) mount. The former can be left up to run all the time while the latter is used only at anchor. However, the large portable type has greater output (Figure 12-16). Handle this unit carefully when demounting, as a rap on the arm or skull could be lethal. I've read that the turbine blades can be

Fig. 12-16 *This graph illustrates the dramatic difference in output between portable and permanently mounted wind-driven generators. The portable type can only be used at anchor.*

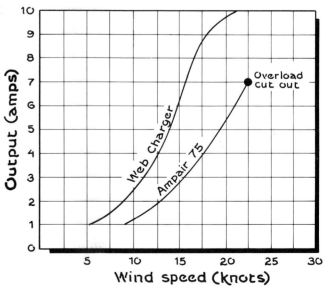

5½ pounds and measures just 15 inches high. It is quite compact and the blades revolve around a vertical axis as opposed to a horizontal one. At 15 knots of wind the Eodyn produces about 90 milliamps (about two amp-hours per day) and will produce about 340 milliamps at 40 knots. As with the others, AC is converted to DC, in this case with a rectifier containing four diodes. The rectifier is a separate unit housed inside the boat, and is protected by a one-amp, four-volt fuse box. The virtue of a smaller unit is that there's less wind resistance while sailing.

Wind-driven generators have been favored by some singlehanded ocean racers, including Walter Greene and Tom Grossman, because they produce less drag than water-driven generators. But any unit that produces just a few hundred slowed by unhooking the electrical lead wires and crossing them, however, I've never tried it. The simplest way is to turn the unit 90 degrees to the wind by means of the rudder. In any case, some sort of remote brake is strongly recommended. Tom Colvin, who lives on *K'ung Fu-Tse*, a 48-foot junk, told me that he tries to sneak up on his wind-powered generator from behind. But usually the wind direction changes and the turbine turns to face him, catching him red-handed with his gloves on!

SOLAR

A significant departure from the "active" generator/alternator types has been the development in recent years of the "passive" solar panel. The heart of the photo-voltaic energy concept is the solar cell.

The solar cell is a semiconductor device that converts light energy directly into electrical energy. Silicon solar cells are made by doping silicon crystals with other chemicals. When phosphorus is added during the growth of the crystal, the silicon develops negatively charged electrons; when boron is added, positively charged carriers appear. The crystals are then sliced into wafers. Incoming light particles called photons are absorbed by the electrons within the silicon wafer and create both positive and negative charges. A photocurrent flows, voltage develops and electricity is produced. All silicon solar cells produce about the same amount of voltage—about 0.5V—so many of them are used in series to produce an amount of electricity sufficient to be of use in charging batteries. The more solar cells, the bigger the panel, the more output obtained.

Just a few of the companies producing solar panels for marine application are Solarex, Free Energy Systems (Figure 12-17), Solar Marine Systems and PDC Labs (Figure 12-18). A typical small panel, suitable for mounting on a hatch, will provide about 600 milliamps (about 30

Fig. 12-17 *Free Energy Systems' Model 129SL solar panel produces about 600 ma.*

amp-hours per week), weighs about six pounds and costs between $300 and $400.

Panel temperature affects output, both extreme heat and cold. Providing ventilation space behind the panel to keep it cool in hot weather is a good idea, though not always practical (Figure 12-19). Mounting the panels so they can be adjusted to face the sun directly will increase output, though this is not always feasible, especially on a narrow monohull. Most panels have blocking diodes that prevent discharge of the battery at night.

John Campbell, Caribbean cruiser/boating journalist, says, however, that tests show the amount of current lost by the diode when charging exceeds the amount lost at night when the diode is removed. The main reason diodes are used to prevent current flowing out at night is to save the skipper the trouble of switching off the circuit. So, if one is willing to wire in a switch and merely flip it off at dusk, the diode can be eliminated altogether with no trade-off in current losses.

French filmmaker Gerard Pesty has experi-

Fig. 12-18 *Solar panels are usually arranged in "arrays" to produce more power. These four PDC Labs Solarcharger units combine to produce about 2½ amps.*

Fig. 12-19 *Aboard his 54-foot trimaran, Architeuthis, Frenchman Gerard Pesty locates his solar panels wherever they give him the most output. Tilting the angle toward the sun and leaving an air space behind the panels maximizes output (Gerard Pesty photo).*

mented with many types of alternative energy devices, including solar panels, aboard his 54-foot trimaran, *Architeuthis* (Figure 12-20). He conducted tests measuring the output of two 40-watt solar panels, one mounted horizontally, and the other rotated to track the sun. Figure 12-21 shows the results.

Fig. 12-20 *The* Architeuthis *obtains power from the wind, water and sun. Note the Aerowatt wind generator at the mizzen masthead and the Motorola Hydroalternator on the transom. Solar panels and a prop shaft-driven water generator are not visible in this photo (Gerard Pesty photo).*

Fig. 12-21 *To determine the difference in output between a flat, fixed solar panel, and one continually tilted toward the sun, Gerard Pesty and Jean Philippe Malice conducted an experiment aboard* La Malicieuse. *The table and graph show the results: about 35 percent more power from the tilted solar panel.*

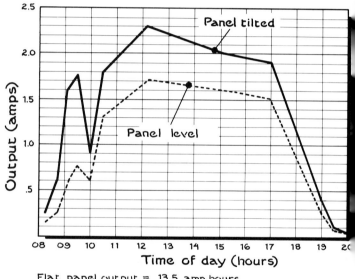

Flat panel output = 13.5 amp hours
Tilted panel output = 18.25 amp hours
DIFFERENCE: 4.75 amp hours

EFFECT OF TILTING PANELS ON OUTPUT

Local Time	Sky Condition	Sun Elevation Above Horizon	Lying on Deck	Tilted*
8:15 AM	Veiled	10°	0.15	0.25
8:45	Slightly Veiled	15°	0.25	0.60
9:10	Clear	21°	0.60	1.60
9:30	Clear	25°	0.75	1.75
10:00	Veiled to Overcast	30°	0.60	0.90
10:30	Clear	35°	1.30	1.80
12:15 PM	Veiled (Bright)	55°	1.70	2.30
3:00	Clear	45°	1.60	2.00
5:00	Clear	39°	1.50	1.90
7:00	Slightly Veiled	16°	0.25	0.40
7:30	Veiled to Overcast (Grey)	—	0.07	0.10
8:00	Veiled to Overcast (Grey)	—	0.03	0.03

* Perpendicular to Sun's Rays

Common causes of solar panel failure are breaking or crazing of the glass cover (Figure 12-22) and corrosion of the wires at the solar panel terminals (Figure 12-23).

INSTALLATION

Solar, wind and water generators are no more difficult to install than a car stereo; only basic tools and attention to instructions are required. On the other hand, auxiliary generators and high-powered AC alternators may require custom metal mounting brackets. And the wiring of a 110-volt system should adhere to ABYC specifications.

Installing Solar Panels

The orientation of the solar panel to the sun directly affects the amount of charge to the battery. The conclusion of Pesty's tests is that solar

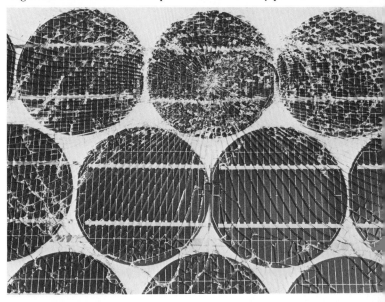

Fig. 12-22 *The glass cover of this solar panel aboard Olivier de Kersauson's* Kriter VI *was cracked by a sharp blow. Not only will this reduce performance, moisture will soon creep in and begin the insidious corrosion process (Gerard Pesty photo).*

Fig. 12-23 *Marc Pajot installed solar panels on his record-setting* Elf Aquitaine, *but due to poorly sealed terminal wires, the panels failed in less than two years (Gerard Pesty photo).*

Fig. 12-24 *Aboard* Nike 11, *Richard Konkolski had a specially molded mount for his array of solar panels (Gerard Pesty photo).*

Fig. 12-26 *Guy Bernardin, another BOC competitor, installed this solar panel on* Ratso *(OSTAR spelled backwards!) (Herb McCormick photo).*

panels must be rotated to follow the path of the sun in order to deliver maximum charge. Leaving them flat on deck, as so many cruisers do, means about 35 percent less charging power.

Round the world racer Richard Konkolski has a specially molded mount on *Nike II* that provides air space behind the panels, and allows a certain degree of rotation (Figure 12-24). On the Valiant 40 *Fantasy*, sailed by Dan Byrne in the BOC round the world race, stainless steel mounts at the stern pulpit and alongside the cockpit were made to hold four solar panels (Figure 12-25). These could be rotated by hand to any desired angle, and though they look flimsy,

Fig. 12-25 *BOC competitor Dan Byrne used four solar panels on adjustable ball-socket mounts. One was swept away in the Southern Ocean (Herb McCormick photo).*

he lost only one in gale-force winds. Guy Bernardin's *Ratso*, another BOC entrant, is similarly fitted for rotating solar panels (Figure 12-26).

Corrosion can be partially prevented by using a good quality bedding compound where the wires enter the panel housing, and around the terminals inside the housing. Silicone rubber is okay, but doesn't adhere well to surrounding surfaces.

Because each solar cell is connected in series to the rest, a shadow across only a small part of the panel can reduce output of the array by a significant amount—80 percent or more. Therefore, it is necessary to locate the panels where rigging, sails and lifelines aren't likely to cast their shadows across the panels. If mounting in an exposed area, some sort of detachable mount is a good idea for removal when the wind picks up.

Once a suitable mounting site is found, the panel can be wired to the battery. The closer to the battery the better, because the longer the connecting wires, the greater the loss of current flowing through them. Insulated wire of at least #18 AWG should be used; the farther the distance, the thicker the wire.

If mounting on deck or on a hatch, make a template of the panel to transfer the holes for the mounting screws from the panel to the

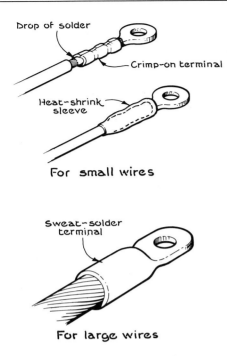

For small wires

For large wires

Fig. 12-27 *Terminal wires should be connected to the battery with crimp lugs, soldered for good connections, and protected with heat-shrink sleeves.*

hatch. Drill holes and secure with stainless steel screws.

Remember to apply a bedding compound to the hole and threads of the screws to prevent water from creeping in, especially if the deck is cored. On many panels, the screws will be put in from inside the boat, coming up through the deck or hatch and into the holes in the frame of the panel's back. An additional hole is required for the lead wires to pass through and the same precautions should be taken here to make it waterproof.

If one wire is red, or marked with a "+", it should be taken to the positive terminal on the battery; the other wire is led to negative. If the wires aren't fitted with terminals, pick up some crimp lug eyes at your local chandlery or electrical supply shop. They are crimped on, and a drop of solder on each ensures a good connection. A plastic heat-shrink sleeve protects the joint (Figure 12-27).

Besides a blocking diode on the positive wire, some solar panels manufacturers also advise placing a fuse on the positive side to prevent damage to the panel in the event of shorts. Small in-line fuses are available at most chandleries or electronic stores. Figure 12-28 diagrams a typical installation.

About the only maintenance solar panels require is an occasional washing with a mild detergent and fresh water.

Installing Wind and Water Generators

The electrical hook-ups of wind and water generators generally will follow those just given for solar panels. Permanently mounted wind generators can be fitted high up in the forward side of mizzen masts, at the masthead, or on a pedestal attached to the stern pulpit. Figures 12-29 through 12-31 illustrate some of the possibil-

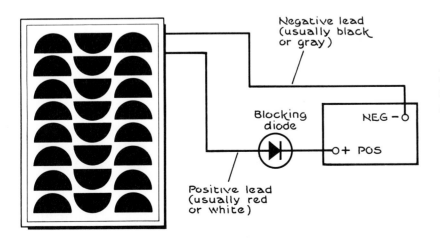

Fig. 12-28 *This schematic shows a typical solar panel electrical hook-up to the battery.*

Fig. 12-29 *This Windco generator is mounted halfway up the mizzenmast (Gerard Pesty photo).*

Fig. 12-30 *A closer view of Gerard Pesty's wind generator atop the mizzenmast (Gerard Pesty photo).*

Fig. 12-31 *The Ampair 50, like the newer 75, can be mounted just about anywhere it isn't in the way—in this instance it's mounted on it's own special davit mount (Gerard Pesty photo).*

ities. The only other word of caution is that objects this size are subject to considerable stress from the wind, and so should be securely mounted with thru-bolts (see Chapter 10). The vibration caused by many units is substantial, and will loosen bolts and wear out bearings if not properly installed and inspected regularly.

Most water generators are designed to mount on the stern pulpit, and assuming the stern pulpit isn't about to fall off, this should be a sufficiently strong place for installation.

SUMMARY

The type of cruising you do is a major factor in choosing your power-generating equipment. For many cruisers, the majority of time is spent at anchor, with intermittent passages ranging from one day to several weeks.

Under way, water generators are hard to beat for power output. There is some drag caused by towing a water generator, but for the cruising man, with a boat 35 feet and larger, it shouldn't be a great concern. Considering that a unit like the Greenwich Power Log can generate up to 12 amps, you could run a stereo, a low-amp refrigerator and lights without depleting the battery.

At anchor, water generators are useless, so another system is necessary. Here you can take your pick of solar or wind generators. The attractive feature of solar panels is that they are passive—meaning there are no moving parts. Small permanently mounted wind generators, such as the Eodyn, approximately equal the solar panel in terms of output and, like the solar panel, there's no fussing with them. To obtain greater power, a unit like the Web Charger can be hoisted in the rigging while at anchor. It will produce about six amps whereas the smaller, permanently mounted wind generator may give only 150 milliamps, about 40 times less. My choice would be a medium sized, permanently mounted unit of the Ampair 75 type—other makes are available.

Permanently mounted systems—solar and wind—can complement the water generator while under way as well. If you're committed to alternative energy, the most effective system will combine two different types.

The key to your decision will in part be affected by possible mounting sites for each of the three types. If you've no place to mount a solar panel or wind generator, consider something else.

Achieving independence afloat is one of the true joys of the cruising life, and making your own electrical power is at the very heart of this independence. Advances in technology are certain to make this task easier, more economical and more reliable in the future.

FURTHER READING

How To Make Your Own Solar Electricity by John W. Stewart; Tab Books Inc., Blue Ridge, Summitt, Pennsylvania 17214.
The Solar Boat Book by Pat Rand Rose; Ten Speed Press, P.O. Box 7123, Berkeley, California 94707.

CHAPTER 13

Instruments and the Electrical System

The moment man cast off his age-long belief in magic,
Science bestowed upon him the blessing of the
Electrical Current.

JEAN GIRAUDOUX

The first rule about marine electronics is that electricity and salt water don't mix. Once electrical wiring and appliances are wet, corrosion is swift and insidious.

The only way to avoid the hassle and frustration of failed electronics is not to have them. Considering that for 99.9 percent of human history electrical power was unharnessed (yet sailors voyaged round the world), it should be a worthwhile sacrifice for any of us to live at least a short while without it. Living simply better prepares one to cope with the exigencies of nature and the vagaries of man-made equipment.

Yet electrical conveniences have become so much a part of our daily lives, it is almost unthinkable to try doing without them. The size and scope of one's electrical inventory is a controversial subject among cruising people. Purists burn oil lamps, toss the engine overboard and eat out of cans until fresh meats and vegetables can be purchased. At the other end of the spectrum, large yachts cruise the world with air conditioning, satellite navigation and a deep freeze filled with steaks and frozen fish.

I find myself somewhere in the middle, partly because even if I wanted SatNav, I couldn't afford it, and partly because I don't understand electronics well enough to repair the more sophisticated equipment. As much of the boat's gear as possible should be repairable by the crew. In many parts of the world, parts are simply unavailable.

A good spare parts inventory and the ability to install them increases independence afloat. If an electrical item cannot be repaired, a backup should be available; or you should have the ability to do without it for the duration of the cruise. SatNav is nice, to be sure, but know how to use a sextant as well. To take off on a long passage without the knowledge or skill to navigate without electronics is plain dumb. Yet, who would deny the luxury of punching a few buttons to obtain a precise position fix?

Some "purists" like Lin and Larry Pardey believe that sailors who have such devices on board gradually develop unconscious dependencies on them, which reduces their ability or readiness to handle problems without the aid of electronics. While this may be true to a certain extent, it's not *wrong* per se to have electronics on your boat— it's more a function of your confidence in basic skills (such as using a sextant), how much you want to be in contact with the world, how much frustration you're willing to put up with when they fail, and how much money you're willing to spend. But one shouldn't overlook the advantages of such equipment, such as SSB, which in the event of a medical emergency at sea may be your only means of communicating with a physician.

NAVIGATION INSTRUMENTS

There is no doubt that a great deal of money can be spent on electronics. But, like pocket calculators, television sets and home computers, the price of sophisticated items has come down dramatically in recent years. This trend will continue. Several years ago, the cheapest and virtually only SatNav on the market was made by Magnavox and cost about $10,000. Today, there are numerous brands available, and the cost of some are under $2,000. Before going off cruising, one should plan carefully for the electronics he desires on board. If the list gets too lengthy, it could delay departure by several years. So let's concentrate on the minimum requirements.

Compass

The compass isn't really an electrical device in the conventional sense. But a good quality compass is the single most important piece of navigational equipment on a boat. Coastwise and even mid-ocean navigation is predicated on being able to tell what direction the boat is sailing. The ancient Polynesians could navigate by the stars and sea alone. And Marvin Creamer, the New Jersey man who is sailing around the world without instruments, has developed a method of celestial navigation without instruments. Hopefully, his arcane techniques soon will be explained to the rest of the world where they can be well utilized, at least for lifeboat navigation. Meanwhile, the rest of us remain dependent on the compass.

Don't skimp on the quality of compass you put on board. When buying a new or used boat, the compass that comes with it is often the least expensive "nice-looking" unit available. And for knocking about the bay, it probably does the job. But what a difference a good compass makes, with several 45° lubber lines, a large well-gimballed card and a red night-light.

The best compass, however, does little good if it isn't corrected. Three relatively simple methods of correcting the compass and completing a deviation card can be found in the *Cruising World* Notebook, "Compass Deviation Card", August, 1983.

Locate the compass parallel to the centerline of the boat, yet easily read from both port and starboard helm positions. Be careful to mount it where it can't be damaged by an errant foot or sheet. Nor should it be near ferrous metals or electrical wiring. Wiring that, by necessity, must be run close to the compass should be twisted to minimize their effect. Typical mounts are on the cabin facing the cockpit, and atop binnacles or wheel steering pedestals (Figure 13-1). On *Adriana*, the red night-light wires are led to the bus bar and tied in with the navigation light circuit. When the running lights are turned on, the compass light comes on as well.

Fig. 13-1 *The compass mounted on* Isabelle's *brass binnacle is in a convenient-to-read location.*

Knotmeter and Log

A basic aid to dead reckoning (DR) is knowing how fast the boat is moving. The equation, speed x time elapsed = distance traveled (e.g. 5 mph x 1 hr = 5 miles) is fundamental. After you've sailed your boat awhile, you learn to estimate the speed of the boat fairly accurately even without a knotmeter. But to learn, you need some help, and a knotmeter is the instrument to use.

For a generation of cruisers, the patented Walker Log (Figure 13-2) was the log to own. By knowing the distance traveled and time elapsed between readings, average speed can be determined. The propeller sending unit was trailed over the transom on a long line and it was very accurate. The only problem was that it was fouled with seaweed and sharks liked to eat them. Hiscock and others always advised carrying several spares. One of the reasons the trailing log is more accurate than sending units mounted on the hull is that turbulence from water passing around the hull can distort the readings. Stowe manufactures trailing log units with an accuracy of plus or minus 3 percent—very good indeed. Many taffrail logs are mechanical, meaning that the propeller at the end of the line turns a cable inside (just like bicycle speedometers) which turns dials in the readout unit. In contrast, electronic logs tell the indicator how fast the boat is traveling by the frequency and/or strength of electronic impulses generated by the sending unit.

While a log is an invaluable navigational aid, it's also nice to have the speed function to help determine the most efficient set and trimming of the sails. For years *Adriana* had a finely cali-

Fig. 13-3 *Like many companies, Swoffer's knotmeter sending units originally were propeller types, which were reliable and difficult to foul. Swoffer now uses paddle wheel sending units.*

brated knotmeter made by Swoffer in Seattle, which had a propeller-type sending unit mounted low on the keel (Figure 13-3). The sending unit should be mounted near the bow, but not too near the centerline of the boat, as the speed of passing water varies here. Being low and mounted aft, it is relatively free from turbulence caused by the bow wave, and it does not come too close to the surface when the boat is heeled.

When we were hit by lightning in Green Bay in 1979, the unit was damaged beyond repair (more on this later). I wrote to Swoffer and had them send me a replacement sending unit. What I got was one of the new breed of paddle wheels (Figure 13-4) and a hull plug.

At first glance, this looked like an improvement to the old propeller-type unit, which for me at least never fouled, presumably because it was heavier, larger, and not partially tucked away in a cavity. About two weeks in salt water, however, was all it took for barnacles and grunge to jam the paddle wheel. It was then that I discovered why they had sent me a plug. The idea is that when the paddle wheel fouls, you reach into the bilge, yank it out, and before the boat sinks (remember, a 1½-inch hole two feet below the waterline admits 71 gallons of water per min-

Fig. 13-2 *The Walker Log is a mechanical distance-measuring device hung over the stern and trailed behind the boat. By measuring distance and elapsed time, speed also can be determined (Kathy Bray drawing).*

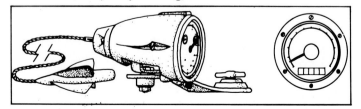

Fig. 13-4 *This paddle wheel-type sending unit is very sensitive and gives accurate knotmeter readouts. But barnacles and other marine organisms can foul it easily, which is why the plug is sold with the unit. (Ray Jefferson, Model K-12 inset.)*

ute), you jam in the plug. Then you clean out the paddle wheel, chip off the barnacles, and frantically reinstall it. Cleaning was so frequently required that I stopped cleaning it. What if I dropped the plug while the paddle wheel was out? Fishing around the bilge while water gushes in seems an iffy proposition at best. Special transducer antifoulants are now available to reduce organic growth.

The stern pulpit-mounted trailing-type log requires no installation. If you select the thru-hull type, begin by carefully studying your hull for a suitable location. Many new boats have next to no bilge at all, so you may have to drill your hole through the hull beneath a berth, somewhere near the middle of the boat. The safest position from grounding damage is in the concave garboard curve.

Use a hole saw for this purpose (Figure 13-5). Drilling from inside out usually chips the gel coat on the outside, but not so much that it won't be covered by the flange of the sending unit. If concerned about this, drill only until the pilot bit goes through the hull, then go outside and complete the hole.

Obviously, the size of the hole saw is dictated by the diameter of the sending unit. The manufacturer generally will specify that dimension, something like 2⅜-inches, just the sort of dimension you'll never need again. Hole saws are very useful, and most hardware stores sell seven-blade kits that are supposed to meet all requirements. But I find that there's seldom use for the same hole saw twice. Consequently, I buy a standard chuck and pilot bit, and purchase the hole saws individually, according to the job at hand. When installing something through the hull, especially below the waterline, the hole must be cut to exact specifications to ensure a tight fit. A quarter-inch of slop around a knotmeter sending unit is simply too much. Bedding compound may keep water out for a while, but what happens if you ground the boat or come hard off a wave? I want to know that everything below the water is well secured and watertight.

Use generous amounts of bedding compound, such as polysulfide, enough so that when you tighten down the backing plate, compound oozes out both inside and outside the hull. It can be cut away after it dries, so don't worry about how messy it looks.

Use a hole saw also to cut the hole in the bulkhead where the indicator readout will be mounted. The wire between the two should be

Fig. 13-5 *A hole saw attached to a power drill is used for cutting holes for depthsounder transducer and knotmeter sending units. The bit centers the hole saw.*

run out of the way, behind bunks and cabinetry. Avoid pulling the wire tight because it could chafe on sharp edges. If there is any doubt about this, wrap tape around the wire where it might chafe, or better yet, slip plastic tubing over the wire. The ultimate protection is to run the entire wire through PVC tubing, but generally the wires for knotmeters are well-insulated and tough.

Knotmeters need calibrating (be suspicious of a unit that has no adjustment knob). This is best done by running the boat over a measured course free of wind and current. Any known distance between two buoys or other land or sea marks is suitable. For example, if the distance between two buoys is 1.2 miles, and the time elapsed during the run (with steady throttle) is 18 minutes (0.3 hour), the knotmeter should read 4 knots (1.2n.m. ÷ 0.3h. = 4.0kn.). Keep running the boat at the same throttle while you figure the equation, so you can adjust the knotmeter while running at the speed used during the test.

Depthsounder

You can do without depthsounders; traditionalists will tell you to use a leadline. Charge the hollow tip of the leadline with wax and you can even bring up a sample of the bottom—mud, coral, sand or gravel? It makes a difference in your anchoring strategy.

But depthsounders can help prevent groundings by alerting the skipper to changing depths. Today there are a few sonar units that read ahead of the boat, giving even more advance warning of impending danger.

I've found that navigation is the most useful function of my depthsounder. Look on any chart at the contours of depth approaching a shoreline. Usually, the contours will read something like: 40 feet, 25 feet, 5 feet. Suppose you're feeling your way along a coast at night or in a fog. You know the shore is near. Turn on the depthsounder and see what reading you get— 41 feet, after a few minutes 23 feet. You can look at the chart and estimate your proximity to shore by comparing the depth on your sounder with the depth on the chart.

Wherever you mount the transducer, note how far beneath the surface it is and figure this into your readings. For example, if the transducer is two feet below the waterline, add two feet to any reading you get (four feet on the readout is actually six feet of depth). But, don't assume there is six feet beneath your keel! If your boat draws four feet, then there's only two feet beneath your keel. That's the bottom line!

There's no real difference between installing a depthsounder transducer and a knotmeter sending unit. Use the right size hole saw, use a good quality bedding compound, and run your wires so they won't be damaged by water or chafe. A fairing block (Figure 13-6) between the transducer and hull probably will be required to aim the transducer straight down to prevent erroneous readings.

Depthsounders, such as the Seafarer flasher-type, are best located inside the cabin on a hinged arm so they can be viewed from the cockpit. It's best if the helmsman can view the readout while he steers. Of course the depthsounder could be located in the cockpit, but often there

Fig. 13-6 *Depthsounder transducers must be mounted vertically, and because few hulls are flat bottomed, hardwood fairing blocks must be fashioned to correctly position the transducer against the hull.*

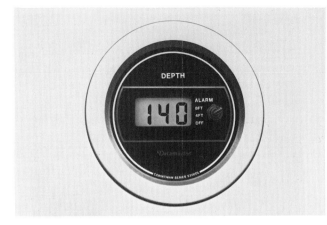

Fig. 13-7 *Ray Jefferson digital depthsounder*

just isn't room, nor is there any point in exposing a piece of electronics to the weather when it isn't absolutely necessary. Many depthsounders are too bulky to place in the cockpit, except the new breed of low-profile digital depthsounders that are mounted on the cabin bulkhead (Figure 13-7). With experience, it is possible to determine bottom material.

The business of digital versus flasher is an interesting one. Manufacturers will tell you now that digital readouts have better service records. But I just can't get the hang of them. A large-scale dial tells you the same information as a precise number, and you can gauge numbers by glancing at the relation of the indicating finger with the graduated facing. Also, the finger falls and rises in a perceptible and predictable manner, whereas the numbers on a digital readout change capriciously, so you're never really certain what number will appear next.

However, Bruce Bingham tells me that if you study your digital sounder readouts, you can discern patterns in the seemingly erroneous numbers and learn to read bottom conditions.

Some models of each type run on their own nine-volt batteries, which simplifies installation. In the end, it's really a matter of personal preference. But a depthsounder is an inexpensive and very valuable piece of navigational equipment. There's no reason why you can't install the unit of your choice.

RDF

Not long ago I received a call at *Cruising World* from a physician who had just completed a pas-

sage from Bermuda to Watch Hill, Rhode Island. His 31-foot cutter had been badly damaged by gale-force winds and high, steep seas in the Gulf Stream. The outboard rudder stock had snapped, the companionway hatch busted open (the weather-boards smashed and the hatch jammed open), the boat half filled with water and all their electrics shorted out.

They had called the U.S. Coast Guard before losing power in their radio. An airplane flew over, dropped a large barrel with pumps and other gear astern, and left. Without a rudder, however, the crew was unable to maneuver back to pick up the package, so they continued on, using the sails to steer the boat. The *only* piece of navigational electronic gear that worked was the RDF, which they used to find their way into Watch Hill.

Why did the RDF work when all else had failed? Because their model, like many others, used its own "D" size batteries and therefore was not dependent on the ship's batteries. Also, it was located high on a shelf where water could not reach it.

Many good RDF's are on the market, some manufactured by Pearce-Simpson, Ray Jefferson (Figure 13-8), Aqua-Meter and others.

Fig. 13-8 *Ray Jefferson RDF, Model 670*

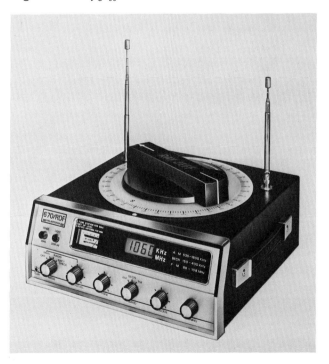

Prices range from about $250 to $600. The more expensive models prevent 180-degree bearing error, and automatically rotate to pick up the desired radio signal or beacon. The less expensive models are tuned manually.

The fortunate doctor was correct in mounting the instrument high on a shelf. Further, it should be well secured so it won't be damaged by sliding around. By the same token, it should be easily moved for use on the chart table or wherever is most convenient, assuming it cannot be read or tuned on its shelf. Because it has its own power supply, no other installation is necessary.

Loran C

Loran is an extremely accurate means of navigation that utilizes pairs of pulsed radio signals from land-based transmitters to give the yacht's receiver a position fix. Accuracy is generally within an eighth of a mile, which makes it extremely useful for coastwise navigation. Range is up to 700 miles from transmitting stations during daytime, and about 1,400 miles at night.

Most of the U.S. coastline and some of the European coastal waters are covered by Loran C (Figure 13-9). Parts of the Caribbean are still uncovered, likewise the South Pacific and much of Asia.

Like other electronic equipment, price has come down dramatically, while at the same time the capabilities of Loran C have increased tremendously. Now it is possible to purchase a Loran C unit that will tell you what course to steer to reach the destination (way point) you desire, how long it will take to get there, how fast you're going toward that destination, and so forth. They can even be interfaced with autopilots so that all you have to do is punch a few buttons and then watch while the boat and all its marvelous electronics do the rest. All you've got to do, it seems, is get the docklines ready.

The type of Loran C system you select depends mostly on the thickness of your pocketbook. As you add options, the price rises. Many coastal cruisers in the U.S. use Loran C, as do the America's Cup 12-Meter boats and IOR racers: If you can afford it, why not? Of course, Loran C is no substitute for basic piloting skills, but then, if you own a more expensive set with pre-programmed waypoints, you'll probably have to know something about piloting to program the darned thing. Manufacturers provide detailed operation manuals that should be self-explanatory to the person with basic piloting and navigation skills.

Initially, some persons were intimidated by the special charts with overlaid Loran C lines. Some sets now convert the Loran C lines of po-

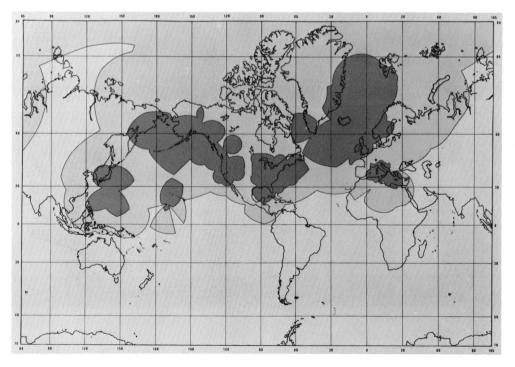

Fig. 13-9 *Range of Loran C coverage*

Fig. 13-10 *Micrologic Loran C, Model ML-3000*

Fig. 13-11 *The NCS Meridian satellite navigator displays the boat's position in latitude and longitude, distance run between satellite passes, course and speed made good. It has an eight-inch whip antenna and emergency battery pack. (Navigation Communication Systems).*

sition to latitude and longitude (Figure 13-10), which are printed on all charts and are more readily understood by the body public.

Loran C often is more accurate than satellite navigation and unlike SatNav, provides continuous readouts. For the coastal sailor, Loran C is the thing to have, for the blue-water passage-maker, it's SatNav. Installation is best done by a qualified technician, but if you're familiar with electronics, the manufacturer's instructions should be sufficient to guide you in installing the antenna and various components on your boat. These generally include the control unit, alternator capacitors to eliminate interference, the antenna and a ground wire. Loran is often wired directly to the battery for maximum power and minimum interference. Typical full operating load is several amps.

SatNav

As mentioned earlier, the price of SatNav (Figure 13-11) has decreased remarkably in recent years, and today it is probably the most accurate means of navigation for ocean crossings. The Navy Navigational Satellite System (known as TRANSIT) has five satellites orbiting the Earth, which transmit signals to your receiver. The mini-computer in your SatNav unit measures the Doppler frequency shift as the satellite swings into range, and gives a precise position fix based on this data. By 1988, there may be operational units available for use with the new Global Positioning System (GPS), that may incorporate as many as 18 satellites.

A fellow I met in California sailed his Alajeula 38 from Southern California to the Marquesas with a borrowed SatNav. He checked its accuracy with a sextant on a daily basis, and was quite impressed with the SatNav. In fact, he believes that he shaved a few days off his passage time because of the SatNav's ability to tell him exactly where he was each day. Fixes can be obtained with each pass of the orbiting satellite, and as the number of satellites in this system are increased, the frequency of fixes also will increase. Again, it's probably best to have a qualified technician install a SatNav unit on your boat unless you have a bent for these things.

MARINE RADIOTELEPHONES

The two principal means of communication for boats at sea are VHF (Very High Frequency) and SSB (Single Sideband) radiotelephones. VHF radios are used by all types of commercial and recreational watercraft for ship-to-ship and ship-to-shore conversations. Their range is limited to line of sight, and so are used mostly for coastal cruising.

The jump to SSB is a major one—in terms of cost, installation, sophistication of circuitry and operation. With the right equipment and atmospheric conditions, the range of an SSB radio is thousands of miles (Figure 13-12).

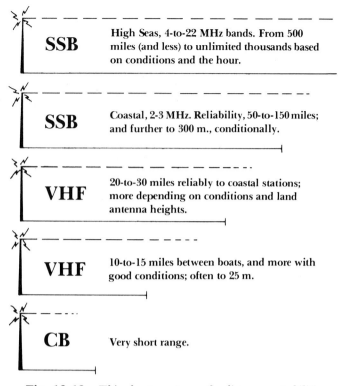

SSB — High Seas, 4-to-22 MHz bands. From 500 miles (and less) to unlimited thousands based on conditions and the hour.

SSB — Coastal, 2-3 MHz. Reliability, 50-to-150 miles; and further to 300 m., conditionally.

VHF — 20-to-30 miles reliably to coastal stations; more depending on conditions and land antenna heights.

VHF — 10-to-15 miles between boats, and more with good conditions; often to 25 m.

CB — Very short range.

Fig. 13-12 *This chart compares the distance capabilities of different radiotelephones.*

Regulations require the use of VHF whenever its range is sufficient to establish communications; SSB therefore can be used only offshore or in the more remote areas of the world, but for the itinerent cruiser, it could prove invaluable. Figure 13-13 shows the spectrum of radio frequencies used on ships, from very low frequency omega to super high frequency radar.

While the levels of skill required to operate VHF and SSB vary greatly, there is a protocol involved in the proper use of each. Government publications detail these more specifically for VHF and SSB, and are available to the user (see reading list at end of chapter).

VHF

Anyone who can operate a CB can operate a VHF. For calling the U.S. Coast Guard while cruising the coast, or talking to a fisherman or freighter passing by, its utility is unsurpassed.

Today, $350 to $500 will buy a fully synthesized VHF (Figure 13-14) that picks up 50 or more channels. The older, non-synthesized types require crystals for every channel. If you leave your particular region some of the crystals will need to be replaced so you will have the channels most useful in the new geographic area (Figure 13-15). Fully synthesized types don't use crystals—just dial the channel number and there you are.

VHF radios are almost always mounted inside the cabin, such as above the navigation station or, in the case of a smaller boat like *Adriana*, under the deck or under a shelf on the bulkhead separating the cabins. Fixing the unit to the shelf is just a matter of drilling in a few screws through the bracket into the wood.

The antenna is the key to a good hook-up. Because the range of VHF is line of sight, the higher the antenna the farther the range. This means that a masthead antenna has a longer range than an antenna mounted on deck. Just how much is determined by the table in Figure 13-16.

Fig. 13-13 *This chart shows the different radio frequencies assigned to various types of equipment. Frequencies are measured in megahertz. (Twentieth Century Publications, Inc.).*

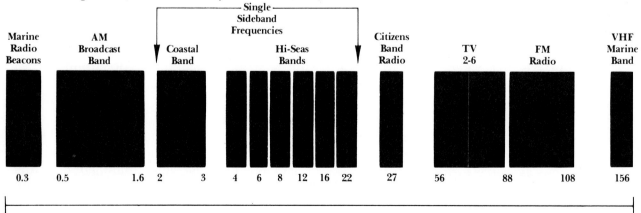

Fig. 13-14 *Ray Jefferson VHF, Model 7800*

For example, assume that the tip of a deck-mounted antenna is 12 feet above sea level and the height of the receiving antenna at a Coast Guard Station on shore is 50 feet above sea level. From the table, the distance in nautical miles is 12.1. A masthead antenna 44 feet above sea level extends that range to 15.8 n.m.—about 30 percent greater.

When reading about VHF radios you usually see maximum distances of 25 or 35 miles. Several reasons exist for the discrepancies between these distances and the 12 to 15 miles just mentioned. First, a maximum range of 25 to 35 miles depends on good weather conditions, an excellent antenna installation and no obstacles—such as an island—between the transmitter and re-

FCC RECOMMENDED VHF-FM CHANNELIZATION

Channel Designators	TYPE OF COMMUNICATIONS Points of Communications
16 (Mandatory)	DISTRESS, SAFETY & CALLING— Intership & ship to coast
06 (Mandatory)	INTERSHIP SAFETY—Intership
65, 66, 12, 73 14, 74, 20	PORT OPERATIONS—Intership & ship to coast
13	NAVIGATIONAL—Intership & ship to coast
22	Liaison communications only with U.S. Coast Guard ship, coast, or aircraft stations
07, 09, 10, 11, 18, 19, 79, 80	COMMERCIAL—Intership & ship to coast
67, 08, 77, 88	COMMERCIAL—Intership
09, 68, 69, 71, 78	NON-COMMERCIAL—Intership & ship to coast
70, 72	NON-COMMERCIAL—Intership
24, 84, 25, 85, 26, 86, 27, 87, 28, 88	PUBLIC CORRESPONDENCE— Ship to public coast
162.4 MHz & 162.55 MHz	NOAA WEATHER SERVICE— Ship receive only

Fig. 13-15 *FCC Recommended VHF Channels*

DISTANCE TO OBJECT JUST VISIBLE ON HORIZON

Height of Transmitting Antenna in Feet	0	4	8	12	16	20	30	40	50	75	100	200	300	400	500	1000	
4	2.3	4.6	5.6	6.3	6.9	7.4	8.6	9.6	10.4	12.3	13.8	18.6	22.2	25.3	28.0	38.7	4
8	3.3	5.6	6.5	7.2	7.9	8.4	9.6	10.5	11.4	13.2	14.8	19.5	23.2	26.3	29.0	39.6	8
12	4.0	6.3	7.2	8.0	8.6	9.1	10.3	11.3	12.1	13.9	15.5	20.2	23.9	27.0	29.7	40.3	12
16	4.6	6.9	7.9	8.6	9.2	9.7	10.9	11.9	12.7	14.6	16.1	20.9	24.5	27.6	30.3	41.0	16
20	5.1	7.4	8.4	9.1	9.7	10.3	11.4	12.4	13.3	15.1	16.6	21.4	25.1	28.1	30.9	41.5	20
24	5.6	7.9	8.9	9.6	10.2	10.8	11.9	12.9	13.8	15.6	17.1	21.9	25.6	28.6	31.3	42.0	24
28	6.1	8.4	9.3	10.1	10.7	11.2	12.4	13.4	14.2	16.0	17.6	22.3	26.0	29.1	31.8	42.5	28
32	6.5	8.8	9.8	10.5	11.1	11.6	12.8	13.8	14.6	16.5	18.0	22.8	26.4	29.5	32.2	42.9	32
36	6.9	9.2	10.2	10.9	11.5	12.0	13.2	14.2	15.0	16.9	18.4	23.2	26.8	29.9	32.6	43.3	36
40	7.3	9.6	10.5	11.3	11.9	12.4	13.6	14.5	15.4	17.2	18.8	23.5	27.2	30.3	33.0	43.6	40
44	7.6	9.9	10.9	11.6	12.2	12.8	13.9	14.9	15.8	17.6	19.1	23.9	27.5	30.6	33.3	44.0	44
48	8.0	10.3	11.2	12.0	12.6	13.1	14.3	15.2	16.1	17.9	19.5	24.2	27.9	31.0	33.7	44.3	48
52	8.3	10.6	11.5	12.3	12.9	13.4	14.6	15.6	16.4	18.3	19.8	24.6	28.2	31.3	34.0	44.7	52
56	8.6	10.9	11.9	12.6	13.2	13.7	14.9	15.9	16.7	18.6	20.1	24.9	28.5	31.6	34.3	45.0	56
60	8.9	11.2	12.2	12.9	13.5	14.1	15.2	16.2	17.0	18.9	20.4	25.2	28.8	31.9	34.6	45.3	60
64	9.2	11.5	12.5	13.2	13.8	14.3	15.5	16.5	17.3	19.2	20.7	25.5	29.1	32.2	34.9	45.6	64

Header row: Height of Receiving Antenna in Feet

Note: Values in table are in nautical miles.

Fig. 13-16 *VHF range is line of sight; this table of distances to the horizon will help you determine your unit's range, depending on height of transmitter and receiver.*

ceiver. Second, radio waves do tend to curve slightly around the Earth's surface.

The distance to the horizon is determined by this formula:

$$D = 1.144 \times \sqrt{H}$$

(where D is distance to the horizon and H is the height of the observer above sea level)

The formula is different for VHF radios, based on the knowledge of how much the wavelengths bend:

$$1.4 \times \sqrt{H}$$

The difference in formulas is about 22 percent, and this increases our previous figures of 12.1 and 15.8 to 14.7[1] and 19.3.

The key to having a VHF that works at peak efficiency and reliability is the antenna hookup. Marine electronics dealers carry a variety of antennas, one of which is suitable for your installation. Usually, masthead antennas are 3 db gain and deck-mounted antennas 6 db gain. The higher the gain, the longer the antenna, and the greater the range. However, the signal also becomes flatter and this can cause receiving difficulties in rolly seas.

The distance from the antenna to the radio in part determines the size of cable needed—wire that's too thin, run over a long distance, loses power. So, for 6 db gain deck-mounted antennas, about 20 feet of ¼-inch cable is provided. It is too small however, for the 3 db gain masthead antenna, which preferably is ½-inch RG-8/U-type coaxial cable with a polyethylene core.

The masthead antenna should be securely mounted on the side of the mast with the bracket provided; the wire enters the mast through a hole, travels down to the base where it exits the mast again and passes through the deck, through the cabin to the set (Figure 13-17). Rub-

ber ferrules in the spar holes prevent cable abrasion. An alternative is to run the cable entirely inside the spar. The choice is essentially whether you want the connectors inside, out of the weather (but where any banging against the mast walls will be horrendous), or outside, where if a problem occurs—and it usually occurs at the connectors (Figure 13-17)—it is more readily accessible. *Adriana*'s coaxial cable exits at mast and step, but I don't know if in the long run it is any better. Some weatherproofing with silicone and duct tape over the connectors certainly helps.

I also carry a spare cable and short hand-held antenna, available from Radio Shack, for emergency use. You never know when the mast might come down or be struck by lightning, and it's comforting to have a backup.

Figure 13-18 shows several methods of secur-

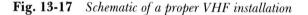

Fig. 13-17 *Schematic of a proper VHF installation*

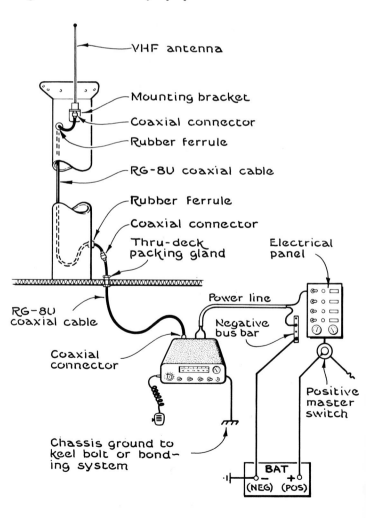

---

[1] To determine distance from the observer, or antenna, to the object sighted beyond the horizon, you also need to know the distance from the horizon to the tip of the receiving antenna. Distance from transmitter to receiver is:

$1.4 \times \sqrt{H}$ of transmitter + $1.4 \times \sqrt{H}$ of receiver. Assume 12′ transmitter, 50′ receiver:

$1.4 \times \sqrt{12} + 1.4 \sqrt{50} = 4.8 + 9.9 = 14.7$ n.m.

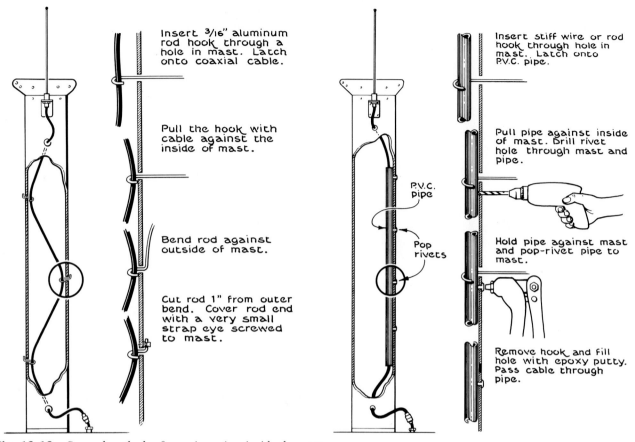

Fig. 13-18 *Several methods of securing wires inside the mast*

ing the wires inside the mast (including the mast-head light wire and any others), so they won't rattle. This noise drives me nuts, and it obviously bothers others, because no other on-board problem has generated more suggested solutions from *Cruising World* readers.

I haven't tried all of these solutions, but they seem as good as any.

Barry Conacher suggests drilling small holes in the mast and using metal clips to grab the wire and secure them in a diamond pattern.

Don Casey suggests running all wiring through a PVC tube screwed or glued to the inside of the mast. I like the idea of glue better, as no holes are involved, but getting a good bond seems iffy to me, though I'm told it can be done. Kim Houghton of Rig-Rite in Warwick, Rhode Island, says his company retrofits spars with pop-riveted PVC pipe. They drill two holes, one to insert a coat hanger through to hold the PVC tight against the second hole. The PVC is drilled and pop-riveted, then the wire removed and a pop rivet put in the first hole to cover it.

A final note on installing the VHF radio—the closer the unit is to the battery, the shorter the power wires and therefore the less potential power loss. For runs up to about 12 feet, use #10 AWG wire with crimp lugs or eye terminals (Figure 12-27), and plastic ties to hold them in place as you run them through the boat. The power wires can be led directly to the battery or to the main switch, but not the distribution panel, as too much power will be lost through the additional circuitry of narrow-gauge wires.

Single Sideband Radios (SSB)

For about the same price as a good Loran C receiver, a Single Sideband radio (Figure 13-19) can be purchased that will give the cruising couple communications with at least part of the "other" world, whether the boat is in the middle of the Pacific or rounding Antarctica. However, purchasing SSB is not to be taken lightly—you don't simply identify the model that has an at-

Fig. 13-19 *A single-sideband radio (upper right) for world-wide voice communication aboard Gypsy Moth V, sailed by Desmond Hampton in the BOC Challenge (Jim Gilbert photo).*

tractive case, pull it off the shelf and screw it into your navigation station. Research SSB radios at your local library, write for the government publications detailing the regulations governing their use, and consult with the technicians and sales persons at your nearest marine electronics store.

Models range from 50 watts to 1,000 watts, but the largest are really intended for use only on large commercial ships. More power doesn't necessarily mean greater range or clarity. More important is the user's knowledge of frequencies, daily and seasonal effects and his ability to tune the set properly. With the improved solid-state circuitry available today, a typical SSB for the cruising sailor might be rated at 150 watts, and have the same range as the 1,000-watt sets.

SSB frequencies begin with the Middle Frequency (MF) coastal bands at 2 and 3 MHz. From 4 MHz to 22 MHz are known as the High Frequency (HF) or High Seas bands. High frequency transmissions result in groundwaves that hug the Earth, and are limited in range to about 150 miles, depending upon conditions (Figure 13-20) and skywave propagation bounced off the ionosphere anywhere from 30 to 250 miles

Fig. 13-20 *SSB radios transmit both ground waves and sky waves. Note the skip zones where there is little or no reception.*

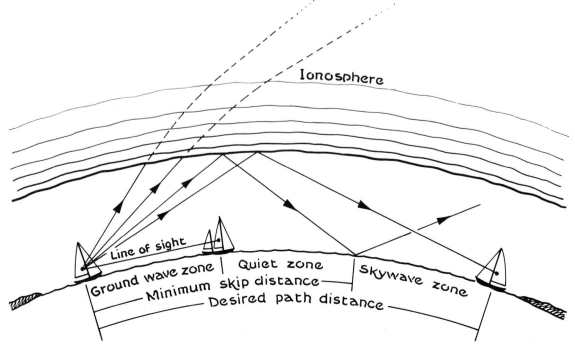

high. Under good conditions, you can get reception via skywaves up to about 5,000 miles. There is a Skip Zone between the groundwaves and skywaves in which the SSB radio is ineffective. Typical frequency propagation for the different reasons is shown in Figure 13-21.

The effectiveness of SSB is very much dependent upon a good installation, and skilled technicians are required to do the job right. A ground plane must be established (Figure 13-22) that may involve adding ground screens beneath berths, and tying together metal components (such as engine and tanks) inside the boat with woven copper straps. The antenna may be a whip type, or utilize the backstay or, on ketches, the triatic stay, both of which must have insulators no closer than four feet from the mastheads or deck. An antenna coupler electrically changes the antenna's length to match the desired frequency. The coupler, plus the radio itself, must be properly located and installed.

While the time and money investment in SSB

TYPICAL FREQUENCY PROPAGATION SPRING AND SUMMER

Frequency (KHz)	4000		8000		12000		16000	
Propagation (Miles)	Min	Max	Min	Max	Min	Max	Min	Max
Hours after sunset								
1	50	250	200	1000	500	3500	750	6000
2	100	600	250	1500	500	3500	750	6000
3	100	600	250	2000	500	3500		
4	100	800	250	2500				
5	100	1000	250	2500				
6	100	1500	400	3000				
7	100	1500	500	3500				
8	250	2000	750	4000				
9	250	2500	750	4000				
10	250	2500	750	4000				
11	100	1000	500	2500				
Hours after sunrise								
1	100	500	400	2000				
2	0	100	400	2000				
3	0	100	250	1500				
4	0	100	250	1500	500	1000		
5	0	100	250	1500	500	1500		
6	0	100	250	1500	500	2500	750	4000
7	0	100	250	1500	500	3500	750	4000
8	0	100	250	1500	500	3500	750	4000
9	0	100	250	1500	500	3500	750	4000
10	0	100	250	1500	500	3500	750	4000
11	0	100	150	500	500	3500	750	6000
12	0	200	150	500	500	3500	750	6000
13	50	250	150	750	500	3500	750	6000

TYPICAL FREQUENCY PROPAGATION FALL AND WINTER

Frequency (KHz)	4000		8000		12000		16000	
Propagation (Miles)	Min	Max	Min	Max	Min	Max	Min	Max
Hours after sunset								
1	100	600	400	2000	500	3500	750	6000
2	100	800	400	2000	500	4000	750	6000
3	100	1000	400	2000	500	4000		
4	100	1000	400	2500	500	4000		
5	100	1000	400	3000	500	4000		
6	100	1500	400	3500				
7	250	2000	400	4000				
8	250	2500	500	4000				
9	500	3000	500	4000				
10	500	4000	500	4000				
11	500	3000	750	5000				
12	250	2500	750	5000				
13	250	1500	500	2500				
Hours after sunrise								
1	100	1000	400	2000				
2	100	500	400	2000				
3	0	100	400	2000	500	3500	750	4000
4	0	100	400	2000	500	3500	750	4000
5	0	100	250	1500	500	3500	750	4000
6	0	100	250	1500	500	3500	750	4000
7	0	100	250	1500	500	4000	750	5000
8	0	100	250	1500	500	4000	750	5000
9	0	100	250	1500	500	4000	750	6000
10	0	100	250	1000	500	3500	750	6000
11	0	250	250	1500	500	3500	750	6000

Fig. 13-21 *Typical frequency propagation for different seasons (Twentieth Century Publications Inc.)*

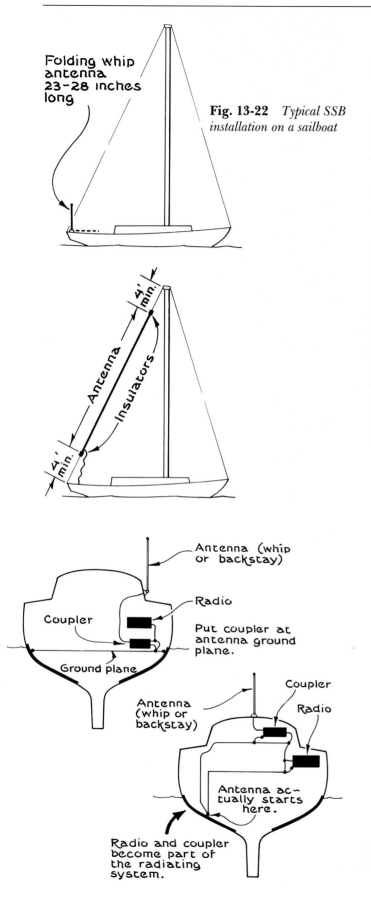

Fig. 13-22 *Typical SSB installation on a sailboat*

Folding whip antenna 23-28 inches long

4' min.

Antenna

Insulators

4' min.

Antenna (whip or backstay)

Radio

Coupler

Put coupler at antenna ground plane.

Ground plane

Coupler

Antenna (whip or backstay)

Radio

Antenna actually starts here.

Radio and coupler become part of the radiating system.

is considerable, it is worth noting that here at *Cruising World* we have received numerous stories from both ocean racers and cruising folks about how SSB saved a life or expedited medical treatment. The majority of sailors might spend a lifetime at sea never needing SSB, but for those who have, it is difficult to imagine that they would go to sea again without it.

Weather and Time

Obtaining accurate, up-to-the-minute weather forecasts is important for anyone sailing even a few miles offshore. Similarly, the ocean navigator must know exact time (Greenwich Mean Time) for his celestial navigation calculations. Both weather and time signals can be obtained with the right radio equipment—VHF picks up the NOAA weather broadcasts (WX1, 162.50 MHz; WX2, 162.400 MHz; WX3, 162.475 MHz), and SSB picks up time signals (WWV—Fort Collins, Colorado, 2.5, 5.0, 10.0 and 15.0 MHz; WWVH—Kauai, Hawaii, 2.5, 5.0, 10.0, 15.0 and 20.0 MHz) (Figure 13-23.) If you don't

Fig. 13-23 *WWV and WWVH broadcast format for transmitting time signals*

WWV (Ft. Collins, Colo.)

Frequencies—2.5, 5, 10, and 15 MHz

Times of Broadcast	Broadcast Area
8 minutes past the hour	Storm information for
9 minutes past the hour	western North Atlantic, including Gulf of Mexico and Caribbean Sea
10 minutes past the hour	Storm information for
*11 minutes past the hour	North Pacific east of 140° W.

WWVH (Kauai, Hawaii)

Frequencies—2.5, 5, 10, and 15 MHz

Times of Broadcast	Broadcast Area
48 minutes past the hour	Storm information for
49 minutes past the hour	North Pacific; also
50 minutes past the hour	the South Pacific to
*51 minutes past the hour	25°S., 160°E–110°W.

*An additional segment may be broadcast when there are unusually widespread storm conditions.

have VHF and SSB aboard, the least you should do is purchase a radio receiver, not only for NOAA weather broadcasts and WWV time signals, but also to pick up local weather and news in your area.

EPIRB

EPIRB is an acronym for Emergency Position Indicating Radio Beacon. A typical model is about the size of a Thermos bottle, and is used by sailors to send emergency signals when the boat is in danger of sinking and radio communications have proven fruitless.

There are now three types of EPIRBs: Class C is recommended for coastal sailing no more than 20 miles offshore as it broadcasts on VHF channels 15 and 16 (156.75 and 156.8 MHz). Because the U.S. Coast Guard and other government and private groups monitor these channels 24 hours a day, your signal stands a reasonable chance of being picked up. The Coast Guard would then attempt a rescue by ship or helicopter, or ask a ship in your vicinity to lend assistance. As long as the EPIRB is transmitting, your searchers can home in on your position. So, leave the EPIRB on once it has been activated, and don't try to conserve the batteries by periodically shutting it off. Because VHF is line of sight, the higher you can hold the EPIRB, the better its range will be.

Class B EPIRBs transmit on 121.5 and 243 MHz and are manually activated. The signals' effective range is about 200 to 300 miles, hopefully enough for passing airplanes, satellites and ships to detect. Class A is identical to Class B, except that it is automatically activated when it comes into contact with water. They cost several hundred dollars, but are vital equipment aboard any boat venturing offshore.

Color Radar, Weatherfax and Computers

By now it should be clear that there is no end to the type and variety of electronic equipment available today. Unfortunately, the realities of economics dictate that I confine my electronics to bare essentials: Depthsounder, knotmeter, EPIRB, VHF radio, compass and RDF—that's it. But just when I think *Adriana* is pitifully primi-

tive, Danny Greene, who has sailed 30,000 Atlantic Ocean miles on a 26-foot boat, tells me he just bought his first VHF radio!

ELECTRICAL BONDING

Once you have electricity on board, even if it's just an engine, battery, cabin lights and VHF radio, the possibility exists of electrolytic corrosion to metal parts of the boat.

The American Boat and Yacht Council (ABYC) is quite specific as to how bonding should be accomplished. ABYC's Standard E-1 applies to all direct current systems under 50 volts.

The purpose of bonding, as described by ABYC, is to: 1) provide a low-resistance electrical path inside the hull between otherwise isolated metallic objects, especially those in common contact with sea water, 2) prevent the possibility of electrical potential on exposed metallic enclosures of electrical equipment, 3) provide a low-resistance path for excessively high voltages, such as when the boat is struck by lightning, and 4) to minimize radio interference. Boats *without* permanently installed electrical systems do not need bonding.

The heart of the bonding system is a "common bonding conductor," which is generally a length of bronze or copper metal at least a half-inch wide and no less than 1/32-inch thick. It is laid inside the hull from stem to stern and those metallic objects that are to be connected are done so by using #9 AWG wire or larger (Figure 13-24).

Items to be bonded include engines (use the engine negative terminal), metallic enclosures of electrical appliances, motors, generators and pump frames, fuel tanks, fuel-deck fittings and lead-lined battery trays.

It is *not* necessary to include in the bonding system electrically isolated thru-hull fittings, if they are all of the same metal, or if they are protected by sacrificial anodes, as is common with propeller shafts. Warren Thompson of ITT Jabsco, told me that his company will not recommend bonding of sea cocks because of conflicting data.

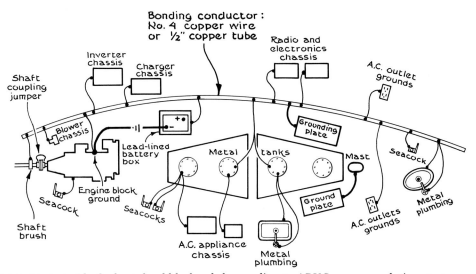

Fig. 13-24 *Metal objects inside the boat should be bonded according to ABYC recommendations to prevent corrosion, radio interference and to provide a low-resistance path for excessively high voltages, such as from lightning.*

On steel and aluminum hulls, the hull itself can serve as the common bonding conductor. In this instance, items to be bonded that are not in contact with the hull should be wired directly to the hull.

LIGHTNING GROUND PROTECTION

During a cruise to Green Bay one summer, *Adriana* was struck on the masthead by lightning. Though we didn't know it at the time, the reason we weren't hurt was because the boat was grounded. The shrouds were wired to a plate in the hull that gave a path for the lightning to follow to ground (Earth). Nevertheless, the lights burned out, the diodes in the VHF were fried, the points in the engine were closed, and the battery casing was literally blown apart. Whether bonding these items to a common conductor tied in with the lightning ground would have prevented this damage, I am still uncertain.

What I do know is that I never want to be struck again, and this presents a curious problem. Naval architect John Letcher told me that a grounded mast in fact increases the odds of your boat sustaining a lightning strike. Lightning doesn't actually "strike" the way it appears; rather a path from the atmosphere to ground must be present for the charge to pass through. Of course, an ungrounded mast also can be hit, and if it is, the damage will be much greater.

I have seen two boats hit by lightning that did not have grounded masts—one sank because the lightning exited the boat at the waterline, perforating the hull in a thousand tiny places. The other lost its mast when the lightning blew out the chainplates.

In any case, it's a sticky-wicket—ground the mast and increase the odds of being struck, or go ungrounded and pray you're never struck. As terrifying as it was to be struck by lightning, I'd opt for the grounded system.

Our crew was saved from injury for two reasons: We were not touching the rigging or any part of the ground system or metal objects inside, and because, in the words of the ABYC Standard E-4, "A grounded conductor, or lightning protective mast, will generally deflect to itself direct hits which might otherwise fall within a cone-shaped space, the apex of which is the top of the conductor or lightning protective mast and the base is a circle at the surface of the water having a radius of approximately two times the height of the conductor." The probability of protection, ABYC reports, is 99 percent (Figure 13-25).

If your boat is not grounded, and you wish it to be, run #8 AWG wire from each shroud of an aluminum mast to a plate in the hull, such as a Dynarod® (Figure 13-26), of at least one square foot. Tom Colvin recommends grounding only the mast, not the shrouds. The spar is more vertical and there's presumably less danger to the chainplate if there's a poor wiring connection.

But on deck-stepped spars without compression posts or bulkheads directly underneath,

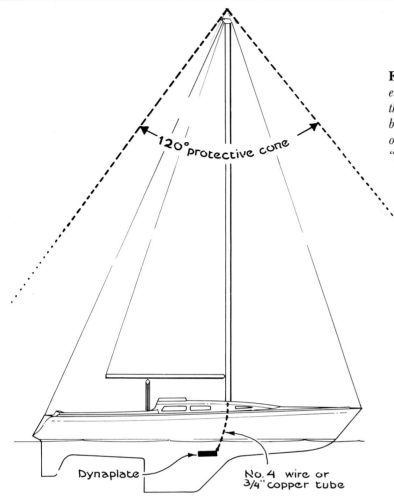

Fig. 13-25 *A lightning ground system routes electricity from the spar to a ground plate in the hull, and may be incorporated with the bonding system. When struck, the lightning rod or masthead deflects the lightning, creating a "cone of protection" underneath.*

120° protective cone

Dynaplate

No. 4 wire or 3/4" copper tube

there's no way to run the ground wire straight down to the ground plate. Propellers, large metal rudders or radio transmitter ground plates also can be used for grounds. However, I don't like using the prop shaft or any other ob-

Fig. 13-26 *A Dynaplate makes an excellent ground for bonding or lightning protection (Aquadynamics, Inc.).*

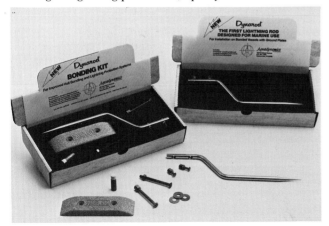

ject that requires the lightning to make an abrupt turn—the system must be as vertical as possible. *Adriana* has a plate in the hull with a bolt protruding into the bilge, to which the wires are connected. For this reason, do not use the engine as the ground, as the only electrical path to earth is horizontally via the propeller shaft.

Wood masts require a lightning rod at least six inches higher than the mast connected to #8 AWG wire or larger run down the mast to the ground plate. All wires should run as vertically as possible and avoid sharp bends. Sailtracks also should be protected.

With wood and fiberglass hulls, the lightning ground system can be connected to any bonding system that exists to prevent surges of voltage through metal and electrical objects inside the boat. Steel boats can use the hull itself.

Read the ABYC recommendations in Appendices A and E carefully before installing a bonding or lightning ground system.

SOME BASICS ABOUT 12-VOLT DC ELECTRICAL SYSTEMS

The boat's wiring system is all too often taken for granted, and it's not until you're tracing down a bad connection, trying to install a new piece of electrical equipment, or sniffing acrid smoke in the cabin that you begin to consider the merits of a well-planned and executed wiring system.

The two principal sets of standards for wiring on small sailboats are: the ABYC *Safety Standards for Small Craft* (mentioned earlier), and the National Fire Protection Association's *National Electric Code*. Anyone considering major work with electrical systems would do well to read these documents beforehand.

Just because your boat's electrical system is only 12 volts (24 and 32 volts often appear as separate circuits on larger yachts), doesn't mean there isn't enough juice to pose danger on board. We've received numerous manuscripts at *Cruising World* from readers reporting electrical fires in their 12-volt fuse panels. Shoddy workmanship here, as anywhere else, soon tells. Because of this potential hazard, it is important to be able to pull off the cover of your fuse panel quickly, or better yet, quickly reach the main switch to shut off power.

Unless your boat is very old, or some previous owner has botched up the wiring, chances are it will require little attention. If you are installing a new DC system from scratch, or modernizing an old one, be sure it is installed with the negative polarity grounded, which is now accepted practice and recommended by ABYC (Figure 13-27). Positive-ground electronic gear is difficult to come by.

Wiring systems on boats are two-wire systems, with the hot or positive wire carrying power to

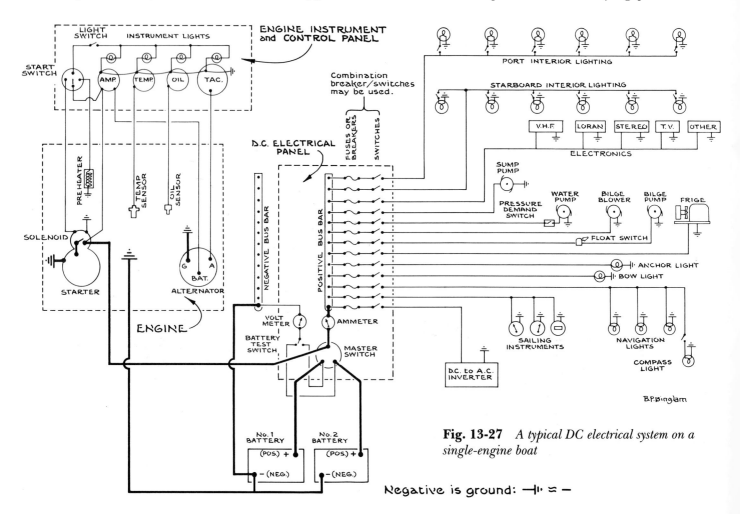

Fig. 13-27 *A typical DC electrical system on a single-engine boat*

Negative is ground: ⊣⊢ ≃ ─

lights and appliances, and a separate, insulated wire returning to ground, generally the negative bus bar in the distribution panel, which in turn is connected to the common ground such as the engine block. If the boat is bonded, as described earlier, the bonding strip is *not* to be used as ground.

Most important to the average sailor is determining how to add electrical equipment. If there is room on the positive bus bar (distribution panel) and negative bus for a new circuit, this is preferable. This way, the new VHF or cabin fan will have its own circuit, fuse or circuit breaker and switch. The possibility of overloading is, of course, reduced. Future trouble-shooting will be vastly simplified if you follow ABYC's recommended color coding system when adding new equipment (Figure 13-28). Don't run wires in the bilge. Run them under the side decks, supported every 18–24 inches. And near the compass, twist the positive and negative wires around each other over their entire length to minimize their influence.

If there is not room for a new, separate, circuit, the appliance can be added to an existing circuit. But care should be taken in selecting which one. For example, it would be unwise to use the same circuit for too many appliances that are likely to be used at the same time. If an electric bilge pump, spreader lights and VHF radio are all on the same circuit, transmitting on VHF (especially at the 25-watt setting) while the other items also are in use, could overload the system. Common appliances could be grouped as follows:

- Cabin lights, fans, navigation station light.
- Running lights, masthead tricolor, compass light and other instrument lights, such as depthsounder.
- VHF, SSB, etc.
- Electric pumps
- Autopilot
- Stereo, T.V.

If the distribution panel cannot accommodate as many circuits as seems necessary, it might be a good idea to add a new bus with additional circuits. To determine whether you will be overloading a circuit, you need to know the total load (in amps) on the circuit, and the wire size (gauge)

RECOMMENDED MARINE WIRING COLOR CODE DIRECT CURRENT SYSTEMS—UNDER 50 VOLTS

Color	Item	Use
Yellow w/Red Stripe (YR)	Starting Circuit	Starting Switch to Solenoid
Yellow (Y)	Generator or Alternator Field	Generator or Alternator Field to Regulator Field Terminal
	Bilge Blowers	Fuse or Switch to Blowers
Dark Gray (Gy)	Navigation Lights	Fuse or Switch to Lights
	Tachometer	Tachometer Sender to Gauge
Brown (Br)	Generator Armature	Generator Armature to Regulator
	Alternator Charge Light	Generator Terminal/Alternator Auxiliary Terminal to Light to Regulator
	Pumps	Fuse or Switch to Pumps
Orange (O)	Accessory Feed	Ammeter to Alternator or Generator Output and Accessory Fuses or Switches
	Accessory Common Feed	Distribution Panel to Accessory Switch
Purple (Pu)	Ignition	Ignition Switch to Coil and Electrical Instruments
	Instrument Feed	Distribution Panel to Electric Instruments
Dark Blue	Cabin and Instrument Lights	Fuse or Switch to Lights
Light Blue (Lt Bl)	Oil Pressure	Oil Pressure Sender to Gauge
Tan	Water Temperature	Water Temperature Sender to Gauge
Pink (pk)	Fuel Gauge	Fuel Gauge Sender to Gauge

Fig. 13-28 *ABYC's recommended wiring color code for direct current electrical systems under 50 volts*

CONDUCTOR SIZES FOR 10% DROP IN VOLTAGE

TOTAL CURRENT ON CIRCUIT IN AMPS

12 Volts—10% Drop Wire Sizes (gage)—Based on Minimum CM Area

Amps	10	15	20	25	30	40	50	60	70	80	90	100	110	120	130	140	150	160	170
5	18	18	18	18	18	16	16	14	14	14	12	12	12	12	12	10	10	10	10
10	18	18	16	16	14	14	12	12	10	10	10	10	8	8	8	8	8	8	6
15	18	16	14	14	12	12	10	10	8	8	8	8	8	6	6	6	6	6	6
20	16	14	14	12	12	10	10	8	8	8	6	6	6	6	6	6	4	4	4
25	16	14	12	12	10	10	8	8	6	6	6	6	6	4	4	4	4	4	2
30	14	12	12	10	10	8	8	6	6	6	6	4	4	4	4	2	2	2	2
40	14	12	10	10	8	8	6	6	6	4	4	4	2	2	2	2	2	2	2
50	12	10	10	8	8	6	6	4	4	4	2	2	2	2	2	1	1	1	1
60	12	10	8	8	6	6	4	4	2	2	2	2	1	1	1	0	0	0	0
70	10	8	8	6	6	6	4	2	2	2	2	1	1	1	0	0	0	2/0	2/0
80	10	8	8	6	6	4	4	2	2	2	1	1	0	0	0	2/0	2/0	2/0	2/0
90	10	8	6	6	6	4	2	2	2	1	1	0	0	0	2/0	2/0	2/0	3/0	3/0
100	10	8	6	6	4	4	2	2	1	1	0	0	0	2/0	2/0	2/0	3/0	3/0	3/0

Length of Conductor from Source of Current to Device and Back to Source—Feet

Fig. 13-29 *This table indicates the size wires required to keep voltage drop 10 percent or less. Loads (amps) and length of wires are shown.*

and length of those wires. The table in Figure 13-29, reprinted from ABYC's standard E-9, will help.

The 10-percent voltage drops in the table of conductor sizes are acceptable if the wire is heavy enough to handle the load. Compare the wire size in this table with the sizes in Figure 13-30, which allow for only a three percent drop. The latter is preferable for appliances such as VHF, for which you might always want full

CONDUCTORS SIZES FOR 3% DROP IN VOLTAGE

TOTAL CURRENT ON CIRCUIT IN AMPS

12 Volts—3% Drop Wire Sizes (gage)—Based on Minimum CM Area

Amps	10	15	20	25	30	40	50	60	70	80	90	100	110	120	130	140	150	160	170
5	18	16	14	12	12	10	10	10	8	8	8	6	6	6	6	6	6	6	6
10	14	12	10	10	10	8	6	6	6	6	4	4	4	4	2	2	2	2	2
15	12	10	10	8	8	6	6	6	4	4	2	2	2	2	1	1	1	1	1
20	10	10	8	6	6	6	4	4	2	2	2	2	1	1	1	0	0	0	2/0
25	10	8	6	6	6	4	4	2	2	2	1	1	0	0	0	2/0	2/0	2/0	3/0
30	10	8	6	6	4	4	2	2	1	1	0	0	0	2/0	2/0	3/0	3/0	3/0	3/0
40	8	6	6	4	4	2	2	1	0	0	2/0	2/0	3/0	3/0	3/0	4/0	4/0	4/0	4/0
50	6	6	4	4	2	2	1	0	2/0	2/0	3/0	3/0	4/0	4/0	4/0				
60	6	4	4	2	2	1	0	2/0	3/0	3/0	4/0	4/0	4/0						
70	6	4	2	2	1	0	2/0	3/0	3/0	4/0	4/0								
80	6	4	2	2	1	0	3/0	3/0	4/0	4/0									
90	4	2	2	1	0	2/0	3/0	4/0	4/0										
100	4	2	2	1	0	2/0	3/0	4/0											

Length of Conductor from Source of Current to Device and Back to Source—Feet

Fig. 13-30 *This table indicates the size wires required to keep voltage drop three percent or less. Loads (amps) and length of wires are shown.*

power. For example, a circuit carrying 25 amps a distance of 15 feet, requires #14 AWG wire to keep the possible voltage drop at 10 percent; for a three percent drop, the size of wire increases to #8.

Each circuit should be protected by a fuse or trip-free circuit breaker, which is magnetically or thermally opened when an overload occurs. The circuit breaker is more convenient because it doesn't need replacement. Sometimes a piece of equipment, such as a stereo, will come with its own in-line fuse in the hot wire, and while this protects the stereo, it doesn't protect the other equipment on the same circuit.

Battery Selector Switches and Isolators

Every cruising boat should carry more than one battery, perhaps several. A 30-foot boat might have a 105-amp deep-cycle battery for lights and electronics, and an 80-amp or larger heavy-duty battery for starting the engine. It should be the rule on board *never* to use the engine's battery for any other purpose. A three-way switch allows you to select the battery you have designated for cabin lights or engine starting. With this switch you also can select which battery you wish to charge—one at a time. Figure 13-31 diagrams the wiring necessary to hook

up a three-way switch. The Guest Corporation offers a free booklet explaining installation of its switches, which is very handy. Consider a few variables before hooking up the switch: brand of alternator, internal or external regulator, and whether or not the alternator has isolating diodes built in.

It is more convenient if both batteries can be charged at the same time, and you'll be more secure knowing that one battery isn't discharging into the other. Guest also makes a battery isolator that can be installed in conjunction with a three-way switch. Without an isolator, when the switch is set for both batteries there is the danger the more fully charged battery will discharge into the lesser charged battery. An isolator isn't necessary if you charge battery #1 for a while as the engine runs, then switch to battery #2 for awhile before shutting off the engine.

INSTALLING SHORE POWER

Since most of us find ourselves alongside a dock from time to time, it's nice to have 110-volt AC power even for a short time. This is not to say the boat shouldn't be capable of generating its own DC or AC power under way, at anchor

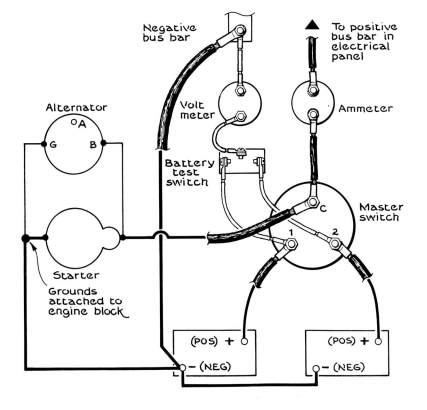

Fig. 13-31 *A Guest three-way battery selector switch enables you to determine which battery you want to use for a given purpose—lighting and electronics, or engine starting.*

or on the mooring. But it's generally easier and less expensive to use shore power when it's available.

Adriana spends most of each year on a mooring, and there we rely on the 12-volt DC ship's electrical system and kerosene and diesel to supply our energy needs. When she comes into the dock for the winter, 110-volt AC shore power runs the small Intermatic heater and electrical blanket that keeps us warm. Some day I might install a diesel-fired heater and dispense with the electrical heater. But we won't ever want to do away with the electric blanket!

The size of the extension cord from the AC outlet on the dock to the receptacle on your boat depends on the amount of juice you need. Most boats in the 30 to 40-foot range use 30-amp wire, though some opt for the larger 50-amp wire. Good quality connectors, such as those made by Hubbell and Marinco, should be used on either end; cord kits with these three-prong connectors already attached are available from most chandleries or mail-order houses (Figure 13-32).

The female receptacle should be located somewhere on deck where it is relatively free from spray and other sources of moisture. A common location is on the side of the footwell, perhaps near the after end of the cockpit.

Fig. 13-32 *Hubbell shore power connectors are made for 30-amp and 50-amp wire. Note the three prongs—one for ground—and weather protective case.*

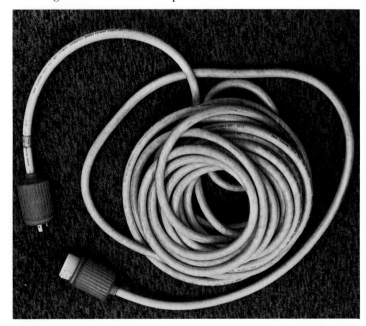

The boat's internal AC system of wires and outlets should be entirely separate from the DC system. However, you may wish to add a battery charger so that your AC shore power charges your DC battery when you're at the dock. In every case, you should also install a polarity indicator that will warn you if the polarity of the system has reversed itself. And, it is important to install a main shore power circuit breaker disconnect that will shot off all power coming into the boat with the throw of one switch. Each appliance or outlet should have its own branch circuit breaker as well.

Faults in an AC power system on board can be lethal, and for this reason, ground fault circuit interrupters (GFCI) have become quite popular. Hubbell makes a portable GFCI into which you plug appliances rather than directly into outlets. Pass and Seymour and the Square D Company make GFCI's that are incorporated into the circuit breakers and trip open with a leak as little as five milliamps.

Figure 13-33 follows the ABYC recommended wiring installation of a shore power system using 120 volts.

SUMMARY

Electronics and salt water don't mix. Equipment and wiring that isn't protected from moisture begins to corrode quickly, with failure right around the corner. For this reason, considerable care should be taken when installing electrical wire and equipment, and one should always be prepared to pilot or navigate by means other than electronic.

• Depthsounder transducers and knotmeter sending units mounted beneath the waterline should be tightly mounted and well bedded.

• Carry an EPIRB for offshore cruising.

• Boats with permanent electrical systems should be bonded.

• A lightning ground system incorporating a red, #8 AWG wire or ground plate, protects the boat and the crew.

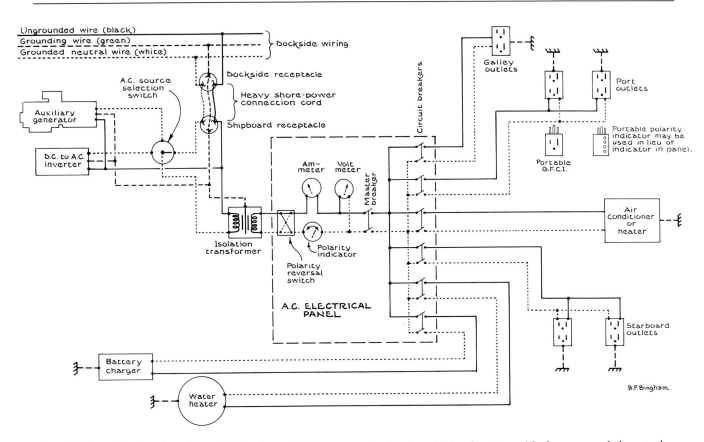

Fig. 13-33 *This drawing of an ABYC schematic illustrates a single-phase 120-volt system with shore-grounded neutral conductor and grounding conductor.*

• Electrical wires shouldn't be run through the bilge; support wire bundles every 18 or 24 inches; twist positive and negative wires near the compass; use the ABYC recommended color coding system; and avoid running wires over sharp edges, which could cause chafe.

• Avoid overloading circuits by carefully determining the equipment that is run off each circuit, and by using the correct size wire for the load and distance from the battery.

• Each circuit should have a fuse or circuit breaker for protection against overloading.

• The boat should have at least two batteries—a deep-cycle battery for lights and electronics and a heavy-duty battery for engine starting. A three-way selector switch safeguards against draining the engine start battery.

• If you have 110-volt shore power on board, a ground fault circuit interrupter (GFCI) prevents potentially lethal shocks.

FURTHER READING

Your Boat's Electrical System by Conrad Miller & E. S. Maloney; Hearst Books, 959 Eighth Avenue, New York, New York 10019.

Electrical And Electronic Equipment for Yachts by John French; Dodd, Mead & Company, 79 Madison Avenue, New York, New York 10016.

How To Install Everything Electronic In Cars, Boats, Planes, Trucks And RV's by Clayton L. Mallmark; Tab Books, Blue Ridge Summit, Pennsylvania 17214.

Radio And Radar In Sail And Power Boats by Kenneth Wilkes; Nautical Publishing Company Ltd., Nautical House, Lymington, Hampshire S04 9BA, England.

A Mariners Guide To Single Sideband by Frederick Graves; Stephens Engineering Associates, Inc., 7030 220th S.W., Mountlake Terrace, Washington 98043.

A Mariner's Guide To Radiofacsimile Weather Charts by Dr. Joseph M. Bishop; Alden Electronic & Impulse Recording Equipment Company, Alden Research Center, Westborough, Massachusetts 01581.

Owner Repair Of Radio Equipment by Frank W. Glass; Los Gatos, California 95030.

Marine Electrical Practice by G. O. Watson; Butterworth & Company, Borough Green, Sevenoaks, Kent TN15 8PH England.

Marine Radiotelephone Users Handbook by the Radio Technical Commission for Marine Services; P. O. Box 19087, Washington, D.C. 20036.

How To Use Your VHF Radio—FCC Rules for Recreational Boaters; Part 83, Subpart CC; Superintendent of Documents, U.S. Government Printing Office, Washington, D.C. 20402.

The 12-Volt Doctor's Practical Handbook—For the Boat's Electric System; Spa Creek Instrument Co., 616 Third Street, Annapolis, Maryland 21403.

CHAPTER 14

Beating the Heat and Cold

A capital ship for an ocean trip
Was the Walloping Window Blind—
No gale that blew dismayed her crew
Or troubled the captain's mind.
The man at the wheel was taught to feel
Contempt for the wildest blow.
And often it appeared, when the weather had cleared,
That he'd been in his bunk below.

CHARLES EDWARD CARRYL

No matter where you live or cruise, temperatures rise and fall enough to require most sailors to manipulate the temperature inside the cabin of their boat. Unless you live year round in Tahiti, where the mean temperature, season to season, night to day, varies only about 20 degrees, heating and cooling devices, however simple, make life aboard more comfortable.

Exposure to extreme hot and cold temperatures is unhealthy, and the cruising sailor should equip and fit his boat with the climates of his cruising areas in mind. A healthy, rested crew is less likely to make the stupid kinds of mistakes that often result from decisions made under fatigue.

Depending on boat size, cruising area and climate, heating and cooling systems may be sophisticated and expensive or simple and less costly. Whatever the need, reasonable solutions are possible with a little effort and investment.

AIR CONDITIONING

During the winter of 1981, I went sailing with friends on a plush C&C Landfall 48 out of Port O'Connor, on the Texas Gulf Coast. One day it would be hot, and Jon Reeves, the skipper, would turn on the air conditioning. The next day a Blue Norther would blast down from Oklahoma and we'd run the heater every few hours to stay warm.

These operations were carried out by pushing buttons and flicking switches—as simple as keeping cool or warm at home. In reality, heating and air conditioning on boats is probably more complicated than in houses, if only for the reason that cramped spaces make installation and maintenance more difficult.

Large marine air conditioners require 115-volt or 240-volt electrical power, obtained at the dock, or from the ship's auxiliary generator. No juice, no air conditioning. Obviously, the first consideration in adding air conditioning is whether sufficient time will be spent at docks to make the expense worthwhile, and/or whether you have the space and money to invest in a diesel-fueled auxiliary generator. Using the main engine for this purpose, in my opinion, results in more wear and tear than it's worth to a very important and expensive piece of machinery. If the answer to either question is "no", then skip the rest of this section and start reading "Simpler Solutions".

Aqua-Temp, Grunert, Marine Air Systems and Marine Development Corporation ("Cruisair") are four companies making air conditioning systems for yachts, and I would imagine that most of their business is fitting out power boats and only the largest sailing yachts.

Aqua-Temp markets a system that it says is advantageous because the boat does not need to be hauled for installation. Existing sea cocks are tapped for the raw water cooling intake and discharge hoses. Two sources of raw water are mentioned, the engine intake and head intake. Of the two, I'd opt for the head intake, because taking water off the engine intake—even if you're trying to be careful by not running the engine and air conditioning at the same time—always poses the potential danger of running the engine with the Y-valve closed.

All of the above-mentioned systems work similarly to galley refrigerators; that is, sea water is used to cool (remove heat from) Freon or another refrigerant gas in a condenser and an evaporator/blower is used to get rid of the heat and provide cool air through the ducts and vents.

Cruisair™ components are self-contained and are precharged with Freon so they don't require charging in the field.

Before purchasing a system, consult the manufacturer for the number of BTUs required to cool and heat your cabin space. Large yachts may require more than one unit, or at least a larger than normal condenser with several remote evaporator units. The Marine Development Corporation has a chart to help determine the BTU capacity necessary to cool a given cabin space (Figure 14-1).

HEATING

For about 15 percent extra cost, most air conditioners may be fitted with heating coils and pumps to provide heat as well as air conditioning. However, the Cruisair people warn that heat pumps don't work very well in waters "much less than 38°F". For winter liveaboards in northern regions, kerosene and diesel heaters are probably a better idea.

The Complete Live-Aboard Book by Katy Burke has an excellent chapter on heating. In it she gives another formula for determining BTUs: volume of cabin x climate factor = BTUs.

Volume is the cubic feet of space to be heated; the climate factor she gives as 10 for warm (Florida) climates, and 20 for northern (New England) climates. As an example, a cabin such as *Adriana*'s measures about 8' x 8' x 6' or 384 cubic feet. Newport, which is on an island surrounded by the relatively warm waters of Narragansett Bay, averages about 5 to 8 degrees warmer than the nearby mainland. Here we can use a climate factor of 15: 384 x 15 = 5,760 BTUs. This figure jibes fairly closely with the chart for air conditioning (8' x 8' cabin = 64 square feet; 5,000 BTUs).

BTUs REQUIRED TO COOL CABINS

CAPACITY BTU/HR	Below Deck Cabins		Mid Deck Cabins		Above Deck Cabins	
	Square Feet	Square Meters	Square Feet	Square Meters	Square Feet	Square Meters
5,000	70	6.5	50	4.5	35	3.2
7,000	100	9.5	75	7.0	50	4.5
10,000	140	13.0	100	9.5	70	6.5
12,000	200	18.5	150	14.0	100	9.5
16,000	270	25.0	200	18.5	135	12.5
20,000	338	31.2	250	23.3	167	15.8
24,000	405	37.0	300	28.0	200	19.0
30,000	500	46.2	375	35.0	250	23.7
36,000	600	55.5	450	42.0	300	28.5
48,000	800	74.0	600	56.0	400	38.0

Fig. 14-1 *This table, which gives an approximate number of BTUs necessary to heat different size cabins, was prepared by the Marine Development Corporation.*

Fig. 14-2 *The Wallas-Thermotron kerosene bulkhead heater with fan (Viking Leisure Products)*

Notice that the figures for my cabin don't include the head or forward cabin. To heat those areas, while not as important, almost doubles the space and BTUs. Convection or radiant-type heaters won't circulate air efficiently from one cabin to the next, so more than one outlet is necessary for an even distribution of heat. Forced-air heaters do a much better job, and on a small boat such as mine, a small electric heater in the main cabin pushes enough air into the forward cabin to keep it moderately comfortable. But then I spend winters at the dock, where I have access to shore power.

The best heating system for boats on the go, especially those not large enough to carry an auxiliary generator and those in near-freezing waters, are heaters using kerosene or diesel fuel. Wallas-Thermotron is a Swedish outfit that makes a very nice, quiet, kerosene-fueled cabin heater that mounts on a bulkhead or in a lazarette (Figure 14-2). A combination intake/outtake pipe must be run through the cabin roof.

Outside air is sucked in, heated by a kerosene burner, and a fan blows the warm air into the cabin.

Several ducts may be led to different cabins. The fan runs off 12 volts and, depending on model, draws between 1.5 and 2.5 amps. A gallon of fuel lasts between 11 and 22 hours. Obviously, the larger the tank the less often filling will be necessary. A five-gallon jerry jug could be strapped into a seat locker. Or a larger permanent fiberglass tank can be fabricated for installation in the cabin, under the cockpit or on deck.

Kerosene (called parrafin in Great Britain) is one of the most universally available fuels. If you've chosen it for cooking, you also may decide to use it for heating as well. More than likely you'll already have kerosene lighting on board, and the fewer fuels carried, the simpler your task of procuring fuel, stowing it and keeping spare parts.

A permanent gravity feed system as pictured in Figure 14-3 can be filled through the same sort of deck fill used for water and engine fuel —just be certain the fill is labeled correctly! A tank vent tube is necessary and this may be routed through the deck or inside the cabin (Figure 5-6, Chapter 5).

Fig. 14-3 *A basic, gravity-feed kerosene storage system*

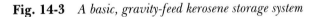
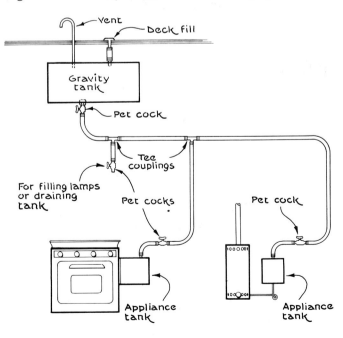

Nylon hose can be used to run kerosene from the gravity feed "header" tank to the stove and heater tanks as can copper tubing and some types of PVC (other types can become brittle after prolonged contact with kerosene). Each tank should have a positive action valve, such as an in-line ball-valve. It's also handy to have a tap for filling lamps (use rigid tubing, not nylon); this is much less messy than pouring kerosene from a portable tank.

The tank end of the outlet pipe inside the fiberglass or stainless steel tank should *protude up an inch* from the bottom so that sediment doesn't reach the stove and heater burners. Otherwise, install a filter in the system. Figure 14-4 diagrams a slightly more sophisticated system, not only with a filter, but with a large main tank and pump to fill the day tank, which in turn feeds the stove and heater by gravity. A couple living aboard in a warm climate might expect to use about a gallon of kerosene each week for the stove/oven and cabin lamps. A 30-day supply could be contained in a five-gallon gravity feed tank; obviously a larger main tank, such as pictured in Figure 14-4, with a 20 to 30-gallon capacity, would give several months of fuel, though less in colder climates with a heater running.

Espar makes heaters similar to the Wallas-Thermotron that run off gasoline, kerosene and diesel. They look more like a vacuum cleaner and are quite compact (Figure 14–5). During *Adriana*'s first winter in Newport, a neighbor on a Southern Cross 28 installed an Espar diesel heating system in his boat. Even when we were iced in, Charlie reported that he and his wife were quite comfortable. To save fuel, he didn't run the heater all day when they were at work, but it ran in the evenings and on weekends. At night they turned it off, relying on their Airex-cored hull to retain the warmth a few hours, and on their electric blanket when sleeping. Before getting up each morning, Charlie hopped out of bed to turn on the heater for 15 minutes, then back to bed until things warmed up. He reported no problems with the heater and fuel costs were affordable.

Like the Wallas-Thermotron, the Espar fan is 12-volt or 24-volt, and ranges from 40 to 220 watts, depending on the model. Fuel consumption ranges from 20 hours per gallon for the smallest gasoline model, to six hours per gallon for the largest diesel model.

These systems are highly efficient and not all that difficult to install, though a few days of planning and work are indicated.

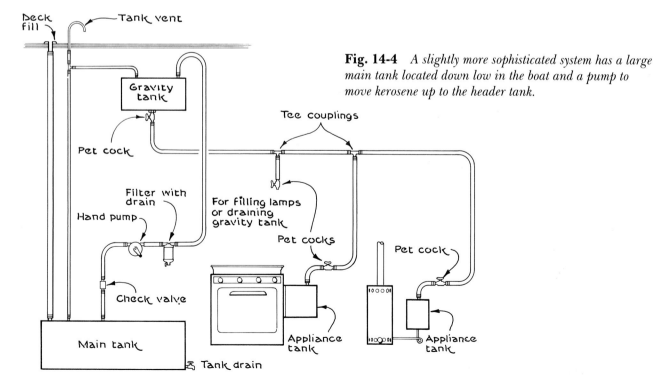

Fig. 14-4 *A slightly more sophisticated system has a large main tank located down low in the boat and a pump to move kerosene up to the header tank.*

Fig. 14-5 *An Espar diesel heater with fan; the company also makes gas and kerosene models.*

climates where heaters and float coats just aren't necessary. This is the simplest way to beat the cold. Danny Greene spends summers in Newport (May to September) and winters in the Caribbean. There's a whole flock of migrating sailors like him, but even they are subject to shivering cold and perspiring heat while tarrying on the Chesapeake to watch the birds, or enjoying decent sailing winds and secluded anchorages. And at night, some small source of heat is always appreciated.

The intake and/or exhaust pipe through the cabin roof must be drilled with a hole saw. The core material—end-grain balsa or plywood—should be sealed with epoxy or carved out and filled with epoxy resin thickened with chopped strand (see Figure 4-7, Chapter 4).

Wires should be led to an extra circuit on the distribution panel (see Chapter 13). Both Wallas-Thermotron and Espar heaters require no special insulation on the mounting surface, as do most solid-fuel heaters. Some typical installations for either type are shown in Figure 14-6.

SIMPLER SOLUTIONS

There's a line in the Harry Nilsson theme song from the movie *Midnight Cowboy*, that says, "Going where the weather suits my clothes." I've always taken this to recommend living in tropical

Small Cabin Heaters

When cooking, the stove puts off a bit of heat, but this is a very inefficient way to warm the cabin, and expensive when compared with most other methods. The usual trick is to put a clay pot on top of the stove to radiate heat.

The next most primitive method is to rely on the kerosene cabin lamps. The conventional wick-type lamps and barnyard lanterns don't put out much heat, but the Alladin mantle kerosene lamps do. On summer nights in Newport, which typically are cool, my bulkhead-mounted Alladin lamp gives off sufficient heat to warm *Adriana*'s cabin. When it is warmer the Alladin is sometimes too hot to use, and so I reluctantly resort to the inferior quality of 12-volt electrical lighting.

For a bit more heat than lamps and stoves, consider a floor or bulkhead-mounted cabin heater using solid or liquid fuel. Ratelco and

Fig. 14-6 *This drawing shows one possible installation of forced-air kerosene or diesel heaters.*

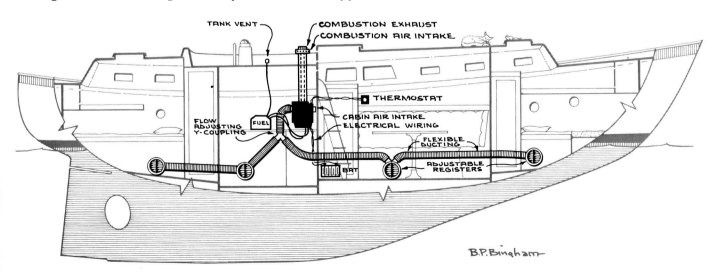

Shipmate manufacture small stoves that burn wood, coal or charcoal briquets. The former is lightweight stainless steel weighing 10 pounds, the latter is heavy cast iron and weighs 38 pounds. As a permanent heating source, solid fuel stoves aren't very practical because of the amount of fuel that must be stowed.

David Markell's Pearson Vanguard has a Tiny Tot wood/coal burning stove mounted in the port quarter area (Figure 14-7), where there used to be a quarter berth. The berth was removed and a bulkhead installed separating the main cabin from the under cockpit area. A navigation station was fitted outboard, using the engine box as a seat. The stove is mounted against the new bulkhead. A coal bin under the cockpit is filled from the deck (Figure 14-8), ushering coal to a small hinged bin, accessible through a trap door next to the stove. It's a clever arrangement and does the trick in removing the chill from the air when Dave's cruising Rhode Island Sound and the Elizabeth Islands. Heat from the smoke pipe is reflected by stainless steel plates on the cabin bulkhead, and smoke and fumes are exhausted through a Charlie Noble on deck (Figure 14-9).

Fig. 14-7 *This Pearson Vanguard has a Tiny Tot coal/wood stove under the bridge deck. Notice the coal bin at bottom.*

Fig. 14-9 *The Tiny Tot's deck exhaust, popularly known as a Charlie Noble.*

Fig. 14-8 *A deck-loading coal bin in the Vanguard's cockpit.*

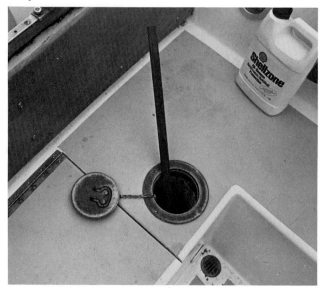

Increases in the cost of energy in recent years have prompted many homeowners to purchase portable kerosene heaters. These have been in use aboard boats for years, most notably in England where the Alladin floor heater is quite popular (Figure 14-10). I use one on *Adriana* during the winter, but there's little floor space for it. A bulkhead heater would certainly be more suitable. Also, these portable kerosene heaters *must* be vented, such as cracking the main hatch an inch or so, in order to get rid of dangerous carbon monoxide fumes.

However, I *never* go to sleep with an open flame burning of any kind. My daughter and I once went to sleep with an alcohol heater burning softly between our bunks. During the night, Adria kicked off one of her blankets and it fell on top of the heater. I began dreaming of fire,

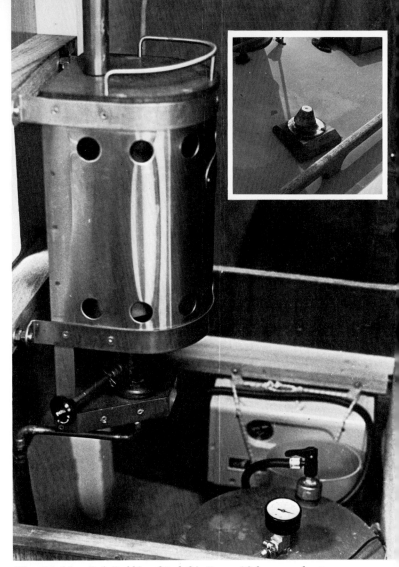

Fig. 14-11 *Bob Dobbins fitted this Force 10 kerosene heater, rated at 6,000 to 9,000 BTUs inside his hanging locker; the fuel tank is beneath, and on deck there's a small vent.*

Fig. 14-10 *An Alladin portable kerosene heater. It does not have a thru-deck exhaust, so it must be vented by cracking open a hatch for fumes to escape.*

awoke in the middle of the night unable to breathe, and with the cabin full of smoke. Only quickly tossing the blanket and Adria out into the cockpit saved us from certain suffocation.

Bob Dobbins, who lives aboard a Triton in Bristol, Rhode Island, installed a Force 10 diesel heater in his hanging locker (Figure 14-11). A separate 10-gallon fuel tank is sold as an option. But Bob had a small auxiliary diesel tank already installed for the stove/oven, which he tapped to supply fuel to his new heater. The burner is a modification of the standard Primus burner, and according to Bob, works quite well, though it requires regular cleaning. And because there is no fan to spread the heat, he does need to supplement the Force 10 with an electric heater when the temperature dips into the 20's. It is rated at 6,000 to 9,000 BTUs, and is vented through the cabin roof, so hatches can be kept

Fig. 14-12 *The Chesapeake diesel heater by Dickinson is mounted on a bulkhead and can run on briquets, wood and coal.*

closed. The popular Dickinson line of drip-feed diesel heaters are another alternative to bulkhead-mounted heating (Figure 14-12).

A small 12-volt cabin fan helps circulate warm air throughout the boat. Most solid and less expensive liquid fuel heaters do not have fans to push air around, and this limits heating to the immediate area. If the heater doesn't have an internal fan, an external fan can be used for cooling in summer as well.

Opening Ports

Keeping the cabin cool in summer is easier and much less costly than heating it in winter. Good cross-ventilation is a starting point. It amazes me that more boats aren't equipped with opening ports to help accomplish this. A major reason is the cost-cutting measures of boatbuilders. When opening ports are installed, they often are of the cheap, plastic variety.

Fortunately, *Adriana* has six opening ports—two in the forward cabin, one each in the head and hanging locker/vanity, and two facing forward on the riser of the main cabin roof. These last two are of immense value because when lying to anchor, the wind blows straight through them.

Portlights aren't too expensive to purchase and install yourself. I'd opt for bronze ports, such as those available from Spartan Marine, the gear-manufacturing arm of Cape Dory in East Taunton, Massachusetts. They're a bit more expensive, but much stronger and certainly better looking.

A new opening port can be installed where no present port exists or, if the opening port is larger than an existing fixed port, the old one can be removed and an opening one put in its place (Figure 14-3).

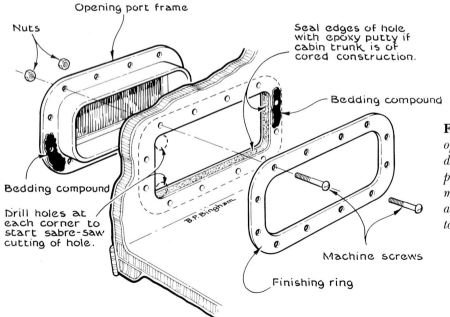

Fig. 14-13 *If you can substitute opening ports for fixed ports without dangerously increasing the size of the port, make a template of the new port, mark it on the cabin and cut out with a saber saw. Use a bedding compound to prevent leaks.*

If the port doesn't come with a template to mark the size hole to be cut, make one out of cardboard. Use a pencil to mark the outline and then drill pilot holes large enough to accept a saber saw blade.

Small cutting errors of ⅛-inch or so can be covered by the port flanges. Be sure to seal off any core material as described earlier in this chapter and in Chapter 4. Use a good quality bedding compound to prevent leaking around the port—surely the most common source of leaks. When the screws are tightened, the compound should ooze out everywhere. Don't worry, it can be cut away later. Rainhoods keep rain out when you want the port open for ventilation (Figure 14-14). You can form your own by heating thin sheets of Plexiglas with a torch. Simple windscoops can be cut from Clorox bottles or any other plastic container that can be jammed into a port. The open end should face into the cabin; outside, on the forward side of the container, cut a large hole to funnel the wind.

Thought might also be given to fitting larger ports with storm plates that can be quickly and easily fastened with machine screws (Figure 9-56, Chapter 9).

Adding two or four-way opening hatches also aids ventilation. The forward cabin hatch can be modified in this manner (Figure 9-18, Chapter 9), or, if there is sufficient room between the main hatch and mast, an extra hatch can be placed in the ceiling of the main cabin.

Fig. 14-14 *Port covers, such as this plastic one by Sailing Specialities, Inc., keeps rain out when the port is open.*

Several items can be fabricated from canvas that improve cabin coolness. None are very difficult to make, and each will improve your handiness with a needle and thread.

Awnings

A cockpit awning keeps the cockpit and cabin cool. We made one for *Adriana* using white Dacron sailcloth, though a UV-treated cloth will last longer. Measure the distance from the mast to the end of the boom, or, if you're willing to be a little fancy, to the stern of the boat.

Everyone seems to have their favorite method of supporting awnings, and I've found PVC tubing to be ideal. It's lightweight, doesn't rust, cheap, and bends to form a very attractive dome over the cockpit area. The lower sides keep more sun and rain out than flat awnings. Extending the awning to the mast might seem unnecessary, but shading the cabin top lowers temperatures inside. And when it rains, the extra length usually keeps the cockpit dry. While you're at it, you might consider a rainwater catchment system in your awning. (See also Figure 9-31, Chapter 9.)

Wind Scoops

Wind scoops funnel air into hatches quite efficiently, especially at anchor. Incidentally, one of the best ways to keep cool and avoid bugs is to stay away from shore as much as possible. In hot weather, it's always more comfortable at anchor than at a dock.

The familiar, brightly colored Windscoop™ marketed by Pastime Products is well worth its modest price. However, if you'd like to make your own, there are easy patterns available. A four-sided scoop was made for me by Anne Correll, a costume maker at the University of Windsor. The advantage of her design is that it works without adjustment even at the dock when the direction of wind changes.

Dodgers and Biminis

A cockpit dodger gives protection against wind and spray when it's cold, and shields two

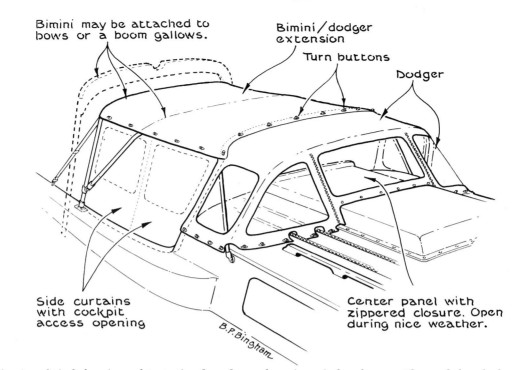

Bimini may be attached to bows or a boom gallows.

Bimini/dodger extension

Turn buttons

Dodger

Side curtains with cockpit access opening

B.P.Bingham

Center panel with zippered closure. Open during nice weather.

Fig. 14-15 *A cockpit dodger is good protection from forward-coming wind and water. If extended to the boom gallows, it also can function as a bimini.*

corners of the cockpit from the sun on hotter days.

Dodgers can be installed by professional canvas makers for about $500, including the aluminum or stainless steel tubing, snap fasteners and canvas work. Sailrite sells a dodger kit for under $200, and would make a good introductory project to canvas making—a worthwhile skill for the cruising man or woman.

If the boat is fitted with boom gallows, the dodger may be extended aft over the cockpit and function as a bimini as well (Figure 14-15). In inclement weather, side curtains allow the cockpit to be used as a sort of bastardized porch, though they should probably be taken down when sailing as they impair visibility and won't hold up in higher winds.

In the tropics, a bimini minimizes exposure to the torrid sun and to unnecessary exposure from ultraviolet rays. Bright, hot sun not only ages your skin, but tires the crew more rapidly. In contrast to the sunbathing mania, people living in the equatorial regions generally wear more clothing than we do and avoid standing in the sun when possible.

Hull Color

As everyone knows, light colors are cooler than dark colors because they reflect rather than

absorb the sun's rays. White decks, however, cause glare that can be hard on your eyes. Painting the decks (Chapter 15) with a light grey or green substantially reduces glare while making little difference to temperatures inside the cabin.

Insulation

Heating or cooling the cabin is one thing, but keeping it that way is quite another. The answer is insulating the hull. Some of the newer fiberglass boats use Airex or Klegecell foam cores, which in effect adds an insulating layer between the inner and outer layers of fiberglass. Condensation is virtually eliminated, and heat and cold are preserved long after the temperature has changed.

Styrofoam™ is one of the first materials people think of when the subject of insulation arises. There are three difficulties with it, however: it is rigid and does not conform well to the shape of the hull; it is brittle and must be covered with something to prevent it from chipping away; and if it ever burns, toxic fumes are given off.

Urethane foam works well—two inches of it would turn the hull into a Thermos. However, it is expensive. *Cruising World* contributor Michel Savage used a product called Ethafoam in his Westsail 32 ("Install Your Own Insulation",

Cruising World, December, 1982). The Ethafoam is rated at R-2.5, which is not as good an insulating factor as some other products, but definitely better than none at all. And, it is only ½-inch thick, so it is not difficult to work with. It comes in rolls five feet by 25 feet, and reportedly has good compression resistance.

Savage cut the expanded polyethylene foam with an X-Acto knife and glued it in place with Flintkote 200-32. Both the hull side and foam must be coated for good adhesion. "Don't kid yourself," he wrote, "it sounds simple but this job is extremely messy. You may have to dismantle wall panelings or ceilings." A small electric heater to remove moisture from the cabin helps achieve a good bond.

Don Lakenmacher, also using a material from the home building industry, ("Consider a Radar-Reflective Material," *Cruising World,* December, 1982), used a foil-clad polystyrene product called Texcon Reflecto-Foam with an R factor of 5.9. It is ¾-inch thick. A major reason for his choice was that the material is radar-reflective. His assumption is that he has turned his entire hull into a radar-reflective surface that large ships will easily spot on their radars. Contact cement was used to adhere it to the hull. But always check with the manufacturer of your foam before buying glue. Contact cement, for example, will melt Styrofoam.

In the forepeak and under cockpit areas, exposed foam poses no real aesthetic problem. But in the living quarters, you'll probably want to cover it with something—contact paper, paint or wood. A wood ceiling as described in Chapter 3, with foam glued to the hull, would look very attractive (Figure 14-16).

There is much to be said for insulation, but there is a down side, too. If the backing nuts and plates of thru-deck fittings are covered, gaining access to them will require removing the insulation and possibly ruining your beautiful job. If water does ingress through leaky thru-deck bolts, closed-cell foam will not allow the water to migrate throughout the material. But if the glue hasn't bonded the foam to the hull absolutely everywhere, there could be room for water and condensation to collect.

The previous owner of *Adriana* installed indoor/outdoor carpeting on the hull sides of the forward cabin. This has a rubber backing and does possess some insulating properties. But if it should ever become wet, it might never dry. The ensuing odor could be disagreeable. Luckily, this hasn't been the case—so far.

Howard Chapelle, the late marine historian of the Smithsonian Institute in Washington, D.C., once wrote, "exposed piping in a boat is a seamanlike feature." The same could be said for

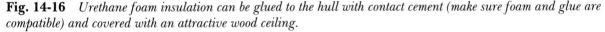

Fig. 14-16 *Urethane foam insulation can be glued to the hull with contact cement (make sure foam and glue are compatible) and covered with an attractive wood ceiling.*

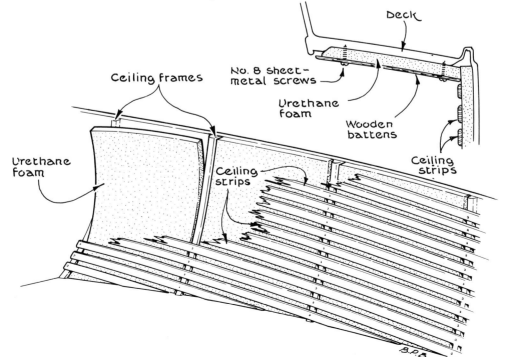

wiring, deck fittings, etc. The easier you can get to something, the quicker you can isolate the cause of a problem and fix it. On today's new boats you're supposed to be impressed if no part of the hull is visible. I remain skeptical.

SUMMARY

People who sail learn to adapt and find comfortable a greater range of temperatures and weather conditions than people who live on land. Nonetheless, for comfort and health, the cruising boat should have on board some methods of heating and cooling, whether sophisticated fuel-powered devices, simple awnings to shade the cockpit and cabin or insulation to retain warmth. After all, the idea is to have fun, not test the limits of your physical endurance.

- Kerosene and diesel-fueled heaters are fairly efficient, the fuel is almost universally available, and installation is simpler than large marine heating systems.

- In cold climates, radiant heat often won't warm the entire boat; a fan of some sort is recommended to circulate warm air.

- Opening ports generally provide better ventilation than deck opening hatches, and screens keep out the bugs.

- A dodger offers valuable protection against wind and spray.

- A hull cored with foam (e.g. Airex, Klegecell) has better insulating properties than a wood, steel or solid fiberglass hull. Insulation is almost always added to the insides of steel and aluminum boats, never to wood (potential for dry rot is enhanced), and more commonly to solid fiberglass hulls now that thin, closed-cell urethane foams are available.

FURTHER READING

Boat Canvas From Cover To Cover by Bob & Karen Lipe; Seven Seas Press, 524 Thames Street, Newport, Rhode Island 02840.
Canvas Worker's Library by James L. Grant; Sailrite Enterprises, Route 1, Columbia City, Indiana 46725.
The Complete Live-aboard Book by Katy Burke; Seven Seas Press, 524 Thames Street, Newport, Rhode Island 02840.
Air Conditioning: Home and Commercial by Edwin P. Anderson and Roland E. Palmquist; Theodore Audel & Company, 4300 West 62nd Street, Indianapolis, Indiana 46268.

CHAPTER 15

Painting and Varnishing

Painting, n. The art of protecting flat surfaces from the weather and exposing them to the critic.

AMBROSE BIERCE

Boats of almost any material—fiberglass, wood, steel and aluminum—can benefit from protective coatings of paint. While rig and gear may represent more than half the cost of the vessel, the hull and deck comprise the boat in itself, and ultimately are the most costly and difficult to replace or repair.

Most production fiberglass boats are laid up in a mold that is first covered with a polyester resin gel coat. This is the hard shiny surface you see on the exterior of the hull. Gel coat is usually about 18 to 22 millimeters thick and can be waxed and buffed to protect it from the sun's ultra-violet rays and to maintain an attractive high-gloss finish.

Conventional isophthalic (ultra-violet resistant) gel coats have suffered some because of their brittleness. This is most evident where voids or air pockets exist between the gel coat and the first layers of fiberglass mat.

As the air inside expands and contracts, blistering can occur. Or, if water migrates through the gel coat (yes, it is slightly porous) to the void, blistering also occurs. Some advances in gel coat technology have been made by modifying thixotropic polyester coatings ("thixotropic" means that additives to the gel coat or paint have given it more body and an ability to be applied more thickly) with urethane and increasing film thicknesses to 40 to 50 millimeters. As yet, however, the results of these studies have yet to find their way into the boatbuilder's yard.

These problems aside, gel coats, especially dark colors, eventually chalk and fade. At some point in the life of a fiberglass boat, refinishing the hull surface becomes necessary. Re-gelcoating is possible, though probably beyond the skills and equipment of most do-it-yourselfers.

With the advent of the new copolymer paints such as Awlgrip®, Interthane® and Imron®, a new finish can be applied to the hull's surface by anyone willing to do the surface preparation and follow the manufacturer's instructions in applying the paint. In fact, some boatbuilders such as Hatteras have now dispensed with gel coats altogether in favor of copolymer paints.

Wood boats require repainting every several years, depending on the quality of the initial paint job, environment, working of the hull and degree of abuse. The initial coatings may be repairable or coverable with a minimum of surface preparation for a period of years. But at some point, the hull will have to be taken down to bare wood and fresh, fault-free coatings applied.

Steel and iron rust very quickly exposed to salt water and oxygen, and rely almost entirely on surface coatings for protection against corrosion. The Dutch have been building steel sailboats for more than a hundred years—many of them are still afloat—and while the old paint systems did the job with conscientious application and maintenance, new developments in the chemistry of painting can mean almost indefinite lifespans for steel boats—shotblasting, zinc undercoats and two-part linear polyurethane paints. Chlorinated rubber paints have also been used with some success as have aliphatictars.

Aluminum can be left uncoated without immediate concern for the integrity of the hull. Many of the so-called French "escape machines" are simply the strongest, most maintenance-free hulls available—hard-chined bare aluminum. After all, there are literally thousands of masts and booms made of aluminum out there doing just fine—some with paint, some anodized, and some just bare aluminum. However, aluminum is subject to an oxidizing film when exposed to oxygen in air or water. The result is minor pitting corrosion, which is arrested as the film covers the surface; clean the surface and the pitting begins anew. Painting eliminates any sort of corrosion or oxidizing film, and gives a better appearance.

Even in this fast-paced, high-tech world besieged by new wonder materials such as Kevlar, Mylar, and carbon fibers, there is still a place for good old-fashioned painting. And if you get right down to the chemistry of today's paints, you'll find them just as much a part of the space age.

BOTTOM PAINTING

Antifouling paints are made from two basic ingredients: 1) a binder or matrix that is durable enough to hold the biocide (antifoulant chemical) for the life of the paint, yet release it at a controllable rate over a period of time, and 2) a biocide that has sufficient toxicity to control fouling of the bottom (Figure 15-1). In formulating the paint, it is primarily the choice of a proper binder system and biocide that determines the quality of an antifouling paint.

There are three principal types of antifouling paints used today: 1) soluble matrix in which the binder literally dissolves over a period of time, releasing the biocide (usually cuprous oxide) as it goes; 2) diffusion-type organo-tin, in which the biocide diffuses through the binder, killing organisms as it reaches the surface; and 3) copolymer, using either copper or tin, mostly with acrylic binders, that are united (copolymerized) by means of a chemical reaction in which the molecules of each ingredient are cross-linked.

Each type has its pros and cons (Figure 15-2). Soluble matrix paints are fairly effective and inexpensive, yet can't be used on aluminum hulls; diffusion-type organo-tin paints perform well in fresh water—not as well in salt water—and don't set up glavanic cells on aluminum hulls; and copolymer paints, while expensive, have a straight-line release rate, meaning that as long as there's any paint on the bottom, the biocide will be just as effective as when it was new.

Today, there is little doubt that the copolymer bottom paints made by Interlux, Petit and others are the most effective for most boats in most areas. But much depends on the type of use a boat receives, where it is sailed, and how much of the year it is in the water. For the weekend summer sailor who doesn't race, soluble matrix and organo-tin paints may be the most cost effective. If some of these words like organ-tin and copolymer sound incomprehensible, ask your paint salesman to show you a spec sheet or brochure on the product you're considering. The chemical composition of the paint by volume, will be listed.

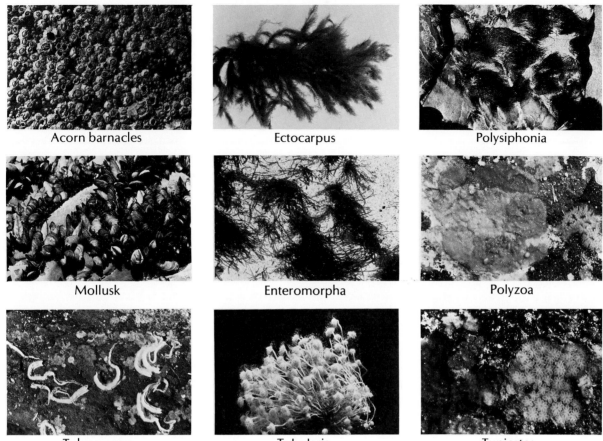

Fig. 15-1   *Common fouling organisms in saltwater (Interlux Yacht Finishes)*

Fig. 15-2   *Characteristics of different antifouling paints (Robert Wilkinson)*

	Soluble Matrix Type	Diffusion Type	Copolymer Type
Surface Condition (After prolonged use)	Rough	Smooth	Smoothest
Service Life	6 months to 2 years depending upon biocide level release rate.	Approximately 1 year. 2 years + possible.	Usually dependent upon film thickness. 4 years + possible.
Cost	Cheap to expensive.	Usually more expensive than soluble matrix type.	Most expensive.
Color Range	Limited to dull, dirty colors.	Very clean, even pastel shades possible.	Depends upon use of co-biocide. Color range can be clean to dirty, dull colors.
Compatible Solvent	Mineral spirits, aromatic solvents and ketones. Depends on modifying resin.	Ketones and/or aromatic solvent.	Hi *Flash* aromatic solvents and/or xylol.
Current Binder Systems	Rosin always present. Rosin may be modified with ester gum, vegetable oils, epoxy ester, vinyl, chlorinated rubber, etc.	Usually vinyl rosin or acrylic.	State of present art is arcylic, but may be other type in future.
Market Popularity	General use. Used on all substrates except aluminum. Has potential to set up galvanic cell on dissimilar metals.	Popular with sailboat racing enthusiasts. Recommended for freshwater as an anti-fouling paint. Safe to use on aluminum hulls. Wide range of colors possible.	Multi-seasonal paints. Excellent antifouling performance. Favorite of professional sailboat racers. Excellent film integrity.

Surface Preparation

As with most other paint jobs, a good-looking, effective coating of antifouling paint depends to a large extent on surface preparation.

Some types of bottom paints aren't compatible with others (i.e. vinyls and non-vinyls), so it is wise to be sure what type of new paint you intend to apply to the old surface before sanding. If the two paints aren't compatible, it may be necessary to take the surface coatings down to the bare hull or to use a tie coat that is compatible and bonds well to both the old and new paint. If they are compatible, cleaning and roughing up the surface may be all that's required.

If taking a hull down to the bare substrate, a power tool such as a grinder (Figure 15-3) is quicker than hand-sanding. Fitting a foam pad between the disc and sandpaper helps in preventing gouges from using too much force or using sandpaper that is too coarse. Home power drills also can be used, but generally aren't built to stand up to the constant non-stop, high-speed use necessary over large surface areas. Orbital and vibrating sanders may be used to clean and rough up old paint, but are too slow in removing entire coatings. Belt sanders should never be used as they are capable of removing a great deal of material in a hurry, and it is very difficult to prevent cutting lines in the hull with them.

On power grinders, try to avoid grit size coarser than about #100 to #120. Eighty-grit will do the job faster, but unless you are ex-

Fig. 15-3 *A grinder, with a foam pad inserted between the disc and sandpaper, helps prevent gouging the hull. This paper is glued to the pad with a special type cement that allows peeling off the paper when it gets clogged.*

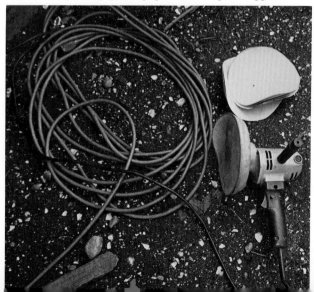

tremely conscientious, you run the risk, with a momentary lapse in concentration, of gouging the hull. If you're not taking the hull down to bare substrate, hand sanding is a reasonable alternative. There is no danger of damaging the hull, there's less obnoxious dust to breathe and, if you're in a pleasant country boatyard where the fruit trees blossom and the birds sing, you don't have to listen to a whining motor.

I prefer wet sanding fiberglass hulls rather than using dry sandpaper. There aren't any particles of paint in the air to breathe (the copper tastes sweet and suspiciously unhealthy in your mouth), the sandpaper doesn't clog as fast, and it seems that you get a smoother surface than with dry sandpaper. I fill a plastic bucket with fresh water, put #120 grit sandpaper on a rubber block that conforms nicely to the hand and hull, and use a sponge in my left hand to occasionally clean the hull where I've been sanding and to clean the sandpaper when it loads up. Both are dunked in the bucket every five or six strokes for cleaning. With the hull wet, it's sometimes difficult to see where you've sanded, so you learn to use your fingertips to identify unsanded areas. When done, hose down the entire underbody and when dry, inspect both visually and by touch for areas you might have missed.

The bottom of the keel is often dented or gouged from those inevitable groundings, and if severe, I usually fill them up with Marine-Tex. This is a white two-part compound that trowels in nicely with a putty knife. When hardened—usually within a few hours—I sand with a grinder, or if the area is inaccessible, with a coarse file and then sandpaper. A sanding block *always* insures more even pressure on the surface and therefore a smoother, more uniform finish.

Also, take the opportunity at this time to inspect all thru-hulls and transducers to make certain they are still well bedded. If you've had minor leaking around one, or if the compound seems to have worn away, either remove the thru-hull and rebed (if the problem is serious) or sand all the paint from the surface around the fitting and squeeze in a good bedding compound such as polysulfide or Life Caulk. Smooth the compound around the fitting and scrape off the excess. If it looks messy, wait until it's hardened to sand or cut smooth.

Paint Application

Before painting, wipe down the hull with the paint manufacturer's recommended prewash solution, thinner or solvent. If in doubt, an acetone-soaked cloth usually works fine. Not only does this clean the hull of dust and other impurities, but it also softens the old paint for better adhesion to the new coat.

Use masking tape (Scotch "Fine-Line" works best) to mark the line between the bottom and boot. With the roll of tape in one hand, unroll it as the other hand presses the tape into place. Unroll about a foot at a time to help determine a straight line and to speed up the job. Be sure to run your finger along the edge to be painted to ensure good adhesion of the tape, thus preventing paint from getting underneath.

I usually paint bottoms with a roller, hitting hard-to-get-at places with a throw-away brush (they're hard to clean well enough for use topsides later, and since you don't really care if a few bristles fall out, why waste the money on an expensive camel hair brush?).

Soluble matrix paints may require just one coat if there's a base underneath of old paint; organo-tin and copolymer paints depend on film thickness to work effectively and so two coats are generally better than one. In fact, Interlux suggests two coats of Micron 33 (the brushable version of Micron 22, the first copolymer antifouling paint), each a different color, so that when you next haul out, you can gauge the amount of paint left on the hull. Because hydrolysis and the speed of passing water are major factors in the release of some copolymer paints, you may find that some areas of the hull expose the undercoating, while other areas still show the topcoat.

When done painting, remove the masking tape the same day, even while the paint is wet. Failure to do so will probably result in some of the tape sticking to the hull. While it can be removed with lighter fluid or alcohol, it's an unnecessary job.

Aluminum and steel bottoms require special protection. Common practice is to sandblast first. Steel bottoms can then be sprayed with an epoxy lead paint; Interlux recommends following with several coats of Intergard Mastic Black

4413/4414. A primer is then applied as well as an additional coat of 4413/4414 and another coat of primer. Then two coats of the desired bottom paint finish the job. The procedure is similar for aluminum bottoms, but always be sure to read manufacturer's instructions and use the products recommended in the sequence and manner suggested. Remember that bottom paints using copper as a biocide should not be used on aluminum hulls due to electrolytic action. For the same reason, zinc paints are never used underwater.

Let the bottom dry for a day before taping off the boot stripe; this prevents the tape from peeling off the bottom paint when it's removed. Sand the boot stripe area. A hard antifouling paint keeps the boot cleaner than an enamel. If your cruising gear and stores have lowered the waterline, now's the time to raise the boot a few inches. If necessary, use a ruler to periodically measure the distance between the old waterline and the tape.

With the possible exception of the new copolymer bottom paints, most paints will necessitate hauling the boat at least once each year for sanding and painting. Again, frequency is determined by the quality of the paint job, effectiveness of the biocide in the waters being sailed, how much time is spent under way versus sitting at anchor in dirty harbors, etc.

For many cruising people, these haulouts and servicings are major expenses that must be planned with a degree of care and forethought. If you can't reach a suitable port with adequate haulout facilities, you may be faced with careening the boat or letting her dry on a tide so you can sand and paint before the tide comes back in. The easiest do-it-yourself method is probably drying out along a pier or wall (Figure 15-4). Check the tide tables for those days with the maximum rise and fall, but be certain there will be enough water to float you off when done— you could find yourself stranded for the next four weeks!

Inspect the bottom where you expect your keel to touch. Is it hard enough? If there are obstacles, don a face mask and snorkle to aid in your vision and breathing and clear them first. When you've determined the day, hour and exact location, rig a sturdy fender board over

Fig. 15-4 *An economical haulout can be accomplished by positioning the boat next to a wall as the tide goes out, or by supporting the hull on both sides with timbers. This big ketch did the trick in a corner of Newport Harbor. (Steve Krous photo).*

two tough fenders and add a stout line to a masthead halyard for inclining the boat slightly towards the pier or wall. The line can be led to an anchor sunk into the adjacent land. Take up on the line with the mast winch as the boat settles. Have ready additional fenders, cushions and whatever else seems necessary to shove in between the pier and boat as it may be difficult to predict exactly how the two will meet. As the water recedes, start scraping barnacles and sanding with wet or dry sandpaper (don't use power tools standing in the water). You may not be able to do the absolute bottom of the keel effectively if the water doesn't completely expose the entire surface, but with a scraper and wet sandpaper, you can do a fair job. Be sure to allow time to paint the entire hull before the water rises again.

As long as you're working on the bottom, remember bare hulls covered with metal keels and centerboards, and old paints incompatible with the new coating may require barrier or tie coats before the new paint can be successfully applied. Check with the manufacturer of your chosen paint to be sure, and use the product he recommends. Once you select a paint, you're best advised to use his entire product line for such things as surfacing compounds, solvents and barrier coats as they are chemically designed as part of a unique system, and may not work with other brands of paints.

VARNISHES AND OILS

Keeping up with brightwork is a never-ending job, and while most persons won't argue the attractiveness of satin-finish coamings, toe rails and handrails, it can become burdensome for the cruiser on the go.

Nonlive-aboards and live-aboards who stay more or less in one area will probably have a different attitude toward varnishing than the itinerant cruiser on a tight budget. When cruising poor, hostile and Third World countries, nothing says, "rich American yacht" quite so much as sparkling brightwork. Former *Cruising World* managing editor Betsy Hitz wrote an August 1982 article, "Are Cruising Sailors Sitting Ducks?" after she and her companion were attacked in Bequia. "Even in an affluent nation like the U.S.," she wrote, "a yacht is erroneously thought to be a symbol of untold wealth, a toy of the idle rich. What must this same vessel represent to a man from Haiti, St. Vincent or Trinidad, whose annual income is less than the value of a winch?"

She then recounted the following conversation with a fellow cruiser moored nearby. "Richard Roderick, a sage Australian who is completing a seven-year circumnavigation with his family, learned long ago that the myth of the wealthy yachtsman creates a sometimes-dangerous image problem for cruising sailors. Lounging in a hammock strung between his masts, Richard would look up from his magazine at Jim and me varnishing our rails and polishing the hull in Bequia before our mishap.

"You got it all wrong, Mates," he'd sigh, shaking his head. "Those blokes in there are going to think you're bloody *millionaires*. You've got to poor it up. Let the varnish go. Look at that tight furl. Slop-it-up, Mates! Why that dinghy of yours hasn't even any *patches*. Look at that American flag—that's really asking for it. Might as well be flying a green dollar sign. When cruising, there's one thing you've got to learn about money: Never, but never, let anyone know you've got any."

This anecdote isn't intended to scare you, but Mr. Roderick isn't alone in his thinking. Many other cruisers have arrived at the same conclusion, and it's offered here as an incentive to people who already hate varnishing to paint it over! If you get a few scratches on a painted surface, just dab a bit of paint over the damaged area and it looks as good as new. When this happens to varnish, however, water discolors the wood underneath and the only way to restore the surface to its original state is to remove all the varnish, sand and possibly even bleach the wood, then start applying varnish all over again. I've owned several wood boats and though I love fashioning wood, I hate sanding it—it's no mystery to me why some people decide to paint varnished surfaces.

Where it's safe to look yachtie, or when you have the time and inclination to varnish, by all means do so. And, of course, there are usually dozens of places in the cabins that benefit from varnishing.

Surface Preparation

New wood requires only a light sanding—by hand or power sander, such as a vibrating type, that cuts with the grain—before varnishing, though if it's porous, you might consider brushing on a filler coat—wood paste or clear acrylic —to fill up the grain and give your varnish the most mileage. Sand with the grain as much as possible, and if you must go across the grain to remove a spot, do so as lightly as possible because it will require more sanding with the grain to remove the cuts. Again, a sanding block assures a flat surface.

Varnishing Tips

- Use paint and varnish remover with care, as it can eat through the gel coat if dropped on deck.
- Bleaching wood to remove water discoloration is possible, but very tricky, and in my mind usually not worth the effort.
- Inside the cabin, vacuum as you sand to remove dust from the air.
- Avoid very coarse sandpaper because it is too difficult to remove the cut lines.
- Strain varnish with a lady's nylon to remove dirt and blobs—don't assume it comes from the can free from contamination.
- Saturate the wet brush (good quality bristle) thoroughly before applying varnish to prevent air bubbles.
- Use a piece of wire across the top of the can to "tap off" varnish, rather than using the lip of the can; again, air bubbles can result.
- Don't let the brush dry between uses as dried varnish will flake off the bristles and ruin your next coat.
- Use a brush cleaner compatible with your varnish after every use.
- Don't shake cans of varnish—yup, air bubbles again.
- Never apply varnish in full sun because it dries too quickly and the finish will blister.
- Outside, use a varnish with a UV screen.
- Similarly, basements are often too damp for good varnishing. Use a dehumidifier if you must, and run a vacuum cleaner to keep dust out of the air.
- Sand in-between coats to knock off bumps and pieces of dust. Use a tack cloth or cheesecloth to wipe the surface before applying the second coat.
- Use wood filler paste or clear acrylic filler before varnishing to fill the grain and minimize the number of coats required.
- Five coats of varnish is a minimum on surfaces exposed to moisture, six to eight better. One or two annual coats on furniture is probably sufficient.
- Apply coats thinly on inclined surfaces, otherwise sag can occur.
- Store cans of varnish and paint upside down so scum forms on bottom of unused portion.
- Suspend varnish brush on wire run through top of cleaner can so bristles aren't crushed.

Over the years I've observed on my boats that vertical varnished surfaces hold their film thickness much longer than horizontal surfaces. For this reason, if I were looking for bright work to paint over, I'd attack the horizontal surfaces first.

Teak oils to me are just as much a nemesis as varnishing. Cleaning teak is a thankless task that leaves yellow hands, painful cuts, and discolors the topsides as it is washed off (though this is not so much a problem on dark-colored hulls). Most of these oils don't last very long, requiring reapplication about every three to four weeks. Otherwise you'll have to go through the first step of cleaning again.

However, there are today a few oils that are the product of advanced technology, and are supposed to last several months. Some can be wiped or brushed on, but brushes seem to reach corners better and use less varnish. The trouble with vegetable oils has been that while they allow the wood to breathe, they often mildew and wear off. Synthetics, such as polyurethanes, don't allow the wood to breathe and keep moisture in. Matthews is an all organic oil, and I highly recommend it.

TOPSIDE PAINTING

Running down to the nearest chandlery or paint store and purchasing a quart or two of a marine enamel, any old can of thinner or solvent and a few brushes is not the most intelligent way to approach a painting project. When companies refer to various "systems" of paints they market, they're not kidding. The chemistry of formulating paints has developed so radically in recent years it is important now to familiarize yourself with the types of paint available and their appropriate applications. Most of these paints—be they alkyd enamels or cross-linked polyurethanes—require prewashing the surface with cleaners, perhaps applying a primer coat, and thinning the paint with a compatible solvent. The technique used in applying the paint makes a difference, too, as well as maintaining the pristine cleanliness of the surface to be painted.

Surfacers

Surface nicks and dents should be filled before painting. They are most easily detected after the initial sanding of the hull or deck because they appear as bright spots, indentations that sandpaper cannot reach.

Clean the surface with the product recommended by the manufacturer of your paint and then fill in the spots with a surfacing putty. The smoother you apply it, the easier it will be to sand later on. There are several types: nitrocellulose lacquer, polyester two-part, acrylic lacquer and modified vegetable oil types. For strength and durability, the two-part epoxies probably are best. When the putty has cured, sand to a smooth finish.

After the sanding residue has been removed with a tack cloth, and any grease, wax and oil removed with a cheesecloth soaked with solvent (preferably the same type used with the paint), it may be advisable to coat the surface with a primer. One reason to do this is gel coat porosity. Test for gel coat porosity by brushing a small amount of any kind of paint on the surface. If the gel coat is porous, tiny pinholes or craters of paint will be visible.

Surface primers vary considerably in both chemical and physical make-up. They can dry and/or cure by oxidation of a vegetable oil (alkyd types), by solvent evaporation (lacquer types), or by a chemical cross-linking (epoxy or polyurethane types). Each has its advantage and disadvantage. Lacquer types dry quickly, but shrink and consequently have little film buildup. These types have little solvent resistance and can be used only with spray-applied finishes or with brush-applied finishes that have weaker solvent systems than are required for lacquer.

Alkyd surface primers are used almost exclusively with alkyd finish enamels. Film buildup is very good as are brushing characteristics. Alkyds are the simplest system for most persons.

Two-part catalyzed epoxy or polyurethane primers are superior primers when used with the new two-part linear (aliphatic) polyurethane enamels. They have excellent physical strength and solvent resistance.

Hard primers such as this give better end results, but are difficult to sand. Soft primers are easier to sand because they have been loaded with more pigment. But they tend also to act like blotters when the finishing coat is applied. Porous surfacers also absorb moisture, and moisture is one of the worst enemies of a good paint job. Select a surfacer that is fairly hard (two-part epoxy), but not so hard that it can't be sanded reasonably well.

Above the water, two coats of surfacing primer generally should be used. Between coats, sand with 120-grit sandpaper. Wipe residue clean with cheesecloth and solvent. Again, be certain that the surfacing primer you have chosen is compatible with the paint you intend to use; if it isn't, you've got a real problem on your hands.

Choosing a Paint

The oldest and best-known enamels are the alkyd types (Figure 15-5). These paints almost always contain mineral spirits as a solvent sys-

CHARACTERISTICS OF DIFFERENT TOPSIDE PAINTS

Product Type	Ease of Application	How Paint Dries	Solvent Type	Cost	Durability	Toxicity
Old Line Marine Enamel	Very good. Can be brushed or sprayed	By solvent evaporation and oxidation of a vegetable oil	Usually mineral spirits. Does not require strong solvent	Moderate	The standard from which other improvements are made	Low. Mineral spirits solvent only
Silicone Alkyd	Same as alkyd	Same as alkyd	Same as alkyd	More expensive than alkyd	Gloss retention excellent; superior to other products of this type	Same as alkyd
Oil-Modified Polyurethane	Similar to alkyd, usually slightly better flow	Usually faster than alkyd, by oxidation of vegetable oil	Same as alkyd	More expensive than alkyd	Better abrasion resistance than alkyd	Same as alkyd
Acrylic-Modified Alkyd	Similar to alkyd	Similar to alkyd, usually slightly faster	Same as alkyd	More expensive than alkyd	Gloss retention and color usually slightly better than alkyd	Same as alkyd
Two-Part Polyurethane	Can be finicky; requires more attention to detail	By chemical cross-linking and solvent evaporation	Usually strong solvent: esters, ketones, and aromatics	Very expensive	Best	Very hazardous when sprayed; no problem when brush or roller used
Epoxy	Can be finicky; requires attention to detail	By chemical cross-linking and solvent evaporation	Same as urethanes	More expensive than alkyds; not as expensive as polyurethanes	Excellent for primers and putties not used for finish coat	Has a hazard potential from solvent and epoxy constituents
Lacquers	Mostly used in putties	By solvent evaporation	Usually ketones and aromatic solvents	Moderate	Best feature is fast dry; has excessive shrinkage	Not usually a factor because of amounts used

Fig. 15-5 *Characteristics of different topside paints (Robert Wilkinson)*

tem. They are easy to apply and economical to use. But they do not possess the overall durability and gloss of some of the newer cross-linked polyurethanes.

From alkyd technology other types of enamels have been developed. For example, silicone resin is added to modify some alkyds to enhance gloss retention. While it may approach polyurethane paint in terms of gloss retention, it is not as resistant to abrasion. Oil-modified polyurethanes also are examples of modified alkyd technology and possess good drying properties and better abrasion resistance than standard alkyd types. Acrylic resins can be used as alkyd modi-

fiers to improve "dust free" time and give whiter whites.

Alkyd enamels are compatible with most generic-type primers, however, the manufacturer's literature should be read carefully. (For example, when alkyd enamels are used over epoxy primers, special techniques should be used to ensure adhesion, such as the application of a tie-coat primer.)

Epoxy paints are very strong solvent- and chemical-resistant coatings, and provide excellent binder resins for primers and sanding surfacers. As a class, they do have some shortcomings: They have a tendency to yellow quickly and lose gloss. They also require strong solvent systems and can be applied only over bare substrate or other well cross-linked coating systems. Because of these characteristics, they seldom are used in the yacht finishing business as a topcoat enamel. But, because of their binder strength and water-resistant properties, they often are used as binders for high quality primers and sanding surfacers.

Above the waterline, epoxy sanding surfacers almost always are recommended with two-part linear polyurethanes. The combination of a high-quality epoxy sanding surfacer and polyurethane enamel is an excellent paint system, the best all-around system currently available.

Two-part, cross-linked polyurethane enamels fall into two chemical classifications. There are aromatic and linear types. The aromatic polyurethanes have physical characteristics somewhat similar to epoxy resins inasmuch as they yellow and do not hold their gloss. Very good primers can be made from them, but they are not suitable for high quality topcoat enamels. A big advantage of this type of primer, as opposed to an epoxy primer, is that the polyurethane generally will cure at lower temperatures.

Linear polyurethanes have excellent all-around properties, including gloss and color retention, in addition to resistance to scratch abrasion, solvents and chemicals. Properly applied, these products represent the finest available air-cured paints for finishing above the waterline.

Surface Preparation

Painting fiberglass usually is complicated by the fact that the gel coat retains mold-release agents used in the production process to pop the hull and deck out of their molds. This wax must be removed; otherwise, it will cause the paint to form a soft waxy film, prevent the proper layout of the paint (crawling), and prevent the paint from adhering properly. Failure to remove this wax with the appropriate solvent wash compromises all paint applications that follow (Figure 15-6).

Examine the hull for surface imperfections and repair with surface putties and/or primers as mentioned earlier.

The grit size of the abrasive is important, though there are two schools of thought on this. Some persons specify using a fine paper of 220-grit or finer so as not to penetrate the "float" layer on the surface, thereby exposing the porous layer beneath. This condition, as was mentioned earlier, requires the use of a primer to fill up the pores. On the other hand, fine-grit abrasives do not sufficiently rough up the surface, which is necessary for good adhesion of the paint. Sanding with coarser paper assures good adhesion. If porosity occurs, so be it. At least the paint system will not peel from the gel coat.

Paper as coarse as 80-grit can be used on gel coats without causing problems. Usually, 120-grit or 150-grit paper is used. Sand the gel coat

Fig. 15-6 *Before painting, the topsides must be sanded smooth, whether the original surface is gel coat or old paint.*

until all traces of gloss have been removed, but not so much that the paint won't cover the sanding tracks.

If a surface putty and/or primer is to be used, apply it at this time. If not, proceed directly with the finish coatings.

Working With Two-Part Polyurethanes

Linear polyurethanes are distant cousins of the polyester resins used to build fiberglass sailboats. They harden, set and cure by means of a chemical process called polymerization, in which long, skinny molecules cross-link to form a hard, impervious solid. These paints are prepared for polymerization by adding a catalyst (part A) to a base (part B).

The rate of polymerization is subject to temperature; the higher the temperature, the faster the cure. Allowing the paint to cure overnight is usually sufficient time between coats, and with linear polyurethanes, two coats are always required if applied by brush or roller. The full cure may not be completed for a number of days, and so it is wise to be gentle with the painted surface until it has finally cured.

Linear polyurethanes are relatively quick drying. But don't confuse surface dryness with the curing process. Sanding too soon after the first coat has been applied could result in gumming up the sandpaper and botching the job.

Professional spray applications of linear polyurethanes almost always will achieve better results, but the brushable versions of these paints can produce excellent results as well. Chances are, however, your second experience with these paints will produce better results than the first. So it never hurts to experiment a bit with a piece of fiberglass, or at the very least, with a small area of the boat such as the transom.

Here are some tips to follow.

- Follow manufacturer's instructions to the letter.
- Dewax hull with specified solvent wash.
- Sand gel coat with grit between 80 and 150 (Figure 15-7).
- Fill dents and nicks with specified surface filler putty (Figure 15-8).
- Sand putty with 80-grit or finer Production paper (Figure 15-9).

Fig. 15-7 *In this sequence of photos, courtesy Interlux Yacht Finishes, a boat is being prepared for painting with Interlux Polythane®. Here, the gel coat is being sanded with an orbital sander.*

Fig. 15-8 *A two-part surfacing putty is mixed and then applied over dings and gouges using a putty knife.*

Fig. 15-9 *The surfacing putty is sanded smooth with an orbital sander.*

Fig. 15-10 *A primer is used between the bare gel coat and finish coatings to ensure good bonding.*

- Apply two coats of surface primer, sanding with 120-grit paper in between (Figure 15-10).
- Sand surface primer with fine-grit paper until perfectly smooth, preferably with 340-grit wet paper or finer. Remove scum with freshwater rinse (Figure 15-11).
- The "ideal" day for painting is 75°F, no wind, relative humidity between 40 and 50 percent, and a work area out of the sun. Plan your day to start and finish on the shady side of the hull.
- Find the right mixing ratio of paint to thinner and experiment on a small area not readily noticeable. The right ratio will keep the paint wet so that overlaps flow together (Figure 15-12).
- Only mix as much paint as needed to coat a continuous surface area, such as one side of the boat.
- You can pre-mix batches, and refrigerate them to save time, improve flow and minimize the amound of reducer required
- Thin paint with specified solvent (in many ways, the proper use of solvents separates the professionals from the amateurs).
- One way to apply paint is to have a helper on hand. One can paint with a ⅛-inch-nap polyurethane roller while the other tips off the area with a fine bristle brush (Figure 15-13).
- Objective is to put enough on to level out, but not so much that it will sag (Figures 15-14 and 15). Surface tension varies with color. Dark colors sag more easily than light colors. White is easiest to work with.
- If painting decks, use a flattening agent to reduce gloss. Mixing in a non-skid compound also helps reduce gloss.
- For small touch-up jobs, use measuring spoons for accurate mixing of the two parts.
- Store brushes in paper towels after cleaning. Never hit the brush on wood to clean; use a pet comb to unclog bristles.

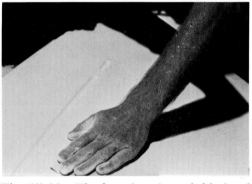

Fig. 15-11 *The dry primer is sanded by hand (a sanding block would be better). Afterwards it is wiped clean with a tack rag*

Fig. 15-12 *Mixing the Interlux Polythane®*

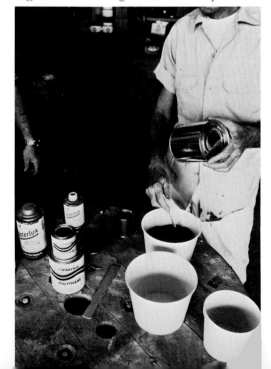

Wood, Steel and Aluminum Hulls

When the time comes to paint the topsides of a wood boat, the surface should be sanded smooth to bare wood or nearly so. Apply a wood preservative such as Interlux's 1370 Wood Preservative Clear and allow to dry for a few days. Sand with 80-grit paper. On plywood hulls only, Interlux recommends next using a wood sealer. For a really smooth, fair hull, apply two coats of a sanding surfacer (light sand after the first coat), and allow each coat to dry overnight. Finish coats of enamel can then be applied, sanding lightly with 220-grit paper in between.

John Scarlett, author of *Wooden Boat Repair Manual,* prefers oil-based (alkyd) paints to epoxy and polyurethane types because they allow the wood underneath to breathe a bit. He writes, "Since boats have a nasty habit of damaging their paintwork, and any damage will let in moisture, it seems wise to use a finish which will let it out again."

Steel hulls, according to Interlux's specifications, should be sandblasted and within an hour sprayed with a red lead epoxy paint, followed by one coat of Intergard Barrier Kote Gray 4404/4414. Sand with 120-grit paper and wipe with a reducing solvent. Imperfections can be faired

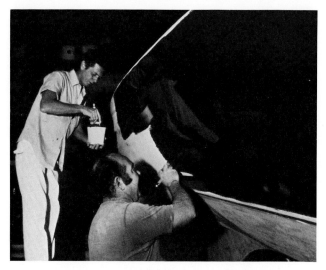

Fig. 15-13 *Two men brush on the first finish coat, carefully thinning the paint as they go.*

Fig. 15-14 *Make sure while painting that sagging is not occurring from applying too much paint.*

Fig. 15-15 *With the second and final coat applied, this once dingy-looking boat now looks brand spanking new.*

with microballoons, sanded and wiped with solvent again. Then spray a second coat of Barrier-Kote Gray and allow to dry before sanding and wiping.

Depending on finish paint type, wipe the surface with the correct reducing solvent, then apply the paint (see manufacturer's instructions for exact details), and wet sand with 320-grit paper in between. With some paints, a primer coat may be required as well.

Aluminum hulls can also be sandblasted in which case a barrier coat is applied (Interlux's is a two-part epoxy). If it can't be sandblasted, disc sand for an anchor pattern, then apply a deoxidizer, any primer specified, and clean with the appropriate solvent. Fair the surface with microballoons and apply another barrier coat and sand. Interlux says it is important to end up with at least six millimeters of barrier coating even after sanding on all hull areas. No microballoons should be used after the top coat. If finishing with an enamel, use a primer first; if using a polyurethane, check with the manufacturer for exact instructions.

Spars

It is becoming common practice now to coat spars with two-part polyurethanes. Different companies have different systems, so again, stick with the products recommended by the company you select.

The basic procedure for painting aluminum spars is to remove all fittings and sand with a medium-grit emery cloth to remove oxidation and to form a light anchor pattern to help the paint adhere. Wipe down the spar with a zinc-chromate, self-etching vinyl butyral wash, and then cover with two coats of paint. Allow the first coat to dry overnight, and then sand with 320-grit dry or wet paper before applying the second coat.

Decks

When the molded non-skid pattern on fiberglass decks wears smooth, you can either glue on new non-skid pads, or paint them with the hard, durable polyurethane paints mentioned for topsides. Surface preparation is the same. Sand can be mixed with the paint, or specially formulated synthetic granules, such as Interlux's Noskid Compound. Before painting, also take the time to repair gel coat dings with one of the many kits available in chandleries.

The decision to incur the extra expense and time of using copolymer paints versus enamels is largely one of how much scuffing the topsides receive and how much importance you attach to a high gloss. Copolymers are much harder and can withstand far greater abuse than enamels. But if your boat receives so much abuse—from dinghies smashing alongside (fit a protective rubber gunwale guard to it) or rubbing pilings at docks—that you end up wanting to paint every year anyway, enamel is certainly more economical. High gloss finishes are a matter of personal preference; actually I like the slightly duller finish of enamels better.

The first year I owned *Adriana* her gel coat was a chalked and faded robin-eggshell blue, and I didn't hesitate to paint the topsides with a Sears two-part catalytic urethane. This lasted several years, and when it came time to repaint, I used enamels—partly because using two-part paints requires practice in thinning correctly, and partly due to cost. Close up, my enamel paint jobs didn't look as good as they might have, but from 10 feet they looked great, and people were often surprised that the finish wasn't the original gel coat.

PAINTING THE BOAT'S NAME

The technique employed by decorators of vans and plastic sign painters is a comparatively inexpensive way to apply your boat's name on your transom or topsides.

1. Draw your boat's name full-size on a piece of paper. Use rulers, French curves, and whatever other tools you find helpful in achieving the desired finish. Here you can make mistakes and they won't hurt. But what you see here is what you get on the boat.

2. Place the paper with your boat's name on the kitchen table with a cotton blanket beneath.

Then, use a pounce wheel (which you can purchase for several dollars at an art supply store) or a common pin to perforate all the lines. When finished, lightly sand the backside of the paper to fully open the holes.

3. With acetone, Fantastik®, or similar cleaner, clean the area on your boat which is to be painted.

4. Use masking tape to mark off the area to be painted. Leave a little more space than will be required by the name. Cover all areas outside the tape heavily and tightly with newspaper.

5. Purchase a quart of brushable or spray mask at an art supply store or auto body shop and apply to the exposed area. When dry, the mask is a thin film which is easy to cut away for your lettering. The rest peels off easily when the paint job is done.

6. Tape the boat's name over the mask in the correct location. Using a cloth and pounce powder, pat the cloth over the perforation so that the outline of your letters is shown on the mask. An alternative to pounce powder is the blue chalk powder used on carpenters' plumb lines; it's available at most hardware stores.

7. Using a razor blade or sharp knife, such as an X-acto, lightly cut out your letters from the mask along the outline created by the pounce powder. A straightedge is helpful for straight lines.

8. Paint the exposed surface areas. Commendable results can be had with a brush or spray can. Dabbing with a stipple pad or wadded-up, fine mesh cheesecloth will remove most of the brush marks. Good quality enamel paints are suitable for lettering.

9. Allow the paint to dry for about four hours or longer, then remove all masking tape, mask and newspaper. Masking tape which is left on the hull for several days can be hellish to remove. Do not wax the lettering for about one week.

Large, bold lettering, especially super-graphics, could discourage would-be thieves from pilfering your boat. But should your boat vanish anyway, the thin cut lines made by your knife when cutting away the mask could eventually help identify your boat.

If using a pounce wheel and powder seems like too much hassle, a simple alternative is to cover the back of the paper (which contains the boat's name) with charcoal chalk. Then tape the paper to the hull and trace the lettering with a pencil. Cut away the lettering along the outline as before.

This method allows you to demonstrate your creative talents, but with calculated safeguards. For most amateurs, freehand is just too risky and stick-on letters too blah. Even if you don't want a dreamy mood mural on the side of your boat, you can learn something from the fellows who decorate vans.

Richard Fritzler, a friend of mine who is a medical illustrator, showed me a simpler variation of this method. The boat's name was drawn on a piece of brown paper exactly the way we wanted to see it on the transom. We then cut out each letter using a straightedge and X-acto

Fig. 15-16 *An illustrator friend made a stencil for* Adriana's *name, temporarily glued it to the transom, and used a spray can of enamel to paint the name.*

knife. Spray mask was used to temporarily glue the brown paper stencil to *Adriana*'s transom. We then used a spray enamel paint to coat the areas cut away. Spray acrylics can be used also. It is most important to spray the paint on thinly, or else sagging inevitably occurs. You will probably have to go over the surface several times, but the whole process shouldn't take more than a few hours. The result is surprisingly professional looking. Take your time in drawing the name, cutting it out and applying the paint, and there's no reason you can't do just as nice a job as in Figure 15-16.

SUMMARY

Contrary to popular belief, fiberglass gel coats are porous—with time, the colors chalk and fade, and some water may migrate through to the laminate. While painting is not a panacea for gel coat problems, it is better than leaving it to deteriorate further. Epoxy copolymer paints offer the best protection and the highest gloss and durability, though they may not allow wood hulls to breathe sufficiently.

Bottom painting should be undertaken on a periodic basis, and again, the new generation of copolymer paints give the best, longest lasting results.

One's approach to painting and varnishing is largely an individual matter, subject to each person's preferences regarding preparation time, ease of application, color and maintenance. I'm not one to try saving the original gel coat of a fiberglass boat as long as possible, nor one for retaining the beauty of natural wood at all costs. Good quality paints are relatively inexpensive, enable you to play with color schemes, reduce maintenance and offer important protection to your all-important investment.

Epilogue

During the seven years I owned *Adriana,* spending countless hours on many of the projects in this book, my single purpose was to make her the safest, most comfortable boat possible for extended cruising. But wouldn't you know, just when she was ready to go, and just about the time this book was nearing completion, I decided I needed a Pearson Vanguard so there'd be more room for the kids and friends who would be sailing with me from time to time.

The best laid plans. . . .

Adriana was sold to a family in New Hampshire who intend to cruise the New England coast. They commissioned the yard in Bristol to paint her with a dark green Awlgrip, and on her transom were the neatly printed letters of *Phaedra*—hardly the do-it-yourself jobs she had been used to. But I must say I was pleased, and at the same time a little saddened that her new owners had taken her from my hands looking better than at anytime I'd owned her.

Fortunately, the Vanguard was well-equipped by a previous owner who sailed her in the Caribbean for a few years. So I won't be starting from scratch. But at the moment there's a box of propane fittings for the oven to sort out, UV patches to be sewn on the roller furling twin jibs, and a forward cabin in need of a double berth and more storage. The list is long, but manageable.

The same can be said for the wait.

Like sending grown children off to seek their fortunes, there is satisfaction in knowing you've done your best preparing them for the adventure of life. And a life at sea—for children and for boats—is one worth all the hard hours.

Adriana rests quietly at Bowen's Wharf, Newport, Rhode Island, awaiting her winter wraps.

ABYC: BONDING OF DIRECT CURRENT SYSTEMS

PROJECT E–1 (ADOPTED WITH PROPOSED REVISIONS MAY 30, 1972)

E–1.1. PURPOSE

This standard establishes requirements and recommended methods for bonding direct-current electrical systems:

—to provide a low-resistance electrical path, within the confines of the hull, between otherwise isolated metallic objects, particularly those in common contact with sea water and potentially subject to electrolytic corrosion due to stray currents:

—to prevent the possible existence of an electrical potential on exposed metallic enclosures of electrical equipment:

—to provide a low resistance path to ground for voltages that may be considerably in excess of those for which the system is designed, as might occur when lightning strikes, and

—to minimize radio interference.

E–1.2. SCOPE

This standard applies to all boats equipped with direct-current electrical systems operating below 50 volts.

E–1.3. DEFINITIONS

a. *Ground*—A surface or mass at the potential of the earth's surface, established at this potential by a conducting connection (intentional or accidental) with the earth, including any metal area which forms part of the wetted surface of the hull.

b. *Bonding*—The electrical connection of the exposed, metallic, non-current carrying parts to the ground (negative) side of the direct current system.

c. *Common Bonding Conductor*—An electrical conductor, usually running fore and aft, to which all equipment bonding conductors are connected.

d. *Bonding Conductor*—A normally non-current-carrying conductor used to connect the non-current-carrying metal parts of a boat and the non-current carrying parts of direct current devices on the boat to the boat's bonding system.

e. *Engine Negative Terminal*—The point on the engine at which the negative battery cable is connected.

E–1.4. BONDING SYSTEM

a. *General*

(1) All boats equipped with a permanently installed electrical system shall be equipped with a bonding system.

(2) A bonding system shall consist of:
—Common Bonding Conductor
—Common Bonding Conductor connection to negative side of electrical system
—Individual Bonding Conductors connected to the Common Bonding Conductor
—Individual Bonding Conductor connections to the non-current-carrying metallic parts of electrical equipment.

(3) Bonding conductors shall be color coded according to ABYC E–3 "Wiring Identification on Boats"

(4) Bonding conductors shall be separate from the AC and DC electrical system grounded conductors. (See E–8, "Alternating Current Electrical Systems" and E–9, "Direct Current Electrical Systems".)

(5) Bonding conductors shall be permanent, continuous, and at least of the same size as the conductors leading to the equipment to conduct safely any currents likely to be imposed on them due to stray-current leakage or short circuits; and in all instances shall be of sufficient size to permit operation of over-current devices in the associated circuits. The engine bonding conductor shall have a current-carrying capacity at least as great as the largest bonding conductor in the bonding system.

(6) In multi-engine installations with cross-over

313

starting systems, the engines shall be bonded together with a cable large enough to carry the starting current. The connections of this bonding cable shall be independent of any other electrical connections to the engines. This bonding cable shall be independent of current-carrying conductors as provided in ABYC E–9, "Direct Current Electrical Systems."

Note: the bonding wire (or cables) to the engine(s) must be large enough to carry cranking current, because a break in the cranking circuit could cause the cranking current to flow in an alternate path (such as fuel lines).

(7) The common bonding conductor shall be un-insulated copper or bronze strip, copper tubing, bare tinned-copper wire or insulated copper wire of the proper gauge. Copper braid shall not be used for this purpose.

    (a) Common Bonding conductors fabricated from copper or bronze strip shall have a minimum thickness of 1/32 inch and be no less than 1/2 inch in width.

    (b) Wire, where used as the common bonding conductor, shall be at least no. 8 AWG.

       Note: These requirements are based on both physical strength and the ability to make and maintain low-resistance connections, as well as current ratings.

(8) Where the bonding system is used as a part of the lightning protective system, conductor sizes shall be as specified in ABYC E–4, "Lightning Protection."

b. *Items to be Bonded*—Exposed, metallic non-current-carrying parts of the following items shall have provision for, and be connected to, the bonding system.

(1) Propulsion and auxiliary engines. It is recommended that this bonding conductor be connected to the engine negative terminal.

(2) Metallic enclosures of all electrical apparatus including:

    (a) Motor, generator and pump frames or enclosures.

       Note: When the metallic frames of electrical accessories are directly attached to the frame of an engine, the engine bonding connection will serve to bond all such accessories.

    (b) Cabinets and control boxes.

    (c) Radio-equipment cabinets and enclosures of other electronic devices.

    (d) Metallic conduit, cable sheaths, or armoring.

(3) Fuel tanks, fuel-fill deck fittings, and electrically operated fuel pumps and valves.

(4) Battery trays (lead-lined).

c. *Items Not Required to be Bonded*

(1) Electrically isolated thru-hull fittings need not be connected to the bonding system. (See ABYC E–2, "Cathodic Protection".)

(2) Other electrically isolated metallic items except as recommended in ABYC E–4, "Lightning Protection."

E–1.5. INSTALLATION OF BONDING SYSTEM

a. *General*—The method of installation of the bonding system should be as illustrated in Figure 1.

b. *Common Bonding Conductor*—The common bonding conductor shall be installed in a fore-and-aft direction such that it will not be totally or partially submerged in bilge water and in a manner that will permit bonding conductors to be as short and direct as possible.

(1) Splices in the common bonding conductor shall provide electrical continuity and mechanical strength equivalent to the original conductor.

(2) Metal fastenings, when used to secure the common bonding conductor to the hull, shall be equivalent to or more noble than the copper conductor.

(3) Connections shall be accessible for inspection and maintenance.

c. *Bonding Conductor*—Bonding conductors need not be insulated. Installation and connections shall be in accordance with ABYC E–9, "Direct Current Electrical Systems."

E–1.6. METAL-HULL VESSELS

a. *General*—The hull of a metal-hull vessel may serve as the common bonding conductor.

(1) Any item to be bonded (See paragraph 4.b.) not in contact with the hull requires a bonding conductor to the hull.

(2) If the item to be bonded is connected to a thru-hull fitting galvanically incompatible with the hull, it shall be insulated from the thru-hull fitting and the thru-hull fitting shall be insulated from the hull.

NOTE: This standard is reprinted with permission of the American Boat and Yacht Council, Inc. Readers wishing to know more about the above standard and other standards published by the ABYC should write: PO Box 806, 190 Ketcham Ave., Amityville, NY 11701.

CHARACTERISTICS OF COMMON WOODS

BASIC STRESSES FOR CLEAR LUMBER UNDER LONG-TIME SERVICE AT FULL DESIGN LOAD UNDER WET CONDITIONS.

Species	Extreme fiber in bending or tension parallel to grain	Maximum horizontal shear	Compression perpendicular to grain	Compression parallel to grain L/d = 11 or less	Modulus of elasticity in bending
1	2	3	4	5	6
	P.s.i	P.s.i.	P.s.i.	P.s.i.	1,000 p.s.i.
SOFTWOODS					
Baldcypress	1,900	150	220	1,450	1,200
Atlantic and northern white cedar	1,100	100	130	750	800
Douglas-fir, coast type, medium-grain	2,200	130	235	1,450	1,600
Pine:					
Eastern white, ponderosa, sugar, and western white	1,300	120	185	1,000	1,000
Southern yellow	2,200	160	235	1,450	1,600
Spruce, red, white, and Sitka	1,600	120	185	1,050	1,200
HARDWOODS					
Ash, commercial white	2,050	185	365	1,450	1,500
Birch, sweet and yellow	2,200	185	365	1,600	1,600
Elm, American and slippery	1,600	150	185	1,050	1,200
Hickory, true and pecan	2,800	205	440	2,000	1,800
Mahogany	2,200	175	450	1,500	1,300
Maple, black and sugar	2,200	185	365	1,600	1,600
Oak	2,050	185	365	1,350	1,500
Teak	2,750	200	600	1,900	1,600

BASIC STRESSES FOR 1- AND 2-INCH NOMINAL CLEAR LUMBER UNDER LONG-TIME SERVICE AT FULL DESIGN LOAD UNDER DRY CONDITIONS.

Species	Extreme fiber in bending or tension parallel to grain	Maximum longitudinal shear	Compression perpendicular to grain	Compression parallel to grain	Modulus of elasticity in bending
1	2	3	4	5	6
	P.s.i.	P.s.i.	P.s.i.	P.s.i.	1,000 p.s.i.
SOFTWOODS					
Cedar:					
Atlantic and northern white cedar	1,400	115	195	1,050	900
Douglas-fir, coast type, medium-grain	2,750	150	350	2,000	1,800
Pine:					
Eastern white, ponderosa, sugar, and western white	1,600	135	275	1,400	1,100
Southern yellow	2,750	180	350	2,000	1,800
Spruce, red, white, and Sitka	2,000	160	330	1,450	1,300
HARDWOOD					
Ash, commercial white	2,550	210	550	2,000	1,600
Birch, sweet and yellow	2,750	210	550	2,200	1,800
Hickory, true and pecan	3,500	235	660	2,750	2,000
Mahogany	2,750	200	675	2,050	1,400
Maple, black and sugar	2,750	210	550	2,200	1,800
Oak	2,550	210	550	1,850	1,600
Teak	3,450	230	900	2,600	1,800

CHARACTERISTICS OF COMMON METALS

Stainless Steel

Contrary to its name, stainless steel is not totally stainless. While there are many types of stainless steel, those of most interest to the sailor are alloys of iron, chromium and nickel. When chromium content exceeds 12 percent, corrosion resistance increases rapidly. Adding nickel, usually between six and 22 percent, improves resistance to acids.

Depending on the crystal structure of the alloy, stainless steels are grouped into three main types—*austentitic, ferritic* and *martensitic.* There are many differences between them, but the most important for the majority of boat owners is that the marine grades used on boats are austentitic and are basically non-magnetic. Ferritic and martensitic stainless steels are both magnetic, so it is often wise to test fasteners or gear with a magnet to determine that they are suitable for marine use.

Types 304 and 316 are the most widely used for boats, with the latter preferred for its extra corrosion resistance obtained from small amounts of molybdenum. They may be used on deck exposed to the atmosphere, but should not be used underwater as they are subject to pitting corrosion. When they start to stain, they can be wiped down with dilute nitric acid, but rinse the deck with water first and immediately after wiping down to avoid damage to other materials on the boat. Commercial cleaners also may be used.

New varieties of stainless steel such as Nitronic 50 (the steel Navtec uses for rod rigging and Universal uses for "Super Stainless" wire rigging—see Chapter 10), are stronger and less prone to tarnish than even Type 316. At present, Nitronic 50 is prohibitively expensive for many applications.

Copper, Brass and Bronze Alloys

Copper and nickel alloys are commonly used on boats for fittings, propeller shafts and heavy gear castings. There are many variations and only some are truly suitable for reliable service on the cruising boat.

Copper by itself is a soft metal with a long life span in the seawater environment. Though copper fasteners and sheathing on the bottom of wood sailing ships were once common, its use on boats today is largely limited to piping.

A copper and zinc alloy is called brass. Because it dezincifies in a marine environment, (the zinc dissolves and leaves the copper soft and spongy) it should not be used for anything on deck—perhaps its best use is the ship's clock. Manganeze bronze is actually a brass (60/40 copper to zinc), and therefore

These samples of rod were placed in warm salt water off North Carolina for 18 months with a rubber band around each. From left to right: Monel, 304 stainless steel, 316 stainless steel and Nitronic 50, a new more corrosion-resistant form of stainless steel. The Monel was pitted everywhere except under the rubber band. The 304 and 316 sections were victims of crevice corrosion, while the Nitronic 50 is clean.

should not be used underwater and is not as wise a choice as some other metals above the water.

Bronze, zinc-free copper alloys using tin, aluminum, silicon and nickel, are more corrosion resistant than brass. Gunmetal is an 88/12 alloy of copper and tin, and not as strong as aluminum bronze (90/10) and silicon bronze (96/4).

Copper-nickel alloys have been used to build boats that are reputedly free from bottom fouling due to organic growth and though they are quite strong, they are expensive. Monel, a proprietory name, is a copper-nickel alloy (70/30) and is both strong and corrosion resistant. It is frequently used for fuel tanks and propeller shafts.

Because copper alloys tarnish to a dirty green color in sea air, fittings and other finished objects are often plated with chromium. A good chrome job provides excellent protection against corrosion and tarnish, but it's not always easy to come by. The process involves several critical steps that must be done correctly to be effective. For instance, if the chrome layer exceeds 0.00001 inch, it may develop cracks. In his book, *Metal Corrosion in Boats,* Nigel Warren says that while regularly rubbing with an oily or waxed cloth will prolong its life, one usually has to buy on trust. Warren advises it isn't worth the risk.

Aluminum

Some aluminum alloys are well suited for boats. They are lightweight (about one-third the density of steel, copper, etc.), strong enough when engineered properly, and corrosion resistant due to the white oxide film that develops on the bare metal when exposed to the oxygen in air or water. While not exactly pleasing in appearance, this film prevents aluminum from literally melting in seawater.

Aluminum can be cast (poured into a mold), wrought (forced into shape), rolled (pressed into plates), and extruded (pulled through a die to form a section such as a mast). Different alloys are used for each method of shaping aluminum. Aluminum is combined with magnesium, manganese or silicon to produce marine-grade alloys.

If the white powder is removed from oxidized aluminum, the oxidization process begins again on exposed surfaces. While this is not necessarily harmful, it is customary to anodize or paint aluminum. Anodizing is done by submersing the metal in a chemical bath and running an electrical charge through it. Aluminum must be etched before painting, but paint does last well on it. A chip in the paint won't cause the metal underneath to start rusting as with steel.

On aluminum boats, bottom paints containing lead, mercury or copper should never be used because the metals are galvanically incompatible (See Galvanic Series). Aluminum corrodes rapidly when in contact with more noble metals. Many spinnaker poles have cast aluminum jaws with stainless steel pistons—the result: galvanic action between these dissimilar metals causing pitting corrosion, which in short work makes the pistons impossible to open or close without mechanical advantage (hammers, Vice-Grips, screwdrivers). Larry Pardey has suggested that in these instances the piston surfaces be filed down so that the fit is actually sloppy.

If it is necessary to use stainless steel or bronze fastenings with aluminum, the fastener should always be insulated from direct contact by using a bedding compound coating on the threads and under the head, plastic tubing over the threads, or a plastic washer to prevent the fastener head from touching the surface (most appropriate when screwing through a thin layer of aluminum into wood or other material).

Steel and Iron

Steel and iron are both manufactured from the same ore, but steel has less than 1.7 percent carbon added, iron has more. Both tend to rust rapidly in the marine environment, but their low price and high strength has encouraged boatbuilders to devise methods of protecting the metals to make them viable for boats.

The Dutch have been building boats in steel for over a century, and in this country steel is rapidly finding favor among cruising people desiring the ultimate protection against holing. Mild steel and Cor-Ten (with 0.5 percent copper and 0.6 percent chromium added) are both used for boatbuilding; the mill scale is removed by shotblasting, the surface covered with a self-etching primer and then a durable painting system is used as a finishing coating.

As with other metals, the speed of water passing over steel increases its corrosion rate. In still seawater, mild steel deteriorates at a rate of about five millimeters a year. Protected, it can virtually be brought to a halt.

Galvanizing is the most common method of protecting steel and iron gear. This process involves dipping the metal into molten zinc, and is much more effective than electroplating (usually done with cadmium), largely because of the greater thickness of the coating and the self-healing nature of zinc.

Before the development of stainless steels, galvanized wire rigging was common, but required periodic varnishing or wiping with linseed oil to prevent corrosion. There is still a place for galvanized steel on cruising boats, such as anchor chain and windlass housings, but for the most part it has been displaced on board by stainless steel, bronze and aluminum.

GALVANIC SERIES OF METALS IN SEA WATER   METALS AND ALLOYS

(Anodic or Least Noble)

Magnesium and Magnesium Alloys

Zinc

Galvanized Steel

Aluminum Alloys

Cadmium

Mild Steel

Wrought Iron

Cast Iron

13% Chromium Stainless Steel, Type 410 (active in still water)

18-8 Stainless Steel, Type 304

Ni-Resist

18.8, 3% Mo Stainless Steel, Type 316

78% Ni—14.5% Cr—6% Fe (Inconel)

Aluminum Bronze (92% Cu—8% Al)

Naval Brass (60% Cu—39% Zn)

Yellow Brass (65% Cu—35% Zn)

Red Brass (85% Cu—15% Zn)

Muntz Metal (60% Cu—40% Zn)

Tin

Copper

50-50 Lead—Tin Solder

Admiralty Brass (71% Cu 28% Zn 1% Sn)

Aluminum Brass (76% Cu 22% Zn 2% Al)

Manganese Bronze (58.5% Cu 39% Zn 1% Sn 1% Fe 0.3 MN)

Silicone Bronze (96% Cu Max, 0.80 Fe, 1.50 Zn, 2.00 Si, 0.75 MN, 1.60 Sn)

Bronze-Composition G (88% Cu—2% Zn—10% Zn)

Bronze-Comp. M (88% Cu—3% Zn—6.5% Sn—1.5% Pb)

13% Chromium Stainless Steel, Type 401 (passive)

90% Cu—10% Ni

75% Cu—20% Ni–5% Zn

Lead

70% Cu—30% Ni

78% Ni—13.5% Cr—6% Fe (Inconel)

Nickel 200

18-8 Stainless Steel, Type 304

70% Ni—30% Cu Monel 400, K-500

18-8, 3% Mo Stainless Steel, Type 316

Titanium

Hastelloy C

Platinum

Graphite

(Cathodic or Most Nobel)

NATIONAL FIRE PROTECTION ASSOCIATION, INC. PLEASURE CRAFT SAFETY STANDARDS

COOKING, HEATING, AND AUXILIARY APPLIANCES

6-1 Cooking Equipment.

6-1.1 Galley stoves shall be manufactured, approved, and labeled for marine use. Printed instructions for proper installation, operation, and maintenance shall be furnished by the manufacturer. A durable and permanently legible instruction sign covering safe operation and maintenance shall be provided by the manufacturer and installed on or adjacent to the stove where it may be readily read.

6-1.2 Stoves using gasoline for fuel shall not be used aboard boats.

6-1.3 Stoves shall be installed in adequately ventilated areas to comply with 2-1.5.

6-1.4 Stoves shall be securely fastened when in use and when stored.

6-1.5 Any burner system that may affect safety by reason of motion of the boat shall not be used.

6-1.6 All woodwork or other combustible materials above stove tops and all woodwork or combustibles immediately surrounding stoves shall be effectively insulated with noncombustible materials.

6-2 Coal, Charcoal, and Wood Burning Stoves.

6-2.1 Coal, charcoal, and wood burning stoves shall be either mounted on a noncombustible base (preferably hollow tile) or mounted on legs providing clearance of at least 5 in. between stove bottom and deck and the deck shall be effectively insulated with a noncombustible material or sheathing.

6-2.2 Stove sides and backs shall have a minimum clearance of 4 in. from the insulation provided in accordance with 6-1.6.

6-2.3 Smoke pipes and stacks shall have a minimum clearance of 9 in. from combustible materials, including painted surfaces, or shall be separated by fire resistant thermal insulation.

Exception: At decks equipped with water irons.

6-2.4 Smoke pipes or stacks shall terminate with approved smoke heads designed to prevent water entry, spark emission, and back draft.

6-2.5 Fuel shall be stowed in a ventilated, metal-lined locker or bin.

6-3 Alcohol, Fuel Oil, and Kerosene Stoves.

6-3.1 Both pressure or gravity fed burners shall be permitted.

6-3.2 Fuel supply tanks shall be constructed of corrosion resistant metal with welded or brazed joints and fittings.

6-3.2.1 Pressure tanks integrally installed with stoves shall withstand a test pressure of at least 200 psig. They shall be effectively protected from the heat of burners.

6-3.2.2 Pressure tanks for remote installation shall be approved and shall be able to withstand a test pressure of at least 100 psig. They shall be rigidly secured in an accessible location permitting convenient filling and pump operation.

6-3.2.3 Gravity tanks shall be substantially secured. They shall be so located or shielded that, under continuous operation at maximum output, the temperature of contained fuel will not be substantially raised by heat from the burners.

6-3.2.4 No gravity tank shall have a capacity exceeding 2 gal. Tanks of larger capacity shall meet the requirements of Section 5-3.

6-3.2.5 Gravity tanks shall have provisions for filling and venting outside the galley space.

6-3.3 If fuel tanks are remotely located, as is preferred for gravity feed systems, approved stop valves shall be installed close to tanks and fuel lines shall be installed with as few fittings as practicable between valves and stove connections.

6-3.4 If solidified fuel is used, the containers shall be properly secured on a fixed base to prevent sliding or overturning due to a sudden roll of the vessel.

6-3.5 Stacks and uninsulated stoves shall comply with the requirements of Section 6-2.

6-4* Liquefied Petroleum Gas Systems.
6-4.1 General Requirements.

6-4.1.1 Liquefied petroleum gas systems shall be designed and installed in accordance with provisions outlined herein and shall be subject to the inspection and approval of the authority having jurisdiction.

6-4.1.2 The use or storage of stoves with attached LPG containers is prohibited on boats having enclosed accommodation spaces.

6-4.1.3 Comprehensive printed instructions and a labeled diagram covering details of proper installation and operation shall be furnished with each system installed on a boat and shall be kept on board for ready reference.

6-4.1.4 All liquefied petroleum gases shall be effectively odorized by an approved agent of such character as to indicate positively, by a distinctive odor, the presence of gas down to a concentration in air of not more than 20 percent of the lower limit of flammability.

6-4.1.5 All component parts of systems other than containers and low pressure distribution tubing between regulators and appliances shall be approved for marine use and shall be so listed or labeled.

6-4.1.6 All component parts of systems subject to container pressures shall have a rated working pressure of not less than 250 psig.

6-4.1.7 With each liquefied petroleum gas system installed on a boat, at least two of the signs required by 6-1.1 shall be provided. These signs shall include the following information statements:

(a) the signal word "WARNING"
(b) the statement "To Avoid Fire and Explosion"
(c) the following directions:

1. Keep container valves closed when boat is unattended. Close them immediately in any emergency.
2. Be sure all appliance valves are closed before opening the container valve.
3. Always apply lit match or other flame to burner before opening burner valve.
4. Close master valve on appliance whenever appliance is not in use (if applicable).
5. Test system for leakage at least twice a month and after any emergency in accordance with the following procedure.

With appliance valves closed, the master shutoff valve on the appliance open, and with one container valve open, note pressure on the gage. Close container valve. The pressure should remain constant for at least 10 minutes. If pressure drops, locate leakage by application of soapy water solution at all connections. Repeat test for each container in multi-container systems. Never use flame to check for leaks.

NOTE: If a leak detection device is installed, these instructions shall be modified as appropriate.

6-4.1.8 The required warning signs shall be installed in plainly visible locations on the outside of each container enclosure and adjacent to each consuming appliance.

6-4.2 Containers.

6-4.2.1 Containers shall be constructed, tested, marked, maintained, requalified for continued service, and refilled:

(1) in accordance with the regulations of the U.S. Department of Transportation for containers in LP-Gas service or
(b) in accordance with equivalent specifications or regulations determined by the authority having jurisdiction.

6-4.2.2 Containers shall be condemned and withdrawn from service when they leak, when corrosion, denting, bulging or other evidence of rough usage exists to the extent they may be weakened appreciably, or when they have been involved in a fire.

6-4.3 Valves and Safety Relief Devices.

6-4.3.1 Each container shall have a manually operated shutoff valve installed directly at the container outlet, which shall be equipped with a securely attached hand wheel for convenient operation without the use of a separate wrench.

6-4.3.2 All containers shall be provided with safety relief devices as required by U.S. Department of Transportation regulations or equivalent regulations.

6-4.3.3 Container valves and safety relief devices shall have direct connection with the vapor space of the cylinder.

6-4.3.4 In addition to the valve required at the container, a dual container system shall be provided with a two-way positive shutoff valve of manually operated type, or equivalent, at the manifold.

6-4.3.5 Discharge of the safety relief valves shall be vented into the open atmosphere.

6-4.4 Reducing Regulators.

6-4.4.1 Each system shall be provided with a pressure-regulating device, so adjusted as to deliver gas to the distribution piping at a pressure not to exceed 18 in. of water (approximately 0.653 psig).

6-4.4.2 A relief valve on the low pressure side of the system shall be integral with each regulator. It shall be set to discharge at not less than twice and not more than three times the delivery pressure.

6-4.4.3 The regulator vent termination shall be turned downward to prevent water entering the discharge line.

6-4.4.4* Each reducing regulator shall be fitted with a pressure gage or leak detector. If a gage is used, it shall be on the high pressure side of the regulator.

6-4.5 Piping and Fittings.

6-4.5.1 All low pressure distribution piping between the regulator and appliances shall be either copper tubing of standard type K, L, or equivalent or flexible hose listed or labeled for use with LPG.

6-4.5.2 Flexible sections used to allow free swing of gimballed stoves shall be approved for marine use.

6-4.5.3 Connecting fittings shall comply with applicable requirements of 5-6.2. Connections may be soldered or brazed with a material having a melting point exceeding 1000°F (538°C).

6-4.6 LPG Appliances.

6-4.6.1 All gas-consuming appliances shall be labeled as suitable for marine use.

6-4.6.2 Cooking stoves, service water heaters, cabin heaters, and similar appliances shall comply with applicable provisions of 6-1.1 and with the following:

(a) Appliances designed for operation with continuous pilot lights or automatic glow plugs are prohibited.

Exception: Cabin heaters complying with 6-4.6.2(b).

(b) Cabin space heaters shall be of the sealed combustion chamber type, designed to provide complete separation of the combustion system from the atmosphere in the boat. A combustion air inlet and flue gas outlet shall be provided as integral parts of the appliance.

6-4.7 Location and Installation.

6-4.7.1 Containers, regulating equipment, and safety equipment shall be rigidly secured, readily accessible, and so located that escaping vapor cannot reach the bilges, machinery space, accommodations, or other enclosed spaces.

6-4.7.2 Except as permitted by 6-4.7.3, locations of containers and regulators shall be confined to open deck, cabin top, outside of cockpits, or semi-enclosures. Equipment shall be protected by a housing vented to open air near the top and bottom.

6-4.7.3 If construction or design prevents compliance with locations specified above, the container, regulating equipment, and safety equipment shall be mounted in a locker or housing that is vapor-tight to the hull interior and located above the waterline in an open cockpit, provided the locker or housing is constructed of or lined with corrosion resistant material. It shall open only from the top by means of a cover seated on a gasket and tightly latched but capable of being conveniently and quickly opened for operation of container valves and for testing of the system for leakage. It shall also be vented at the bottom by a pipe of at least ½ in. internal diameter, led outboard without pockets through the hull sides to a point lower than the locker or housing bottom but above the waterline.

6-4.7.4 Installation of gas equipment in lockers or housing shall be such that when the means of access to the lockers or housing is open, the container valves can be conveniently and quickly operated, and the system pressure gage dials are fully visible.

6-4.7.5 Lockers or housings shall not be used for storage of any other equipment nor shall quick access to the gas system be obstructed in any way.

6-4.7.6 Provisions for storage of unconnected reserve containers, filled or empty, shall be the same as for containers in use. Valves to containers, even those considered empty, shall be kept tightly closed.

6-4.7.7 Distribution lines shall be protected from physical damage and shall be accessible for inspection.

6-4.7.7.1 Lines shall be secured against vibration.

6-4.7.7.2 Lines shall be protected from abrasion wherever they pass through decks or bulkheads.

6-4.7.7.3 Lines shall be continuous lengths of tubing from the tank location to the appliance.

6-4.7.8 After installation, distribution tubing shall be tested prior to its connection to the regulator and appliance by an air pressure of not less than 5 psig. The container valve shall be checked for leakage at its outlet and at its connection to the container by application of liquid detergent or soapy water solution prior to connection of the system. After these tests and when appliances and high-pressure equipment have been connected, the entire system shall be subjected to the following test.

    (a) With appliance valves closed, the master shut-off valve (if provided) on the appliance open, and with one container valve open, note the pressure on the gage.

    (b) Close the container valve.

    (c) Pressure should remain constant for at least 10 minutes.

    (d) If pressure drops, locate leakage by application of soapy water solution at all connections.

    (e) Never use flame to check for leaks.

6-4.8 Precautions.

6-4.8.1 A container shall not be charged with fuel unless it bears the proper markings of the code under which it was fabricated, its water weight capacity, and its tare weight.

6-4.8.2 No container which is due for requalification shall be charged with fuel until it has been retested or otherwise qualified for service in accordance with U.S. Department of Transportation requirements.

6-4.8.3 Container valves must be tested for leaks before the charged container is shipped from the filling plant, and it shall not be shipped with leaking fittings.

6-5 Heating Equipment.
6-5.1 Service Hot Water Heating Units.

6-5.1.1 Open flame heating units shall be installed within the galley area only, well above accommodation flooring and in compliance with applicable requirements of Sections 6-1, 6-2, 6-3, and 6-4.

6-5.1.2 A vent stack shall be fitted at the top of each heating unit and led to the atmosphere with an effective device for preventing flame extinguishment or flareback from back draft.

6-5.1.3 Dampers shall not be installed in vent stacks.

6-5.1.4 Use of water heaters designed for operation with continuous pilot lights or automatic glow plugs is prohibited.

6-5.2 Cabin Heaters.

6-5.2.1 Cabin-heating equipment shall comply with applicable provisions of Sections 6-1, 6-2, 6-3, and 6-4.

6-5.2.2 Burners and burner feed arrangements shall be such that safe operation is not affected by motion of the boat.

6-5.2.3 Heaters shall be rigidly secured.

6-5.2.4 Use of heaters designed for operation with continuous pilot lights or automatic glow plugs shall be prohibited.

Exception: As permitted in 6-4.6.2(b).

6-5.2.5 Gasoline shall not be used for fuel in open flame liquid or vapor burners.

6-5.2.6 Heating boilers shall be approved for marine use.

6-5.2.7 Sealed combustion chamber heaters burning gasoline or fuel oil may be used provided they comply with applicable parts of this standard.

6-6 Auxiliary Appliances.
6-6.1 Lamps and Lanterns.

6-6.1.1 Gasoline shall not be used for fuel.

6-6.1.2 Oil lamps and lanterns shall be approved for marine use.

6-6.1.3 Oil lamps shall have metal bodies and shall be hung in gimbals.

6-6.1.4 Oil lamps shall not be located directly over galley stoves or heating units.

6-6.1.5 Metal shields shall be secured above chimneys.

6-6.1.6 Oil lanterns, if suspended, shall be secured by clips or lashings.

6-6.1.7 Lanterns not in use shall be stowed in a noncombustible enclosure.

FIRE PROTECTION EQUIPMENT

9-1 General Requirements.

9-1.1 All portable fire extinguishers and extinguishing systems shall be approved by the U.S. Coast Guard for marine use.

9-1.2 Brackets used to secure portable fire extinguishers shall be approved for marine use.

9-2 Equipment.

9-2.1 All boats shall be equipped with portable fire extinguishers at least to the extent of the minimum requirements of Table 9-2.1 and the requirements of this section.

On boats having galley stoves, one of the required extinguishers of suitable types shall be readily accessible thereto.

TABLE 9-2.1 **NUMBER AND DISTRIBUTION OF FIRE EXTINGUISHERS**

Type of Boat	Class of Extinguishers[1]	Minimum Required	Recommended Locations
Open boats under 16 ft	B-I	1	Helmsman's position
Open boats over 16 ft	B-I	2	Helmsman's position and passenger space
Boats under 26 ft	B-I	2	Helmsman's position and cabin
Boats 26–40 ft	B-I	3	Engine compartment, helmsman's position, and galley[3]
Boats 40–65 ft	B-I	4[2]	Engine compartment, helmsman's position, crew quarters, and galley[3]
Boats 65–75 ft	B-I	5[2]	Engine compartment, helmsman's position, crew quarters, and galley[3]
Boats 75–100 ft	B-I	6[2]	Engine compartment, helmsman's position, crew quarters, and galley[3]

Notes to Table 9-2.1:

[1] One of the required extinguishers shall additionally have the capability of extinguishing Class A fires.

[2] If more than three B-I units are recommended, the extinguishing capacity may be made up of a smaller number of larger units, provided each recommended location is protected with an extinguisher readily accessible, e.g., 3 B-II units may be used in lieu of 4, 5, or 6 of the smaller B-I units.

[3] Extinguishers recommended for "engine compartment" should not be located inside such compartment but near an entrance to the compartment unless someone is normally present in the compartment.

9.2.2* All inboard-powered boats with the engine compartment enclosed shall have provisions for discharging the extinguishing agent directly into the space immediately surrounding the engine without opening the primary access. Where portable equipment is to be used, a small, suitably labeled, readily accessible port to the enclosure shall be provided for this purpose.

9-2.2.1 If the above extinguisher is portable and readily movable from its fixed mounting, it may also be credited as one of the extinguishers required in Table 9-2.1.

9-2.2.2 Portable fire extinguishers required for the engine compartment shall be a gaseous type.

9-2.2.3 If carbon dioxide is used as the extinguishing agent for fixed systems, the quantity of gas required shall comply with Table 9-2.2.3.

TABLE 9-2.2.3 **REQUIRED WEIGHT OF CARBON DIOXIDE**

Volume of Space (cu ft net)	Carbon Dioxide in lb
90 (or less)	5
140	10
220	15
300	20
375	25
525	35
800	50
1,200	75
1,600	100

and up to 4,500 cu ft at the rate of 1 lb of gas per 18 cu ft of space and above 4,500 cu ft at 1 lb per 20 cu ft. *(See NFPA 11A, Standard for High Expansion Foam Systems; NFPA 12, Standard on Carbon Dioxide Extinguishing Systems; NFPA 12A, Standard on Halogenated Fire Extinguishing Agent Systems—Halon 1301; and NFPA 17, Standard for Dry Chemical Extinguishing Systems.)*

9-2.2.4 If Halon 1301 is used as the extinguishing agent, the system shall be installed in accordance with the manufacturer's U.S. Coast Guard approved installation specifications and NFPA standards and shall incorporate the following:

(a) a means of indicating that the system has discharged

(b) if an automatic shutdown is provided, an easily operable engine restart feature

(c) for systems not incorporating automatic shutdown, a warning label advising the operator to immediately shut down engines when the system discharges.

9-2.2.5 If bilges are open or communicating to more than one space, such spaces, together with the bilge, shall be considered as one in determining the capacity of the system.

9-2.2.6 Systems may be manually or automatically operated. Automatically operated systems which are installed to protect accommodation compartments or to protect engine compartments which are normally attended shall be equipped with a predischarge alarm.

9-3 Installation.

9-3.1 Portable fire extinguishers shall be placed so that they are readily accessible from outside the compartment which they are intended to serve.

Extinguishers shall be secured with a marine bracket to permit immediate release.

9-3.2* Fixed extinguishing systems shall be installed in accordance with the manufacturer's U.S. Coast Guard approved installation procedures and with applicable NFPA standards.

9-3.2.1 Extinguishing agent cylinders shall be mounted a minimum of 2 in. above moist or wet surface to reduce danger of corrosion.

9-3.2.2* Manual controls shall be placed so they are readily accessible outside the spaces served by the systems.

9-3.2.3 Spaces to be protected by such systems shall be enclosed except for ventilation openings, means of access, and closable ports.

9-3.2.4 Systems shall be designed for one of the following modes of application (see 9-2.2.5). Modes (a) and (b) are preferred.

(a) Independent systems installed to cover the various spaces required.
(b) Single system of sufficient capacity for all required spaces simultaneously.
(c) Single system of sufficient capacity for the largest required space, distributed by valves at the controls.

NOTE: Reprinted with permission from NFPA 302-1980, Fire Protection Standard for Pleasure and Commercial Motor Craft, Copyright 1980, NFPA, Quincy, MA 02269. This reprinted material is not the complete and official position of the NFPA on the referenced subject, which is represented only by the standard in its entirety.

ABYC: LIGHTNING PROTECTION STANDARDS AND PRACTICES

RECOMMENDED PRACTICES AND STANDARDS COVERING LIGHTNING PROTECTION PROJECT E–4 (ADOPTED NOV. 3, 1959)

1.0 Scope

1.01 WHEREIN standards and recommended practices outline the means whereby all types of craft can be afforded a high degree of protection against lightning.

2.0 General Principles

2.01 In view of the wide variation in structural design of boats, the following basic guides should be considered and used in designing and installing a lightning protection system for any given craft: (See Fig.1.)

2.1 A grounded conductor, or lightning protective mast, will generally divert to itself direct hits which might otherwise fall within a cone-shaped space, the apex of which is the top of the conductor or lightning protective mast and the base is a circle at the surface of the water having a radius of approximately two times the height of the conductor. The probability of protection is considered to be 99.0 percent for the 60 degree angle shown in the illustration. The probability of protection can be increased to 99.9 percent by increasing the height of the mast so that the 60 degree angle becomes 45 degrees.

2.2 To provide an adequately grounded conductor or lightning protective mast, the entire circuit from the top of the mast to the ground should have a conduction equivalent to a No.8 A.W.G. copper conductor and the path to ground followed by the conductor should be effectively straight.

2.3 If there are metal objects of considerable size within a few feet of the grounding conductor, there will be a strong tendency for sparks or side flashes to jump from the grounding conductor to the metal object at the closest point. To prevent damage from such side flashes an interconnecting conductor should be provided at all places where they are likely to occur.

2.4 Large metallic objects within the hull of superstructure of a boat should be interconnected with the lightning protective system, or the bonding system, to prevent a dangerous rise of voltage due to a lightning flash. Items which are not part of the electrical system of the boat may be independently grounded, provided it is not practical to interconnect with the lightning protective or bonding systems.

2.5 Since a lightning conductor system is expected to remain in working condition for a long period of time with relatively little attention, the mechanical construction should be strong and the materials used should offer high resistance to corrosion.

3.0 Installation Recommendations

3.1 *Lightning Protective Mast*—A lightning protective mast should be of adequate height (Section 2.1.) and should be mechanically strong in order to withstand exposure to use and weather. If the mast is of nonconducting material, the associated lightning or grounding conductor should be essentially straight, securely fastened to the mast, should extend at least 6 inches above the mast, should preferably terminate in a sharp point and should meet the requirements of Section 3.3.

3.2 *Radio Antenna*—A radio antenna may serve as a lightning protective mast provided it is equipped with transmitting type lightning arresters or means for grounding during electrical storms. The grounding of metal rod type radio antennas constitutes sufficient protection for wooden boats, without masts and spars, provided the following conditions are met:

3.21 All conductors in the grounding circuit of the antenna are at least No.8 A.W.G. copper or equivalent in accordance with Section 3.31.

3.22 A line drawn from the top of the antenna downward toward the water at an angle of 60° to the vertical does not intercept any part of the boat. (Section 2.1).

3.23 Antennas with loading coils are considered to end at a point immediately below the loading coil unless this coil is provided with a suitable gap for by-passing the lightning current.

3.24 Non-conducting antenna masts with *spirally* wrapped conductors are not considered suitable for lightning protection purposes.

3.3 *Materials*—The materials used in the making of a protective system should be resistant to corrosion. No combination of metals should be used that forms a galvanic couple of such a nature that in the presence of moisture or direct submersion, corrosion is accelerated. Except for the use of conducting materials which are otherwise part of the structure of the boat, only copper should be used as the conductor. Where copper is used, it should be of the grade ordinarily required for commercial electrical work, generally designated as being of 98 percent conductivity when annealed.

3.31 Copper Conductor

Copper conductor should weigh at least 50 lbs. per thousand feet.

Copper cable conductors should be of a diameter not less than No.8 A.W.G. The size of any wire of a cable should be not less that No.17 A.W.G. The thickness of any copper ribbon or strip should be not less than No.20 A.W.G. (0.032 inch).

Where other materials are used the gauge should be such as to give conductivity equal to or greater than No.8 A.W.G. copper cable.

3.32 Joints

Joints should be mechanically strong and should be so made that they have an electrical resistance not in excess of that of 2 feet of conductor.

3.4 Interconnection of Metallic Masses

3.41 *Interconnection or Grounding*—Metallic masses aboard boats which are a permanent part of the boat, or are permanently installed within or about it, should with the exception of those of comparatively small size, be made a part of the lightning-conductor system by interconnection with it (see Paragraph 2.4) or independently grounded, or both, depending upon their location with respect to the lightning conductors and their surroundings, as more fully described in Sections 3.42 to 3.44, inclusive.

Note: The object of interconnecting the metal parts of a boat with the conductor is to prevent damage from side flashes especially in the case of rather extensive metal objects that *are near by. The main principle to be observed in the prevention of such damage is to pick out on a boat the places where side flashes are most likely to occur and provide metallic paths for them.*

3.42 *Exterior Bodies of Metal*—Metal situated wholly on the exterior of boats should be electrically connected to the grounding conductor at its upper or its nearest end, and, if of considerable length, should be also grounded or electrically connected to the conductor at its lower or its farthest end.

Note: Exterior metal bodies on boats include any large masses such as horizontal handrails on cabin tops, smoke stacks from galley stoves, davits or metal signal masts.

3.43 *Interior Bodies of Metal*—Metal situated wholly in the interior of boats which at any point comes within 6 feet of a lightning conductor should be electrically interconnected with it. The bonding required to prevent *electrolysis* should be considered adequate.

Note: Interior bodies of metal include engines, water and gasoline tanks, control rods for steering gear or reversing gear. It is not intended that small metal objects such as compasses, clocks, galley stoves, medicine chests, and other parts of the boat's hardware should be grounded.

3.44 Metal which projects through cabin tops, decks or sides of boats above the sheer should be bonded to the nearest lightning conductor at the point where the metal emerges from the boat and should be grounded at its lower extreme end within the boat. Spotlights and other devices projecting through cabin tops should be solidly grounded regardless of any other type of lightning protection. Personnel should refrain from operating this gear when lightning is in the immediate vicinity.

3.45 Radio transmitter antenna should be (1) equipped with means for grounding during electrical storms or (2) the transmitter and antenna should be protected by transmitting type lightning arresters.

3.5 *Ground Connection*—A ground connection for a boat may consist of any metal surface which is normally submerged in the water and which has an area of at least one square foot. Propellers and metallic rudder surfaces may be used for this purpose. The ground plate as required by FCC for radio transmitters should be considered adequate. A steel hull itself constitutes an adequate ground.

3.6 *Vessel with Metal Hulls*—If there is an electrical contact between metal hulls and metal masts or other metallic superstructure no further protection against lightning is necessary. Boats with non-conducting or ungrounded objects projecting above the metal masts or superstructure should have these objects grounded in order to protect them.

4.0 Protection of Sailboats

4.1 *Sailboats*—Sailboats with metallic standing rigging will be adequately protected provided that all rigging is grounded, so that the mast and rigging meet the requirements of Section 3.1 and 3.3.

4.2 *Open Day-Sailers*—Open sailboats will be adequately protected if the shrouds and back stays or preventors are grounded. These should be electrically connected at the lower end and grounded to a copper plate on the hull or to a metal rudder, or center board or keel. *For the protection of personnel*, it is recommended that any continuous metallic track on the mast and boom be connected at the lower or forward end of the grounding system. *For protection of the boat only*, it is necessary to ground but one pair of shrouds.

4.3 *Cruising Sailboats*—All stays and all sail tracks should be grounded on cruising sailboats since it is assumed that persons will be in proximity of fore-stays as well as after-stays. Grounding of other objects on cruising boats should be in accordance with the foregoing paragraphs.

5.0 Protection of Power Boats

5.01 Power boats may be adequately protected by a grounded radio antenna or other suitably grounded lightning protective mast as specified in Section 3.1., provided the height of the mast meets the requirements for the specified cone of protection. Interconnection and grounding of metallic masses should be in accordance with this specification.

5.1 Where the size of the boat is such as to render the use of a single mast impractical, additional lightning protective masts should be erected to form overlapping cones of protection. It is recommended that the provisions of the United States Department of Commerce Handbook No.46 "Code for Protection Against Lightning" be followed.

6.0 Protection of Small Boats

6.01 Small boats may be protected by means of a temporary lightning protective mast which may be erected under lightning conditions. Grounding provisions may be made by means of flexible copper wire and a submerged ground plate of approximately one square foot in area.

7.0 Suggested Precautions for Personnel

7.01 Inasmuch as the basic purpose of protection against lightning is to insure the safety of personnel, it is appropriate that the following precautions be listed in this report.

7.1 One should remain inside a closed boat, as far as practical, during a lightning storm.

7.2 One should avoid making contact with any items connected to a lightning conductive system and especially in such a way as to bridge between these items. For example, it is undesirable that an operator be in contact with reversing gear levers and spotlight control handle at the same time.

7.3 No one should be in the water during a lightning storm.

7.4 If a boat has been struck by lightning, compasses and electrical gear should be checked to determine that no damage or change in calibration has taken place.

NOTE: This standard is reprinted with permission of the American Boat and Yacht Council, Inc. Readers wishing more information about the above standard and other standards published by the ABYC should write: PO Box 806, 190 Kectham Ave., Amityville, NY 11701. Readers also should be advised that at the time of this printing, the ABYC was considering major revisions to its lightning protection standard.

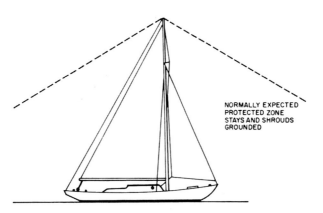

NORMALLY EXPECTED
PROTECTED ZONE
STAYS AND SHROUDS
GROUNDED

MANUFACTURER'S LISTING
(Foreign companies listed by U.S. distributor)

Adler-Barbour Marine Systems, Inc.
"Cold Machine"
511 Fifth Avenue
Pelham, NY 10803

Alladin
kerosene lamps, heaters
P.O. Box 100255
Nashville, TN 37210

Alternatives
AC generator
P.O. Box 235
Valley Springs, CA 95252

American Bosch Diesel Products
  Corp.
hydraulic starters
3664 Main Street
Springfield, MA 01107

American Bureau of Standards
WWV/WWVH time broadcasts
Boulder, CO 80302

American International Marine Corp.
"Barbarossa" blocks
P.O. Box 405
Millersville, MD 21108

American Klegecell
204 North Dooley
Grapevine, TX 76051

Ampair Products
wind/water generators
76 Meadrow
Godalming
Surrey GU7 3HT
England

Aqua Drive Inc.
"Scatra CVA System"
3340 Highway 37 East
Toms River, NJ 08753

Aquadynamics Inc.
"Dynaplate"
168 Rockland Avenue
P.O. Box 1049
Woonsocket, RI 02895

Aqua-Meter Instrument Corp.
radio direction finders
465 Eagle Rock Avenue
Roseland, NJ 07068

BMW of North America
diesel engines
Montvale, NJ 07645

Cape Dory Yachts
160 Middleboro Avenue
East Taunton, MA 02718

Catalina Yachts
21200 Victory Boulevard
Woodland Hills, CA 91367

C.F. Horton & Co.
"Sea Frost" refrigeration
P.O. Box 36
Dover, NH 03820

Cetec Benmar
autopilots
3000 West Warner Avenue
Santa Ana, CA 92704

Coast Navigation
"Walker Logs"
1934 Lincoln Drive
Annapolis, MD 21403

Compton, William
welded thimbles
2320 Wooster Lane
Sanibel Island, FL 33957

Corbin les Bateaux Inc.
Corbin 39
300 Berge Du Canal
Ville Street Pierre
Quebec
Canada H8R 1H3

Corp Brothers
CNG/LNG gas appliances
1 Brook Street
Providence, RI 02903

Cruising Yacht Systems
windvanes
39368 West Archer
Mt. Clemens, MI 48045

Danforth
anchors
500 Riverside Industrial Parkway
Portland, ME 04103

Aqua-Temp Corp.
air conditioners
421 North Line Street
Lansdale, PA 19446

Armco Inc.
Nitronic 50 stainless steel
703 Curtis Street
Middletown, OH 45043

Attwood Corp.
bilge pumps
1016 North Monroe Street
Lowell, MI 49331

Baltek Corp.
Contourkore end-grain balsa core
10 Fairway Court
Northvale, NJ 07647

Basic Designs
"Sun Shower"
P.O. Box 479
Star Route
Muir Beach, CA 94965

Beckson Marine
"Siphon-Mate" pump
P.O. Box 3336
Bridgeport, CT 06605

Boat Life
"Life Caulk" sealant
205 Sweet Hollow Road
Old Bethpage, NY 11804

Bomar
hatches
P.O. Box W
Charlestown, NH 03603

Bosworth Co.
"Guzzler" bilge pumps
195 Anthony Street
East Providence, RI 02914

Bremer Manufacturing
"Sea Swing" stove
P.O. Box 100
Elkhart Lake, WI 53020

Bristol Yacht Co.
1 Franklin
Bristol, RI 02809

Defender Industries, Inc.
discount marine merchandise
255 Main Street
P.O. Box 820
New Rochelle, New York 10801

Dickerson Boatbuilders
R.D. 2
P.O. Box 92
Trappe, MD 21673

Dickinson Marine Products, Inc.
diesel heaters and stoves
4611 11th Avenue N.W.
Seattle, WA 98107

Dow Chemical Co.
"Styrofoam"
Midland, MI 48640

DuPont
"Xytel" and "Imron" paints
Polymer Products Department
Wilmington, DE 19898

D.W. Follansbee
"Enkes" winches, "Zwaardvis" tables,
    "Stavo" steering wheels
4168 Main Road
Tiverton, RI 02878

Dynamote Corp.
inverters
1200 West Nickerson Street
Seattle, WA 98119

Edson Corp.
steering systems
492 Industrial Park Road
New Bedford, MA 02745

EPSCO Inc.
"Seafarer" depthsounders
411 Providence Highway
Westwood, MA 02090

Espar
diesel and gas heaters
P.O. Box 2346
Naperville, IL 60566

Fatsco
"Tiny Tot" wood/coal heating stove
251 N. Fair Avenue
Benton Harbor, MI 49022

Fel-Pro Inc.
"Pro-Lock"
7450 N. McCormick Boulevard
P.O. Box C1103
Skokie, IL 60076

Force 10 Marine Ltd.
23080 Hamilton Road
Richmond, B.C.
Canada V6V 1C9

Forespar
R.C. Marine Xytel sea cocks
2672 Dow Avenue
Tustin, CA 92680

Fram Corp.
filters
105 Pawtucket Avenue
East Providence, RI 02916

Free Energy Systems
solar panels
Holmes Industrial Park
Holmes, PA 19043

Freedom Yachts
Tillotson-Pearson
Bend Boat Basin
Newport, RI 02840

Galley Maid Marine Products
pressure water systems
P.O. Box 10417
Riviera Beach, FL 33404

Gas Systems
CNG/LNG appliances
5361 Production Drive
Huntington Beach, CA 92649

Gibb Yachting Equipment
Gibb-Henderson pumps
415 Tamal Plaza
Corte Madera, CA 94925

Globe Rubber Works Inc.
"Drive Saver"
254 Beech Street
Rockland, MA 02370

Goiot U.S. Inc.
hatches
889 Production Place
Newport Beach, CA 92663

Goldberg's Marine
discount marine merchandise
202 Market Street
Philadelphia, PA 19106

Gougeon Brothers
W.E.S.T. System epoxy
706 Martin Street
Bay City, MI 48706

Greenwich Corp.
"Power Log" water generator
9507 Burwell Road
Nokesville, VA 22123

Grunert Co.
195 Drum Point Road
Osbornville, NJ 08723

Guest Corp.
130 Shield Street
West Hartford, CT 06110

Haarstick Sailmakers
100 Pattenwood Drive
Rochester, NY 14617

Hamilton Ferris
wind water generators
P.O. Box 129
Dover, MA 02030

Harvey Hubbell Inc.
shore power cables
P.O. Box 3999
Bridgeport, CT 06605

Heath Co.
Benton Harbor, MI 49022

Henry R. Hinckley & Co.
Shore Road
Southwest Harbor, ME 04679

H&L Marine Woodwork Inc.
2965 East Harcourt Street
Compton, CA 90221

Hood Sailmakers U.S.A.
P.O. Box 928
Little Harbor Way
Marblehead, MA 01945

Howe & Bainbridge
sailcloth
220 Commercial Street
Boston, MA 02109

Hunter Marine
P.O. Box 1030
Route 441
Alachua, FL 32615

Hydrovane Yacht Equipment Ltd.
windvanes
117 Bramcote Lane
Chilwell
Nottingham
England NG9 4EV

IMTRA Corp.
"Whale" pumps, Nauta tanks, etc.
151 Mystic Avenue
Medford, CA 02155

Industrial Formulators of Canada
"Cold Cure Epoxy"
3824 Williams St.
Burnabey, British Columbia
Canada V5C 3H9

International Marine Instruments
"Combi-Autohelm" autopilots
40 Signal Road
Stamford, CT 06902

ITT Jabsco
pumps
1485 Dale Way
Costa Mesa, CA 92626

Jay Stuart Haft
"Simpson-Lawrence" windlasses,
    "Stowe" logs, "Sta-Lok" terminals,
    and other English imports
8925 North Tennyson Drive
Milwaukee, WI 53217

Lewmar Marine
hatches, winches
P.O. Box 390
125 Wilbur Place
Bohemia, NY 11716

Loctite Inc.
705 North Mountain Road
Newington, CT 06111

Lucas Marine Ltd.
spring engine starter, solar panels,
    prop shaft generators
Frimley Road
Camberley, Surrey
England GU16 5EU

Macwhyte Wire Rope
"Norseman" terminals
2992 14th Avenue
Kenosha, WI 53141

Magnaflux Corp.
"Spot Check"
7300 West Lawrence Avenue
Chicago, IL 60656

Magnavox Advance Products
Satnav
2829 Maricopa Street
Torrance, CA 90503

Mainstay Designs
"Cold Blanket"
42 Margaret Court
Tom's River, NJ 08753

Marinco Marine Industries Co.
shore power
92 Hamilton Drive
Ignacio, CA 94947

Marine Air Systems
air conditioning/heating
P.O. Box 21708
Ft. Lauderdale, FL 33335

Marine Development Corp.
air conditioning/heating
P.O. Box 15299
Richmond, VA 23227

Marine Energy Systems, Inc.
propane locker
104 Epping Road
P.O. Box 988
Exeter, NH 03833

Marine Vane Gears
"Aries" windvane
Cowes, Isle of Wight
England

Matthews Oil
2 Tews Court
Newport, RI 02840

Mayfair Molded Products
bilge pumps
3700 North Rose Street
Schiller Park, IL 60176

Mercantile Manufacturing Co.
"Auto Gen"
P.O. Box 895
Minden, LA 71055

Merriman/Yacht Specialties
steering systems
301 Olive Street
Grand River, OH 44045

Meta
JNF 38
BP 109
69170
Tarare, France

Michigan Wheel Corp.
1501 Buchanen S.W.
Grand Rapids, MI 49507

Minnesota Mining Manufacturing
    (3M)
bedding compound, tape, etc.
3M Center
St. Paul, MN 55144

Morgan Yachts Inc.
7200 Bryan Dairy Road
Largo, FL 33543

Motorola Marine
water generators, solar panels
1313 East Algonquin Road
Schaumburg, IL 60196

Navtec
rod rigging
527 Great Road
Littleton, MA 01460

New Found Metals
bronze deck hardware
240 Airport Road
Port Townsend, WA 98368

Onan
auxiliary generators
1400 73rd Street N.E.
Minneapolis, MN 55432

Origo USA
1121 Lewis Avenue
Sarasota, FL 33577

Pacific Seacraft
Flicka-class sailboats
3301 South Susan
Santa Ana, CA 92704

PDC Labs International
solar panels
P.O. Box 603
El Segundo, CA 90245

Pearce-Simpson Gladding Corp.
navigation instruments
1051 East 32nd Street
P.O. Box 520800 GMF
Miami, FL 33013

Pearson Yachts
West Shore Road
Portsmouth, RI 02871

Petit Paint
36 Pine Street
Rockaway, NJ 07866

Plastimo
bilge pumps
P.O. Box 3333
Annapolis, MD 21403

Racor Industries
fuel filters
P.O. Box 3208
Modesto, CA 95353

Radio Shack
inverters, electronic instruments
One Tandy Center
Fort Worth, TX 76102

Ratelco
"Cole Stove"
1260 Mercer Street
Seattle, WA 98109

Ratsey & Lapthorn
sailmakers
250 City Island Avenue
City Island, NY 10464

Ray Jefferson
electronic equipment
Main & Cotton Streets
Philadelphia, PA 19127

Rockall Sails
222 Severn Avenue
Annapolis, MD 21403

Ronstan Marine
"Latchway Safety System"
805 Court Street
Clearwater, FL 33515

Rule Industries
pumps
Cape Ann Industrial Park
Gloucester, MA 01930

Sailing Specialties
fiberglass anchor well
P.O. Box 527
Lexington Park, MD 20653

Sailrite Enterprises
Route 1
Columbia City, IN 46725

Sails U.S.A.
P.O. Box 542
Portland, ME 04112

Scanmar Marine Products
"Sailomat" windvane
298 Harbor Drive
Sausalito, CA 94965

Shipmate Stove Division
Richmond Ring
P.O. Box 375
Souderton, PA 18964

Shore Sails
7 Merton Road
Newport, RI 02840

Sika Corp.
"Sikaflex 241" adhesive sealant
460 Rand Road
Des Plaines, IL 60016

Solar Marine Systems
10965 Normington Way
San Jose, CA 95136

Solarex
1335 Piccard Drive
Rockville, MD 20850

South Pacific Associates Ltd.
"Fleming" windvane, "Fynspray"

pumps, Murray winches, "Snap-
  Apart Hinges"
3827 Stone Way
Seattle, WA 98103

Spartan Marine Products, Inc.
160 Middleboro Avenue
East Taunton, MA 02718

Square D Inc.
ground fault circuit interrupters
  (GFCI)
P.O. Box 654
Pinebrook, NJ 07058

Surrette Storage Battery
P.O. Box 3027
Salem, MA 01970

Swoffer Marine
knotmeter/log
1048 Industry Drive
Seattle, WA 98188

Tatoosh Marine
Quicksilver Corp.
3040 West Commodore Way
Seattle, WA 98199

Tiller Master
774 West 17th Street
Costa Mesa, CA 92627

Torin Inc.
distributors of Airex foam cores
125 Sheridan Terrace
Ridgewood, NJ 07450

Travaco Labs
"Marine-Tex" sealant
345 Eastern Avenue
Chelsea, MA 02150

Universal Motors
gas/diesel engines
P.O. Box 3008
Oshkosh, WI 54903

Universal Wire Products
222 Universal Drive
North Haven, CT 06473

U.S. Paint Co.
"Awlgrip" paint
831 South 21st Street
St. Louis, MO 63103

Viking Leisure Products
"Wallas-Thermotron" kerosene
  heaters
8898 Clarimont Mesa
San Diego, CA 92123

Viscom International Inc.
"Eodyn" wind generator
244 Farms Village Road
West Simsbury, CT 06092

Web Charger
Old Ships Way
P.O. Box 586
Provincetown, MA 02657

Wesmar Marine Electronics
801 Dexter Avenue North
P.O. Box C 19074
Seattle, WA 98109

Westerly Yachts
2 Sound View Drive
Greenwich, CT 06830

W.H. Den Ouden (U.S.A.)
"Vetus" marine products
P.O. Box 8712
Baltimore, MD 21240

Wilcox-Crittenden
seacocks, pumps, etc.
699 Middle Street
Middletown, CT 06457

Windline Marine
anchor rollers
P.O. Box 25876
West Los Angeles, CA 90025

Index